Ch 5 ✓
7
9
10
15

ENRICHING ESOL PEDAGOGY

Readings and Activities for Engagement, Reflection, and Inquiry

ENRICHING ESOL PEDAGOGY

Readings and Activities for Engagement, Reflection, and Inquiry

Edited by

Vivian Zamel
University of Massachusetts Boston

Ruth Spack
Bentley College

LEA LAWRENCE ERLBAUM ASSOCIATES, PUBLISHERS
2002 Mahwah, New Jersey London

Lawrence Erlbaum Associates, Inc., Publishers
10 Industrial Avenue
Mahwah, NJ 07430

Cover design by Kathryn Houghtaling Lacey

Library of Congress Cataloging-in-Publication Data

Enriching ESOL pedagogy : readings and activities for engagement, reflection, and inquiry / edited by Vivian Zamel, Ruth Spack.
p. cm.
Includes bibliographical references and index.
ISBN 0-8058-3939-9 (pbk. : alk. paper)
1. English language—Study and teaching—Foreign speakers.
I. Title: Enriching ESOL Pedagogy. II. Zamel, Vivian.
III. Spack, Ruth.
PE1128.A2 E58 2002
428'.0071 —dc21 2001057763
CIP

Books published by Lawrence Erlbaum Associates are printed on acid-free paper, and their bindings are chosen for strength and durability.

Printed in the United States of America
10 9 8 7 6 5 4 3 2 1

Contents

Preface

Enriching ESOL Pedagogy: Readings and Activities for Engagement, Reflection, and Inquiry is a collection of thought-provoking articles and activities designed to foster reflection and inquiry. Its twofold purpose is to provide a theoretical perspective and to offer ways for making the teaching of English to speakers of other languages (ESOL) meaningful for both teachers and learners. Underlying the activities we have designed and the readings themselves is the assumption that teachers need to play a role in exploring, shaping, and theorizing the work they do. This volume embraces the notion that a philosophical perspective and an inquiry-based stance on pedagogy are critical for understanding the context and content of English language teaching and for envisioning alternative perspectives and approaches.

Enriching ESOL Pedagogy is based on an understanding of the reality of the classroom experience. Through our own research on and teaching of ESOL learners and teachers, we have come to understand that classroom contexts are complicated by an array of factors, including the expectations and goals of students and teachers, institutional constraints, and assumptions about language and identity. Classrooms and the teaching that takes place within them are therefore neither amenable to simple description nor responsive to prescriptive advice. This book provides theoretical insights and activities for framing and interrogating the teaching of language and literacy and for making sense of the complex reality of classroom phenomena. It also includes concrete examples of classroom contexts that are compelling demonstrations of how these theories and perspectives inform and enable practice.

AUDIENCE

The field of ESOL teaching has come to be represented by an extraordinary range of teaching situations. Accordingly, the typical ESOL methodology course includes a diverse group of practicing and prospective teachers who teach or intend to teach in different settings (e.g., ESOL, bilingual, or linguistically diverse mainstream classrooms), at different levels (elementary, secondary, college, adult), and in different countries. In our effort to address this range of circumstances, we have gathered material that takes into account the various kinds of challenges teachers may face in the classroom and that provides opportunities for addressing their particular issues and needs. At the same time, the readings and activities are informed by a common philosophical ground and thus promote principles for practice that apply to diverse teaching situations and student populations.

THE READINGS

The articles in this collection have influenced and defined our own ESOL theory and practice, contributing to our understanding of language teaching and learning while at the same time challenging us to interrogate what we do and why. These articles represent a range of genres, including research reports, scholarly arguments, ethnographies, classroom narratives, and personal essays, as well as pieces that cut across these genres. This rich mix of published writing allows the pieces to inform and speak to one another in intriguing and unpredictable ways. For this volume, we have organized the articles into five integrated units:

• Unit 1, "Questioning the Nature of Methods," begins by raising questions about conventional descriptions of teaching methodology. It offers a critique not only of methods that do not take into account the complex reality of teaching but also of attempts to prescribe methods in an ahistorical, apolitical, and underconceptualized way. Mark Clarke and Sandra Silberstein encourage teachers to challenge the notion that classroom problems can or should be solved by professional advice and instead to tap into their own understandings of the complexity of the language learning process based on the reality of their own classrooms ("Problems, Prescriptions, and Paradoxes in Second Language Teaching"). Noting the gap between students' and the teacher's expectations in the language class, especially when the teacher is an expatriate, Adrian Holliday argues for an approach that allows for negotiation so that both students and teachers can fulfill their respective agendas ("Teachers' and Students' Lessons"). Observing that the IRE pattern in the classroom—teacher initiates, student responds, teacher evaluates—precludes authentic communication and tends to exclude students whose backgrounds do not match the teacher's, Cathy Roller emphasizes the need for approaches that promote literacy as a tool for exploring meaning rather than as a tool for assessment ("Classroom Interaction Patterns: Reflections of a Stratified Society"). Looking at language teaching from a historical perspective, Alastair Pennycook shows that methodologies reflect a cyclical pattern rather than a linear movement toward progress, favoring those who stand to benefit from them, and he exhorts teachers to interrogate any form of knowledge that is presented to them in the guise of scientific objectivity ("The Concept of Method, Interested Knowledge, and the Politics of Language Teaching").

• Unit 2, "Seeing the Classroom," connects to and builds on the first set of readings by taking into account the complicated nature of real classrooms. It points to the problematic notion of prescription, underlining the importance of observing what is actually happening in the classroom and suggesting productive possibilities for undertaking this kind of exploration. Arguing that prescriptive advice can serve to close down rather than foster exploration of teaching, John Fanselow offers ways to provide feedback on classroom visits that enriches the pedagogy of the observer as well as the observed ("Let's See: Contrasting Conversations about Teaching"). In her ethnographic study of a community college writing course, which focuses on student/teacher and student/student interactions in different settings, Kay Losey challenges past generalizations about students based on their cultural group and suggests ways to take students' backgrounds into account in planning curricula ("Gender and Ethnicity as Factors in the Development of Verbal Skills in Bilingual Mexican American Women"). In her ethnographic study of a high school, Linda Harklau discovers how ESOL and non-ESOL teachers promote or constrain second language acquisition and calls for a collaborative dialogue to draw on the expertise of each faculty group ("ESL Versus Mainstream Classes: Contrasting L2 Learning Environments"). Observing how teachers' preconceptions about students' intellectual abilities and cultural background can undermine learning, Glynda Hull, Mike Rose, Kay Losey Fraser, and Marisa Castellano emphasize the need to talk about difference without subscribing to a deficit model of education ("Remediation as Social Construct: Perspectives from an Analysis of Classroom Discourse"). Celia Genishi encourages teachers to be alert to the nonverbal signs of a student's linguistic growth in order to recognize and design activities that are most likely to promote second language acquisition for each child ("Observing the Second Language Learner: An Example of Teachers' Learning").

• Unit 3, "Theories into Practice: Promoting Language Acquisition," provides the theoretical underpinnings for the kind of teaching and learning that promote language acquisition. It extends the notion that theorizing of this sort, rather than implementation of a particular set of methods or curricula, is critical to teachers' understanding. Stephen Krashen presents a set of hypotheses about adult second language acquisition that takes into account the distinction between learning and acquiring a language, the natural order of acquisition, and the roles of self-monitoring, comprehensible input, attitude, aptitude, anxiety, and silence ("Theory Versus Practice in Language Training"). Karl Kranke and Mary Ann Christison draw on their review of empirical research to extract a set of principles for classroom instruction that emphasizes language acquisition activities, encourages risk taking, builds on students' abilities to acquire language from natural interaction, and acknowledges that error is a natural product of the acquisition process ("Recent Language Research and Some Language Principles"). Tracing the development of one of his teaching techniques to the ideas of several "gurus" who influenced him, Mark Clarke emphasizes the authority of the teacher in selecting, integrating, and applying appropriate theoretical perspectives in the classroom ("On the Nature of Technique: What Do We Owe the Gurus?"). Drawing on theories in adult learning, second language acquisition, and literacy, Elsa Auerbach offers principles for establishing a content-based participatory curriculum for adult ESOL instruction that connects with students' lives in such a way that literacy becomes a tool for addressing real life concerns and taking action ("What is a Participatory Approach to Curriculum Development?").

• Unit 4, "Theories into Practice: Keeping Language Meaningful," draws on the theories and principles presented earlier and chronicles the ways in which a variety of classrooms have enacted these theories and principles. These articles include rich descriptions of actual classroom experiences. Noting that young children actively construct their first and second languages by observing and engaging in real communication rather than through explicit instruction, Judith Lindfors uses the examples of show and tell, story time, and dialogue journals to suggest ways to create classrooms that offer authentic language acquisition environments ("The Classroom: A Good Environment for Language Learning"). Through specific examples of public school curricula and activities that invite students to grapple with concepts and information in the areas of math, science, health, and social studies, Sarah Hudelson demonstrates how to use content-area material as a vehicle for language development ("'Teaching' English Through Content-Area Activities"). Describing a thematic college composition course that explores the myth and reality of the American Dream, Vivian Zamel demonstrates how language acquisition and critical thinking are fostered—and how educational institutions are enriched—when students' realities and perspectives are acknowledged and privileged ("From the Margins to the Center"). Describing the curriculum that she and fellow prisoners created on the subject of AIDS, Kathy Boudin demonstrates that language and literacy acquisition are promoted when a curricular issue has charged meaning and is linked to learners' experiences ("Participatory Literacy Education Behind Bars: AIDS Opens the Door").

• Unit 5, "Questioning Assumptions About Language and Identity," raises questions about the kinds of assumptions about language and identity that teachers bring into their classrooms. We believe these assumptions, often left unexamined, need to be explored and addressed, for they inevitably contribute to the expectations teachers hold for both themselves and learners. In a talk to a TESOL convention audience, Henry Widdowson challenges prevailing notions about who qualifies as a native speaker, what qualifies as standard language, and who is qualified to teach English to speakers of other languages ("The Ownership of English"). Through student interviews and literacy narratives, researchers Yuet-Sim Chiang and Mary Schmida find that the linguistic and cultural identities of the children of immigrants have blurred boundaries and thus question the legitimacy of applying binary categories such as native/nonnative speakers and mainstream/ESL learners to such students ("Language Identity and Language Ownership: Linguistic Conflicts of First-Year University Writing Students"). Reflecting on her experience as a child of missionaries in India, teacher Stephanie Vandrick wonders about the extent to which the ESOL field and its teachers have unwittingly embraced and transmitted a sense that Western culture and the English language—especially the British and American versions—are superior ("ESL and the Colonial Legacy: A Teacher Faces Her 'Missionary Kid' Past"). Resistance to this colonial legacy led writer Simon Ortiz to use the English he was forced to learn in U.S. government schools not to reject his past, as he was expected to do, but rather to transmit the concepts and values he learned through the oral tradition of the Acoma Pueblo people ("The Language We Know"). Reflecting on the different Englishes that immigrants and their children use to communicate in different settings in the United States, writer Amy Tan argues that language that is typically labeled "limited" is as natural and as rich in imagery and thought as language labeled "standard" ("Mother Tongue").

While the division of five units lends itself well to a ten-week or fifteen-week semester, we do not assume that the readings will be assigned or read in a straightforward or linear way. Each unit offers a number of selections that can be chosen according to the goals of a course or of an individual teacher or student. Particular readings in one unit cam be explored in conjunction with those in another unit. The issues raised in a later unit can be addressed earlier.

ACTIVITIES FOR ENGAGEMENT, REFLECTION, AND INQUIRY

Enriching ESOL Pedagogy is designed to allow for engagement with the readings in unique and meaningful ways. Acknowledging the reality and complexity of actual classrooms, we suggest activities and pose questions that do not call for neat or predictable solutions. In order to generate an interactive and recursive process of engagement, reflection, and inquiry, we offer a wide range of options. Each unit of readings is accompanied by four sets of activities:

- **Before Reading.** These prompts call for reflection on issues even before they are addressed in the readings.
- **Reflecting on the Reading.** These prompts allow readers to connect with and respond to the issues that are presented by the readings.
- **Reading for Further Reflection.** These prompts introduce short texts such as poems or autobiographical excerpts to extend the ideas presented by the longer readings.
- **Suggested Projects for Inquiry.** These prompts offer ways to reconsider these issues as a basis for an investigation of teaching and learning.

ACKNOWLEDGMENTS

We deeply appreciate the ongoing encouragement and support we receive from our editor, Naomi Silverman. We are also grateful to the graduate students we teach and the colleagues with whom we work; their experiences, reflections, questions, and discoveries continue to shape our thinking, enrich our pedagogy, and remind us that we too are learners.

Introduction

A major aim of our work in teacher training and faculty development is to help prospective and practicing teachers make sense of the complex nature of English language teaching and learning. Central to this work is the notion that all learning is promoted when it is viewed as meaningful and purposeful and when it contributes to a sense of engagement with and ownership over what is being studied. For English language learning, this means that students need ongoing opportunities to use language in the context of making meaning and constructing knowledge and that their attempts to use language in this way should be encouraged. And because acquiring another language is inextricably linked to learners' past experiences and issues of identity, classrooms need to be responsive to students' sense of who they are and what they know and the complicated ways these experiences and identities are related to acquiring new ways with words.

The conditions that foster learning in students apply as well to the learning of teachers. The process of acquiring an understanding of teaching, too, needs to be viewed as meaningful and purposeful and ought to encourage teachers' sense of ownership over their teaching practice. Accordingly, our work provides prospective and practicing teachers with opportunities to question conventional approaches to teaching methodology, explore how classrooms operate, select among and apply appropriate theoretical perspectives, envision acquisition-rich classroom environments, theorize their own practices, interrogate their own unexamined assumptions about language and identity, and thus to come to value their own knowledge and knowledge-making. Our own experiences have demonstrated that this kind of firsthand engagement with and examination of teaching and learning issues are powerful sources for gaining insights into and transforming teaching. Furthermore, as is the case with language acquisition, learning to teach is not a matter of finding simple and neat solutions. Rather, we believe that understanding teaching involves a recursive process of observing, reflecting on, and theorizing about practice. It is this vision of teaching, as an ongoing process of learning, that *Enriching ESOL Pedagogy* means to promote.

CONNECTING OUR THEORY WITH PRACTICE

In our own classrooms, we encourage students to write because we understand that writing is a generative source for thinking, speculating, questioning, and learning. Writing not only makes it possible to record thoughts but actually gives rise to connections and ideas that can be considered, expanded, revised. Thus students in our classes use writing to explore the associations and experiences they bring to particular themes and issues, to reflect on what strikes them, to extend their understanding to their observations and practice, and to grapple with the multiple factors that impinge on teaching. They themselves often remark on the ways that writing contributes to their reading, understanding, sense of authority, and practice. Here, for example, graduate student Shannon Parker reflects on the role that writing played in her ability to theorize about teaching and to integrate theory, practice, and personal experience:

> As I was rereading my reflections I was struck by how much I had written! More importantly, I feel I have created a text of my own reflections that will be useful for me as I continue to define and explore my own pedagogy through practice. For me writing has always been an essential way to process information. This has certainly proved true as I have retained more knowledge about the pieces that I responded to in comparison with other texts that were engaged in class. Not to say that all is lost on the readings that I did not respond to but writing solidifies my voice in relation to the text and that has always helped me in my learning process.
>
> . . . The most rewarding thing about reflecting in writing is that we were able to explore alternatives to theory. In rereading my reactions, I was able to link theories about language learning and the pedagogical approaches to autobiographical experiences and classroom methods. This provided a unique synthesis that I do not believe you can achieve if committed to only reading about theory.

Students' written responses are central to the work of our courses, for they function as course texts alongside the other texts assigned. We ask students to discuss and refer to their written reflections during whole class and small group discussions. Their own writing thus provides a basis for their contributions to these discussions. When they share their reflections with each other, they typically find that they have produced a myriad of responses that are productive for further thinking. Importantly, this process of sharing responses provides insight into the very nature of reading. Reading is a process that is informed and shaped by what each person brings to a text and thus inevitably gives rise to multiple interpretations and unpredictable reactions. This is a lesson we hope prospective and practicing teachers will bring to their own teaching.

Students' written reflections have the added benefit of extending, enriching, and challenging our own thinking about ESOL theory and practice. This writing becomes our reading, and we respond to selected pieces in the same way we invite students to respond to the assigned readings: by indicating what we have found compelling, intriguing or puzzling. In asking students to write, in valuing their written work, and in giving them to understand that their writing contributes to the construction of knowledge, we aim to establish in our classes a collaborative community of teaching and learning. Through this process of acknowledging and sharing students' written work, we are again modeling a practice that we hope will inform their own teaching contexts.

BEFORE READING

Each unit of readings begins with a section titled "Before Reading," which calls for consideration of experiences with and assumptions about the issues that will be addressed in the unit. Among the variety of prompts from which to choose are these suggestions:

- Describe past teaching or learning experiences.
- Recollect times when issues related to language have had a personal impact.
- Think about what certain terms or concepts bring to mind.

Exploring issues and ideas before reading the articles in each unit allows for the opportunity to identify and consider experiences and beliefs and to bring these individual perspectives to the reading. These experiences and beliefs, we believe, are precisely what give the reading relevance and resonance. Furthermore, these opportunities for reflection before reading makes it possible for prospective and practicing teachers to activate their own knowledge and experiences as resources to draw on for their future teaching.

We offer as an example the following reflection written by graduate student Cheryl Lynch in response to a "Before Reading" prompt in Unit 3, a prompt that asked students to think of a language learning experience and explain why it was successful or not:

> I don't speak another language. I have taken the usual smattering of foreign languages (Latin in junior high, French in junior and senior high school and two years of German in college) . . . all without too much success. All my language classes were taught traditionally without emphasis on communication or context. After college I worked evenings at a hospital where there were a lot of Spanish speaking people working that shift. I saw this as a great opportunity, so I took a "conversational" Spanish course at night with my sister. I had always wanted to speak language fluently and I thought this was my big chance. I was frustrated after years of French and German, that I couldn't speak a word, but I blamed it on not being able to "Use" it. I thought this was my opportunity to really use the language. . . . Although I only took a few months of Spanish, I think I retained as much usable Spanish in that time as almost 5 years of French. I know Conversational Spanish was the closest I ever came to enjoying a foreign language class. The class was casual and fun. My outstanding memory was the Spanish teacher having the whole class to her house for paella. That type of thing had never happened in any of my classes before.

By drawing on her own recollected experiences of language instruction, Cheryl has a basis for connecting with, confirming, or challenging the readings in Unit 3. And when she finally does turn to these readings, they will give her a way to rethink, theorize, and name her experiences.

REFLECTING ON THE READINGS

Each unit of readings is followed by a section titled "Reflecting on the Readings," a series of questions and prompts for reflecting on the ways in which the readings relate to, contribute to, or challenge one's understanding of the issues addressed. We offer an array of questions and prompts, including these possibilities:

- Make connections across readings.
- Revisit personal experiences in light of the readings.
- Reflect on the extent to which individual experiences confirm or refute the perspectives presented in the readings.
- Apply the concepts of the readings to observations or explorations.
- Focus on a particular section of a reading that has particular resonance.

- Imagine scenarios that draw on individual understanding and conviction.

The kinds of questions and activities we have suggested are intended to guide prospective and practicing teachers to examine and question their experiences, beliefs, and observations. They offer possibilities to theorize about teaching and learning while considering individual interpretations, associations, and reactions. They provide opportunities to actively engage with and explore the issues presented in the readings.

The following written reflections reveal what two readers found most compelling in the readings in Unit 1 on "Questioning the Nature of Methods." In the first excerpt, novice teacher Nicole Lasas indicates how the article by Mark Clarke and Sandra Silberstein, "Problems, Prescriptions, and Paradoxes in Second Language Teaching," gives her insight into the complexity of her own teaching experiences:

> Clarke and Silberstein's article speaks to me as a new teacher. Initially, I was always (and still am to some degree) convinced that there must be a right way to do things. Their reference to double binds helped me to see that this is not necessarily true. Sometimes there is a better way to do something. However, there are inherent contradictions in almost everything we feel and do, at least to some extent. What worked for my students one day in class is no assurance that it will work next time. Knowing this and allowing for the occasional "chaotic" realities to exist sends me to less of a panic.

Another, more experienced teacher, Alma Pezo, reflects on Cathy Roller's article, "Classroom Interaction Patterns: Reflections of a Stratified Society," and explains how it encouraged her to explore an alternative possibility for promoting genuine language use in her teaching:

> I especially liked Roller's article in which she suggested how to create an environment that will encourage children to use language. Some of these activities I have been using in my classroom. One of these is the dialogue journal. The students used to write to me, but a few days ago I decided to try note writing. I told them they could write to each other if they wanted. It was interesting that all of them but one student wrote to each other. Then they exchanged notebooks and took them home to write back. The following day, they asked me if they could do it again. How could I turn them down when they asked me if they could write, which is always a big issue? I was so happy that they asked to write that we did it again but I asked them to exchange notebooks in the class and write back to each other. . . . While I was walking around, I saw that Miki wrote in her journal, "You always put P.S. at the end, what does that

> mean?" It was powerful how much meaningful, contextualized language was going on between them.

In our own classes, we promote collaboration not only through discussions of students' responses to the readings—which we occasionally reproduce and distribute as class texts—but also through their written dialogues with one another. We offer as an example the following exchange, which begins with graduate student Carla Foote's reflection about the conflicting expectations of students and teacher, a topic addressed in Adrian Holliday's chapter in Unit 1, "Teachers' and Students' Lessons":

> I do feel that my teaching reflects, in part, my experiences. For example, I feel extremely comfortable when I am standing in front of the class and all my students are in neat little rows. However, I take myself out of my comfort zone, partly due to necessity. (I have 31 students for Advanced ESL) and partly due to my graduate training (the emphasis on student-centered, cooperative learning approaches). I also have witnessed that the experiences of my students were similar to mine except for one aspect. They did not have the classes that showed me the benefits of transitioning to a more communicative approach. As such, I am frequently asked when we are going to start learning. This question is asked while in small groups doing pre-listening discussions. Thus, some of my students are also being taken out of their comfort zone when we do participate in non-traditional approaches/activities that they are not familiar with.

When Carla's reflection was reproduced along with other students' reflections for the class to consider and respond to, another student in the course, Tony Pereira, chose to respond to her because the issue that Carla raised spoke to his own concerns:

> Dear Carla,
>
> As I read your journal entry I could only admire that you would make an effort to use approaches that go beyond the teacher-centered curriculum in a class of 31 students. As an ESL teacher of groups of similar numbers, I often find myself gravitating towards the easier avenue, which is to disseminate information and hope that some will be absorbing what is happening in the front. Grouping students and assigning activities that will allow all to engage in learning is a lot more time consuming, but at the end I have found that it allows me to walk around the classroom, observe what is happening, listen to students' arguments and see how they progress. You are absolutely right when you say that some students are also affected by the change of scenario and seem not to be as productive perhaps due to the unfamiliarity of the situation. We all act different in different circumstances, but I do feel that it is our responsibility to allow them to experience what they will have to

> confront. Real life situations require that they listen, respond, act in different ways depending on the circumstance.
>
> Tony

We have come to value these written exchanges for the ways in which they allow prospective and practicing teachers to share their experiences and perspectives and to establish their own authority around teaching issues. Furthermore, we hope that the experiences of responding to one another in thoughtful ways will come to represent a habit of mind that will continue beyond our own classes into their work experience with colleagues and with students.

READING FOR FURTHER REFLECTION

After inviting responses to the full-length readings in each unit, we include short texts such as poems and excerpts from essays, autobiographies, and interviews in a section titled "Reading for Further Reflection." The vivid images and evocative vignettes of these short texts can deepen an understanding of the theoretical perspectives promoted in the longer scholarly articles. Among the variety of prompts from which to choose are these suggestions:

- Connect the short text to the longer readings.
- Compare the short text to individual teaching and learning experiences.
- Consider what the short text reveals about teaching and learning.
- Theorize about a personal experience discussed in the short text.

These pieces extend the range of readings to provide an enlivened sense of the issues in the field and suggest the numerous possibilities for examining these issues.

Here, for example, graduate student Vanda Figueiredo—who herself acquired English as an additional language—responded to a passage from Maxine Hong Kingston's *The Woman Warrior: Memoirs of a Girlhood Among Ghosts* (from an excerpt reprinted in Unit 2).

Copied Text from Maxine Hong Kingston:

> *When I went to kindergarten and had to speak English for the first time, I became silent. A dumbness—a shame—still cracks my voice in two, even when I want to say "hello" casually, or ask an easy question in front of the check-out counter, or ask directions of a bus driver. I stand frozen, or I hold up the line with the complete grammati-*

cal sentence that comes squeaking out at impossible length. "What did you say?" says the cab driver, or "Speak up," so I have to perform again, only weaker the second time. (Kingston)

Vanda's Reactions:

I identified myself with Kingston when she talks about her silence in the classroom. She reminded me of how silent I was in my first year of school. I was so afraid of talking. My first grade teacher used to punish the students who spoke in class without his authorization. We were given time out if we opened our mouths without his permission. I felt so intimidated by his authoritarian presence. This year, I ended up failing. During my middle school and high school I remained silent. I used to have butterflies in my stomach when I was supposed to read something out loud in class.

In college, the teachers used to say that my voice was so soft that they couldn't understand me. They frequently asked my classmates "What is she saying?" or "She speaks so quietly." They used to say that they needed to see the movement of my lips to try to understand what I was saying. One time I had to do a presentation for my Literature class and after I had been rehearsing a lot, I simply lost my voice and I was not able to perform the presentation. I was also very silent when I first came to the U.S. I had to speak English, though I had some knowledge of the language. Not being able to communicate was very hard. In my first ESL class, I was so afraid to talk and make mistakes. I also felt intimidated by the teacher who would try to force me to talk. And when I tried, she would embarrass me correcting my errors in front of everybody. Sometimes, I still avoid speaking out in class because I fear making pronunciation errors. The question "What did you say?" still bothers me a lot. Often times, I feel that native speakers don't make an effort to understand me. I am aware of the stereotype that arises from the moment I begin to speak English. I feel that I have to perform most of the time to make myself understood.

This activity of selecting, copying, and reacting to a short passage, often identified as "double-entry notes," allows readers in a sense to re-write their reading in light of what they bring to it.

SUGGESTED PROJECTS FOR INQUIRY

Each unit of readings ends with a section titled "Suggested Projects for Inquiry," a series of different kinds of investigations that can be undertaken in order to explore and examine issues raised by the readings. These projects involve firsthand inquiry, providing an opportunity to test out theory. Engaging in this kind of research can also generate knowledge and build theory. The kinds of projects we recommend include these possibilities:

- Interview or survey students and/or teachers.
- Observe classrooms.
- Undertake case studies.
- Tape-record (classroom) interactions.
- Examine students' papers and teachers' responses.
- Analyze classroom textbooks or institutional tests.

We expect that projects will be chosen on the basis of what a particular student- or teacher-researcher finds interesting, intriguing, or even perplexing.

Each set of projects grows out of the particular issues addressed in each unit, but these projects have relevance for and can be revisited in light of issues raised in subsequent and previous readings. A project in one unit can build on a project suggested in another unit. For example, Cheryl Lynch, who had undertaken an observation of an ESOL writing classroom, continued to observe that classroom after reading articles related to the issue of classroom interaction:

Cheryl's Class Observation:

> After the second class, I began to notice in the responding patterns that, in fact, very often it was the same people responding. There were fewer people in this second class than the first, but many of the same students were silent. . . . Other things were the same as well. The questioning patterns: Always a "what" or "why" or "how" question not a "yes/no" question. The teacher is the Queen of the Right Question. There were always open-ended, "what do you think" questions. If a student posed a question it was almost immediately thrown back for the class to ponder. The same enthusiasm on the part of the teacher was there, even when there were bumps.

Cheryl subsequently interviewed the teacher in order to gain an understanding of her philosophical perspective on teaching writing. The following is an excerpt from Cheryl's account of and reactions to this interview:

Cheryl's Interview with the Teacher:

> In the interview I asked the teacher what her goals were in this class. She thought for a while and finally answered that she wanted the students engaged. That means you, as a teacher, have done several things right. And it also means that several things will logically follow. If students are engaged you have picked the right theme and you are probably using approaches that keep the students interested. What will follow is participation in discussions. Students will bring their knowledge to class; ideas will be generated, elaborated and acted upon. . . . When I asked about correction, she said she

> "doesn't." I push, "How does it improve if you don't correct?" "By writing more," was her answer. She emphasized that you must first focus on content. She went on to talk about interlanguage and how it is rule driven and how the student must have an internal understanding of the error before it can be self-corrected. She spoke of error analysis and that the only way to approach correction is in a one with one conference. She encourages the students to see her or the tutor. Although she doesn't correct, I get the feeling that through comments on journals and first drafts of papers and during the process of revision, the students' writing improves.

A series of explorations of this sort can provide the basis for a longer project, for example a paper that pulls together, builds on, and makes sense of the projects already undertaken. And, as is the case of other course work, we encourage practicing and prospective teachers to share these projects as well. In this way, we are promoting the critical notion that acquiring an understanding of teaching English language learners inevitably involves an ongoing and recursive process of inquiry, a process that is enhanced when it is in dialogue with the work of other practitioners.

ENRICHING TEACHING, TEACHING THAT ENRICHES LEARNING

In its attempt to enrich ESOL teaching through readings and activities that engage practicing and prospective teachers in reflection and inquiry, this collection promotes principles of learning that we hope teachers will reenact in their own classrooms. It is our conviction that as teachers are immersed in the kind of work we have envisioned, and as they experience firsthand how this work fosters and shapes their own thinking and learning, they will come to see this approach as productive for students in their classrooms as well. By giving teachers opportunities to connect with and reflect on texts that resonate for them, by inviting them to draw on and contribute their own experiences and perspectives, by validating their interpretations and associations, by asking them to undertake meaningful explorations, by making room for them to revisit issues in light of new concerns, we are very deliberately enacting a pedagogy that we believe will enrich not only their own practices, but also the learning of the students in their classrooms.

Unit I

QUESTIONING THE NATURE OF METHODS

BEFORE READING

Respond to one or more of the following:

- What do you think is meant by the term *method* or *methodology*?
- Recall a positive experience teaching or learning language, in or outside the classroom. Reconstruct the details that stand out in your memory. Thinking back on this experience now, does it suggest that a particular method was being employed? How would you characterize that method?
- Recall a negative experience teaching or learning language, in or outside the classroom. Reconstruct the details that stand out in your memory. Thinking back on this experience now, does it suggest that a particular method was being employed? How would you characterize that method?

Chapter 1

Problems, Prescriptions, and Paradoxes in Second Language Teaching

Mark A. Clarke
Sandra Silberstein

As teachers who have worked in a variety of settings during most of the past two decades, we have struggled to find answers to problems that confront language teachers everywhere. Now, as teacher trainers in Denver and Seattle, we find that we are routinely asked to give advice to teachers, to offer suggestions concerning activities and program goals.

We are just beginning to appreciate the extent to which teachers are bound up in giving and receiving advice, and recently we have become intrigued by the realization that prescriptions are implicit in virtually all discussions of the relationship between theory and practice. Our profession seems to subscribe to the notion that embedded in every new insight into language learning and teaching lies advice to be followed.

One has only to look at a sampling of journals in education to discover that most research articles conclude with "implications for teaching," containing explicit and implicit prescriptions for teachers. However, it is rare for an article on teaching practice to contain "implications for researchers." This unidirectional flow of knowledge and insight is also evident at professional conferences: Researchers are frequently sought as plenary speakers for teachers, but it is rare for researchers to request classroom teachers to address them.

Perhaps as a response to this situation, the past several years have witnessed an increasing number of calls for teachers to be given greater autonomy and discretion in their jobs. *Language Arts*, for example, recently devoted two issues (Vol. 64, No. 7, November 1987; Vol. 65, No. 4, April 1988) to an examination of the roles and relationships of teachers in education. A number of writers have begun to acknowledge the prescriptiveness of the literature, the authoritarian nature of centralized decision making, and the subservient status of classroom teachers (see Clarke, 1982, 1983, 1984; Giroux & McLaren, 1986; Silberstein, 1984, 1987; Stevick, 1980, pp. 283–295; Wilden, 1980).

Consider also the implicit assertion of teachers' incompetence, and the call for prescription and guidance from experts, policymakers, and administrators, to be found in the national studies on American education (see, for example, Gross & Gross, 1985; Karp, 1985). And finally, one need only reflect on the approach of school boards and administrations of schools when conducting program reviews and renovations. The standard procedure is to require an explanation of how current curriculum, materials, and teaching practice conform with "the available knowledge" in the profession concerning language learning and teaching. This tendency to look to the literature for authoritative descriptions of how languages are learned and how they should be taught is a deeply ingrained trait in all of us, which begins with our first course work as neophyte teachers.

We believe that teachers need to challenge the assumption that professional advice should be perceived as prescriptions for language learning and teaching. We argue, moreover, for the need to reexamine the relationship between advice givers and advice receivers. Finally, we assert that the connection between problems and solutions does not necessarily include prescriptions.

PROBLEMS

For teachers, day-to-day reality can be characterized as a series of "problems" to be solved: obtaining some level of orderly progress, covering the material, attacking persistent language problems. Although these are important and compelling aspects of our daily existence, they are not our focus here. This article addresses issues that seem to endure over time, problems that consistently characterize second language teaching. For our purposes, we will define *problems* as persistently troublesome aspects of the teacher/learner relationship or as frustrating and perplexing conditions of the process of second language teaching.

The following vignettes provide examples of these problems in modern guise. These anecdotes, which represent composite descriptions drawn from numerous conversations with teachers in a variety of situations, are intended to evoke the atmosphere in which teachers work. They are not equally representative of the day-to-day world of all teachers; some reflect public school contexts, others intensive English programs. Each vignette is intended to illuminate a type of problem teachers regularly face. Do you recognize yourself in any of the following situations?

1. Teachers: Love your students! You are a professionally trained, experienced teacher who daily invests many hours conscientiously preparing classes. Increasingly, you encounter the suggestion from supervisors and colleagues, as well as in the literature and at conferences, that this is not sufficient, that your competence as a teacher will be judged by how "involved" you are with your students. You suddenly realize that all the work you do to accommodate individual problems is not considered relevant. Apparently, only public displays of involvement with and concern for students will qualify you as a humanistic teacher.

2. Students: Feel good about yourselves! You have also been told that the key to successful teaching (and, incidentally, an important part of your evaluation) is the cultivation of students' sense of personal self-worth. You have been handed a packet of materials and a list of activities designed, you are told, to improve your students' self-concepts. You thought you were teaching language; now you discover that you must perform "psychological manipulation and emotional rehabilitation."[1]

3. Students: Take responsibility! You want your students to take responsibility for their learning, to take an active part in setting goals for the class and in staging and evaluating class activities. Yet they resist your attempts at democratizing the curriculum; they appear content to allow you to exercise total control.

4. Students: Communicate! Although your students excel in structured practice and other class activities, you are consistently frustrated when you encourage them to express their inner feelings and true opinions in the target language. Despite your best efforts, they remain students in a class employing the language of the classroom. They do not use language for anything resembling real communication.

5. Teachers: Trust me/Trust your instincts! You are regularly confronted by experts of various kinds—professors, mentors, older colleagues, supervisors, superintendents, gurus, and so on—who profess to have the knowledge, experience, or insight necessary to help you solve particular teaching problems. You have found many of their ideas helpful as you attempt to construct a theoretical/philosophical foundation for your teaching. When you press for specific solutions to complex or recurring problems, however, they chide you for your lack of independent thinking and assure you that you will know what to do when the time

---

[1]This language may seem excessive, but these are in fact the words of a teacher at an intensive English center who believed he was being judged on "a lot of touchy-feely mumbo jumbo" rather than on his abilities as an English teacher. He had just been chided by the director for not participating in the school's international picnic. This phenomenon has its institutional manifestations as well. It is not uncommon to find "improve self-concept of students" listed among the goals of ESL and bilingual education programs in large metropolitan school districts.

comes. In other words, "I am the expert, and therefore it is appropriate for you to ask my advice on this matter. Trust me. My advice is 'Don't worry; you know the answer. Trust your instincts.' " This problem surfaces in discussions with public school teachers who are required to attend a certain number of "inservices" each year. They are often confronted with an expert who, because of the size of the audiences and time constraints, presents only general information. Frequently, the expert has time only to assure teachers that they can adapt the information to their own situations. This problem arises as well for teachers in training, who are constantly faced with the paradox of being evaluated on their ability to apply insights from experts while being told to trust their instincts.

6. Teachers: The best classroom is a nonclassroom! You are told, and perhaps you believe, that the best second language classroom is the one in which students encounter the language in "real" situations rather than by consciously focusing on learning the language. You spend an enormous amount of time and energy (before and during class) attempting to structure your lessons to be unstructured. The closer you come to reaching this ideal, the more your classes resemble total chaos.

Of course, one explanation for the scenarios described in Vignettes 3, 4, and 6 is that the teacher has merely failed to execute an activity properly or to prepare students adequately for the techniques he or she is using. We are not criticizing efforts to produce more interactive activities in L2 classes, but rather the uninformed, generic assumption that *all* techniques and materials must meet the single criterion that the best classroom does not look like a classroom, a criterion that by logical extension cannot be met. Every generation of teachers must face similar prejudices; for example, E. W. Stevick (personal communication) reported that as a young teacher, he faced considerable pressure to conform with audio-lingual practices.

7. Teachers: Test, test, test! You are an ESL/bilingual education teacher in a school district where student and teacher competence is a hot issue. Your students are making steady progress in their ability to use English, but your superiors are only interested in students' performance on standardized tests. You find that you are spending an increasingly greater amount of time administering tests to your students and in disputing the value of those tests in meetings with colleagues and administrators.

8. Teachers: Stick to the curriculum! You are teaching in an intensive English program that has a good reputation for preparing students for university-level academic work. A great deal of time and effort has been devoted to developing and refining the curriculum and materials, and teachers are expected to push students to their limit with academic tasks. Lately, you feel so pressured by the demands of the curriculum that you

have come to look upon communicative language use—class discussion and small-group interaction—as a waste of time.

PRESCRIPTIONS

You may recognize yourself in one or more of these situations. In fact, the descriptions may seem so familiar that you may have difficulty seeing them as problems—perhaps you think of them merely as "conditions of existence" or "life in the trenches." But we submit that these eight vignettes are the behavioral correlates, the "real-life" manifestations, of difficulties that have always confronted the language-teaching profession. In the current literature these problems can be found under such headings as "learner anxiety," or "affective factors in language learning"; "developing communicative competence"; "integrating theory and practice"; and "teacher accountability."

And, of course, wherever we find problems, we will find suggestions and advice for solving them. These may take the form of specific behavioral directions ("Speak more clearly" or "Allow a few seconds of silence before rephrasing the question") or general guidelines ("Establish a predictable rhythm and pace in your teaching"). Sources of advice include colleagues, mentors, supervisors, journal articles, and conference presentations. In general, teachers welcome help in solving problems. And the role of advice receiver presents no problem when we are under no obligation to follow it.

However, we believe that the profession has encouraged all of us, in our roles as givers and receivers, to perceive professional advice as prescription. Prescription carries (by implication, at least) more authority than does advice. It implies that the prescriber is in a position of authority over the receiver or is in a better position to know the truth of the matter. The exact nature of this authority varies from the real power of a director or department chair to the less direct influence of a friend or guru.

Prescription also implies that the problem will yield to frontal assault, to a simple cause/effect sort of solution. This is precisely the issue. We submit that when people find themselves in situations such as those described in the vignettes above, they are placed in what Bateson (1972b, 1972d), Watzlawick, Beavin, and Jackson (1967), and others have described as pragmatic paradox, or double bind.

PARADOXES

There are three conditions for pragmatic paradox. First, individuals find themselves in a significant relationship, and one of them perceives himself or herself as being in the inferior position. That is, there exists a difference in status or power between the individuals. Second, an injunction is issued that cannot be obeyed, disobeyed, or ignored. And third, the situation cannot be explained away; no amount of talk will extricate the individuals from the problem (for elaboration, see Bateson, 1972b, 1972d; Watzlawick et al., 1967).

Pragmatic paradoxes develop in a number of ways. A few familiar examples will help us make our point. Consider, for example, the case of exasperated parents who would like their child to be just a bit more independent. They might be heard to mutter, "Jane, don't be so obedient!" Or there is the lover who complains, "You don't bring me flowers anymore." The receivers of these injunctions find themselves in a peculiar position: If they comply with the command, they have done so not because they felt motivated to do it, but only to please the person who uttered it. Because the behavior is not spontaneous, their efforts are not likely to satisfy the person who demanded the behavior. But refusing to comply indicates a lack of cooperation, which is equally unacceptable. In other words, the behavior is required to maintain the relationship, but it will be appreciated only if it is spontaneous. However, since it has been commanded, it cannot be spontaneous.

Furthermore, people caught in this situation are not usually in a position to explain the bind in which they have been placed, even if they understand what has happened. Lovers and children are a captive and, in this situation, an inarticulate audience. This is the "Be spontaneous!" paradox: One cannot comply with the command, cannot refuse to comply, and cannot explain away the problem.

Another type of pragmatic paradox occurs when individuals confuse levels of abstraction. This is called *confusion of logical type* and is the focus of considerable philosophical inquiry (see Bateson, 1972b, 1972d; Watzlawick, Weakland, & Fisch, 1974). This is the error made by a child who measures the distance between two points on a map using his or her fingers and concludes that the trip to the beach will not take long. Another example of this type of error is the schizophrenic who enters a restaurant and eats the menu. The error is in confusing the real thing with the representation of the thing, and the pragmatic paradox occurs when someone is required to act as if the map were the territory or the menu were the meal.

Although the clinical literature demonstrates that these double binds can result in mental illness, ordinarily they are merely annoying characteristics of human interaction. And, we argue, they are a subtle and pervasive aspect of the language-teaching profession, especially with regard to the relationship of problems and prescriptions.

The eight vignettes described above illustrate these binds. Vignettes 1–4 qualify as examples of the "Be spontaneous!" paradox. In each of these situations, individuals are commanded (either directly or indirectly) to behave in a manner that will be meaningful only if their behavior is spontaneous. Because it is impossible to improve one's attitude under compulsion, injunctions to teachers to "love your students" or to students to "feel good about yourselves" (Vignettes 1 and 2) are worse than nonsensical; they are dangerous because the receiver of the command is placed in the untenable position of the double bind, in which it is impossible either to act meaningfully (one cannot plan to be spontaneous) or to ignore the command. We place students in a similar situation when we tell them to take control over the classroom (Vignette 3). Students know that teachers are ultimately in charge. The pretense that we are not makes it impossible for students to act and ultimately strengthens the authority of the teacher. The same thing occurs when we ask students to communicate about something of personal importance to them when, from their perspective, the classroom may be an inappropriate context for such behavior (Vignette 4).

Vignettes 5–8 provide examples of the confusion of logical type. In each case, one level of abstraction is confused with another. In addition, Vignettes 5 and 6 represent paradoxical definitions. "Teachers: Trust me/ Trust your instincts!" rests on a paradoxical definition of *the expert*: If I am an expert, you should heed my advice; I am telling you that you are the only one who knows what to do. If I am right (if you are the only one who knows), then you should not be listening to me; however, if I am wrong (if you can learn from me), then I am not an expert. This becomes a confusion of logical types. When experts claim that the only good advice is the advice we take, they are asking us to pay attention to two situations at the same time: the generic conditions for certain behaviors and the specific situation in which we find ourselves. To accept advice from experts suggests that an individual who has never been in our classroom can give us advice of a general nature for handling the day-to-day difficulties with which only we are familiar.

Vignette 6 ("Teachers: The best classroom is a nonclassroom!") also begins as a paradoxical definition: The best class is just like life. But if it is life, it is not a class. The class can be what it claims to be only if it is not a class. And it can be a class only if it is not what it claims to be. This paradox, too, rests on a confusion of logical types. The reality of the classroom is confused with the reality of the "real world." In our zeal to improve the verisimilitude of our classroom activities, we begin to behave as if the classroom has no legitimate reality of its own.

Obviously, we are not referring here to those techniques and procedures that teachers can implement to simulate genuine communication in their classes. Rather, we are commenting on the "tyrannical" aura of authority that has accompanied many recent movements in the field (see Clarke, 1982). As innovative ideas take hold in the profession, an increasingly wider circle of individuals (administrators, policymakers, etc.) become aware, at least superficially, of the implicit demands of the new ideas. At this point in the development of a movement, it is common for a prevalent assumption to develop that good language teaching will always display certain key characteristics. In the case of communicative approaches, the value of drill and explicit language instruction has decreased dramatically, so that teachers are made to feel that all good teaching can be measured against the "unteachiness" of activities. As ideas reach the level of acceptance as common sense (see Geertz, 1977), there is less explicit discussion of the value of certain procedures because everyone assumes that this is what teachers are striving to accomplish. Communicative activities lose their status as one of the many techniques a teacher can utilize and become, instead, the implicitly mandated reality to which all teachers are expected to aspire.

The situations illustrated by the last vignettes ("Teachers: Test, test, test!" and "Teachers: Stick to the curriculum!") have become increasingly common in recent years. In these times of limited educational funding, schools are pushed to justify their effectiveness by demonstrating that students are learning. This pressure has led to a confusion of logical types—a confusion of test scores and curriculum guides with the language competence and behaviors of individual learners. Teachers find themselves caught between pieces of paper and actual behavior as they are asked to ignore the evidence of their senses and to believe that completed syllabuses or test scores reflect the language abilities of their students.

We acknowledge several possible objections to the foregoing characterization. It may seem to stretch credulity to suggest that well-intentioned advice has the unfortunate effect of producing pathological conditions in teachers' day-to-day lives. By invoking the concept of the double bind, originally intended for use in clinical settings, we may have released a cave-load of bats from psychology's belfries. In addition, we run the risk of exaggerating the already difficult task that teachers face in attempting to translate theory into practice by suggesting that the task is inherently paradoxical. Furthermore, to the extent that we capture attention with our comments, we may deflect the debate from more important issues. Let us examine each of these objections in turn.

With regard to the first objection, we must look at human interaction in general before focusing more specifically on language teaching. The concept of the double bind is appropriately applied to everyday interaction because all human intercourse is, to some extent, double binding: Face-to-face interaction constitutes an important event, and even the simplest exchange entails some negotiation of the hierarchical relationship so that we are constantly negotiating not only the topic but also the relationship. Furthermore, in many conversations, this second negotiation is the more important of the two, and it is the one that we cannot explicitly address.

Human interaction requires, by definition, the contact of private worlds. The double bind occurs because the individual is placed in the position of having to reconcile the demands of public and private spheres of constraint (see Scollon & Scollon, 1981, pp. 344–355). The physical and interpersonal constraints on participants in a conversation force them to focus their attention and effort on the ongoing situation; they must negotiate a satisfactory interaction. At the same time, however, each individual must channel internal forces, the kaleidoscope of emotions, perceptions, and interests of his or her individual consciousness.

The everyday, commonplace status of conversation should not lead us to diminish the importance of this conflict between the public and private spheres of interaction. In fact, it is precisely because of its ubiquity that communication is the matrix of mental illness (see Ruesch & Bateson, 1968). Thus, although some would claim that it is an exaggeration to broaden the definition of the double bind to include more than strictly clinical cases, we tend toward the other extreme. We argue that if it is descriptive of psychotic interaction within a culture, then it is also, by definition, true of all human interaction.

Most of the differences between the conversations of "normal" individuals and those of "abnormal" individuals are differences of degree, not of kind (see, for example, Geertz, 1977; Goffman, 1961, 1963; Ruesch & Bateson, 1968). Conversations can be located at points along a particular cultural continuum (such as normal/abnormal, sane/insane, or social/antisocial, for example), if that should prove useful for analysts or linguists or playwrights, but all conversations are of a piece. This is the conceptual context in which we generalize the notion of the double bind beyond its original clinical application.

To the charge that we run the risk of exaggerating teachers' difficulties, our response is the following: Teachers, like all employees, must negotiate conflicts between public and private spheres of interaction, between explicit and implicit communications. However, teachers, especially ESL and bilingual teachers, whose status within educational hierarchies is often marginal, frequently find themselves in double-binding situations. The reason for this is that teachers, like clergy, nurses, and doctors, are subject to unrealistic expectations by society at large. Teachers are expected not only to fulfill the letter of contracts but also to conform to mythical standards of moral stature. This has always been true, but we contend that the recent trend in language teaching toward so-called humanistic and communicative approaches has increased the pressure on teachers to be more than merely the efficient managers of students' learning. Teachers are therefore placed in a position of having to reconcile conflicts between public and private demands, explicit and implicit expectations. (See Watzlawick, 1977, and Watzlawick et al., 1967, for elaboration on the occurrence of paradoxes in everyday life.)

With regard to the final objection, that discussions of fine points such as these deflect attention from the more important issues in the field, we make the following assertion: The subordination of teachers to other professionals constitutes the single most crippling problem of the profession today, and the problem is greatly increased by the fact that it is generally not recognized as a problem at all, but merely as a fact of life. That teachers unconsciously accept this status is everywhere evident: in journal articles and conference workshops, where the speakers are usually "experts" from universities and state or federal departments of education, whereas the listeners are teachers, precisely the people who know enough about their situation and its difficulties to be able to offer advice to each other; in schools, where administrators and other decision makers are typically individuals who left the classroom because of their interest in things other than teaching; in the larger sphere of society, where legislators, school boards, and the public consistently demonstrate that teachers are not the experts at all, but rather the instruments of the system, who will merely put into effect whatever decisions the governing bodies deem necessary after consulting with the expert. This situation reveals critical flaws in our thinking that result from the following fundamental epistemological errors.

EPISTEMOLOGICAL ERRORS

1. *It's all quite simple.* This error can be found at all levels of education. Legislators, echoing public outcry, want to know the answer, without qualification or temporizing, to the problems in education. Policymakers and administrators implement one educational innovation after another in the search for the quick fix. This error may be the result of the technological advances of this century, which have led us to believe that all problems have solutions that can be derived by the straightforward application of simple principles (see P. Berger, B. Berger, & Kellner, 1974; P. Berger & Luckmann, 1967).

This is *The One-Minute Manager* (Blanchard & Johnson, 1982) mentality, reflecting an underlying assumption that problems have single sources: If we can merely locate that source, we will be able to cut the Gordian knot. It further reflects the assumption that people can be programmed, that people respond like billiard balls: Pointed in the right direction, they will reach their goal. These assumptions are strengthened by the tendency to demand instant action and immediate results and by the practice of assigning people hierarchical roles with rigid job descriptions.

2. *The experts have the answers.* This is another outgrowth of modernized, technologically advanced society: The complexity of life seems to demand specialization and rigid role definitions (see P. Berger et al., 1974; P. Berger & Luckmann, 1967). In education, this means that experts are the source of information and insight, leaving teachers as the receivers and appliers. In other words, the people who have the most contact with learners, and therefore the greatest amount of experience, are relegated to a relatively passive role in the profession.

3. *Problems have generic solutions.* It is perilously easy to assume that the existence of labels such as *affective variables in education, learner initiative*, or *communicative competence* guarantees the existence of generic solutions that can be applied without regard to individual situations. But pedagogical problems manifest themselves in specific circumstances with unique individuals. The only appropriate response to a problem is therefore specific to the situation. Although this should seem obvious, virtually all educational decisions these days reflect the assumption by commissions, policymakers, and administrators that solutions can be generalized to contexts other than those from which they arose. Increases in centralized decision making, curriculum coordination, and standardized testing are just three examples of the result of this trend.

4. *Solutions can be mandated.* Generic, "simple" solutions suggested by experts easily become mandates. The assumption is that solutions can be prescribed, like a universal public health program, to cure entire populations. Individual and specific problems are addressed by large-scale educational mandate; appropriate in theory, these programs may in practice serve no individual learner's needs. A case in point is the recent spate of "excellence reports"—*A Nation at Risk* (National Commission on Excellence in Education, 1983), *Action for Excellence* (Task Force on Education for Economic Growth, 1983), and so on—which consistently recommend solutions that ignore the special characteristics of the populations for which they were developed (see Gross & Gross, 1985; Karp, 1985). For example, recommendations for more homework, longer school days, more rigid evaluation, and so on, based on Japanese high-school performance, ignore vast differences between the two countries in terms of cultural traditions, governmental participation in schools, and curricular options and goals (Stedman & Smith, 1985).

5. *Stability in the form of uniformity is possible and desirable.* Implicit in educational mandates is the assumption that homogeneity is an achievable goal, that a desirable solution to a pedagogical problem would be a uniform program for a large number of teachers and learners.

We contend that these errors give rise to attempts at problem solving that create the behavioral paradoxes described above. The errors result from the apparently human propensity for reductionism, the pervasive tendency to accommodate the complexity of life by making it less complex. We have attempted to demonstrate the seriousness of this tendency by focusing on relatively common situations from what we hope is an uncommon perspective.

We are not unaware of the ironic situation in which we place ourselves: We argue that widely disparate problems can be reduced to the single problem of reductionism. We publish our critique of experts and generic solutions in a major professional journal. Nonetheless, we submit that there is a fundamental difference between prescriptions that must be followed and solutions that can be ignored or followed in specific and idiosyncratic ways.

By advocating individual solutions, however, we do not endorse a laissez-faire attitude toward teaching, nor do we deny the importance of formal teacher training. We believe that in most situations, there are good and bad decisions and that these decisions are often informed by research. But decisions specific to a situation can only be developed by the knowledgeable classroom teacher. Thus, we propose the following antidote to the epistemological errors that can place teachers and students in double binds.

BREAKING THE BINDS

We believe that the first steps toward reaching a healthy perspective of the profession and ourselves as teachers can be attained by recognizing certain features of life in the classroom:

First, *language learning is a complex process*. We are reminded of the aphorism credited to H. L. Mencken: "For every complex problem there is a straightforward, simple solution, and it is always wrong." We must learn to live with complexity and to appreciate ambiguity.

Second, *there are problems for which there are no prescriptions, even though they may have solutions*. In these instances, solutions cannot be mandated; they must be discovered by teachers in the messy reality of day-to-day life in the classroom.

Finally, *we can begin to break the bind of paradoxical situations*. This is not always easy, nor is it always possible to do in precisely the manner we would like. But we can break the binds in several ways:

1. *We can deny the validity of hierarchical relationships.* Teachers are professionals with responsibility for making the decisions on which the education system depends. Titles such as *director* or *expert* do not confer wisdom by virtue of being attached to an individual's name. As teachers, we must learn to assert our professional prerogatives.

2. *We can refuse to choose among unacceptable alternatives.* The question is not, This text/curriculum or that? but rather, How do we determine progress? and, How can we accommodate a suitable variety of materials and activities? Perhaps no test or standardized curriculum will meet our needs.

3. *We can recognize paradox when confronted with it.* We cannot expect people to respond to injunctions such as "Be more humanistic!" or "Communicate!" Recall the social worker in *A Thousand Clowns* (Gardner, 1962). She did not like Raymond Ledbetter so she decided to get to know him. Once she got to know him, she decided she hated him. We cannot legislate feelings, but we can create environments that foster humane behavior.

4. *We can step outside of the frame and comment on the situation.* In that way, we can make people aware of the binds in which they place each other. One condition of the double bind is the inability to comment upon it. We break the bind by stepping outside the frame. In instances when we are unable to comment on an unpleasant situation, it is necessary to disengage ourselves mentally, to gain some psychological distance from double-binding situations and win some measure of mental health merely by realizing that we can define roles and relationships differently. We must strive to limit our sense of responsibility for bad situations. Although this is easier said than done, we must resolve to leave school problems at school; it is extremely debilitating to carry home the stress caused by incompetent colleagues, unruly students, or mean-spirited administrators.

5. *We can be content with small, focused solutions.* Our greatest problems are often created by small acts of omission and gradual stages of deterioration, rather than by cataclysmic events. The repair of the education system will come in the same way.

We believe that it is possible to build a humane teaching and learning environment, but this will require a shift in focus. We need to examine the assumptions behind the roles and the relationships behind the system. Most important, we must remember that teachers are the source of energy and information in the system (for elaboration, see Bateson, 1972a, 1972b, 1972c, 1972d; Clarke, 1987). Like the tightrope walker who needs the freedom to be unstable, and thereby remain on the wire, teachers need the slack to make their own decisions—to be wrong on occasion, but to stay on the wire.

REFERENCES

Bateson, G. (1972a). Cybernetic explanation. In *Steps to an ecology of mind* (pp. 399–410). New York: Ballantine Books.

Bateson, G. (1972b). Double bind. In *Steps to an ecology of mind* (pp. 271–278). New York: Ballantine Books.

Bateson, G. (1972c). Ecology and flexibility in urban civilization. In *Steps to an ecology of mind* (pp. 494–505). New York: Ballantine Books.

Bateson, G. (1972d). Toward a theory of schizophrenia. In *Steps to an ecology of mind* (pp. 201–227). New York: Ballantine Books.

Berger, P., Berger, B., & Kellner, H. (1974). *The homeless mind*. New York: Vintage Books.

Berger, P., & Luckmann, T. (1967). *The social construction of reality*. New York: Doubleday.

Blanchard, K., & Johnson, S. (1982). *The one-minute manager*. New York: Berkeley Publishing.

Clarke, M. A. (1982). On bandwagons, tyranny, and common sense. *TESOL Quarterly, 16*, 437–448.

Clarke, M. A. (1983). (The scope of) approach, (the importance of) method, and (the nature of) technique. In J. E. Alatis, H. H. Stern, & P. Strevens (Eds.), *Georgetown University Round Table on Languages and Linguistics 1983* (pp. 106–115). Washington, DC: Georgetown University Press.

Clarke, M. A. (1984). On the nature of technique: What do we owe the gurus? *TESOL Quarterly, 18*, 577–594.

Clarke, M. A. (1987). Don't blame the system: Constraints on "whole language" reform. *Language Arts, 64*, 384–396.

Gardner, H. (1962). *A thousand clowns*. New York: Random House.

Geertz, C. (1977). Common sense as a cultural system. *Antioch Review, 35*(2–3), 5–26.

Giroux, H., & McLaren, P. (1986). Teacher education and the politics of engagement: The case for democratic schooling. *Harvard Educational Review, 56*, 213–238.

Goffman, E. (1961). *Asylums*. Garden City, NY: Anchor Books.

Goffman, E. (1963). *Stigma*. Englewood Cliffs, NJ: Prentice-Hall.

Gross, B., & Gross, R. (Eds.). (1985). *The great school debate: Which way for American education?* New York: Simon & Schuster.

Karp, W. (1985, June). Why Johnny can't think: The politics of bad schooling. *Harper's Magazine*, pp. 69–73.

National Commission on Excellence in Education. (1983). *A nation at risk: The imperative for educational reform*. Washington, DC: U.S. Government Printing Office.

Ruesch, J., & Bateson, G. (1968). *Communication: The social matrix of psychiatry*. New York: Norton.

Scollon, R., & Scollon, S. B. K. (1981). *Narrative, literacy and face in interethnic communication*. Norwood, NJ: Ablex.

Silberstein, S. (1984). *Why ESL teachers are ungovernable*. Unpublished manuscript, University of Washington.

Silberstein, S. (1987). Outtakes from *Reader's choice*: Issues in materials development. *TESL Canada Journal, 4*(2), 89–92.

Stedman, L. C., & Smith, M. S. (1985). Weak arguments, poor data, simplistic recommendations: Putting the reports under the microscope. In B. Gross & R. Gross (Eds.), *The great school debate: Which way for American education?* (pp. 83–105). New York: Simon & Schuster.

Stevick, E. W. (1980). *Teaching languages: A way and ways*. Rowley, MA: Newbury House.

Task Force on Education for Economic Growth. (1983). *Action for excellence: A comprehensive plan to improve our nation's schools*. Denver: Education Commission of the States.

Watzlawick, P. (1977). *How real is real?* New York: Vintage Books.

Watzlawick, P., Beavin, J. H., & Jackson, D. D. (1967). *Pragmatics of human communication*. New York: Norton.

Watzlawick, P., Weakland, J., & Fisch, R. (1974). *Change*. New York: Norton.

Wilden, A. (1980). *System and structure: Essays in communication and exchange* (2nd ed.). New York: Tavistock.

Chapter **2**

Teachers' and Students' Lessons

Adrian Holliday

TWO LESSONS

I wish to argue that classroom events incorporate not just one lesson, but many lessons—one which the teacher plans and administers, and one for each student taking part. Table 2.1 shows this distinction. Because it is not my intention to go into the psychology of individual students, I shall deal with the students' lessons as one, group agenda.

The table shows that the different lessons are marked by different agendas, which are influenced by a mixture of the respective expectations of teacher and student groups and individual abilities and preferences. These are in turn influenced by deep action phenomena—psycho-cultural, informal and micro-political factors which are often hidden from outsider view. In the case of the classroom, the teacher is at least partially an outsider to the culture of the students, and the students to the culture of the teachers.

The influences on each agenda within the classroom derive from the variety of forces outside the classroom . . . the professional-academic cultures of teachers, students and institutions. I have already described how the student culture, with all its constructs on what should happen in classrooms, is formed both inside and outside the classroom through successive generations of students. The significance of seeing what happens in the classroom in these terms is that the teacher's and students' lessons *are*

TABLE 2.1
Teacher's and Students' Lessons

Teacher's Lesson	*Students' Lessons (One for Each Student)*
Teacher's agenda, expressed in a lesson plan:	**Student's agenda:** what each student wants to get out of the lesson:
• what teacher would like to happen	• what each student actually gains from the experience of the lesson
• organised according to teacher's ideas	• organised according to each student's learning style
• a fine production	
Influenced by:	*Influenced by:*
• conventions of methodology	
• textbooks	
• teacher's and institution's expectations about student and teacher roles, and what should happen in lessons	• student expectations about student and teacher roles, and what should happen in lessons
• conventions for organising academic subject matter	• conventions for responding to lesson events (answering questions, drawing attention, taking turns etc.)
• teacher's personal needs, abilities and motivation	• student's personal needs, abilities and motivation
Influenced by:	*Influenced by:*
Deep action	**Deep action**
• tacit rules within professional-academic culture for teacher and student behaviour	• tacit rules within student culture for teacher and student behaviour
• institution micro-politics and informal order	• student micro-politics and informal order

inevitably *different*, and are very likely to be in conflict. The students want one thing out of the classroom process, and the teacher something else.

'The Curse of Caliban'

This notion is inspired by Widdowson's (1984:189–200) allegory about Caliban not learning what Prospero wishes to teach in Shakespeare's *The Tempest*. To cut a long story short, Prospero attempts to teach Caliban, whom he perceives as linguistically uncivilised, how to speak properly. Caliban learns; but he does not learn what Prospero intends to teach. Caliban has his own, student's agenda, and, to Prospero's astonishment, learns instead how to curse.

The moral of Widdowson's rendering of Shakespeare's story is that teachers should not expect their students to be slaves to their lesson plans. Widdowson is really aiming his comments at English for specific purposes

(ESP), which, at the time of writing, was still recovering from the narrow discipline set on it by Munby's (1978) needs analysis régime. The sociolinguistic needs of the target situation, in which the student would eventually use her or his English, would be defined in terms of language functions. These language functions would form the syllabus. The student, on mastering these language functions, would then presumably be able to operate in the target situation. Two problems with this were: i) there are other things going on in target situations than the utterance of prescribed language functions; and ii) students often have far wider aspirations than to be able to operate in limited target situations. This type of linguistically narrow ESP, Widdowson argues, sees students as slaves to syllabus design and implementation, for they are not allowed to learn beyond its specifications. . . .

Deferred Versus Immediate Outcomes

In one case at Lancaster University, with a group of Iranian trainee ships' engineers and a local, native-speaker teacher, it was observed that conflict was caused by a serious rift between the students' desire for spontaneity and the teacher's need to follow a prescribed lesson plan (Holliday 1984:38–9).

Table 2.2 shows how this conflict was manifested. Some of the interpretations in the table are less well founded than others. They are the result of observation of classes and interviews with teacher and students, who, by the way, were all keen to resolve the conflict. However, whether or not the interpretations are fully accurate, there was sufficient evidence to suggest that i) there were widely differing viewpoints held by the various parties, ii) the conflict was influenced by events outside the classroom, and iii) there was a degree of alienation or even anomie, on the part of the students, due partly to ii), and partly to the course purposes, which were too complex and different from what they had been used to.

This situation supports some of the hypotheses I have presented earlier. The micro events of classroom interaction need to be seen in terms of wider macro influences from outside the classroom, and also in terms of the differing viewpoints of the actors. These viewpoints are such that there is clearly a student *real world*, created partly by circumstance and partly by a deeper culture, to which the teacher is outsider. Concerning the latter point, this teacher was eager to understand but found it extremely difficult to fathom what was going on in the students' real world. The research which succeeded in demystifying the situation, at least sufficiently to enable action to be taken, was carried out by a third party, employing an ethnographic approach—although it was not labelled as such at the time. . . .

TABLE 2.2
Classroom Conflict Example

Teacher Behaviour	*Student Behaviour*
Follow step-by-step procedure: i) show slides of a dockyard while students take notes ii) students write a report	Disrupt, talk in own language
Teacher View	*Student View*
The course is 'communicative' in that it addresses student sociolinguistic and learning needs, provides authentic tasks and language data and allows student participation Students' lack of co-operativeness due to belligerence—'the students don't care—talking about other things, don't want to learn'	Want to learn, but frustrated by the way in which the teacher's lesson plan defers the lesson pay-off. The slides are fascinating. Need to talk about them immediately Teacher's failure to appreciate this view due to dislike of students
Background	*Background*
Student reputation for belligerence on campus Local nervousness with regard to early events in the Iranian revolution	Loss of traditional generalised respect for teachers Confusing 'liberating' effect of the 'communicative' course which held teacher-student 'negotiation' as one of its overt principles Unsettling effect of events at home—especially with regard to traditional authority structures

The outcome was arbitration which resulted in a change to a more open-ended methodology that allowed both students and teacher to negotiate what they wanted within the lesson. At the same time, to provide a greater feeling of security for the students, the course was given more structure (Holliday 1984:8–9). The examinations to which the students had been exposed were of a particularly esoteric kind (e.g. highly abstracted problem-solving tasks in which they were assessed on behavioural criteria which were not explained to them), and had not provided a structure of assessment they could recognise.

The 'communicative' régime of the course had insisted that the students should develop an understanding of what it was all about as part of a process competence at which the course aimed. Ironically, their revolution against the course, which their apparent belligerence in effect represented, followed by the change that they later negotiated, meant that the students had succeeded in acquiring sufficient process competence to be highly critical of what was being done to them, but in their *own* terms, rather than in the terms set by the course. Or, perhaps what this process competence really amounted to was a stage in learning the strange culture of the course, to the extent that the students would be able to see its inadequacies. The course had failed to learn *their* culture, despite claims that the 'communicative approach' acknowledges what 'learners bring to the situation' (see Breen and Candlin 1980:93); and it was only when research to investigate the nature of the conflict began, and the two cultures were presented to each party by the third party, that each side began to appreciate the sincerity of the other—the 'want to learn' and the 'want to teach', which had been hidden by anxieties and suspicions—and that the way was paved for reconciliation.

'Anglos' and Eskimos

I have already referred to Collier's (1979) study of the rhythms of movement within the classroom. Although these were not English language classes, the research provides insights into the conflict between teachers' and students' lessons from which we can learn.

Different classrooms with 'Anglo' American and local Eskimo teachers are compared, both with primary level Eskimo pupils. The rhythm of movement of the Eskimo teachers blended with that of the young students—'things took longer and the transitions between activities were less sudden and distinct'. However, the rhythm and movement of the Anglo teachers was very much in conflict. 'Anglo teachers generally ran their classes on a schedule that gave relatively short periods of time to each activity' (ibid.:43). Indeed, the conflict was severe:

> The fast pace and aggressive, linear style of movement of many teachers was deadly. In every case, the students responded with confused behaviour indicative of the failure of the communication process. In extreme examples, the students froze up; the harder the teachers tried, the worse it got. (Ibid.:48)

As with the British teacher and Iranian students above, the Anglo teachers were following agendas which related to their own image of how a lesson should be constructed and carried out, which might have been highly sophisticated and rationalised in terms of methodology, and appropriate to their own professional-academic culture, but were failing to learn the culture of the students.

This appropriateness to their own professional-academic culture at the classroom level might indeed reflect a defence mechanism against the uncertainty of the foreign culture of the students. This parallels the 'busy work' defence mechanism of expatriate staff faced with the uncertainty of local realities in English language projects. Hence, the 'calculated procrastination' which this represents in project work can also be seen in classroom teaching.

Within the context of project work, Swales provides an example of the failure on the part of expatriate personnel to understand and adapt to the real world of students from the Khartoum University project to understand and adapt to the real world of local students. When the project introduced foreign teaching and examination styles, which bore little relationship to their previous experience, the students underwent 'educational shock' as well as 'culture shock' (1980:64). However, the expatriate teachers were unable to address this problem. The outcome was not so much the alienation of the students, but an overall failure of the project 'to convince the students that we were a serious department' (ibid.:66).

THE MYTH OF EXPATRIATE SUCCESS

Because teachers inevitably fail to lesser or greater degrees to address the portion of the classroom culture that belongs to their students, preoccupied as they are with the technology of their perceptions of *their* lessons, much of the 'success' of these technologies is in effect mythical. This can be seen expecially in the case of expatriate lecturers teaching Egyptian trainee teachers in the Ain Shams project.

Short-Term Effectiveness

During the course of the Ain Shams project I saw many examples of expatriate lecturers coping masterfully with difficult classroom conditions, displaying state-of-the-art BANA methodology in producing the learning group ideal (Holliday 1991a:324–36).[1] Furthermore, an integration of language skills and methodology for the Egyptian trainee teachers, who are the students, was admirably achieved. A particular example was of students purposefully and successfully being given responsibility to do classroom tasks, un-monitored, in the class of about 50:

> The [expatriate] lecturer displays excellent classroom management. She . . . successfully has the students working in highly organised groups, doing sophisticated group activities, in two rooms at the same time, during which time she withdraws except as a monitor and achieves decentralisation. . . . The students have to (1) look at blackboard diagrams which indicate a divi-

[1]Editors' Note: BANA = British, Australasian, North American

> sion of labour within each group concerning what they have to do with an authentic extract from the textbook which they will use on teaching practice. They then (2) have to go into groups, men in one room, women in an adjacent room, and prepare sentence types (a different type for each member of the group), which they have to (3) write up on the blackboard and (4) peer teach, the women to the men in their room, and then the men to the women in their room. . . . (5) Students have to copy *all* the sentence types into their teaching practice notebooks before leaving the room. . . . Local students are not supposed to be used to writing in class at all, never mind finishing something completely in class. (Observation notes)

(The descriptions of this and other lessons in Holliday 1991a are supported by photographs.) The final comment in the notes underlines the sense of achievement felt by the expatriates in completely changing indigenous classroom behaviour, away from collectionist lectures. To use Coleman's (1987) terms, the students had been converted from being the audience in a 'teaching spectacle', to being participants in a 'learning festival'. At least, this is the surface perception an observer might get; but how deeply 'successful' was this change?

Despite this apparent success, there is in fact a grave danger here of expatriate lecturers unconsciously disregarding local protocol because of their highly rationalised forms of classroom control. I have already referred to possible inappropriateness in the way in which expatriate lecturers constantly gave explicit classroom instructions. One factor which has to be considered here is that the expatriate lecturers were immune to some of the conservative forces within the local classroom institution which influenced local lecturers. This point was actually made by some local lecturers who saw this immunity as an unfair advantage on the part of expatriate lecturers, enabling them to accept the project's 'unnatural' approach (Holliday 1986a:10). The notion of immunity to local cultural forces grows out of the observation that despite these insensitivities—albeit unconscious—expatriate lecturers *could*, through their rationalised approach, be effective in the short term. In other words, expatriate lecturers could get away with trampling over local protocols in the short time that they were in contact with them. This was all the more possible because of the resilience and hospitality of the local classroom culture. This point is also made strongly by Hawkey and Nakornchai with regard to Thai students' apparent adaptation to foreign methodologies:

> We should beware, however, of over-simplified = equations between what is traditional and expected and what is difficult to accept because it is new. A foreign teacher in Thailand may well find that students revel in the opportunity to be creative and to work independently if they offered it, just *because* it is novel. (1980:73)

Consider another expatriate lecturer's class. He is grappling with his second week in a provincial university, with no previous experience of teaching either in a university or outside Britain:

> British school teacher, down-market clothes, books in ethnic bag (commented on by senior local lecturer colleagues)—a long way from the local PhD image. Refuses to allow janitor to carry things for him (a little embarrassing when he had a *lot* to carry, clearly couldn't manage elegantly, even with my help). Clearly a good teacher, but mechanical authority, constantly asking the students to be quiet. Small voice, therefore had to shout, but no more than necessary. Very cool despite having quite a hard time (janitor dropped 150 × 4 photocopies on the floor, so that he had to spend twenty minutes picking up and collating [without allowing the students to help], at the same time as myself, the head of department and another senior lecturer came in to watch with only one minute's warning). Sweating brow keeps turning into a . . . smile—'It's like a zoo in here; but they're so nice aren't they'. . . . Eyes absolutely fixed to him. The lecturer uses his foreignness to show how he can make sense of the Arabic text (included to demonstrate similarities with English) despite his inability to 'read'. (Observation notes)

Although he did not conform to the local lecturer image with his casual appearance and willingness to carry things by himself, he was carried through by his students' fascination and hospitality, and by the novelty of his approach. Although his teaching style was *mechanical*, and his approach did stimulate some complaint on the part of the students regarding the 'unstructured' nature of the skills-based, discovery-oriented, collaborative approach this teacher employed, the students were:

> very careful to say that he was a marvellous teacher, especially for his keenness to turn up to every lecture for the full time. They were very concerned that their criticisms would not be taken as being against him. (Observation notes)

Moreover:

> It was significant that . . . [he] had very little time to sit and talk because he was teaching three classes in six hours, and was being conscientious enough to attend on time. . . . [My two local co-observers] seemed very impressed with the pace he was able to keep up. (Observation notes)

I wish to suggest that, despite hard work and a genuine concern for the students, the 'success' of this lecturer's highly rationalised approach was largely a myth maintained by the novelty, likeability and the respect for being clearly devoted and hard-working afforded him by his local peers and students. This is reminiscent of the way in which the hospitable Egyptian lecturer gave her expatriate colleague information that would please him, rather than upsetting him with the reality of the situation. In fact, the *apparent* acceptability of expatriate lecturers was in sharp conflict with private conversations I had with the local teaching staff, who seemed to find it hard to take seriously the expatriates' lack of seniority, lack of formal qualifications, lack of university experience, and lack of ability to appreciate and get on with local protocols, regard for the sensitivities of local colleagues and so on.

An interesting case is reported by Szulc-Kurpaska (1992). An evaluation of language and methodology courses for trainee teachers in Poland revealed dissatisfaction on the part of students with regard to the degree of informality practised by expatriate lecturers both in and out of the classroom. Despite the initial attractiveness of this behaviour, students were becoming confused and uneasy over the blurred definitions of teacher and student role. They wanted to know where they stood, and were happier with local lecturers who managed to blend friendliness with a traditional social distance. Szulc-Kurpaska found that although students could go to her home to discuss work, they knew where they stood because she insisted on being addressed by her title and family name and did not extend friendliness beyond the work relationship (personal communication). It took years of experience and knowledge of local protocols to be able to manage such a balance.

Dealing With Student Attitudes

One area where expatriate lecturers in Egyptian faculties of education could not be immune was in dealing with local student attitudes. The ease with which their intentions could be misconstrued by the students is illustrated in one case where:

> One expatriate lecturer who had tried the 'Vegetarian' text in a provincial faculty had complained that the students had accused him of trying to corrupt them with Western ideas—naturally, he suspected, they had identified him too much with the interactants on the recording. (Observation notes)

This text was a conversation between two vegetarians about their diets. The expatriate lecturer believed that the students thought he was suggesting they should become vegetarians—a sufficiently eccentric concept within the local national culture to be considered 'Western'.

The problem was not so much that the text content might have been inappropriate to the so-called national culture, which would have been a dangerous overgeneralisation, but that the expatriate did not know sufficient about the real world of the students to understand their reactions, which seemed confusingly varied and unpredictable. On several occasions, texts in the project materials were criticised by local lecturers on the grounds of being potentially corrupting; but it was difficult to achieve consensus among local lecturers because of widely differing opinions.

Examples of outsiders to the student culture receiving confusing signals can be found in the following three cases. In an essay class which I was observing:

> I was asked to comment on the introduction of one male student. When he said that 'poor people' were an evil which had to be solved, I assumed that he wanted to say 'poverty' was an evil, and not 'poor people'. The more I tried to make my point that what *he* said sounded as though he wanted to eradicate the people rather than their condition, I began to see that he *did* intend the former, and that it was not a language problem that made what he said seem strange but a marked attitude difference that I had not expected. In the same way, when the class began to discuss possibilities for the next essay assignment on the effects of divorce on women, and a female student remarked that society inflicted great suffering on divorced women, I assumed that she meant this in a negative way, and that she was making a plea for women's liberation. However, I soon got the impression that she, and all the others, felt that the women's suffering was a *positive* thing because it was a disincentive for women to get divorced in the first place. Divorce was *bad*, and *women* should not do it, no matter what. The progressive end of the class were the ones who accepted that divorce was common in their society, albeit bad; the conservative end would not accept this and said that women in their society did *not choose* divorce except in rare, and presumably criminal, cases.
>
> I was guilty of . . . grave misinterpretations. I had assumed that the statements by the students were eccentric because of language difficulty rather than because their underlying attitudes were different to my expectations. I did not have the experience of the culture outside the classroom to accurately perceive what was going on.
>
> . . . [Their local lecturer] said that he too was sometimes shocked at his students' attitudes. (Observation notes)

This case illustrates how the attitudes of students are very different from what one expects, and easily misinterpreted. My first reaction to this event was that the local students were conservative in their attitudes. However, this hypothesis was not substantiated in another essay class:

> The students seemed outspoken, the [local] lecturer seemed to be provoking them. The subject matter may have been considered sensitive by an expatriate. There were several references to manwoman relationships in co-ed schools. One woman said that if women found out about men's mentality in co-ed schools they would never marry them, and that normally women never found out about men until marriage because in university they kept apart and at work their roles were very separate. Several men said that they had to be careful of what they said when they got to university (after single-sex

> schools) because women were there. The lecturer asked if he meant bad language and he giggled. Two women said that they preferred single-sex schools because they could sit on the floor and not care about anyone else. Several women said that at university they did not communicate with men. Some said that men kept away from them because they didn't like to admit that the women were not inferior academically. Some men said that they didn't know how to behave with women after single-sex schools and that they felt that this was a lack. One man said that women were superior academically and that he couldn't have known this had he been to a single-sex school. (Observation notes)

In both cases I felt that the issues being discussed with the local lecturer would have to be too sensitive for me as an outsider to handle, that these were areas in which I was out of my depth in an inscrutible student culture, within the context of the classroom where the expatriate lecturer cannot afford to be misconstrued.

In a third class, in which I was giving the guest lesson:

> At the end of the lecture some of the [students] . . . asked how they could learn better English. The women said they watched the foreign serial (which came on the television every night), but found the present one *The Foundation* (a British TV business drama) difficult because everyone talked so fast. I agreed (in fact the acting does seem quite bad and everyone does seem to talk quite fast). One woman asked why I didn't seem to be like the people in *The Cedar Tree* (another British serial about an upper middle class family between the wars). She said that they seemed very conservative and cared too much about traditions. I thought it impressive that she had picked this up (although there *are* Arabic subtitles). I explained that it was set a long time ago and about a very upper class family, not dissimilar to old Egyptian films set in the 40s and 50s. (Observation notes)

Later, in a discussion with one of the students' local lecturers:

> We talked about the interests of the students in the TV and radio. I mentioned the business of *The Cedar Tree* . . . and asked if they listened to a particularly well-known radio local English language broadcaster and disc jockey. She said that although this broadcaster was very popular with the students in the capital, in the provinces she was considered too 'Western' and was not listened to. This didn't seem to fit with the students' talk of *The Cedar Tree* being too conservative. (Observation notes)

These apparent contradictions in student attitude exemplify how far student attitudes are part of a complex deep action within the student culture, and that it is not helpful to explain these things away by referring to national cultural traits.

It was no less confusing to consult local lecturers on the question of text appropriacy. One local lecturer complained vehemently about a text in which there was a 'report on Saudi women's education with reference to a man at the gate keeping men out of the school' (Observation notes). She:

> said that the project's essay and reading comprehension course was completely inappropriate because of the content of this particular text. I had defended myself and the course by saying that several local colleagues had vetted all the texts during the selection process. The head of department had said that these people could not be relied upon. I had also had a similar reaction from another eminent member of an English department who had seen the reference to alcoholic pilots in one of the texts. . . . [He] said that the texts in the course encouraged anti-Western feeling among students by showing a bad side of Western culture. (Observation notes)

It was hard to get consensus however. Another local colleague, who had watched me use the text without difficulty, said that the text was ideal (Observation notes); and other 'local colleagues who had helped select the texts still maintain that the items mentioned are not inappropriate' (Observation notes).

The issue of text appropriacy was not therefore just a matter of inscrutible student culture, but of a wider complex of cultures within the institution and perhaps beyond—a deep action involving perhaps micropolitical, political or religious conflicts beyond the sight of the outsider.

Counterproductive Tinkering

There were cases where expatriate lecturers did not get away with their rationalised approach. I have already referred to Dr Anwar being unimpressed at Beatrice's expertise in the language laboratory and attitude towards the local system. Despite (in my view), her ability to make the language lab lessons work, in terms of the learning group ideal, she was also missing important things about the culture of her students and how they related to other personalities. She failed or refused to understand that a lab technician was available to see students to their places and help them operate the machinery (Holliday 1992a:224). Furthermore:

> The technician and the lab assistant also said that they thought Beatrice was unprofessional in the way in which she favoured particular groups of students who were nice to her and invited her to their homes at weekends, by giving them special classes, and that *these* students would be the ones she would give special sessions to in the lab. They felt that this was not a valid reason for wanting to break regulations by having a personal key or for asking them to work overtime—the only alternative. (Observation notes)

In this way, rationalisation brought to the situation by the expatriate lecturer, oriented as it was to the learning group ideal, failed to either perceive or appreciate other important features of relationships within the local educational environment. Using Widdowson's terms, the quality of the relationship between teacher and student might not be dependent simply on the quality of the learning *transaction* which is taking place, but also on the quality of a wider set of *interactions*. The social perceptions of teacher and student roles, not only by the teacher and students, but also by other involved actors (e.g. the lab technician), although appearing to have little to do with pedagogy, had also to be right. Returning to my insistence on referring to 'student' rather than 'learner', a large part of Beatrice's problem, and of the alienation of many teachers from the culture of their students, was her apparent assumption that her students were there only to *learn*. She might have rationalised her methodology on an understanding of how 'learners' learn, but not on how *students* interact with their world and all the complex social factors surrounding why they are in the classroom.

THE POSSIBILITY OF INTEGRATION

There were, however, cases which proved that the intrusion of expatriate lecturers did not have to be counterproductive. Although Collier suggests that outsider Anglo teachers in Alaska were unable to work to the natural rhythms of their students, he did find an exception to this rule in the case of one teacher, Mr Scout, who 'broke away from the standard Anglo pattern' (1979:48):

> Many activities [in his class] . . . were group activities in which he was only marginally involved. The pacing of these activities was largely in the hands of the children . . . [and this teacher] is highly sensitive to non-verbal signals. (Ibid.:45)

Significantly, Mr Scout created a 'classroom environment . . . in which it was possible for him to learn the movement patterns of the children and them to learn his' (ibid.:40). Collier further speculates that the ability of this teacher to integrate with the culture of the class might have been connected with the fact that he was from a marginal immigrant background (ibid.:33). One might assume that being an experienced marginal person by nature would permit the cultivation of an ability to observe and adapt to other cultures.

Such an ability was also found in the lessons of an expatriate lecturer, Dawoud, in an Egyptian faculty of education. In the first place, he too was able to create a learning environment which put activities in the hands of the students, enabling them to express and capitalise on their natural gregariousness and ability at small-group organisation, and which also gave scope for observation of their behaviour. Secondly, he was a member of an immigrant minority in the United States, and brought up in the Middle East in a culture cognate with the one in which the project was taking place:

> Dawoud was born in the Middle East, and has a PhD in linguistics . . . [thus] his undergraduate educational background is culturally more similar to that of local lecturers and students than that of any of the other expatriate lecturers. . . . Several students were carrying flowers. One of the men gives a flower to Dawoud, which he takes and keeps during part of the lesson—evidence of a profound integration with their culture—he holds it as they do. (Observation notes)

In another class:

> Dawoud showed his cultural integration by being very strict with latecomers, telling them they could not come in, but at the same time knowing when to make exceptions. He managed to make an interesting balance between theory and practice—by turning the practical language learning element of his class around the theory, as though using it as a carrier content. (Observation notes)

From my integrationist point of view, looking for signs of a skills-based, discovery-oriented, collaborative approach, I was concerned that he was being too didactic. However:

> One of Dawoud's arguments for what he was doing is that this was the way he had learnt while in English classes in his youth; and clearly he knew what was interesting and in demand for the students. I was also concerned that although he was masterful at managing learning in a very communicative way he was very worried about letting go and wanted to make every single step lecturer-controlled. He said that it would be very easy to lose the students' attention if he did not work in this way. He was also very concerned about maintaining his professorial status by presenting theory. He might be right about this. This might be where the interface between practice and theory for the local situation lies. (Observation notes)

Here Dawoud manages not only a degree of integration with the traditional aspects of the classroom culture, but also conforms to aspects of the local lecturer image implicit in the prevailing local professional-academic culture. The fact that he possesses a PhD in a theoretical subject helps to enable this; and taking on the expected lecturer image helps integration with the classroom culture as a whole. In addition, his lessons demonstrate not only how he is rationalising his classroom methodology, but also how this methodology can become culturally appropriate. Moreover, he sees that, to become culturally appropriate, the teaching methodology must be part of a wider *ethno*methodology.

There is therefore a capacity for some expatriate lecturers to move towards the traditional requirements of the local classroom culture if their rationalised approach is appropriately directed and expanded.

Exotic British Students

All the cases of classroom conflict cited in this chapter have been of teachers and students from different national cultures. In previous chapters I have argued that it is misleading to think of problems in English language education only in terms of national cultural differences. Conflicts between people of the same national culture, but of different professional-academic cultures, have been described with reference to the Keele University integrated studies curriculum project in Chapter 7 [of my book]. Within the classroom, the history of secondary school teaching in Britain is rife with discipline problems which can be traced to teachers' inability to learn and understand the culture of their students. This inability may possibly but not necessarily be affected by overlays of differences in social class or generation. One of my own recent teaching experiences was particularly revealing in this respect.

I had to take three classes in applied linguistics for another department, on a diploma course for British primary school teachers. The course was already established, and the students had already formed an established culture by the time I arrived. Although they were of the same nationality, similar social class, and generally of the same generation, although we were all 'teachers' of one type or another, I felt as much an outsider to their culture as I would to the cultures of students in other-nationality classes. What was particularly interesting was that, despite sharing the same English language, without any marked differences in accent or dialect, I found their mode of communication almost as mysterious as that of the Egyptian classes already cited. I could understand every word they said, but when it came to monitoring group activities, I was as much at a loss about when it was appropriate, in *their* cultural terms, to make moves to put them on task or to join in their discussion. As with the Egyptian class in which students were apparently *off*-task, but later showed that they were very much in touch with the lesson, I found it difficult, with these British students, to determine whether or not they were *on*-task. There was bantering and laughter between them which represented protocols governing formality and informality which I found difficult to understand. For survival, I had to observe and learn as much as I could about their culture before proceeding.

THE PARAMETERS FOR LOCAL TEACHER SUCCESS

A strong implication of the argument in this chapter is that conflict between student and teacher agendas is increased where the teacher is an expatriate and thus all the more foreign to the culture of the students. The cases of the Anglo teacher and Dawoud, who go some way in succeeding to bridge the gap, are unusual.

A major advantage which local teachers have is that they have in the past been students like their own students. Dalbouni (1992) makes explicit use of this type of inside knowledge in her research on the social context of writing instruction at Damascus University; and one of Dawoud's advantages is that he was brought up as a student in a national culture cognate with that of his Egyptian students.

However, it would be dangerous to be too romantic about the innate ability of local teachers to know their students so well that conflicts are reduced. I have shown that, within the same national culture, students still have very different cultures from their teachers. Indeed, the student group in each class will have a different culture, as the culture of the classroom is different to some degree in each case. The teacher's role, whatever her or his background might be, by its nature will give the teacher a different construction on events within the classroom from those of her or his students: their agendas are essentially different; and the communication they have with each other is essentially limited. An interesting anecdote from a newly initiated teacher trainer in South Africa illustrates this point. He remembered the pleas of his British tutors, while studying in Britain, for the class to let them know how they felt about course content—to make some comment about the issues that were being raised. He now had the same difficulty with his own compatriots while carrying out training programmes in South Africa: it was very hard for him to find out how they felt about things.

Whoever the teacher is, therefore, classroom methodologies need to be developed to increase the teacher's ability to study the culture of her or his students, and to allow students the ability to express their needs to the teacher.

REFERENCES

Breen, M. P. and C. N. Candlin. 1980. The essentials of a communicative curriculum in language teaching. *Applied Linguistics, 1*(2), 89–11.

Coleman, H. 1987. Teaching spectacles and learning festivals. *English Language Teaching Journal, 41*(2), 97–103.

Collier, M. 1979. *A Film Study in Classrooms in Western Alaska.* Fairbanks: Center for Cross-Cultural Studies, University of Alaska.

Dalbouni, H. 1992. *An investigation into the relations between the educational context and the written projects of university EFL students, with implications for the teaching of writing.* Unpublished PhD thesis. Department of Linguistics, University of Leeds.

Hawkey, R. and C. Nakornchai. 1980. Thai students studying. In The British Council. 1980. *ELT Documents 109, Study Modes and Academic Development of Overseas Students.* London: The British Council, 70–8.

Holliday, A. R. 1984. Research into classroom culture as necessary input to syllabus design. In J. Swales and H. Mustafa (Eds.) *ESP in The Arab World,* 29–51. Birmingham: Language Services Unit, University of Aston.

Holliday, A. R. 1986. *Interim Report for 1985-6 for The Phonetics and Grammar Components of The BA in Education with English.* Unpublished report. Cairo: Centre for Developing English Language Teaching, Ain Shams University.

Holliday, A. R. 1991. *Dealing with Tissue Rejection in EFL Projects: The Role of an Ethnographic Means Analysis.* Unpublished PhD Thesis. University of Lancaster.

Munby, J. 1978. *Communicative Syllabus Design.* Cambridge: Cambridge University Press.

Swales, J. 1980. The educational environment and its relevance to ESP programme design. In *Projects in Materials Design,* 61–70. ELT Documents Special. London: The British Council.

Holliday, A. R. 1992. Intercompetence: Sources of conflict between local and expatriate ELT personnel. *System 20*(2).

Szulc-Kurpaska, M. 1992. *Evaluation in Legnica Foreign Language Teacher Training College.* Unpublished Report. Foreign Language Teacher Training College, Legnica, Poland.

Widdowson, H. G. 1984. *Explorations in Applied Linguistics 2.* Oxford: Oxford University Press.

Chapter 3

Classroom Interaction Patterns: Reflections of a Stratified Society

Cathy M. Roller

The focus of this special issue of *Language Arts* is the rapid demographic change that is transforming the face of developed countries. Relatively homogeneous majority populations are being replaced by heterogeneous collections of racial, ethnic, and cultural groups. The question posed by this issue is, "What is the role of language arts instruction in the face of such change?" To answer this question we need to assess the role of language arts instruction in the relatively homogeneous societies of recent decades as a basis for determining what kinds of changes the pluralistic societies of the future will require. Because I am from the United States, I will speak mainly of that society, focusing on reading instruction as it has been implemented in our schools in recent decades.

First, I would like to argue that present reading instructional technology in the U.S.—the basal reader systems used so ubiquitously in our schools—has by some measures served society exceptionally well. Shannon (1985) noted that public schools in the United States have traditionally served two functions: to instruct youths in academic subjects and to develop good citizens for the republic. Since the midnineteenth century, the task of producing good citizens for the republic has required that those citizens be differentiated. With the closing of the frontiers and the increase in population through immigration that came with industrialization, expansionist attitudes were replaced by protectionist ones. The perception that our society required different classes of people to do different sorts of tasks began to grow. Woodrow Wilson wrote in 1909:

> Let us go back and distinguish between two things that we want to do; for we want to do two things in modern society. We want a class of persons to have a liberal education, and we want another class of persons, a very much larger class, of necessity, in every society, to forego the privileges of a liberal education and fit themselves to perform specific manual tasks. You cannot train them for both in the time you have at your disposal. They must make a selection and you must make a selection. (Kozol 1985, p. 89)

The selection process then, as now, seems to have been heavily influenced by class and racial criteria. We have only to look to the rates of unemployment, poverty, infant mortality, and illiteracy among minority groups to recognize that there has been something insidious operating in America. Our commitment to equal opportunity seems to have been undermined, if it ever existed at all. The selection process has not meant a wide variety of opportunity for everyone. Rather, it has encouraged the creation of class barriers based on the racial and ethnic differences that could (or should) be a source of richness and vitality in our public life.

That schools are instrumental in this process of class creation is unarguable; whether it has been intentional or not is open to question. It is interesting to note that since the beginning of public schooling in this country in the nineteenth century, literacy rates have actually gone down (Cook-Gumperz 1986). Scollon (1988) has reported that:

> One of the arguments in support of schooling given then [middle of the nineteenth century] was that literacy was getting to be too widespread among the working classes. They were getting too many dangerous ideas. Public schooling could be used to limit students' access to this literate conversation. It would keep them out of the picture by carefully controlling what they read and how they read it. (p. 30)

I argue, as Shannon (1985) and Fraatz (1987) have that reading instruction as presently delivered has, probably unintentionally, been instrumental in perpetuating and maintaining our class- and race-stratified society.

ONE READING LESSON AS MICROCOSM

The aspect of reading instruction that I will explore in depth is the communication patterns that occur in typical basal reader instruction. Specifically I will focus on how these patterns contribute to the sorting and stratification process. I first became aware of the nature of these patterns when I taught a demonstration classroom in a rural Zimbabwean primary school. I taught third grade students their English reading lessons. This assignment was part of a national effort, Project Zimread, to improve language instruction. I took part in the project from May 1985 through August

1986 while serving as a Fulbright Lecturer at the University of Zimbabwe. I set up my demonstration classroom using the methods and techniques I had been teaching for a number of years to teachers-in-training at the University of Iowa. I divided the children into three reading groups instructed from basal-like readers at the primer, 1–2, and 2–2 levels. The three-day instructional cycle included a series of activities completed Before, During, and After the children read their stories. Each group did two seatwork activities and met with me daily. Because of paper shortages and the unavailability of duplicating equipment, I presented the seatwork on workcards. I made two workcards for each table and put them on stands. The children wrote their answers to the activities in an exercise book. At thirty-minute intervals the children rotated to their assigned activities.

When I met with a group on a "Before" day, I worked mainly with vocabulary introduction (Heimlich and Pittelman 1986) and prior knowledge (Hansen 1981). However, discussion was difficult since I could handle Shona, the children's first language, only at about a first grade level and their English was rudimentary. For the "During" sessions, I checked oral reading accuracy and taught simple question-answering techniques (Raphael 1986). "After" lessons began with the children drawing a picture summary of the story; I then worked with them until they could produce a brief oral summary of the story (Spiegel and Fitzgerald 1986).

The instruction was remarkably "successful," particularly with the top group. Within two weeks, the children, particularly those in the top two groups, learned the seatwork routines and could do their exercises independently. They knew what was expected in the reading circle and they could play the vocabulary games, respond to questions, and provide brief oral summaries of the stories they read. At the end of the five weeks I presented a demonstration lesson to the teachers of the five-school cluster of which this school was a part. The teachers were impressed with the lesson and were amazed that these third-grade children, particularly those in the top group, could perform so well in English.

In many ways I was quite proud of what the children and I had accomplished. However, even as the teachers applauded, I felt dissatisfied and unhappy with what we had done. While I was relatively successful, the teaching was very difficult. My primary recollection of the experience is of how hard I worked and how little I enjoyed the teaching. It seemed that every bit of my attention went into explaining directions, overseeing tasks, and working toward accurate performance. The low group required constant monitoring. There was little joy in that classroom. But the fact that the teaching was difficult was not the only source of my discomfort.

What was so deeply disturbing was that I *was* able to teach those children their English reading lessons when I couldn't really communicate with the children at all. The lack of communication was painfully clear on several occasions. The first day of class, I asked one child where the books were. He responded, "My name is Tonderai. I come from Chikore village." I got similar responses several times. The children responded to an English question with the English they knew. That same day when I dismissed them, the children raced for the door. During the lesson several children had asked for permission to go to the toilet, but I hadn't understood the Shona for "toilet."

We developed a "lesson language" that followed the Initiate-Respond-Evaluate (IRE) pattern documented in several classroom discourse studies (Barnes 1976; Bellack 1966; Mehan 1979; Wells 1986). I questioned; they answered; I evaluated. The pattern got us through the lesson and allowed us to achieve our goals—pronouncing vocabulary words, answering questions, and summarizing stories. But there was no authentic communication occurring. I asked children questions that I knew the answers to, and they knew that I knew the answers. The lessons were an exercise in assessment, not communication. Although I knew their names, could move them around the classroom, could even "teach" them, I knew almost nothing about their lives. We never really established contact with one another. We did not connect.

Perhaps I should not have been surprised at our lack of authentic communication, given the levels of our language skills and the nature of the demonstration project. What was surprising was that this classroom didn't look or sound much different from the ones I was familiar with at home. At home, too, reading lessons are conducted in "lesson language." At home, too, teachers initiate, children respond, and teachers evaluate.

In Zimbabwe I learned that the methods I was using, quite common ones in the United States, accommodated *noncommunication*. The linguistic barriers which separated the children and me forced me to notice and to acknowledge the superficiality of the teaching methods I was using. The experience made me look with fresh eyes at the classrooms I was familiar with at home. The similarity between my Zimbabwean classroom and the classrooms I had observed at home was startling. How much authentic communication occurs around reading predetermined stories, answering predetermined questions, and filling in worksheets? Probably very little. Teachers in U.S. classrooms could conduct lessons and know little more about their children than I knew of the Zimbabwean ones.

TYPICAL TEACHER-LEARNER INTERACTION

Surely language arts lessons that accommodate the learning of a communication skill without communication do not teach children communication skills! A look at the interaction patterns in typical reading lessons leads me to the dismaying conclusion that perhaps in many lessons communication is not even a goal. The transcript that follows comes from a demonstration lesson by one of my finest masters' degree students. For many years, I used this transcript as exemplary in training reading teachers.

The lesson was based on a story from a well-known basal reading series. The story explored the idea of cheating. The main character, Maria, receives help from another child in preparing a project for a science fair. Maria eventually wins a prize and feels quite guilty about not acknowledging the help she received. In the part of the prereading interaction reproduced here, the teacher is exploring feelings of competition in science fair participants:

T: The first question I'd like to ask you about today is whether or not you've participated in a science fair or some kind of contest where you had to make something. Think for a minute. How did you feel when you were entering this contest? Give me a low signal when you're ready to tell about your past experience. OK, C1.

C1: When I was in Cub Scouts we had to make a robot out of boards, bottle caps, and (*unintelligible*). At first I thought I was going to win, but when I got to the judging I saw other things that were a lot better than mine.

T: While you were constructing your robot you thought you probably would win. Were you nervous?

C1: No.

T: Not too nervous. Who else has been in a contest like that?

C2: I was in the same thing. I wasn't, I got it done. I knew I wouldn't win anything.

T: Uh, huh.

C2: Turned out I was sick that night so I never got to take it in.

T: You never got to take it in. C3, have you ever entered a contest or something like that? Some other kind of competition maybe, where you're up against other people and they're doing the same kind of thing you're doing? C4?

C4: In fourth grade where we had a Valentine party. We had to make these boxes. When I first made it, I didn't think I was going to win at all because I just got some old things and put it together so.

T: What kind of box was it?

C4: Just a Valentine's box in fourth grade where we used to put our envelopes into.

T: Uh, huh. I can remember doing that in school too. C5? Have you ever entered a competition?

C5: There was a Halloween where you had to color a picture in or draw it. I entered it but I didn't win anything.

T: How did you feel?

C5: I didn't really care.

T: You didn't care whether you won or not. Well, in the story today is a girl named Maria, and she's entering a science fair, so she has to have a pretty elaborate project. How do you think she feels? Just think about it a minute. The importance of the project. C3?

C3: I think she feels really nervous.

T: Nervous. C4, how about you?

C4: She's anxious.

T: OK. Let me get some of these words down. I like these words. Nervous, anxious (*writing on board*). Anybody else? C1.

C1: Scared.

T: Scared. C5, do you agree with those?

C5: Uh, huh.

T: Is that what you think she probably will be feeling? OK.

Notice how the teacher dominates the exchange. She has thoroughly planned the lesson. She had determined several critical ideas for understanding the story as she interpreted it, and in this transcript she pursued one of these relentlessly with each child. Note the turn-taking pattern here. The teacher initiated the discussion, directed the turns, and, after each child's response, commented. I originally liked this interaction for precisely these reasons. The teacher had given the lesson adequate preparation. She had identified concepts that I, too, thought were important. She had specific objectives on which she focused. She gave attention to the children's prior knowledge and helped them make connections between their own experience and the story.

What strikes me now about this lesson is that it is dominated by the IRE interaction pattern. The teacher Initiated by asking a question, the child Responded by answering, and the teacher Evaluated. Even though many of the questions were directed at the children's experience, it is clear that the teacher was controlling the parameters of the communication and that only certain communications, determined by the teacher, were appropriate. Essentially the children could communicate only what the teacher wanted to hear. It was the teacher's meaning that dominated.

A second characteristic of the exchange that now catches my attention is the "pedagogical register" that dominates it. The tape clearly presents a teaching situation. No one would mistake it for a conversation. Heath (1978) describes this pedagogical register as characterized by the use of high pitch, exaggerated intonation contours, and carefully enunciated speech. The register proclaims not that "we are talking together," but that "I am teaching you."

A third troubling characteristic of typical reading lessons, one which is not evident in this transcript, is the extensive use of worksheets. Barnes

(1976) has noted that worksheets use language as an instrument of control. Upon reflection, I decided that the workcards I used in Zimbabwe were very much an extension of the kind of dominance I exercised in discussion through the IRE interaction pattern. Even when I was not with the children, it was my language and my meanings as presented on the workcards that set the parameters of communication. The workcards, even more than the IRE sessions, provided children with specified blanks to be filled in. Once again the purpose of a communication task—writing—was not actually communication but assessment.

"Success" as defined by the IRE pattern and its extension in worksheets is for the children to match the teacher's meanings. Teachers do not really listen to the children's meanings; rather they determine whether there is a match between their own meanings and the children's. Since teachers are usually a part of the dominant culture, children from the dominant culture have a distinct advantage. They find it easier to match the teacher's meanings because they are more likely to share them. Thus, the reading lessons sort children on cultural and racial characteristics at the level of the smallest interaction. The children who play the "match game" successfully, those who share the teacher's culture or quickly adapt to it, stay with the teacher and move along with him or her as they travel through the curriculum. Those who are unsuccessful at the match game become mystified by the schooling process and inevitably fall behind or tune the teacher out.

Barnes (1976) suggests that the IRE pattern ultimately dehumanizes all the participants in the game—teachers and successful students as well as the unsuccessful players. The pattern teaches students that their purposes, their knowledge, and their reality are insignificant. Knowledge and truth are controlled by the teacher. The sorting that is done through the question-answer routines essentially places students in a competition for approval. The students who match the teacher's meanings come to think of themselves as "better than" those who are unsuccessful. Those who continually miss the teacher's meanings come to think of themselves as "less than" others. Since student's own meanings and contributions have been barred from the schooling process, all learners, whether successful or unsuccessful, are dehumanized. Instead of looking at one another as unique and richly variable human beings, they learn to measure themselves against the teacher's meanings. They exit from our schools believing that the class markers which have been highlighted and exaggerated by the schooling system are just, fair, and inevitable.

It is not only the excessive use of the IRE pattern and worksheets (Durkin 1978–79) that is of concern. Very early in the game the children are placed in low, middle, and high reading groups. Shannon (1985) has shown that this division into groups is related to class and race. Class and race may influence the assignment to groups through the interaction patterns discussed above. There is also evidence, however, that once the assignment to groups has occurred, the interaction patterns of teachers and children within these groups may further widen the achievement gap between the groups (Shannon 1985; Stanovich 1986). Specifically, Allington (1983) has found that in top reading groups teachers tend to focus on meaning and interrupt students infrequently, while in bottom groups they focus on decoding and interrupt often. Teachers ask more questions in low-ability groups (Hoetker and Ahlbrand 1969), and the instruction of lower groups is also characterized by a more pedagogical register (McDermott 1985). Children in the lower groups spend proportionately more time than those in the upper groups in the teacher-dominated interaction patterns that seem to facilitate sorting at the expense of learning.

Whether we lay the blame at the feet of IRE patterns, ability grouping, or both, the important point to be made here is that children who have passed through our reading lessons may well have learned that literacy is not used for authentic communication. They do not experience literacy as a tool for exploring, building, and negotiating corporate meanings in the classroom. Instead they come to know literacy as an evaluation instrument. Is it any wonder, then, that large segments of our society reject literacy? The point of reading lessons as currently delivered is not communication and literacy. It is the sorting of children by the extent to which they match their teacher's meanings. This sorting and grouping process serves to turn racial and ethnic diversity into rigid class divisions.

CHALLENGES WE FACE

What shall we do? If what we want is to maintain our class-oriented society, we should change nothing. As our society becomes more pluralistic we teachers who are currently part of the dominant majority should simply intensify what we are doing. More basals, more worksheets, more question-answer sessions, more sorting. Indeed, if maintaining our privileged position for ourselves and for our children is our objective, we could probably pursue it even more effectively if we were open and honest about our agenda. A number of societies, for instance prerevolutionary Zimbabwe (Rhodesia), have been quite successful in using the schools to promote racial segregation. However, if a society divided along race and class lines and alienated from itself is not our intent, then we must change.

We need classroom structures and organizations that accommodate and, in fact, insist that language be used for constructing meaning rather than as a club to enforce the meanings of a stratified and stultified society. If language arts instruction is to be a positive force in achieving the humanistic, pluralistic society we seek, then it must occur in school settings where language is actually used for communication and learning and is not wielded as an instrument that leaves students silent and dehumanized.

REFERENCES

Allington, Richard L. "The Reading Instruction Provided Readers of Differing Abilities." *The Elementary School Journal, 83* (1983): 548–559.

Barnes, Douglas. *From Communication to Curriculum.* Middlesex, England: Penguin Books, Ltd., 1976.

Bellack, Alan. *The Language of the Classroom.* New York: Teachers College Press, 1966.

Cook-Gumperz, Jenny. *The Social Construction of Literacy.* New York: Cambridge University Press, 1986.

Durkin, Dolores. "What Classroom Observations Reveal About Reading Comprehension Instruction." *Reading Research Quarterly, 14* (1978–1979): 481–533.

Fraatz, Jo Michelle Beld. *The Politics of Reading: Power, Opportunity and Prospects for Change in America's Public Schools.* New York: Teachers College Press, 1987.

Hansen, Jane. "An Inferential Comprehension Strategy for Use with Primary Grade Children." *The Reading Teacher, 39* (1981): 665–669.

Heath, Shirley Brice. *Teacher Talk: Language in the Classroom.* Washington, DC: Center for Applied Linguistics, 1978.

Heimlich, John E., and Susan D. Pittelman. *Semantic Mapping: Classroom Application.* Newark, DE: International Reading Association, 1986.

Hoetker, James, and W. P. Ahlbrand. "The Persistence of the Recitation." *American Educational Research Journal, 6* (1969): 145–166.

Kozol, Jonathan. *Illiterate America.* New York: New American Library, 1985.

McDermott, R. P. "Achieving School Failure: An Anthropological Approach to Illiteracy and Social Stratification." In *Theoretical Models and Processes of Reading*, edited by Harry Singer and Robert Rudell. Newark, DE: International Reading Association, pp. 558–594, 1985.

Mehan, H. *Learning Lessons.* Cambridge, MA: Harvard University Press, 1979.

Raphael, Taffy, E. "Teaching Question-answer Relationships Revisited." *The Reading Teacher, 39* (1986): 516–522.

Scollon, Ron. "Storytelling, Reading, and the Micropolitics of Literacy." In *Dialogues in Literacy Research*, edited by John E. Readance and R. Scott Baldwin. Chicago, IL: National Reading Conference, 1988.

Shannon, Patrick. "Reading Instruction and Social Class." *Language Arts, 62* (1985): 604–613.

Spiegel, Dixie Lee, and Jill Fitzgerald. "Improving Reading Comprehension through Instruction about Story Parts." *The Reading Teacher, 39* (1986): 676–682.

Stanovich, Keith E. "Matthew Effects in Reading: Some Consequences of Individual Differences in the Acquisition of Literacy." *Reading Research Quarterly 21* (1986): 360–407.

Wells, Gordon. *The Meaning Makers: Children Learning Language and Using Language to Learn.* Portsmouth, NH: Heinemann, 1986.

Chapter **4**

The Concept of Method, Interested Knowledge, and the Politics of Language Teaching

Alastair Pennycook

Examining the concept of Method in second language education, this paper argues that both a historical analysis and an investigation of its current use reveal little conceptual coherence. Ultimately, the term seems to obfuscate more than to clarify our understanding of language teaching. While this may seem at first a minor quibble over terminology, there are in fact far more serious implications. By relating the role of teaching theory to more general concerns about the production of interested knowledge and the politics of language teaching, this paper argues that Method is a prescriptive concept that articulates a positivist, progressivist, and patriarchal understanding of teaching and plays an important role in maintaining inequities between, on the one hand, predominantly male academics and, on the other, female teachers and language classrooms on the international power periphery.

It is not uncommon in texts on language teaching to find a discussion of methods prefaced with the phrase "so-called" (e.g., H. D. Brown, 1980, p. 240), suggesting a certain skepticism toward this concept. This suspicion can be found amongst academics who have looked closely at the idea of teaching methods and found it wanting, and amongst teachers who feel frustration at being told how to teach, sensing that there is little concordance between what the concept purports to describe and what is actually happening in their classrooms. In particular, many teachers in an EFL context question the usefulness of supposed methods to their own teaching contexts and resent their imposition by "experts" from abroad. And yet, despite this dissatisfaction, the concept of Method continues to be used by many of those involved in teacher education. In this paper, I shall try to show not only why there is very good reason to be skeptical about methods, but also to show that the concept reflects a particular view of the world and is articulated in the interests of unequal power relationships. Of particular concern will be the hierarchical nature of the relationship between academic theorizing and teaching practice, both within and beyond the confines of North American or European life. Second Language Education (SLE) is involved in a complex nexus of social, cultural, economic, and political relationships that involve students, teachers, and theorists in differential positions of power. I hope the following discussion will show that we must view critically all of the standard orthodoxies of TESOL and investigate the interests served by such orthodoxies.

INTERESTED KNOWLEDGE AND THE POLITICS OF SECOND LANGUAGE EDUCATION

Let me start by making two very basic claims that are central to the arguments of this article: First, that all education is political, and second, that all knowledge is "interested." To say that language teaching is in some sense political would seem uncontroversial since it is clear that many decisions about what gets taught, to whom, how, when, and where, are made at high levels of the political hierarchy. Thus a number of models of factors involved in language teaching reflect the fact that we must always take into account the sociopolitical context of education (see, for example, Mackey, 1970; Strevens, 1977). Here, however, I would like to expand this notion of the political from the narrower concerns of governmental or administrative decision-making to include all societal relationships of power. Thus, what is being argued here is that we should avoid reducing the political either to the liberal emphasis on rules and administration or to the conservative emphasis on politics as a private enterprise in defense of a free-market economy and individualist rights and freedom (Giroux, 1988, p. 29). Rather, we must see the political as involving all relationships within a society, as concerned with all the fundamental inequalities, particularly those based in class, race, and gender differences. Among others, Foucault (1980) argues that power is not simply something possessed by the dominant group, nor is it a question of prohibition and punishment; rather, power is coextensive with the social body. Relations of power are interwoven with other kinds of relations for which they play both a conditioned and a conditioning role (p. 142).

In this view, education is fundamentally political since it is constantly involved in the (re)production of social and cultural inequalities (both within and between nations), and of particular forms of culture and knowledge. Significantly, in the United States and a number of other Western countries, there has been a retreat from this view of education as political. As Giroux (1983) points out, the move in the early 20th century toward scientific management of the curriculum signaled a move away from viewing the school as a political site. Thus, both the conservative view that overtly described schools as training grounds for promoting obedience, punctuality, silence, and industry, and the more radical views of Dewey and the social reconstructionists, that saw the school as a site of democracy and social change, became submerged under a view of education as a rational and technical operation. As Giroux (1983) explains:

> This philosophical shift in the purpose and function of schooling not only abstracted schools from the context of the wider society, it also ushered in a mode of rationality that relegated the political nature of schooling to the anteroom of educational theory and practice. Citizenship education became entwined in a "culture of positivism," one that displayed little interest in the ways in which schools acted as agents of social and cultural reproduction in a society marked by significant inequities in wealth, power, and privilege. (p. 170)

The significance of seeing the school as a site of political struggle lies in the need to recognize that those who wish to deny the political nature of schooling are clearly articulating an ideological position in favor of the status quo. Anyone who holds an alternative view of society must first recognize this before looking at the possibilities for producing change in and through the educational system. Paulo Freire, who has probably done more than any other educator in the service of the disenfranchised, points out the ideological implications in the U.S. of this retreat from the political: "It is necessary to negate the political nature of pedagogy to give the superficial appearance that education serves everyone, thus assuring that it continues to function in the interest of the dominant class" (Freire & Macedo, 1987, p. 122).

While my argument thus far has been concerned with the politics of all forms of education, I would suggest that these arguments are especially relevant to second language education, since it is centered around the highly political concept of *a language* (*langue*) and is bound up in the contentious issues of bilingualism, minority education, and internationalism. Again, some might be willing to admit an element of the political in such "sociolinguistic" areas as language planning, but I would argue that since linguistics is forced to work with a concept that is inherently political, it does not seem unreasonable to suggest that linguistics itself is political. There has, however, been a strong tendency to overlook the political dimensions of the concept of language, ignoring the intimate connections between language and the development of the nation state, and the many implications of distinctions between *language* and *dialect*.

An interesting example of the political implications of the notion of *a language* and *a grammar* can be found in Illich's (1981) account of the presentation of the first Castilian grammar to Queen Isabella at the end of the 15th century. Its author, Nebrija, argued that this new grammar would be a crucial tool in the colonization both of the subjects already within the kingdom and of those in the new lands being discovered. Of fundamental importance was a standardized language for governance and control of the people, a language which, Nebrija argued, would limit the current diversified reading and allow for much stronger centralized control over books. This and the other European grammars were to play a crucial role in the formation of the modern state and its citizens as they were weaned away from the Church. The notion of *a language* and *a grammar* during this period came to take on immense political significance. As R. Harris (1987) argues, "the European post-Renaissance concept of 'a language' was from the outset a political concept, and the 'grammar of a language' no less so. To insist on the worldwide imposition of these concepts as providing the only scientific approach to linguistic inquiry is, at the very least, to confuse science with cultural imperialism" (p. 1373).

There appears to be a strong parallel, then, between attempts to deal with education and language without acknowledging the political. It is important, therefore, to recognize the ahistorical and apolitical stance taken by many linguists as once again an ideological position. It is dangerous to assume, as does Newmeyer (1986), a connection between structuralism and egalitarianism, since as Mey (1985) argues, concepts of equality and democracy in linguistic analysis can easily become tools of linguistic manipulation:

> Abstract considerations of "uniform structures" and general postulates about "equal rights" of dialect speakers can easily lead the way to potentially manipulatory notions about "linguistic democracy" and similar things. . . . Linguistic models, no matter how innocent and purely theoretical they may seem to be, not only have distinct economical, social, and political presuppositions, but also consequences. . . . The veil of linguistic manipulation that is drawn across the consciousness of the underprivileged can only hide, not abolish, the existing state of social inequality. (p. 26)

SLE, then, is inscribed in a complex constellation of educational and linguistic relationships that must be considered in any understanding of the context of language teaching. In the English programs run by the U.S. for refugees in camps in Thailand, the Philippines, and Indonesia before their immigration to the U.S., for example, Tollefson (1988) suggests that there is a covert policy to ensure that immigrants will have enough English to perform adequately in minimum-wage jobs while avoiding any welfare dependency, yet not enough to move beyond these levels of employment:

> The RPCs [Refugee Processing Centers], despite their declared aims, can be expected to continue to limit refugees' improvement in English language proficiency, capacity for cultural adaptation, and preemployment skills, thereby contributing to the covert goal of ensuring that most refugees will only be able to compete effectively for minimum-wage employment. (p. 39)

With respect to bilingual education in the U.S., Cummins (1989) argues that the "overwhelmingly consistent pattern" in the research data clearly showing the efficacy of bilingual programs has been consistently ignored because its acknowledgment would "effectively eliminate the psychoeducational legitimization for eradicating minority children's language and culture" (1989, p. 88). Thus, the reality of domination over minorities could no longer be obscured by appeal to the rhetoric of inequality if it were not for the complicity of academics making recommendations "that are absolutely devoid of empirical evidence and logical coherence" (1989, pp. 88–89). Cummins suggests that many academics are involved in a disinformation campaign that helps to maintain the "covert racism and psychological violence to which dominated minority students are still subjected" (1989, pp. 127–128) and to preserve the political status quo that is being threatened by the changing demographics with the increasing numbers of Spanish-speaking peoples in the U.S.

A similarly intimate relationship between language, language teaching, and power can be seen in the spread of the English language around the world, or as Phillipson (1988) calls it, "the international linguistic hegemony of English." "Linguicism" (cf. racism, sexism, classism), Phillipson argues, has operated during both the colonial and the neocolonial eras to further increase the dependence and subjugation of the Third World. Cooke (1988) and Judd (1983) see the problems posed by the spread of English to be the loss of indigenous languages and the maintenance of social elites. Other writers have emphasized the cultural content that English brings with it: "The spread of English went parallel with the spread of the culture of international business and technological standardization. From there, the jump towards the standardization of international thought becomes easy to make" (Ndebele, 1987, p. 4). As Peirce (1989) argues, we must go beyond views of language as "neutral," since "English, like all other languages, is . . . a site of struggle over meaning, access, and power" (p. 405). The role of language teaching in this process has received little criticism in the West, so that "ELT is largely perceived . . . as being a technical business which is unconnected with cultural imperialism, linguicism, or the global power structure which maintains the Periphery in a state of dependence on the Centre" (Phillipson, 1988, p. 348).

Although this outline of the political in language teaching has been far too brief to give credit to a number of extremely important issues, it has, I hope, suggested the way in which language and language teaching are always inscribed in relations of power, and are therefore political issues. I now turn to the second of the basic issues that frame this discussion: the interested nature of knowledge.

In recent years, a growing number of questions have been raised about the paradigms and ideologies of the social sciences. Doubts have arisen about some of their most basic tenets, especially the predominant positivist (or scientist)[1] orientation, that is the tendency of the social sciences to model themselves after the physical sciences through use of the empirical-analytic approach, thus claiming to arrive at objectivity through the development of standardized, quantitative techniques of analysis. As Popkewitz (1984) suggests, this has led in educational research to the superimposition of technique over theory and therefore to the over-adherence to certain techniques of investigation and the narrowing of the scope of theory. Closely connected to claims that the knowledge thereby produced is neutral and objective has been the removal of the personal and the political from the investigation of human issues. Generally speaking—and these same issues emerged from the preceding discussion of education and linguistics—there has been a tendency to validate only one type of knowledge, to affirm that an ahistorical and apolitical approach is more scientifically sound, and to believe in objectivity (in an objective/subjective dichotomy), in the efficacy of investigative procedures that emphasize quantification and prediction, in the linearly progressive cumulation of knowledge, and in the universal applicability of human rationality.

This position has received strong criticism, however, from a diversity of sources. Critical theorists (e.g., Habermas, 1984; Marcuse, 1964), feminists[2] (e.g., Belenky, Clinchy, Goldberger, & Tarule, 1986; Grimshaw, 1986; Harding, 1986; Keller, 1985; de Lauretis, 1986), Third World writers (e.g., Kothari, 1987; Nandy, 1983), postmodernists (e.g., Hebdige, 1986; Lyotard, 1984), philosophers of science (e.g., Feyerabend, 1988; Kuhn, 1970), anthropologists (e.g., Clifford, 1988), sociologists and philosophers of education (e.g., K. Harris, 1979), and critical pedagogues (e.g., Apple, 1986; Giroux, 1988; Giroux & McLaren, 1989; Simon, 1984, 1987) have all, from their different viewpoints, raised fundamental questions about this view of knowledge: They argue that all knowledge is produced within a particular configuration of social, cultural, economic, political, and historical circumstances and therefore always both reflects and helps to (re)produce those conditions. Furthermore, since all claims to knowledge represent the interests of certain individuals or groups, we must always see knowledge as interested.

---

[1]For a discussion of the these terms, see Williams (1916).

[2]These categories are not, of course, mutually exclusive. One may be both a feminist and philosopher of science, or both a Third World writer and an anthropologist, for example. This list is also but a tiny selection of these areas of work.

These criticisms all address the problems of the dominance of one particular type of knowledge (rational-purposive or scientific-technological), its colonization of other forms of knowledge, and its link to patriarchal, positivist, and progressivist modes of thought. Most important, then, is the need to acknowledge the fact that "all knowledge claims are 'interested' and are modes of intelligibility grounded in the struggles, tensions, and inequalities that mark history's bequest to the present" (Simon, 1984, p. 381). As Popkewitz (1984) and Silva and Slaughter (1984) have shown, furthermore, we need to examine carefully the role of social scientists as it has been historically constituted, since an analysis of their relationship to society and political structures suggests that "contemporary American university-based social science tends to support vested political economic interests" (Silva & Slaughter, 1984, p. 5). For the purpose of our discussion here, the central issues are the roles of positivism and patriarchy, the claims to universality, objectivity, and truth, and the belief in inherent progress, within the domains of linguistics and applied linguistics. What is being argued, then, is that the fundamental challenges being made to the social sciences (questioning the paradigms of research, the roles of intellectuals, and the nature of the knowledge produced) need to be addressed by applied linguists, since they raise serious doubts about TESOL, especially regarding the relationship between the production of academic knowledge and teaching practice, and between central and peripheral institutions in an international context. A number of areas requiring reexamination suggest themselves: an understanding of education and language as fundamentally political; a recognition of the social, cultural, economic, and political forces that inform the problematics and research paradigms of such areas as second language acquisition (for some suggestive work here, see Bourne, 1988; Nayar, 1989); acknowledgment of the serious implications, both pedagogically and politically, of our current use of such concepts as "communicative competence" (see Bourne, 1988; and Peirce's [1989] distinction between what is normatively appropriate and what is politically desirable); an understanding of the implications of the current tendency to trivialize content in SLE (see Brumfit, 1985; Mukherjee, 1986); and an examination of the concept of Method (which will be discussed at some length in this paper).

I have argued, then, that we must emphasize the political in SLE and always look critically at the interests involved in the production of different types of knowledge. As suggested in the introduction, these issues need to be examined carefully if any form of reciprocal relationship is to be developed between academics and teachers in the West, and between the West and other parts of the world. Yet herein lies a major problem, for as Clarke and Silberstein (1988) point out with respect to relationships between academics and teachers, and as others (e.g., Altbach,1981) have indicated concerning international relations in general, rather than a reciprocal relationship, there in fact exists a one-way flow of prescriptivist knowledge. The knowledge produced in the central academic institutions is legitimated through a series of political relationships that privilege it over other possible forms of knowledge. Since my principal concern here is the connection between academics and teachers, in the next section I shall consider in some depth the question of the concept of Method. There are a number of problems with the relationship between the knowledge produced in applied linguistics and that produced through classroom practice—as Gregg (1986) points out, much of second language acquisition theory has been unhelpfully antiteacher—but it is in the area of methods that I feel these issues are in most need of being addressed.

METHODS IN LANGUAGE TEACHING

In this section, I closely examine the concept of Method in language teaching, with a view to showing how the dominance of this notion in the conceptualization of teaching has diminished rather than enhanced our understanding of language teaching. I argue further that we need to investigate the interests served by the construction of this concept. Ideally, it would be useful to attempt a genealogy of Method, but this is clearly beyond the scope of this paper. Nevertheless, some general comments may be useful to set this discussion in a broader context. Feyerabend (e.g., 1988) has examined and criticized at some length what he sees as the modern obsession with Method in the natural sciences, tracing it back to a Cartesian legacy. His attack on Method focuses principally on the serious consequences that it has in limiting the potential of scientific investigation. Similarly, for political science, Wolin (1972) argues that Method "avoids fundamental criticism and fundamental commitment" and that far from being an innocent, epistemological, neutral idea, it is a "proposal for shaping the mind" (pp. 23, 38). It is important, then, that we see the concept of Method as a product of early scientism, an attempt to delineate modes of inquiry and define the problematic. While this tendency to use Method has presumably served a purpose in the investigation of scientific questions, it has also tended to limit the scope of investigation and prescribe the problematic.

With regard to language teaching, Stern (1983) has suggested that there is a "fundamental weakness" in the concept of Method. His suggestion, however, that the "conviction has gradually spread that language teaching cannot be satisfactorily conceptualized in terms of teaching method alone" (p. 474) has not been supported in light of the continuing emphasis on methods. Indeed, as Stern himself noted later, in a review of Oller and Richard-Amato's (1983) *Methods that Work*, "this century-old obsession" was far from dead: "One of the most extraordinary and in some ways totally unexpected phenomena in the recent history of language teaching has been the 'method boom' of the seventies" (Stern, 1985, p. 249). He goes on to argue that "the prolonged preoccupation with the new methods, useful as it has been to widen our horizon, is becoming increasingly unproductive and misguided" (p. 251). Stern's hope that the last great method debate (audiolingualism vs. cognitive code) was over seems to have been unrealized, given its central role in TESOL orthodoxy and the extent to which the concept of Method is interested knowledge. It is part of this orthodoxy (see, e.g., H. D. Brown, 1980; Clarke, 1982; Larsen-Freeman, 1986; McArthur, 1983; Richards & Rodgers, 1986) that there has been a series of language teaching methods over the years, each being succeeded by a better one until we reach the present. Here we find (a) the best method (or approach) to date, (b) a proliferation of new and exciting methods from which to choose, and (c) the promise of even better things to come. As I hope to show, however, the epistemological presumptiveness of this orthodoxy has serious consequences for language teaching and is supported neither by a diachronic nor synchronic analysis of language teaching. As I suggested earlier, positivist and progressivist thought naturally tends to exclude or to make a very particular reading of history, and so it is to a historical overview that we shall now turn.

In the preface to his history of language teaching, Kelly (1969) suggests that "nobody really knows what is new or old in present-day language teaching procedures. There has been a vague feeling that modern experts have spent their time in discovering what other men [*sic*] have forgotten" (p. ix). One thing that emerges from Kelly's comprehensive study is a pattern of cyclical change: The Classical, Renaissance, and Modern periods have been marked by an emphasis on oral communication, while the Middle Ages and Enlightenment placed much more emphasis on analysis of the written text. This cyclic revolution, Kelly argues, is largely based on "alternation between the social and philosophical aims of language teaching with the literary aim acting as a balance" (p. 399). It becomes evident that the goals and therefore the procedures of language teaching closely reflect the social, political, cultural, and intellectual climate of the times. The entrenchment of learning in the monastery of the Middle Ages, with the goal of preserving Latin as the language of religion and scholarship, clearly led to a strong emphasis on the text and its analysis. The sudden influx of new ideas and spread of European scholarship during the Renaissance brought about a swing toward a much more oral-based approach. The Enlightenment emphasis on rational thought and coherent theorizing brought about an increased emphasis on formal and rule-based study that appears to have coexisted with other forms until a strong drive at the end of the 19th century once again moved the spoken language to the fore.

Lambley's (1920) study of the teaching of French in England during Tudor and Stuart times clearly demonstrates how the language taught and the nature of the teaching were affected by sociopolitical changes. In the 15th century, "fluency in speaking French was the chief need of the classes of society in which the demand for instruction was greatest. Correctness in detail was only of secondary importance, and grammar, though desirable, was not considered indispensable" (pp. 27–28). Texts from this period contained dialogues for giving directions, obtaining lodging at inns, and buying and selling goods; they were clearly aimed at providing functional oral skills for merchants (some also included models for writing letters, bills, and other such documents). This pragmatic orientation is clearly spelled out by Caxton in an introduction to a text he published around 1483: "Who this booke shall wylle lerne/ May well enterprise/ Marchandise fro one land to another,/ And to know many wares/ Which to him shall be good to be bought/ Or sold for rich to become" (cited in Lambley, 1920, p. 43).

French in the Tudor period, although needed particularly by courtiers and merchants, was also used by travelers and soldiers. The Counter Reformation in late 16th century France brought, on the one hand, a body of native-speaker teachers to England and, on the other, created a need for instruction in English as a second language (Howatt, 1983). In the English teaching of this period, the use of dialogues and situational teaching were common, and Lambley shows that many of the issues debated today were also hotly argued in the late 16th and early 17th centuries: rule-based learning as opposed to learning through practice, formal study as opposed to informal use.

What is most striking in these histories is the constant recurrence of the same teaching techniques and debates about teaching. Arguments for the inductive teaching of grammar, for example, were made by Saint Augustine in the 4th century, Francis Bacon in the 17th century, and Henry Sweet in the early 19th century (Kelly, 1969, pp. 35–38; Howatt, 1984b, p. 280). In 1415, a treatise entitled *Femina* argued that teaching should follow the natural model provided by mothers with their children (Lambley, 1920), an argument that constantly reappears over the centuries (Kelly, 1969, pp. 34–43). Substitution tables, realia, language games, dialogues, and many other parts of the modern scene have been around for centuries. Kelly (1969) concludes that the "total corpus of ideas accessible to language teachers has not changed basically in 2,000 years" (p. 363). A slightly more detailed look at the teaching principles advocated by Comenius (1592–1670) should illustrate this point more clearly.[3]

[3]The following section on Comenius is based primarily on Caravolas (1984). The translations from the French are my own.

Not only are the enlightened views of Comenius' general educational principles—such as universal education and intercurricular teaching—familiar points of educational debate today, but so too are many of his more practical suggestions. In the "sensory principle," for example, Comenius chides teachers for lecturing too much rather than letting children learn through the direct experience of their senses. The presentation of each new object must be linked to the appropriate sense: As he wrote in 1651, "In our school we follow the rule that everything one needs to know about things should be taught with the help of the things themselves, that is to say that as far as possible, the real objects or pictures of them should be presented so that they can be seen, touched, heard, tasted, etc." (Caravolas, 1984, p. 88). He continually stresses the dictum "you learn by doing" (p. 220). His "pleasure principle" stresses the importance of affect, of motivation, and of interesting activity in the classroom. Classrooms, he suggests, should be "workshops full of ardent activity" (p. 94). He outlines seven principles to improve student motivation: (a) The teacher should be lively and interesting, (b) presentations should be brief, (c) examples should be concrete, (d) students should always be active, (e) activities must be useful and relevant, (f) there should be variety in every class, and (g) games should be used. Other suggestions included students working together and sometimes taking the role of the teacher; the integration of language teaching with other parts of the curriculum as part of an interdisciplinary approach; and the use of dialogues and role plays or sketches in language teaching. Clearly, many of these ideas would find support today, especially the emphasis on experiential learning, inductive presentation, motivational techniques, and the use of games and role plays.

It seems evident from these historical surveys that while there certainly are trends and shifts in language teaching, these tend to be a reordering of the same basic options, and to reflect the social, cultural, political, and philosophical environment. This view does not emerge in many discussions of language teaching; overlooked is the fact that much is not as new as is claimed. On this process of forgetting, Caravolas (1984) has this to say: "It should be recognized that this forgetfulness is not always innocent. These days language teaching has become a colossal enterprise which, like any other industry, defends both its overt and covert interests by any means possible, in the name of profit and glory" (p. 210). Despite the clear implications of the historical works cited, the reading of history by a number of other authors is quite different and appears to support quite different interests.

Other historical surveys tend not to present the cyclical nature of change that Kelly outlines, preferring a much more linear model. While Titone (1968, pp. 1–2) acknowledges that the "so-called 'traditional method' " in language teaching is neither traditional nor classical but very recent, he goes on to describe the period of its use (dating from the beginning of the 19th century) as a "*deviation* [emphasis added] in teaching method." He then argues that "this deviation can most probably be explained by the inevitable lack of linguistic and psychological knowledge on the part of the language teachers in those days; and the traditional inertia or routine-addiction of the school practitioners, who did not care for change or improvement of their teaching habits." This is clearly a very different argument from the ones discussed earlier: Titone is suggesting that there is a definite direction in which language teaching has progressed, apart from the unfortunate deviation. Interestingly, for Titone writing in the mid-1960s, this progress had led to the development of audiolingualism, a proposition at which the modern reader can wrily smile, secure in the knowledge that true progress has in fact led to communicative language teaching, audiolingualism being but a slight deviation from that true path. Titone, then, makes a clearly positivist and progressivist argument: We have continued to make progress in a cumulative fashion toward the present day by the application of scientific principles to teaching.

While making passing reference to the work of Kelly and others, the historical introduction to Richards and Rodgers' (1986) influential book[4] on methods reflects the positivist and progressivist work of Titone far more than it does a historicist orientation. Thus, a historical view emerges suggesting that although oral approaches were originally employed with Latin, these changed once Latin was no longer used as a language of communication. This, in turn, affected the approach toward teaching modern languages until the 19th century, when these deviations were overcome and the reinstitution of the primacy of the oral over the written led to the opening up of the modern era. Richards and Rodgers (1986) are then able to contrast the older approaches in which "tradition was for many years the guiding principle" (p. 14) with the modern era in which there is a "principled approach to language teaching, one based on a scientific approach to the study of language and of language learning" (p. 8).

It is clear that the histories that are supportive of the concept of Method also support a historical view that suggests linear development over time, development which has resulted principally from scientific advance, and a view that is therefore clearly supportive of the position of the social scientist/applied linguist. That is to say, these fundamentally ahistorical readings of history and texts rely on a view of knowledge that validates the position of positivist applied linguistics over other forums of possible knowledge. Furthermore, looking in more depth at the claims made by adherents to the concept of Method, it is tempting to conclude with Clarke

[4]Its popularity is evidenced by its inclusion in a number of applied linguists "top ten" books (H. Douglas Brown, Elliot Judd, Joan Morley, Peter Strevens); see Haskell (1987).

(1983) that "the term 'method' is a label without substance" (p. 109). There are three important aspects to this: First, there is little agreement as to which methods existed when, and in what order; second, there is little agreement and conceptual coherence to the terms used; and third, there is little evidence that methods ever reflected classroom reality.

H. D. Brown (1980) suggests that there has been a new (Kuhnian) paradigm every 25 years of this century, "with each new paradigm a break from the old but taking with it positive aspects of previous paradigms" (p. 244).[5] Thus, according to Brown, we have had the Direct Method, the Grammar-Translation Method, the Audiolingual Method, and now have available the Interpersonal Approaches (which include the "new methods": Community Language Learning, the Silent Way, Suggestopedia, and Total Physical Response [TPR]). Clarke (1982), somewhat hesitantly, also offers four methods: Grammar/Translation, Structural/Audiolingual, Interactional/Humanistic, and Notional/Functional. According to McArthur (1983), there have been five: Grammar-Translation, Direct, Structural, Situational, and Communicative. Stern (1983) hesitantly suggests seven; Larsen-Freeman (1986) and Richards and Rodgers (1986) propose eight. On these last three lists citing seven or eight methods, only Audiolingualism appears on all three. Stern alone mentions the Reading and Audiovisual Methods, and Cognitive Theory (as a method). What, too, are we to make of Brown's reversal of the more usual sequence by placing Grammar-Translation after the Direct Method?

Regarding the second issue, that there is little agreement and conceptual coherence to the terms used, two principal attempts to provide conceptual cohesion to the field have been made by Anthony (1963) and Richards and Rodgers (1982, 1986). Anthony (1963) made a three-part distinction among *approach*, *method*, and *technique*, while Richards and Rodgers (1982) tried to clarify and expand these categories by subsuming *approach*, *design*, and *procedure* under the umbrella term *method*. Reading Richards and Rodgers (1986), however, one is struck by a feeling of strain at attempts to fit disparate concepts into their framework. In many instances, their attempts to demonstrate conceptual unity for methods do not seem justifiable. In their first description, for example, that of the Oral Approach and Situational Language Teaching, we are told that the linguistic theory behind this is "a type of British 'structuralism'," apparently embracing Halliday's work, and that the theory of learning is "a type of behaviorist habit-learning theory" (p. 35). If the concept of Method assumes

---

[5]As one would expect from the foregoing discussion, I take issue with this progressivist description. I would also suggest that this is not quite what Kuhn intended by the concept of *paradigm shift*. In the second edition of his book, H. D. Brown (1987) lays more emphasis on the cyclical nature of change.

coherent theories of language and of learning, surely these descriptions provide inadequate support. The examples used are also inconsistent; in the introduction to one of the books (Alexander, 1967) listed by Richards and Rodgers as apparently situational, the author himself comments on "situational teaching":

> In this method, little structural grading is possible. The situation takes precedence over the structures. The patterns that are included arise naturally out of the situation itself: they have a thematic significance rather than a structural one. *This system has serious drawbacks* [emphasis added]. The dialogues which the student hears are refreshingly natural, but the teaching of basic patterns inevitably becomes much less controlled. (p. xiii)

Alexander furthermore insists on strict adherence to the axioms common to the audiolingual era: "Nothing should be spoken before it has been heard; nothing should be read before it has been spoken; nothing should be written before it has been read" (p. xii). Again, claims to coherency dissolve under close scrutiny.

Among the so-called methods, audiolingualism appears to provide the best example of coherence;[6] there are, nevertheless, a number of reasons to question this. Writing in the early 1960s—at the apparent height of audiolingualism—Mackey (1965) lists 15 methods, one of which, the Mimicry-Memorization Method, he tells us, is also known as the Audiolingual Method. For Mackey at least, it seems that it was not so clear that this method predominated at the time.[7] Bazan (1964), in a strong criticism of the assertions of the time, which, she suggests, "cannot claim any status other than that of assumptions" (p. 337), questions not only the claims to empirical validity, but also the fact that this "new methodology" was indeed new, since it bore so many resemblances to previous oral-based approaches. Howatt (1984a) questions the commonly held tenet that the Michigan Oral Approach, out of which audiolingualism is said to have grown, was based on behaviorism. He argues that Fries never mentioned psychology in his earlier papers and that behaviorism was, in fact, rather more complex than the commonsense notions of repetition and practice.

Further confusion surrounds the linguistic base. While it seems reasonable to state that language teaching in North America used structuralist grammars in the 1950s and 1960s, it is surely erroneous to suggest, as do Richards and Rodgers (1986), that "Chomsky rejected the structuralist approach to language description" (p. 59). Undoubtedly, Chomsky's famous attack on Skinner's work (Chomsky, 1959) marked an important point in

[6]Indeed, is might be argued that much of the development of the concept of Method was based on the fact that this one period seems to have been fairly homogeneous: Historical commentary since has tried to create a myth of homogeneity for other periods both before and after audiolingualism.

linguistic and psychological theory, but his approach to linguistics is surely structuralism *par excellence*. What he rejected were certain particularities of North American structuralism, especially the empiricist method of investigation, in favor of a more rationalist approach. But the claim that the "Chomskyan Revolution" marked the end of structuralism appears to be another myth that has been repeatedly used to demonstrate a positive leap forward in the progressive path of language teaching.

For a time—and especially before the emergence of *communication* as a term around which a new claim to Method could be built—it was argued that the Audiolingual Method had been replaced by the Cognitive Code Method based on rationalist/deductive procedures and transformational grammar. Looking at Carroll's (1966) paper, usually cited as documenting this change, however, the situation becomes far less clear. Carroll calls "cognitive code learning theory" a "modified, up-to-date grammar-translation theory," and also suggests that "in practice, of course, some teachers act as if they believed in both of these theories, appealing to one of them for some of their teaching procedures and to the other for different aspects" (p. 102). What seems ultimately to be implied is that the age-old debate between what Howatt (1984a) calls the "rational" and "natural" approaches to language teaching, or what Rivers (1981, pp. 25–27) calls "formalism" and "activism," was indeed alive and well in the 1960s, as it had been for the past 2000 years.

Of course, the hardest orthodoxy to dislodge is that which suggests that what we are doing today is significantly different from all that has gone before. Raimes (1983), however, suggests that the belief in change is frequently founded on superficial views: "All too often scholars look at classroom methodology rather than the underlying intellectual assumptions which generate methods" (p. 538). Examining orientations to teaching in the early 1980s, she concludes that "the current emphasis on communication has . . . been absorbed neatly into our positivist traditional framework. Far from superceding tradition, it has been assimilated into it" (Raimes, 1983, p. 545; see also Swan, 1985). Clarke (1982) also expresses doubts about many of the apparent changes that are claimed to have occurred in language teaching, warning us of the "tyranny of bandwagons" which "effectively constrains professional thought and debate" (p. 445). Horowitz (1986) has also recently drawn attention to the problems of designating new methods, approaches, or techniques. He suggests that there is in fact far less than is being claimed to "process writing," which he describes as

[7]It should be observed that Mackey, like Stern, has little faith in the concept of Method. His important work (1965), along with that of Halliday, McIntosh, and Strevens (1964) and the two smaller works by Bosco and DiPietro (1970) and Krashen and Seliger (1975), all attempt to construct analytic schemata that overcome the limitations of Method.

one of the new buzzwords of TESOL, "the 'communicative competence' of the mid-1980s" (p. 141).

Richards and Rodgers (1986) in fact suggest that "communicative language teaching is best considered an approach rather than a method" (p. 83) since, despite some theoretical consistency, design and procedure are fairly open to interpretation. Similarly, H. D. Brown (1980, p. 240) shows some general discomfort with the Method concept: "the term *approach* may be more accurately descriptive of these general moods." He argues that the "Audiolingual Method, for example, would be better termed an approach because there is such variation within the so-called method." I would also suggest that the Direct Method, which according to Stern (1983) is characterized by the "use of the target language as a means of instruction and communication in the classroom" (p. 456), is an equally general orientation or approach. This does not leave much else with the status of Method other than the "so-called new methods" (Richards & Rodgers, 1986). If we examine Larsen-Freeman's (1986) description of these so-called methods, however, her examples all occur on the opening day of a beginning class (see van Lier, 1987), suggesting they are of a very different order from the other approaches, for which a much greater variety of examples is given. The "new methods" seem to reduce to a constellation of techniques, which is not to say there is nothing valuable to be gained from them. The other methods seem to expand out to broad educational orientations. As regards the conceptual coherence of methods and attempts to better define them, it is worth concluding by quoting Clarke (1983) at some length:

> I contend that our traditional three-part distinction of approach, method and technique—as commonly interpreted—is inadequate. Approach, by limiting our perspective of language learning and teaching, serves as a blinder which hampers, rather than encourages, professional growth. Method is so vague that it means just about anything that anyone wants it to mean, with the result that, in fact, it means nothing. And technique, by giving the impression that teaching activities can be understood as abstractions separate from the context in which they occur, obscures the fact that classroom practice is a dynamic interaction of diverse systems. (p. 111)

It would seem, then, that despite attempts to clarify the Method concept and to use it analytically, serious doubts exist about its conceptual validity. The third and extremely important doubt exists about whether the claims made in the literature as to the predominance of a certain method at a certain time ever reflected what was actually happening in classrooms. Studies conducted to test the relative efficacies of methods (e.g., Scherer & Wertheimer, 1964; Smith, 1970) remained largely inconclusive, in part because they lacked any element of classroom observation, relying simply on pre- and posttesting. Since, as has been argued, the category of Method is conceptually weak, any study that claims that teachers are adhering to a certain method, without rigorous definition of that method and classroom observation, is ultimately of little value. More recent studies that have included classroom observation (e.g., Fröhlich, Spada, & Allen, 1985; Long & Sato, 1983) have begun suggesting that there is far less concordance than expected among what teachers claim to be doing, what researchers anticipate to be happening, and what actually appears to be occurring in classes.

While a number of writers, such as Rivers (1981), have emphasized eclecticism in language teaching, suggesting that teachers in fact pick and choose from different methods, this idea, as Stern (1983) points out, still has the serious drawback of implying the conceptual unity of methods (even if teachers do not adhere to them). A clearer understanding of the situation, then, suggests that teachers make a whole series of decisions about teaching based on their own educational experiences, their personalities, their particular institutional, social, cultural, and political circumstances, their understanding of their particular students' collective and individual needs, and so on. Any relationship between these decisions and theories about pedagogy and language learning are highly complex and need to be studied without the use of a priori categories, especially when those categories are as clumsy and unspecific as are methods. As any teacher who has taught through any of the alleged upheavals over Method can testify, there is a remarkable disparity between, on the one hand, the dictates of "experts" and teaching textbooks, and on the other, actual classroom practice. This suggests a close relationship between academic thought and textbook publication, but little between these and the knowledge produced by teachers in their daily practice.

Despite the inherent weakness of the concept of Method, extravagant claims have at times been made for different methods. An example of this can clearly be seen in Krashen's use of Asher's evaluation of TPR. Krashen (1982, p. 155) claims that "Asher has done a thorough job in putting his method to the empirical test," in which, comparing TPR students to a control group following a "standard" course, he "reported that after only 32 hours of TPR instruction, TPR students outperformed controls, who had had 150 hours of classtime, in a test of listening comprehension, and equaled controls in tests of reading and writing. Asher's students progressed nearly five times faster!" Krashen then argues that this provides sound empirical proof that "methods that provide more of the input necessary for acquisition, and that 'put grammar in its place,' are superior to older approaches." As Beretta (1986) points out, however, there are serious problems both with the evaluation itself, since TPR teaching materials were used as test materials for both experimental and control groups, and with Krashen's interpretation of the evaluation, since Krashen's implication that TPR students *equaled* controls who had received 150 hours of instruction on a test of reading and writing is "simply not the case" (1986, p. 433).

Krashen's position can be understood more clearly if we look at this work from the point of view of interested knowledge: Namely that he works within a positivist framework that claims such work is objective; his own beliefs strongly support a view of this type of teaching technique as superior to others; and he has committed himself to these ideas by coauthoring another "method," the Natural Approach (Krashen & Terrell, 1983). While Krashen and Terrell acknowledge their indebtedness to the earlier Natural Method—"the approach we will present in this book is in many ways the natural, direct method rediscovered" (1983, p. 17)—their brief historical overview is similar to Titone's (1968); they argue that the earlier Natural Method was indeed a positive move away from the long adherence to the misguided Grammar-Translation Method. Their strongest arguments to support their approach, however, rest on their claims to rigorous scientific backing, that the Natural Approach (unlike the Natural Method) is "based on an empirically grounded theory of second language acquisition, which has been supported by a large number of scientific studies in a wide variety of language acquisition and learning contexts" (1983, p. 1). Interestingly, comments on this method are divided along the lines we observed previously between the progressivists (Method supporters) and the historicists. Thus, while Richards and Rogers (1986) go to some lengths to outline the differences between Krashen and Terrell's Natural Approach and the 19th century Natural Method, Howatt (1984b, p. 281) skeptically makes the following comparison, commenting that "the similarity [of Sauveur's Natural Method] to Krashen and Terrell's 'Natural Approach' goes beyond the almost identical labels":

> Let us count the fingers: one, two, three, four, five, six, seven, eight, nine, ten. We have ten fingers. I have ten fingers; you have ten fingers, mademoiselle. How many fingers have you, madame? (I have ten fingers). And you, monsieur? (And I also). And George? (And George also). Do you see the ten fingers? (Yes). Let us count the fingers together. (Sauveur, 1874, p. 11)

> Let us count the number of students with blue eyes. One, two, three, four . . . Are there any others? (Jim). Oh, of course, we can't forget Jim. Yes, he has blue eyes. Now, who has brown eyes? Does Martha have brown eyes? (Yes). And what color is her hair? (Brown). Is it light brown or dark brown? (Light). Is she wearing a dress today? (No). A skirt? (Yes). What color is the skirt? (Blue). Yes, it's a blue skirt with white stripes. (Krashen & Terrell, 1983, p. 81)

Once again, recourse to historical information starts to erode the claims made by academics in the name of modernism, positivism, progress, and objectivity. Let us, therefore, return to the historicist position and leave the last word of this section to Kelly (1969): "That the expert in language teaching acts with the purity of motive and design expected from a scientist is demonstrably untrue. Discoveries are filtered by social and educational needs, and what suits the circumstances is what is considered proved" (p. 407).

KNOWLEDGE, TEXTS, TEACHERS, AND POWER

The construction of the Method concept in language teaching has been a typical example of the attempt to validate current forms of knowledge at the expense of past forms. While it is clear that language teaching has undergone many transformations over the centuries, a thorough examination of the past suggests that these changes have represented different configurations of the same basic options rather than some linear, additive progress toward the present day, and that these changes are due principally to shifts in the social, cultural, political, and philosophical climate. The Method construct that has been the predominant paradigm used to conceptualize teaching not only fails to account adequately for these historical conditions, but also is conceptually inconsistent, conflating categories and types at all levels and failing to demonstrate intellectual rigor. It is also highly questionable whether so-called methods ever reflected what was actually going on in classrooms.

Serious implications arise from this deconstruction of the Method concept, implications which go far beyond the reassessment of an academic issue. Put another way, if the argument has been that all knowledge is interested, we may indeed want to ask what interests are served by particular forms of knowledge. It is therefore important both to understand the construction of the Method concept within an apolitical, ahistorical, positivist, and progressivist orientation to education, and to investigate the *effects* of the production of that knowledge. This knowledge, then, should be seen within its political context and, more specifically, in its relationship to the political economy of textbook publishing, the hierarchical nature of knowledge production, the gendered issue of teaching practice, and educational imperialism in the teaching of English as an international language.

As I think has been convincingly shown in the previous section, the Method concept is ultimately *prescriptive* rather than *descriptive*: Rather than analyzing what is happening in language classrooms, it is a prescription for classroom behavior. This relationship has been clearly noted by Clarke and Silberstein (1988): "Prescriptions are implicit in virtually all discussions of the relationship between theory and practice" (p. 685). What this immediately suggests is a troubling relationship in which methods serve the advancement of academic careers and limit the practice of teachers. When we look at the question of what knowledge is legitimated in schools, it is essential, as Apple's work (e.g., 1986) has cogently demonstrated, that we look at the political economy of textbook publishing (see also Tollefson in this issue of the *TESOL Quarterly*). Although this question of knowledge or "content" is an important one, especially as regards the trivialization of content endemic to SLE, it is not an issue with which I shall deal here. The significance of looking at the political economy of textbooks for the discussion here lies in establishing that the definition and academic legitimation of methods is clearly beneficial to the publishing industry. As Richards (1984) argues, "The terms *notional-functional* and *communicative* sell. Many an underpaid academic has consequently succumbed to attractive offers to lightly work over an audiolingual or structural course so that it can be published in a new edition bearing a notional-functional or communicative label" (p. 14). The obvious commercial benefits for publishers deriving from methods, the support given for methods by universities and their journals (the example of the involvement of the University of Michigan and its journal, *Language Learning*, in promoting Audiolingualism is significant here), and the pushing of methods through institutions such as the British Council or Berlitz all suggest important political, economic, and ideological reasons for the growth and maintenance of the Method concept.

Defense Department funding for structuralist linguistics and audiolingualism is a strong example of this. Newmeyer (1986) supplies a telling quotation from Mortimer Graves, the executive secretary of the American Council of Learned Societies, a major source of research funding, who in 1950 argued that

> ideological World War III has started and there is no certainty that it is well won yet. In spite of the fact that this is a war for men's [*sic*] minds, there exist no Joint Chiefs of Staff planning such a war, no war production authority concerning itself with material for such a war. These questions are by and large, in our society, left to the private initiative of the type that one sees in the Georgetown Institute of Languages and Linguistics.
>
> In this war for men's [*sic*] minds, obviously the big guns of our armament is [*sic*] competence in languages and linguistics. (p. 56)

Another aspect of the "interest" in Method may be seen in the context of the gradual de-skilling of the teacher's role. As Apple (1986) and Giroux (1988) argue, the rise of scientism and the social efficiency movement in the 1920s, the use of management systems in curricula, the development of behavioral objectives, the increasing state intervention in schools, the development of "teacher-proof" materials and prespecified teaching procedures, and the recent moves, especially in the U.K. and U.S., toward more centralized curricula, have led to a de-skilling of the role of teachers and greater institutional control over classroom practice. While this is a significantly troubling observation in itself, there is a further dimension that Apple (1986), in particular, has emphasized: We cannot understand the nature of and reasons for that control unless we understand *who* is controlling and who is teaching, namely "the state, in concert with capital and a largely male academic body of consultants and developers, intervening at the level of practice into the work of a largely female workforce" (1986, pp. 36–37). If this is true in education in general, it is surely even more so in SLE, where, as G. Brown has recently observed, "the people at the top tend to be men, whereas the people who do most of the day-to-day teaching work tend to be women" (see "Sitting on a Rocket," 1989, p. 171). Thus, as Apple (1986) goes on, "This is not only the history of the control of state employees to bring about efficient teaching, but a rearticulation of the dynamics of patriarchy and class in one site, the school" (p. 40). What I am suggesting is that the Method concept has played a major role in maintaining the gendered division of the workforce, a hierarchically organized division between male conceptualizers and female practitioners.[8]

The same unequal relationship is played out in the international context. A recent study by Burnaby and Sun (1989) suggests that we must examine the teaching context very carefully before promoting communicative approaches, since they may be inappropriate for a number of reasons. Education is always socioculturally embedded; as Hall (1986) argues, "A lifetime's experience has convinced me that no society and no culture should force its educational system on another" (p. 168). Yet, given the unequal power relationships that exist between central and peripheral countries, and the "discourse of development" (Escobar, 1984, p. 378) within which much contact occurs, it is exactly the type of epistemological presumptiveness of the Method concept that allows such impositions to occur.

Sampson (1984) outlines three major problems in the export of Canadian language teaching methods to China: The first stems from the "fallacy of the unidimensionality of development," i.e., the fallacy that *everything* exported from "developed" to "developing" countries is advanced. The second stems from a "confusion between scientific and educational theories," i.e., extending positivism to educational theory. The third stems from "technocratic imperialism," i.e., the export of supposedly value-free

[8]I would like to thank an anonymous *TESOL Quarterly* reviewer for helping me see the full implications of this point.

intellectual goods. These attitudes, along with the status accorded foreign teachers abroad, causes considerable conflict: "Perhaps because foreign teachers are referred to as 'experts' in China, some think they are the only ones who possess teaching expertise" (Wu, 1983, p. 15). Many Western teachers abroad blithely assume the superiority of their methods. When we consider that, as I have argued, these methods are such loose constellations of techniques that they have little coherence, it suggests that Western teachers and teacher trainers frequently promote whatever techniques they happen to prefer, while supporting their views by recourse to the Method concept and its supposedly scientific and advanced backing. Furthermore, teachers from those countries who have studied in the prestigious institutions in the West and, despite misgivings, have imbibed the TESOL orthodoxies, are faced, on their return, with the serious problem of the contradiction between the need to validate themselves and their newly gained knowledge, and the feeling that it is nevertheless largely inappropriate.[9]

CONCLUSION

I have argued that we must see all knowledge claims as interested, that is to say, that knowledge is socially constructed, represents particular ways of understanding and explaining the world, and, since it therefore always reflects the interests of certain individuals or groups, is inevitably inscribed in relationships of power. While this view of knowledge has prompted inquiry in a number of areas of the social sciences, it has done little so far to challenge the positivist and progressivist orthodoxies of linguistics and applied linguistics. Since language teaching, and especially English language teaching, has become such a vast concern, it is imperative that we respond to these challenges to the predominant modes of thinking by reexamining some of our most basic beliefs about the nature of language and language teaching and about the ways in which such questions should be investigated. This is of critical importance, I believe, not merely in terms of theoretical questions concerning conceptual paradigms in language teaching, but, far more importantly, with respect to fundamental questions about the shaping forces of our thought and the interests that those shapings serve. The power of the Western male academy in defining and prescribing concepts—whether it be SLA theory (see Nayar, 1989),

[9]I do not want to suggest, however, that the largely female workforce, teachers in other countries, or these returned teachers unquestioningly accept these dogmas. There is certainly constant resistance, which in part accounts for the disparity between academics' claims and classroom realities.

in maintaining inequities between, on the one hand, predominantly male academics and, on the other, female teachers and language classrooms on the international power periphery.

For all of us, it is crucial that we see the social and political roles we play and the social and political implications of the theoretical paradigms that inform our work. At a time when all education is threatened by the conservative drive toward standardized curricula, and a move "back to basics," a move which threatens all openness and diversity in education and ignores questions of class, race, or gender difference, a move which threatens finally to render the teacher as nothing but a technician trained to transmit a fixed canon of knowledge, it is essential that teachers start to oppose those forms of knowledge that are being thrust upon them under the guise of scientific objectivity. As I have argued, Method is one such concept: An analysis of both the history and the present state of language teaching suggests that it has little conceptual validity and yet is a construct central to many teacher education programs, constantly used to legitimate various educational practices as if they were the newest development in a long line of scientific improvement dating back to the last century.

What is needed is perhaps encapsulated in Giroux's concept of the teacher as "transformative intellectual." This means seeing ourselves "as professionals who are able and willing to reflect upon the ideological principles that inform [our] practice, who connect pedagogical theory and practice to wider social issues, and who work together to share ideas, exercise power over the conditions of [our] labor, and embody in [our] teaching a vision of a better and more humane life" (Giroux & McLaren, 1989, p. xxiii). This definition should, of course, include academics as transformative intellectuals; reciprocal relationships can indeed be developed, and we should either see practice and theory as informing each other, or, better still, do away with this distinction all together. Rather than opting for "reductionist descriptions which are easier to understand but which, by definition, are incomplete and inaccurate" (Clarke, 1983, p. 107), rather than trying to understand our practice according to some form of totalizing or universal discourse, we need to recognize the complexities of language teaching and its contexts, and strive to validate other, local forms of knowledge about language and teaching.

REFERENCES

Alexander, L. G. (1967). *New concept English* (Teacher's Book). London: Longman.

Altbach, P. (1981). The university as center and periphery. *Teachers College Record, 82*(4), 601–622.

Anthony, E. M. (1963). Approach, method and technique. *English Language Teaching Journal, 17*, 63–67.

Apple, M. (1986). *Teachers and texts: A political economy of class and gender relations in education.* New York: Routledge & Kegan Paul.

Bazan, B. M. (1964). The danger of assumption without proof. *The Modern Language Journal, 48*(6), 337–346.

Belenky, M. F., Clinchy, B. M., Goldberger, N. R., & Tarule, J. M. (1986). *Women's ways of knowing: The development of self, voice, and mind.* New York: Basic Books.

Beretta, A. (1986). Program-fair language teaching evaluation. *TESOL Quarterly, 20*(3), 431–444.

Bosco, F. J., & Di Pietro, R. J. (1970). Instructional strategies: Their psychological and linguistic bases. *IRAL, 8*, 1–19.

Bourne, J. (1988). "Natural acquisition" and a "masked pedagogy." *Applied Linguistics, 9*(1), 83–99.

Brown, H. D. (1980). *Principles of language learning and teaching.* Englewood Cliffs, NJ: Prentice Hall.

Brown, H. D. (1987). *Principles of language learning and teaching* (2nd ed.). Englewood Cliffs, NJ: Prentice Hall.

Brumfit, C. (1985). Creativity and constraint in the language classroom. In R. Quirk & H. G. Widdowson (Eds.), *English in the world: Teaching and learning the language and literatures* (pp. 148–157). Cambridge: Cambridge University Press.

Burnaby, B., & Sun, Y. (1989). Chinese teachers' views of Western language teaching: Context informs paradigms. *TESOL Quarterly, 23*(2), 219–238.

Caravolas, J. (1984). *Le Gutenburg de la didacographie ou Coménius et l'enseignement des langues.* Montreal: Guérin.

Carroll, J. B. (1966). The contributions of psychological theory and educational research to the teaching of foreign languages. In A. Valdman (Ed.), *Trends in language teaching* (pp. 93–106). New York: McGraw-Hill.

Chomsky, N. (1959). [Review of *Verbal Behavior*]. *Language, 35*, 26–57.

Clarke, M. A. (1982). On Bandwagons, tyranny and common sense. *TESOL Quarterly, 16*(4), 437–448.

Clarke, M. A. (1983). The scope of approach, the importance of method, and the nature of techniques. In J. E. Alatis, H. H. Stern, & P. Strevens (Eds.), *Georgetown University round table on language and linguistics* (pp. 106–115). Washington, DC: Georgetown University Press.

Clarke, M. A., & Silberstein, S. (1988). Problems, prescriptions, and paradoxes in second language teaching. *TESOL Quarterly, 22*(4), 685–700.

Clifford, J. (1988). *The predicament of culture: Twentieth-century ethnography, literature, and art.* Cambridge, MA: Harvard University Press.

Cooke, D. (1988). Ties that constrict: English as a Trojan horse. In A. Cumming, A. Gagne, & J. Dawson (Eds.), *Awarenesses: Proceedings of the 1987 TESL Ontario Conference* (pp. 56–62). Toronto: TESL Ontario.

Cummins, J. (1989). *Empowering minority students.* Sacramento, CA: California Association for Bilingual Education.

De Lauretis, T. (Ed.). (1986). *Feminist studies, critical studies.* Bloomington: Indiana University Press.

Escobar, A. (1984). Discourse and power development: Michel Foucault and the relevance of his work to the third world. *Alternatives, 10*, 377–400.

Feyerabend, P. (1988). *Against method.* London: Verso.

Foucault, M. (1980). *Power/knowledge: Selected interviews and other writings, 1927–1977.* New York: Pantheon.

Escobar, A. (1984). Discourse and power development: Michel Foucault and the relevance of his work to the third world. *Alternatives, 10*, 377–400.

Feyerabend, P. (1988). *Against method*. London: Verso.

Foucault, M. (1980). *Power/knowledge: Selected interviews and other writings, 1927–1977*. New York: Pantheon.

Freire, P., & Macedo, D. (1987). *Literacy: Reading the word and the world*. South Hadley, MA: Bergin & Harvey.

Fröhlich, M., Spada, N., & Allen, P. (1985). Differences in the communicative orientation of L2 classrooms. *TESOL Quarterly, 19*(1), 27–58.

Giroux, H. A. (1983). *Theory and resistance in education: A pedagogy for the opposition*. South Hadley, MA: Bergin & Harvey.

Giroux, H. A. (1988). *Schooling and the struggle for public life: Critical pedagogy in the modern age*. Minneapolis: University of Minnesota Press.

Giroux, H. A., & McLaren, P. (1989). Introduction to H. A. Giroux & P. McLaren (Eds.), *Critical pedagogy, the state, and cultural struggle* (pp. xi–xxxv). Albany, NY: SUNY Press.

Gregg, K. (1986). [Review of *The input hypothesis: Issues and implications*]. *TESOL Quarterly, 20*(1), 116–122.

Grimshaw, J. (1986). *Philosophy and feminist thinking*. Minneapolis: University of Minnesota Press.

Habermas, J. (1984). *The theory of communicative action* (Vol. 1). Boston: Beacon Press.

Hall, E. T. (1986). Unstated features of the cultural context of learning. In A. Thomas & E. T. Ploman (Eds.), *Learning and development in a global perspective* (pp. 157–176). Toronto: OISE Press.

Halliday, M. A. K., McIntosh, A., & Strevens, P. (1964). *The linguistic sciences and language teaching*. London: Longman.

Harding, S. (1986). *The science question in feminism*. New York: Cornell University Press.

Harris, K. (1979). *Education and knowledge*. London: Routledge & Kegan Paul.

Harris, R. (1987, December 11–17). In and out of the language lab [Review of *The politics of linguistics*]. *Times Literary Supplement*, 1373.

Haskell, J. F. (1987). A bare-bones bibliography bookshelf. *TESOL Newsletter, 21*(2), 37–46.

Hebdige, D. (1986). Postmodernism and "the other side." *Journal of Communication Inquiry, 10*(2), 78–99.

Horowitz, D. (1986). Process, not product: Less than meets the eye. *TESOL Quarterly, 20*(1), 141–143.

Howatt, A. P. R. (1983). Five-hundred years of English language teaching. *ELT Journal, 37*(3), 262–265.

Howatt, A. P. R. (1984a). *A history of English language teaching*. Oxford: Oxford University Press.

Howatt, A. P. R. (1984b). Language teaching traditions: 1884 revisited. *ELT Journal, 38*(4), 279–282.

Illich, I. (1981). Vernacular values. In *Shadow work* (pp. 29–51). Boston: M. Boyars.

Judd, E. L. (1983). TESOL as a political act: A moral question. In J. Handscombe, R. A. Orem, & B. P. Taylor (Eds.), *On TESOL '83* (pp. 265–273). Washington, DC: TESOL.

Keller, E. F. (1985). *Reflections on gender and science*. New Haven, CT: Yale University Press.

Kelly, L. G. (1969). *25 centuries of language teaching*. Rowley, MA: Newbury House.

Kothari, R. (1987). On humane governance. *Alternatives, 12*, 277–290.

Krashen, S. D. (1982). *Principles and practice in second language acquisition*. Oxford: Pergamon Press.

Krashen, S. D., & Seliger, H. (1975). The essential contribution of formal instruction in adult second language learning. *TESOL Quarterly, 9*(2), 173–183.

Krashen, S. D., & Terrell, T. D. (1983). *The natural approach: Language acquisition in the classroom*. Oxford: Pergamon Press.

Kuhn, T. (1970). *The structure of scientific revolutions*. Chicago: University of Chicago Press.

Lambley, K. (1920). *The teaching and cultivation of the French language in England during Tudor and Stuart times*. London: Longman.

Larsen-Freeman, D. (1986). *Techniques and principles in language teaching*. Oxford: Oxford University Press.

Long, M. H., & Sato, C. (1983). Classroom foreigner talk discourse: Forms and functions of teachers' questions. In H. Seliger & M. H. Long (Eds.), *Classroom oriented research in second language acquisition* (pp. 268–285). Rowley, MA: Newbury House.

Lyotard, J. (1984). *The postmodern condition*. Minneapolis: University of Minnesota Press.

Mackey, W. F. (1965). *Language teaching analysis*. London: Longman.

Mackey, W. F. (1970). Foreword to L. Jakobovits, *Foreign language learning: A psycholinguistic analysis of the issues* (pp. vii–xiii). Rowley, MA: Newbury House.

Marcuse, H. (1964). *One-dimensional man*. Boston: Beacon Press.

McArthur, T. (1983). *A foundation course for language teachers*. Cambridge: Cambridge University Press.

Mey. J. (1985). *Whose language? A study in linguistic pragmatics*. Amsterdam: John Benjamins.

Mukherjee, T. (1986). ESL: An imported new empire? *Journal of Moral Education, 15*(1), 43–49.

Nandy, A. (1983). *The intimate enemy: Loss and recovery of self under colonialism*. Delhi: Oxford University Press.

Nayar, P. B. (1989, March). *From Krasher to Ashen: Ethnocentrism and universality in TESOL*. Paper presented at the 23rd Annual TESOL Convention, San Antonio, TX.

Ndebele, N. S. (1987). The English language and social change in South Africa. *The English Academy Review, 4*, 1–16.

Newmeyer, F. J. (1986). *The politics of linguistics*. Chicago: University of Chicago Press.

Peirce, B. N. (1989). Toward a pedagogy of possibility in the teaching of English internationally. *TESOL Quarterly, 23*(3), 401–420.

Phillipson, R. (1988). Linguicism: Structures and ideologies in linguistic imperialism. In J. Cummins & T. Skuttnab-Kangas (Eds.), *Minority education: From shame to struggle* (pp. 339–358). Avon: Multilingual Matters.

Popkewitz, T. S. (1984). *Paradigm and ideology in educational research*. Basingstoke: Falmer Press.

Raimes, A. (1983). Tradition and revolution in ESL teaching. *TESOL Quarterly, 17*(4), 535–552.

Richards, J. C. (1984). The secret life of methods. *TESOL Quarterly, 18*(1), 7–24.

Richards, J. C., & Rodgers, T. (1982). Method: Approach, design, and procedure. *TESOL Quarterly, 16*(2), 153–168.

Richards, J. C., & Rodgers, T. (1986). *Approaches and methods in language teaching*. Cambridge: Cambridge University Press.

Rivers, W. M. (1981). *Teaching foreign language skills* (2nd ed.). Chicago: Chicago University Press.

Sampson, G. P. (1984). Exporting language teaching methods from Canada to China. *TESL Canada Journal, 1*(1), 19–31.

Sauveur, L. (1874). *Introduction to the teaching of living languages without grammar or dictionary*. Boston: Schoenhof & Moeller.

Scherer, G. A. C., & Wertheimer, M. (1964). *A psycholinguistic experiment in foreign language teaching*. New York: McGraw-Hill.

Silva, E. T., & Slaughter, S. A. (1984). *Serving power: The making of the academic social science expert*. Westport, CT: Greenwood Press.

Simon, R. (1984). Signposts for a critical pedagogy [Review of *Theory and resistance in education*]. *Educational Theory, 34*(4), 379–388.

Simon, R. (1987). Empowerment as a pedagogy of possibility. *Language Arts, 64*, 370–383.

Sitting on a rocket. (1989). [Interview with Professor Gillian Brown]. *ELT Journal, 43*(3), 167–172.

Smith, P. D., Jr. (1970). *A comparison of the cognitive and audiolingual approaches to foreign language instruction: The Pennsylvania foreign language project*. Philadelphia, PA: Center for Curriculum Development.

Stern, H. H. (1983). *Fundamental concepts of language teaching*. Oxford: Oxford University Press.

Stern, H. H. (1985). [Review of *Methods that work: A smorgasbord of ideas for language tearhers*]. *Studies in Second Language Acquisition,* 7(2), 249–251.

Strevens, P. D. (1977). *New orientations in the teaching of English*. Oxford: Oxford University Press.

Swan, M. (1985). A critical look at the communicative approach (1&2). *ELT Journal, 39*(1), 2–12, (2), 76–87.

Titone, R. (1968). *Teaching foreign languages: An historical sketch.* Washington, DC: Georgetown University Press.

Tollefson, J. W. (1988). Covert policy in the United States refugee program in Southeast Asia. *Language Problems and Language Planning, 12*(1), 30–42.

van Lier, Leo. (1987). [Review of *Techniques and principles in language teaching*]. *TESOL Quarterly, 21*(1), 146–152.

Williams, R. (1976). *Keywords: A vocabulary of culture and society*. London: Fontana.

Wolin, S. (1972). Political theory as a vocation. In M. Fleisher (Ed.), *Machiavelli and the nature of political thought* (pp. 23–75). New York: Atheneum.

Wu, J. (1983). Quchang buduan—A Chinese view of foreign participation in teaching English in China. *Language Learning and Communication, 2,* 111–116.

Reflection and Inquiry

REFLECTING ON THE READINGS

Respond to one or more of the following:

1. The readings in this unit raise questions about methods as they are typically described in the literature on teaching. What do these authors see as the problems inherent in the concept of method? What surprised, intrigued, or provoked you in these chapters? Why do you think this was the case?
2. To what extent do you identify with any of the perplexing scenarios presented by Clarke and Silberstein (chapter 1)? What kinds of problems, tensions, or conflicts impinge on your own classroom experiences?
3. What issues does Holliday raise about the transferability of methods from one country or context to another (chapter 2)? Which of his examples do you find most compelling? Why? How might teachers begin to identify and examine their own preconceptions about teaching and learning?
4. Roller notes that the Initiate-Respond-Evaluate (IRE) pattern is the typical form of teacher–learner interaction in the classroom (chapter 3). To what extent did the IRE pattern predominate in your own classroom experiences? How might a teacher change this pattern of discourse?
5. Imagine that you've been hired to teach within a program in which everyone is expected to use the same method or textbook. Drawing on Pennycook's historical analysis of method (chapter 4), what concerns might you have about fulfilling these expectations?

6. In what ways do these articles inform one another? For example, what paradoxes might Clarke and Silberstein (chapter 1) find in the classrooms described by Roller (chapter 3)? How does Pennycook's analysis (chapter 4) help to explain Holliday's classroom observations?

7. Imagine that an expert is invited to a faculty development day at your school and discusses a new method that your teaching supervisor urges you to adopt. Imagine, too, that you try the method and it doesn't work. Drawing on some of the arguments from the readings in this unit, create the conversation that you might have with the supervisor.

8. Select a passage (one sentence or several sentences) from one of the readings in Unit One that struck you in some way. For example, it may be a passage that resonates with your own experience, that reminds of you something else you've read or seen, or that makes an important point. Highlight or copy the passage and then reflect on why you chose it.

READING FOR FURTHER REFLECTION

Respond to one or more of the following:

1. Read the following excerpt from Julia Alvarez's *Something to Declare* about her experience in an English-language school in the Dominican Republic. What strikes you?

> School was deadly. I thought I would surely die of boredom sitting on that hard chair listening to Mrs. Brown talk about the pilgrims or *i* before *e* or George Washington cutting down a cherry tree. We were attending the Carol Morgan School because my parents had decided that we should learn English and get "an American education" rather than a Dominican one. To this day, they claim this choice made our transition to the United States so much easier. But how could they have know back then that we would be going into exile in a few years?
>
> So what I was learning in school had nothing to do with the lush, tropical, and dangerous world around me. We were living in a dictatorship, complete with spies, late-night disappearances, torture, and death. What, indeed, did this world have to do with the capital of Alabama and Dick and Jane and a big red bouncing ball? And what on earth was apple pie? Was it anything at all like a pastel de tamarindo? No wonder I shut the doors to my attention and refused to do my homework.

2. Read the following interview with a teacher from Earl Stevick's *Teaching Languages: A Way and Ways*. What do you think accounts for the transformation of the students? In what way did the students transform the teacher's role in the classroom?

> My worst experience in teaching EFL was the year in which I taught first-year junior high school boys for five hours a week. At that time, I believed firmly that (1) language must be modeled and controlled by the teacher in order to avoid errors, and that (2) extensive oral practice was necessary to "set the language" into the students' heads. As the year wore on, I realized that my students were participating less and less in the artfully paced mix of oral drill activities that I had prepared for them. When I would say, "Turn to Chart t," there would be little whines of "Mata ka?" ("Again??"). I became very indignant at this lack of response and interest, especially since I felt that I had rescued these little ingrates through my modern techniques. Against this general background of frustration, I can remember one day on which things went well. I had given the students an assignment to work in twos and threes and write sentences about a picture in their book. That day, I walked around the classroom responding to questions, happily amazed at the transformation of my noisy, nonresponsive students into involved little workers.

3. Read the following excerpt from the *Pedagogy of the Oppressed* by Paolo Freire and consider his metaphor for the educational process. To what extent does Freire's perspective reflect your own classroom experiences? What metaphor would you use to describe your own experiences? What metaphor would describe your ideal notion of teaching and/or learning?

> Education becomes the act of depositing, in which the students are the depositories and the teacher is the depositor. Instead of communicating, the teacher issues communiqués and makes deposits which the students patiently receive, memorize, and repeat. This is the "banking concept" of education, in which the scope of action allowed to the students extends only as far as receiving, filing, and storing the deposits. . . .
>
> In the banking concept of education, knowledge is a gift bestowed by those who consider themselves knowledgeable upon those whom they consider to know nothing.

4. Read the following poem, "English as a Second Language," by Lisel Mueller and write a response. What strikes or moves you? What does the poem reveal about the complicated nature of teaching and learning?

ENGLISH AS A SECOND LANGUAGE
Lisel Mueller

The underpaid young teacher
prints the letters *t, r, e, e*
on the blackboard and imagines
forests and gardens spring up
in the tired heads of her students.

But they see only four letters:
a vertical beam weighed down
by a crushing crossbar
followed by a hook,
and after the hook, two squiggles,
arcane identical twins
which could be spying eyes
or ready fists, could be handles,
could be curled seedlings, could take root,
could develop leaves.

SUGGESTED PROJECTS FOR INQUIRY

Select a project that you would like to pursue:

1. Interview several teachers about their experiences with using particular methods. Some questions to consider: Why have these teachers adopted these methods? To what extent do these teachers believe that these methods work? What do they see as the benefits of a particular method? What do they see as the limitations? To what extent are the teachers faced with the kinds of problems and tensions described by the authors in this unit? How do these teachers address these difficulties? What do your findings reveal about the nature of methods?

2. Interview a teacher about a particular method he or she uses. Ask about goals, choice of materials, and planned activities. Observe the classroom and record what you see. To what extent is the teacher's description of his or her method reflected in what you see? Which activities or interchanges fit the teacher's stated pedagogical orientation? Are there activities or interchanges that do not fit the teacher's stated pedagogical orientation or that shift the focus of the lesson? How do your observations extend your understanding of the readings in this unit?

3. Observe a classroom in which you are a teacher, student, or outside observer. Take fieldnotes in which you record and reflect on what you are noticing. Try to record as much as you can in order to get a sense of the "culture" of this classroom. If it is possible, tape-record the classes you observe. These tapes can help you to "re-see" the classes. If there are course materials (e.g., assignments, handouts, students' papers), try to keep copies of these "artifacts." After recording your observational notes, reread your entries and examine anything else you have collected. What interests, intrigues, or puzzles you? Do you notice any patterns that you want to explore further? Is there a particular aspect of this classroom context that you want to study more closely as you continue to observe?

4. Observe two or more different classrooms in which the same method is reportedly being used. Note what occurs in each classroom. To what extent would you say these classrooms—and their activities and assignments—enact the same method? What questions do your observations raise about the nature of methods?

5. Interview a number of students about their past experiences in ESOL classrooms in order to explore the nature of methods from students' perspectives.

- What kinds of methods did they experience?
- To what extent do they feel these methods promoted language acquisition?
- Did they experience methods that they resisted?

What do these students' experiences reveal about the nature of methods?

Unit II

SEEING THE CLASSROOM

BEFORE READING

Respond to one or more of the following:

- If you have ever been observed and evaluated as a learner or teacher (for example while making a presentation or teaching), what was the experience like? What kind of feedback did you receive? How did it make you feel? What did you learn from it?
- If you have ever observed a classroom, what process did you use? How did you prepare for the observation, what did you do in the classroom itself, and what did you do with the information you gathered in your observation? What did you learn from it?
- From your perspective as a learner or teacher, describe a classroom experience in which the teacher either failed to recognize a student's potential, intelligence, or talent or misinterpreted a student's behavior or performance.

Chapter 5

"Let's See": Contrasting Conversations About Teaching

John F. Fanselow

Two common aims of supervision and observation are to evaluate and to help. Supervisors and observers with these aims provide products to those they visit: "helpful" prescriptions for improvement or a rating of the observed performances. The aims of supervision and observation presented in this article are to explore, to see teaching differently, not to evaluate or help; the emphasis is on a process—visited and visiting teachers sharing ways of looking to discover self. This process includes taping and transcribing excerpts from classes, grouping parts of the excerpts, arriving at a common language to discuss them, and making multiple interpretations about them, based not only on preconceived notions but also on a range of contrasting beliefs and goals. In short, this article tries to provide ways of looking so each of us can see our own teaching differently through observing others, reminding us all that we "are capable of acting on the world, and that these actions can transform the world" (Mehan, 1979, p. 207).

AIMS OF SUPERVISION AND OBSERVATION

When I used to ask teachers to write down comments they recalled from conversations with supervisors or fellow teachers who had visited their classes or had watched videotapes of their teaching, the comments and exchanges between different supervisors/observing teachers and the observed teachers seemed very different from each other. Others have found this too. Gebhard (1984), in a review of different models of supervision—different ways of making comments or of having conversations about lessons between supervisors and teachers—uses these labels: *directive, alternative, collaborative, nondirective, creative*.

Although the conversations I asked teachers to recall often indicated an overall tendency to be, say, more collaborative than directive, or more directive than nondirective, I consistently saw elements of many distinct models in the same sets of comments or conversations. I also began to notice that all the distinct models had the same aim: to provide a means for a more experienced person to help or evaluate a less experienced person. Two articles on supervision in second language teaching use the following words and phrases to characterize the purposes of the supervision models they describe: *functions as an arbitrator, commenting, evaluating, helping, provides* (Freeman, 1982, p. 21); *to direct or guide, to offer suggestions, to model teaching, to advise teachers, to evaluate* (Gebhard, 1984, p. 501). All of these words indicate that the person doing the visiting, no matter whether that person is following a collaborative model, creative model, or any other, is there mainly to help or evaluate the practice teacher, fellow teacher, or inservice teacher in training.

On first thinking about it, what could be more reasonable than designing models of supervision that provide ways for experienced people to help or evaluate inexperienced people? But thinking about the idea of *help* in other contexts provides a different perspective. Haven't you heard children shout to parents or teachers words like "Let me do it—don't show me," or "Don't give me the answer"? When referring to the need of children to be allowed to do things on their own, Montessori (1967, p. 309) made the plea, Let them fill their own buckets. As Alinsky (1971) reminded us:

> It is a human characteristic that someone who asks for help and gets it reacts not only with gratitude but with a subconscious hostility toward the one who helped him. It is a sort of psychic "original sin" because he feels that the one who helped him is always aware that if it hadn't been for his help, he would still be a defeated nothing. (p. 93)

The type of resentment Alinsky mentions is not necessarily universal. Some people seem to like to be helped and expect to be told what to do as well. For them, evaluations containing prescriptions of what to do are welcome. In discussing the appropriateness of different models for teachers at various stages, Freeman (1982) highlights the value of help and evaluation by pointing out that beginning teachers, for example, seem to prefer models and direction to collaboration. But even while pleading for help from the cooperating teacher or supervisor, many practice teachers assert, "The most valuable part of practice teaching was seeing other teachers teach!" Seeing other teachers teach is not the same as being told what to do by an evaluator, nor is it being helped by someone.

As a result of this keen interest that practice teachers and many inservice teachers have in seeing others teach, my fear that helping people can lead to resentment toward the one providing the help, and the fact that prescriptions from supervisor's evaluations can be demeaning and decrease the teacher's authority and responsibility, I see the need for an aim of supervision and observation different from the ones frequently practiced and described in the literature. Whereas the usual aim of observation and supervision is to help or evaluate the person being seen, the aim I propose is self-exploration—seeing one's own teaching differently. Observing others or ourselves to see teaching differently is not the same as being told what to do by others. Observing to explore is a process; observing to help or to evaluate is providing a product.

Besides leading to resentment, help can also lead to "learned helplessness" (Abramson, Seligman, & Teasdale, 1978). Helpful prescriptions can stop exploration, since the receiver, as someone in an inferior position being given orders by someone in a superior position, may easily develop the "ours is not to wonder why" syndrome.

A conversation reflecting the aims of the usual models might go like this: "Here I am with my lens to look at you and your actions and tell you or discover with you what is right and what is wrong and needs to be improved; I will then prescribe better activities or collaborate so we or you alone can discover better activities." A conversation reflecting the aim of observation I am suggesting might go like this: "Here I am with my lens to look at you and your actions. But as I look at you with my lens, I consider *you a mirror*; I hope to see myself in you and through your teaching. When I see myself, I find it hard to get distance from my teaching. I hear my voice, I see my face and clothes and fail to see my teaching. Seeing you allows me to see myself differently and to explore variables we both use." Although supervisors may consider their roles so set that empowering teachers to make decisions seems impossible, such redefinition is possible in any field. The role of managers in relationship to workers, for example, is presently undergoing change in many companies.

Although observing others does not automatically lead to seeing oneself differently, mainly because the aim of seeing others to help them is so usual, over time an increase occurs in comments like these: "That teacher said 'Ok, now' to mark changes in activity just as I do"; "How little each of us walks around"; "That teacher spoke to students at eye level some of the time; I do so only during breaks."

The model I am describing grows out of a range of sources, not only my examination of many transcripts of teacher-supervisor conferences. For example, Jarvis (1972) argued that in order for teacher preparation programs to be truly responsive, they need to shift "the responsibility for the decision-making to the classroom teacher. . . . It is perhaps time to train the teacher to analyze his situation and make his own decision for his situation" (p. 201). As Freire (1970) points out, learning "consists of acts of cognition, not transferrals of information" (p. 67). Each of us needs to construct, reconstruct, and revise our own teaching. He reminds us that for learning to take place we need to resolve the "teacher-student contradiction" (p. 67).

When we observe others to gain self-knowledge and self-insight and when we generate our own alternatives based on what we see others do, we construct our own knowledge and engage in the type of learning Freire has advocated. In a discussion of education, Abbs (1986) has this to say: "Authentic education is to be found in that act of intelligent exploration . . . the first priority of teachers should be to secure the necessary condition for the autonomy of teaching and for the freedom to learn" (p. 21). Using the word *supervisor*—a person with super vision—hardly supports our autonomy. When I observe and when I invite others to observe me, I refer to all of us as *visiting teachers* to avoid the use of the word *supervisor*.

PRACTICES

I and others have used various combinations of the following practices in pre- and inservice MA and adult education programs. Anyone genuinely interested in exploring, in seeing teaching differently, and anyone who believes that we can learn about our own teaching by seeing others can use the practices.

In my experience, trying to observe and supervise with the aim of exploring practices and of gaining insight into one's own teaching does not in itself enable us to stop treating observation and supervision as a means of helping and evaluating others. For people to begin to learn that they can see their own teaching differently by observing others, I and others have found the following practices for collecting, describing, and interpreting observations useful:

1. Short amounts of time have to be set aside for observation and discussion.

2. Segments from observed lessons need to be collected by note taking, taping, or transcribing.

3. The exchanges and activities in the segments need to be grouped in a range of ways.

4. Finally, what was done, as reflected in notes, tapes, and transcripts, needs to be related to notions, beliefs, and goals. Coupling this data collection and analysis with discussions of freedom and the need for each of us to construct our own knowledge helps many visiting teachers to de-

crease their suggestions to others, to increase their descriptive and analytical comments about the lessons observed, and to relate their insights to their own lessons.

Although allowing time for discussions of observations as part of a teacher's load is a policy I advocate, this policy is rare. Even in teacher preparation programs, there are not always long periods of time for discussions. Rather than putting off observations and discussions until sufficient time is available, thereby virtually ensuring that they will never take place, I recommend limiting observations and discussions to as little as 5 minutes.

Obviously, seeing 5 minutes of a lesson prevents us from seeing lesson development. But look how much we notice in 1-minute commercials. In many classes, 30 questions are asked in a minute (Hoetker, 1968). A dozen instances of feedback—both the treatment of errors and communications made after acceptable student moves—can be seen in a minute as well (Fanselow, 1977). In a 30-minute period, hundreds of communications are made, each in split seconds (Jackson, 1968).

Though short segments provide much data, short discussions force a limit to the number of communications that can be considered and the number of alternatives that can be generated. Since one or two communications often affect what is done and since many of our communications are unconscious, we can only hope to see and later try out one or two alternative communications per class period. Short time segments do not of themselves lead to fewer evaluative or helping comments or more exploration, however, and that is why the following activities are used.

Collecting and Describing Data

Transcribing and Note Taking. The first step in our observations, no matter how long, is to capture as many of the specific communications as possible by audio- or videotaping, by taking notes, and by drawing sketches or even taking photographs as communications are observed. Later, tapes can be transcribed to reveal details missed in notes and sketches.

Observers can take notes, sketch, and transcribe as they wish. Many put exchanges in dialogue form in their notes. But now and then, one will put teacher communications in the left-hand column of a page and student communications in the right-hand column to highlight them. Many write one line and pause, forgetting that the purpose of looking is to collect data, not to judge the teacher or think of ways to help the teacher. Some prefer sketches to notes, noting the position of teachers and students, their location, or expressions on faces of teacher or students. Others note what is done rather than what is said—movements, objects used, writing on the board.

Except for the instruction that observers are to write down only what happens, not comments about what happens, no directions are given about what observers are to note. Different observers often note different communications, reflecting differences in the values of the observers. Some observers write down things they are interested in seeing in their own classes that they cannot see while they are teaching. Though two observers are likely to capture some of the same spoken exchanges, they are not likely to have the same account of how the exchanges were said or what other communications were made. Discussing what took place and listening to tapes will make clear a central lesson of observation: What we see is not what takes place but what we value as important to see; observing is selecting.

While transcribing exchanges, drawing sketches, or otherwise noting or capturing specific communications, we cannot write comments such as these: "To make the class lively, this teacher needs more activities"; "This teacher should follow the responses with clearer feedback." When not taking notes or transcribing, we tend to revert to our usual pattern of thinking of ways to help or evaluate another. This is a sure way to miss seeing anything differently, a sure way to limit our observations by trying to relate them to our preconceived notions of good and bad teaching.

Grouping Activities. As data are collected, the observers, and in many cases the teacher observed, begin to group the communications. For example, if the teacher asks the students to give synonyms for some words and to draw sketches to show the meanings of other words, the two types of tasks are grouped. One possible grouping that emerges has to do with the fact that one task requires the students to speak and the other one requires drawing and silence.

A range of groupings of tasks and activities, rather than just one, is aimed for. Looking at the same exchanges again, we can group the questions on the basis of who was asked the question. Were students sitting in particular rows asked to perform some tasks more often than students in other rows? Were males asked to perform more of some types of tasks than females? How many tasks did students perform because the teacher requested them to, either by using names or pointing, and how many did they volunteer for?

The purpose of the questions and the grouping is not to imply that, for example, using names is better than pointing or getting volunteers. The questions are asked so that the same tasks or activities can be grouped and categorized on the basis of a range of characteristics. When we look at, say, a dessert menu, we see many characteristics. We have categories such as high calorie or low calorie, sweet or semisweet, high or low cholesterol, easy or difficult to prepare, for children or adults, and so on. By seeing that there are many ways to group the same communications, we basically are developing a checklist of options and the multiple characteristics of each.

As such lists and groupings expand, ways to vary our teaching—use different options—become more and more evident. Each activity, and the groups it fits in, provides at least one more variable, with a distinct range of characteristics, that we can manipulate in our own teaching. Each grouping also reminds us that communications have multiple dimensions, a fact that is hidden by one-dimensional terms often used to judge teaching, such as *great pace, nice grammar work*, or *fine communications*.

Data are also grouped by making lists. For example, one teacher may give the answer to a question after a student cannot answer, and another may give a clue rather than the entire answer. Thus, we have two specific items on a list of feedback possibilities. Clues, too, may be given in various ways. A teacher may sometimes say, "The word starts with a *g*." Another time the teacher may say, "It has two syllables" or "It is a noun." One of the insights that comes as lists are developed of what is observed in distinct areas of teaching such as feedback, group work, and so on is that the range of activities observed in any one class is often small, but across many teachers the range becomes great.

Using Technical Language. If transcribed communications are merely listed without being grouped or categorized, the list can become very long, of course. By grouping different communications on the basis of inferences we make about them, the value of category labels—technical language—becomes apparent. Thus, from the descriptive statement "Students gave synonyms," an observer and teacher might infer that memory was required but that no motor control was, as in the case of drawing sketches to show the meaning of words. Then, looking at communications from our own or other classes and seeing other activities that require memory alone or memory plus motor control, subsequent communications can be compared with the first ones in the category. The feedback activities listed, such as the distinct clues given, can also be compared and grouped. "Clues given with spoken words" versus "clues given with symbols on the blackboard" would constitute one way to distinguish clues, for example.

After a few discussions between observers (visiting teachers) and the teachers observed (visited teachers), the following general categories inevitably arise: questions that require students to share previous knowledge versus those that require information just presented; tasks done individually or in groups; answers for which the teacher is interested in the form of what is said versus the meaning; questions teachers know the answers to and those they do not know the answers to; communications containing experiences of students and those using language for its own sake; student-to-student communication and teacher-to-student or student-to-teacher communication. Observers are reminded to develop categories that refer to at least two dimensions of any item in order to keep in mind the aim of seeing multiple dimensions of any communication.

The categories for the lists made and the groupings can cover whatever areas that observers and teachers want, as long as the focus is on the data: transcripts, sketches, photographs, notes, and actual recordings as well, when possible. This concentration on the collection and grouping of data makes it difficult to think of helping or evaluating anyone.

Lortie (1975), among others, has said that one of the critical problems that teachers face is that they do not have a language to discuss what they do: "What students [practice teachers] learn about teaching, then, is intuitive and imitative rather than explicit and analytical" (p. 62). Lortie (p. 73) maintains that the absence of a common technical vocabulary limits the ability to analyze as well as the acuity of the observations that teachers make.

Giving category names to the groups of communications and lists of activities provides a technical language, since those noting the similarities and differences between communications and activities constantly have to go back and forth between data and names applied to distinct types of data until they agree on a fit between the terms and the data. Once teachers and observers have developed some technical terms, coding systems developed by others can be introduced. The one I introduce most frequently is my own, called FOCUS (Fanselow, 1987). COLT (Allen, Fröhlich, & Spada, 1984), TALOS (Ullmann & Geva, 1982), or any other coding system can also be used (Long, 1980).

Starting discussions with a published coding system can make the idea of categories clear earlier, but there are some disadvantages to their early introduction. If teachers and observers are unaware of the problem coding systems were designed to deal with, they may use the systems in a mechanical way. Starting with published systems can also imply that the observers and teachers working jointly may not be up to the development of categories. On the other hand, going through the steps of gathering data and grouping data often shows the value of a technical language. It is also more likely that somebody else's categories can be made our own if we develop some of our own along the way. When those doing the observing develop the categories, knowledge is being created, rather than buckets being filled (Montessori, 1967) or information being transferred (Freire, 1970, p. 67).

Interpreting Data

Once a range of communications is captured in the form of data and once activities are listed, grouped, or categorized, interpretations can be made. It must be remembered, of course, that collecting data and listing and grouping them according to jointly developed categories or published ones are not activities free of interpretation. In initial discussions, as in initial collection and grouping of data, most participants interpret data in light of preconceived notions of good teaching. But at this stage, attention is given to showing how the data and lists of categories already reflect values, notions, or theories of teaching and learning. If the data indicate, for example, that the teacher smiled constantly, one participant may point out that a person noted smiles rather than frowns or shaking of the head. As the observer who noted the smiles equates smiles with friendliness, he or she realizes how a belief affected what was observed.

Since it is very common for us all to see, list, and group, as well as interpret, what we see in light of our preconceived notions about teaching, there is no way to prevent such "filtered" data collecting, grouping, or interpreting. But this effect can be counterbalanced. After one observer or teacher says that the teacher's smile showed that the teacher was friendly, other possible interpretations of a smile can be sought. Alternative interpretations emerge from asking what smiles have meant in our classes or by asking for possible negative meanings of smiles. Usually, a comment such as "Well, I often smile when nervous" comes forth. Or one will hear, "I smile sometimes when I want students to like me." Different data from the segment being discussed might also be noted: "The smile was fixed as I recall; I frowned a lot too—look at the sketch you made of me."

To encourage interpretations that are quite different from the normal ones that people with similar preconceived notions offer, participants are taught to ask each other to provide at least one interpretation that is seemingly outlandish or different in intent from the ones given. If all the interpretations are positive, possible negative interpretations can be sought. And if all are negative, positive interpretations can be sought. In the case of the smile, a negative interpretation might be that smiling can be used to keep control. Arguments about the superiority of a particular interpretation are not allowed in the beginning. Rather, the goal is simply to try to remind the participants that each event we see can be interpreted in ways different from our usual ways of doing it because we are each limited by the ideas of reality we have.

Another central lesson that emerges from multiple interpretations of the same event is that each event has more than one cause and that these causes need to be specified precisely. A replay of the videotape or a review of the notes or sketches may reveal some of the exchanges that took place before the smile, exchanges that were not seen because they seemed unimportant: the realization that the smile was perhaps the result of a number of small events that had happened immediately beforehand. By searching for different interpretations, observers and teachers are thrown back to the data, lists, and categories, not to seek support for what they thought when they started, but to seek support for the seemingly outlandish new interpretations. Seeing our own teaching differently is not going to happen if we are simply looking at other lessons and interpreting them in the same way we have been looking at lessons and interpreting them all of our lives.

Data and categories can also be interpreted in relationship to beliefs about teaching the participants have heard about. For example, participants can search for communications that are congruent or incongruent with Smith's (1971) admonition that "information about an error and aid in performing a task correctly are more helpful than discouraging comments about an inadequate performance" (p. 229). If a teacher is heard saying "Why can't you ever do it right?" the participants might respond at first by saying that the communication seems incongruent. *Seems* is used because "Why can't you do it right?" if said humorously and with a smile, could be congruent with Smith's advice. Such tentativeness among the participants is possible because of a self-developed realization based on engaging in the process of collecting data, listing specific communications and activities, and relating them to ideas over and over again in short segments of time.

Isolating beliefs about language teaching that can be related to data and categories is not difficult. Most articles and books are written to further beliefs or theories. By relating beliefs from the literature to what is actually done and observed in specific detail, participants clarify beliefs and see ways to translate the beliefs into practice. To translate Krashen's notion of "comprehensible input" (see Dulay, Burt, & Krashen, 1982) into action, teachers and observers can first examine exchanges in a range of lessons and then group those that seem comprehensible and those that seem not to be. Barnes's (1976) ideas about "exploratory talk" and "finished talk," about "school knowledge" versus "action knowledge," can be understood, seen, and translated into action only when related to data gathered from lessons.

In addition to relating data and categories to beliefs about learning, we can relate them to goals. If our goal is to ensure that students can obtain literal and implied meaning from what they hear and read but we never ask any inference questions of them, then our practices are not congruent with our goal.

Relating data to notions in articles and books brings us to another activity that can be used in the observations and discussions of teaching: reading. Just as one goal of working in pairs and groups is to provide multiple perspectives, so reading is used to provide different angles. When our partners give us a different view of a lesson, we have to take our usual lenses off, for a few seconds at least, to try to see what they have seen. Published notions, both of ways of looking at teaching (Bateson, 1972; Mehan,

1979) and ways of teaching (Haskell, 1987), show us different maps of similar territory that require us to try on a range of different lenses.

Self-Observation and the Notion of Opposites

Transcribing, listing activities, grouping communications, categorizing and relating these activities to our notions, beliefs, and goals—all show the great number of different ways of seeing variables, relationships between them, and consequences, *if* these activities can be done in pairs or groups. However, often we cannot find even one person to observe us or to be observed.

The basis for getting multiple perspectives when we are in a group is simply to juxtapose different individuals' perceptions. This same idea of juxtaposing, of using opposites, can also be used to provide different perceptions when we are alone. If in our own classes we see the students always sitting in chairs during speaking lessons, we can ask ourselves to juxtapose—to give an opposite posture. In this case two opposites come immediately to mind. Students and teacher alike can sit on the floor, if the room is carpeted, or everyone can stand. Though much conversation outside of the classroom takes place when we are standing, the point of juxtaposing or contrasting opposite situations is to see situations not seen before, not to argue about the absolute superiority of a particular format. And although some may object to standing or to sitting on the floor, by precluding alternatives based on what people might think, we close off inquiry and tend to limit what occurs to our preconceived notions of good and bad teaching.

In addition to generating alternatives by looking at aspects of the classroom, we can compare the communications in a class with those we see outside of a teaching setting. Using our chair example, we can compare where we sit in a teaching setting with where we sit in a nonteaching setting, such as a dormitory room, living room, or park. Finding opposites to what we normally do in a teaching setting or comparing what we do in teaching and nonteaching settings can be extremely valuable in providing the alternative perspectives a partner would supply in pair or group work.

The idea of opposites can also help to broaden the range of interpretations. If the first and only interpretation of a teacher's smile is that the teacher is happy and no other interpretations come up in a discussion, an opposite interpretation can be offered: "I have interpreted the smile as a good communication; now let me consider a smile a bad communication. Then what could it mean? What are some disadvantages of smiling?"

In second language acquisition research, learner errors were first attributed to the first language of the learners. Then, some began to explain the errors on the basis of developmental stages. Different types of errors were later considered to be caused by different types of tasks used to elicit the sentences that contained the errors (Ellis, 1985). What are these but opposite interpretations of the same data? Most fields are enriched by multiple interpretations of the same data, and these multiple interpretations can be generated by considering opposite interpretations to those usually provided.

Even with the concept of opposites to provide different perspectives, self-observation is limited. It prevents us from getting distance from our teaching and seeing our teaching through others. Though transcribing our own teaching gives us some distance from what we do, since the written record removes our voice, the transcriptions often remain too much a part of ourselves.

MEANINGS

Given the aim I advocate for conversations about teaching, labels often used to classify conversations about teaching, as well as the words in the conversations, take on new meanings. "Ask questions more rapidly" is *not* necessarily a prescription or an offer of help in a conversation in which exploration and seeing teaching differently are the goals. The meaning need *not* be, "Do this because I who visited your class know more than you do and you need help." Rather, the meaning can be, "Try this to see how it alters what has been happening. I am going to ask questions more rapidly too; perhaps different reasons to ask questions both slowly and rapidly will become apparent. We can compare tapes when we have some descriptions of both quick and slow questions." On the other hand, when a visitor in the role of a person in charge says, "You might try a slower pace," though the modal *might* is used, the meaning can be a "helpful" prescription. The message can mean, "I know, and I want you to do what I say." Exploration can be inhibited or completely stopped because the underlying intention of the words can be to show who is in charge.

Even a comment such as "The quick questions were great" can be seen as a description rather than as a judgment if the aim is exploratory. In such a context, the *great* could refer to the execution of the direction rather than to the technique itself.

Words in our conversations, to be judgments, must imply that the speaker or hearer is attributing good or bad, superiority or inferiority, to a practice. If "good lesson" is said or heard to imply that you or a teacher you visited did what was prescribed—what the speaker or hearer considers to be the right way to do it—then a judgment is probably being made in our communication. The words must be heard in relationship to the aim of our conversation and the role of those having the conversation. In the conversations I advocate, judgments are avoided because they tend to close off exploration. They tend to end, rather than continue, a process.

Some label an emphasis on data and description *objective*. We avoid both the terms *objective* and *subjective*. The meaning of *a lot* in "You asked a lot of questions" is not subjective because of *a lot*. Nor are *42* and *2* objective in "You asked 42 questions in 2 minutes." Both statements can be judgments or descriptions, depending greatly on what the speaker's and hearer's aim is and the role each is assuming. Again, if the words are used to see differently, as a means to explore—suggesting the importance of comparing the asking of 42 questions in 2 minutes with 22 in 2 minutes or a few with a lot—then, they are both simply descriptive. If the words are used because the speaker or listener—the visited or visiting teacher—is against frequent questions or feels that asking a lot of questions is *not* the thing to do, both groups of words are likely to be judgments. Both can be implied helpful prescriptions to use fewer questions if you want to do the right thing and be a good teacher, given the preconceived notion of good teaching held by the visiting teacher or visited teacher.

There is a reason that explanations or proof to support categories or interpretations has not been mentioned. Observers do not request explanations like "Why did you smile?" And teachers do not give such explanations: "I smiled because I thought at that moment the class needed reassurance." These exchanges tend to lead to arguments and can be seen as veiled attempts to support or strengthen the authority of one of the participants. In the model presented here, explanations are replaced by what a person did; what the characteristics were of what was done; how these related to beliefs, theories, or goals; and multiple interpretations of the data and groupings and the relationships among these.

Trying to see how the same words that for so long meant one thing can begin to mean something else is, of course, not something accomplished only by going through a series of steps. Nor indeed is seeing differently—exploration—a point to reach, but rather a tendency, a movement toward.

This tendency, this movement toward, as well as the tendency back toward the usual conversations, is noted by recording the discussions among teachers and observers—visited and visiting teachers. The exchanges in the discussions are dealt with in the same way as exchanges from classes: Short transcriptions are made, communications are grouped and coded, and multiple interpretations are made. They are related to the beliefs upon which this model rests—the trust that can come from joint effort without external evaluation; exploration; multiple perspectives; multiple causation; the idea that much of what we do in classes, just as outside the classroom, is beyond our awareness; and the notion that helping another from a superior position can lead to resentment and dependence.

The discussions of the observations often show confusion, struggles to group and categorize data. They also contain examples of simple causation ("The repetition of the sentence made them learn it"), prescriptions ("You should never put the directions up on the board when they are in their books"), and all the other normal types of conversations we usually have about teaching. But now and then the teaching act is discussed in a way that is congruent with the beliefs of this model.

CONCLUSION

Judgments and predictable prescriptions are *not* limited to conversations about teaching. In a critique of Canby's movie reviews, Carney (1986) reminds us that using words like *charming, sincere, buoyant, funny*, and *clever* to review films "amounts to an alarming aesthetic" (p. 30). He goes on:

> One is accustomed to seeing invocations of charms, etc., as measures of value . . . in ads for Calvin Klein, Christian Dior, Clinique, and Club Med. But these are hardly the supreme values that one would expect in a serious reflection on art. . . . They are, indeed, precisely the values such a reflection should question. (p. 30)

If we discuss teaching with words implying judgments like *exciting, boring, flowed smoothly*—all variations of *good* and *bad*—we limit our perceptions in the same way that such one-dimensional, uncritical words limit our perceptions of film and other forms of art.

The usual conversations, full of prescriptive clichés designed to help or evaluate, no doubt provide more certainty than conversations whose purpose is to see our own and others' teaching differently and to explore reality. In fact, Canby's *buoyant, funny*, and *clever* might be welcome in many conversations about teaching. Conversations between Socrates and others in the Socratic dialogues could not be described in this way! These characters reflect more complexity in their conversations—movement from strongly held opinion to floundering uncertainty to a confused not knowing. Similar stages occur in conversations aimed at seeing teaching differently—exploring. An authentic quest for learning and meaning requires that these stages take place. Neat, pat answers to complex problems were not a part of the Socratic dialogues, nor are they a part of conversations exploring teaching. As Abbs (1986) reminds us in a discussion of Socrates:

> To adopt the Socratic view of education would be to reaffirm that education in our culture is primarily concerned with critical reflection . . . with sustained inquiry into the various forms of meaning, with the lifelong process

> . . . that goes well beyond the enclosing pressures of the ego and the ephemeral clamourings of party politics. (p. 21)

To observe others and ourselves with the purpose of helping implies not only that we know that one set of practices is consistently superior to another, but that we know what needs to be done in each distinct setting. It also implies that there is a simple cause-effect relationship between a communication and a result: "Smile and the class will be relaxed"; "Speak slowly and the class will understand." To help another or ourselves means we know what should be done and what practices produce what results. If experience in classes has taught us nothing else, we have learned that each day we and our students are different as a result of ongoing experiences and that practices that seemed to have particular consequences one day have different ones another day.

To *help* means we have something to give another, a product to sell. The whole thrust of the point of view and activities presented in this article is toward the value of process, not product, and toward the construction of our own knowledge, not the acceptance of the knowledge of others in some type of package, as a product. Freire's (1970, p. 59) use of *banking* as a metaphor for education that stresses product highlights the aim of many conversations about lessons we observe: the passing of information from one person to another. As Mehan (1979) says:

> In sum, providing people with prearranged packages of information is oppressive, for it fails to treat people as responsible for their own lives. Furthermore, these imposed programs often have little to do with the participants' own preoccupations and practical circumstances. Providing people with ways of looking, on the other hand, reminds the participants that they are capable of acting on the world, and that these actions can transform the world. (pp. 206–207)

The model for visiting teachers presented here, like the ideas of Mehan and Freire, all come together in Bronowski's (1956) discussion of the purposes of art and science. For the words *science* and *works of art* in the following quotation, one might consider substituting the words *observation* and *lessons and conversations about lessons*, respectively.

> The discoveries of science, the works of art are explorations—more, are explosions—of a hidden likeness. . . . When a simile takes us aback and persuades us together, when we find a juxtaposition in a picture both odd and intriguing, when a theory is at once fresh and convincing, we do not merely nod over someone else's work. We re-enact the creative act, and we ourselves make the discovery again. At bottom, there is no unifying likeness there until we have seized it, we too have made it for ourselves. (p. 19)

When we collect and interpret data from observations and reconstruct our teaching, we are, of course, reinventing the wheel. But why not? Why deny others or ourselves this pleasure? By providing pat prescriptions to *help*, we not only deny others or ourselves the excitement of constructing knowledge, we also imply that we ourselves or those we work with cannot construct knowledge. Moreover, helping can stop exploration. Again, Bronowski's (1956) comments are appropriate. To him, the process of exploration is the "habit of truth": "In science and in art and in self-knowledge we explore and move constantly by turning to the world of sense to ask, Is this so? This is the habit of truth, always minute yet always urgent" (p. 43).

REFERENCES

Abbs, P. (1986, January 13). The poisoning of the Socratic idea. *The Guardian*, p. 21.

Abramson, L. V., Seligman, M. E. P., & Teasdale, J. D. (1978). Learned helplessness in humans: Critique and reformulation. *Journal of Abnormal Psychology, 87,* 49–74.

Alinsky, S. D. (1971). *Rules for radicals—A practical primer for realistic radicals.* New York: Random House.

Allen, P., Fröhlich, M., & Spada, N. (1984). The communicative orientation of language teaching: An observation scheme. In J. Handscombe, R. A. Orem, & B. P. Taylor (Eds.), *On TESOL '83* (pp. 231–252). Washington, DC: TESOL.

Barnes, D. (1976). *From communication to curriculum.* Harmondsworth, England: Penguin.

Bateson, G. (1972). *Steps to an ecology of mind.* New York: Ballantine.

Bronowski, J. (1956). *Science and human values.* New York: Harper & Row.

Carney, R. (1986, June 30). A critic in the dark. *The New Republic*, pp. 25–33.

Dulay, H., Burt, M., & Krashen, S. (1982). *Language two*. New York: Oxford University Press.

Ellis, R. (1985). *Understanding second language acquisition*. Oxford: Oxford University Press.

Fanselow, J. F. (1977). The treatment of error in oral work. *Foreign Language Annals, 10,* 583–593.

Fanselow, J. F. (1987). *Breaking rules—Generating and exploring alternatives in language teaching*. White Plains, NY: Longman.

Freeman, D. (1982). Observing teachers: Three approaches to in-service training and development. *TESOL Quarterly, 16*, 21–28.

Freire, P. (1970). *Pedagogy of the oppressed.* New York: Seabury.

Gebhard, J. G. (1984). Models of supervision: Choices. *TESOL Quarterly, 18*, 501–514.

Haskell, J. (1987). A bare-bones bibliography bookshelf. *TESOL Newsletter, 21*(2), 37–46.

Hoetker, J. (1968). Teacher questioning behavior in nine junior high school English classes. *Research in the Teaching of English, 2*, 99–106.

Jackson, P. W. (1968). *Life in classrooms*. New York: Holt, Rinehart and Winston.

Jarvis, G. A. (1972). They're tearing up the street where I was born. *Foreign Language Annals, 6*, 198–205.

Long, M. (1980). Inside the 'black box': Methodological issues in classroom research. *Language Learning, 30,* 1–42.

Lortie, D. C. (1975). *Schoolteacher: A sociological study*. Chicago: The University of Chicago Press.

Mehan, H. (1979). *Learning lessons*. Cambridge, MA: Harvard University Press.

Montessori, M. (1967). *The discovery of the child.* New York: Ballantine.

Smith, F. (1971). *Understanding reading: A psycholinguistic analysis of reading and learning to read.* New York: Holt, Rinehart and Winston.

Ullmann, R., & Geva, E. (1982). *The target language observation scheme (TALOS)* (York Board of Education, Core French Evaluation Project). Unpublished report, Ontario Institute for Studies in Education, Toronto.

Chapter 6

Gender and Ethnicity as Factors in the Development of Verbal Skills in Bilingual Mexican American Women

Kay M. Losey

This study describes and analyzes differences in student output across ethnicity and gender in a mixed monolingual English and bilingual Spanish/English class in order to understand how L2 oral language skills are developed in a mixed classroom. Primary participants in the study included approximately 30 basic writing students ranging in age from 18 to 60. Fifty-five percent of the students were bilingual Mexican American, and the remainder were monolingual Anglo Americans. Participant observation, informal interviews, and audiotaped classroom and tutorial interaction provide the data for this classroom ethnography. Data were analyzed to discover patterns of student output in various interactional contexts and to discover how the structure and content of interaction influenced these patterns. The analysis revealed that bilingual Mexican American students spoke significantly less in whole class interaction than monolingual Anglo American students. Moreover, an analysis by gender revealed that Mexican American men contributed four times the amount expected, whereas Mexican American women spoke half as much as expected. In other interactional contexts, however, the bilingual women were quite verbal. The social status of Mexican American women as "double minorities" and negative attitudes toward Spanish/English bilinguals help explain why the Mexican American women alone responded to whole class interaction with silence.

There is little question that opportunities for interaction between bilingual learners and target language (TL) speakers are important for further development of the speaker's second language (Krashen, 1985; McLaughlin, 1985; Swain, 1985; Wong Fillmore, 1982). Researchers have also concluded that the necessary interaction between bilinguals and TL speakers includes not only appropriate input but opportunities for output, as well (Swain, 1985; Wong Fillmore, 1982).

Numerous factors beyond learner proficiency with the TL have been shown to influence bilingual students' output in the classroom. In the case of Mexican American bilinguals, studies have shown that such students often produce little output in the classroom. One group of studies has concluded that this silence is a result of differential treatment by teachers based on ethnicity (Ortiz, 1988; Parsons, 1965; U.S. Commission on Civil Rights, 1973), students' language dominance or students' language preference (Laosa, 1977; Ortiz, 1977, 1988; Townsend & Zamora, 1975). Other researchers have found evidence of a cultural mismatch between the interactional style of the home and of the school (Delgado-Gaitan, 1987; Gumbiner, Knight, & Kagan, 1981; LeCompte, 1981), concluding that Mexican Americans students are more successful in classrooms with collaborative learning structures (Díaz, Moll, & Mehan, 1986; Trueba, 1987) studying topics that draw upon the students' experiences and interests (Díaz, Moll, & Mehan, 1986; Moll, 1988; Trueba, 1987).

However, none of the studies of bilingual Mexican American classroom interaction consider how adult Mexican Americans interact in the classroom or the role of gender in their interaction. But as Swacker (1975) argues, "any sociolinguistic research which does not, at least, specifically give consideration to the sex of the informant might well be of questionable validity" (p. 82). Previously, none of the research on classroom interaction and Mexican American bilinguals has examined this factor. This study looks at both teacher input and student output or response in a mixed monolingual Anglo American and bilingual Mexican American community college classroom in a variety of contexts. It examines the differences in response between monolingual speakers and bilingual speakers and considers the observed differences in terms of language background and ethnicity as well as gender.

BACKGROUND TO THE STUDY

The study of classroom interaction and its role in the success or failure of students rests upon the notion that all learning is a fundamentally social process, the result of interaction between two or more individuals. Vygotsky (1978) has noted that "human learning presupposes a specific social nature" (p. 88). The social process by which learning occurs creates a bridge that spans the learner's "zone of proximal development," such that what one is unable to accomplish alone can be achieved successfully with a more capable peer or adult. The theory of learning as socially constructed has been extended to the study of adults in the work of Lave (1988), who notes that "the processes of learning and understanding are socially and culturally constituted" (p. 2) (see also Elsasser & John-Steiner, 1977; Freire, 1970; Wertsch, Minick, & Arns, 1985, for additional research on the social nature of adult learning).

Likewise, second language learning also occurs through interaction. McLaughlin (1985) concludes that students have the best chance to develop a second language when they "(a) receive a great deal of oral language input (adjusted to their abilities) from staff and native-English-speaking peers, and (b) have an opportunity to use the language in meaningful contexts where they receive feedback from native speakers" (p. 162). Similarly Wong Fillmore (1982) finds that "a major problem for language learners involves getting enough exposure to the new language, and getting enough practice speaking it with people who know the language well enough to help them in their efforts to learn" (p. 284). Research and theory on adult second language acquisition and learning suggests that adults, too, need interaction with native speakers to successfully acquire a second language (e.g., Krashen, 1976). In fact, one reason adults are often considered notoriously poor second language learners may be a lack of interest or opportunity to interact with native speakers relative to school-age learners (Schumann, 1978).

In the classroom, the traditional interaction pattern may prevent students from having opportunities to practice the language or provide output. Every "speech community" (Hymes, 1972) has its own norms for interaction that may differ with varying aspects of the "speech event" (Hymes, 1972). Usually these exchanges are made up of various types of initiations and responses where the initiators ask real questions in which they have a real interest and to which they have no answer but to which the respondents have an answer (Sacks, Schegloff, & Jefferson, 1974). The exact "participant structure" of exchanges in a speech event or the "who will talk and when they will talk" (Philips, 1972/1985, p. 373) varies depending on a multitude of factors, such as language attitudes, power, and status (Sacks, Schegloff, & Jefferson, 1974).

The classroom may be considered a variety of speech community. One typical interactional pattern known and expected in the speech community of the classroom is the Initiation-Response-Evaluation (IRE) exchange (see Cazden, 1988; Mehan, 1979). In this pattern, the teacher initiates (I), the student responds to the initiation (R) and the teacher evaluates (E) the correctness of the student's response. The IRE pattern varies from normal conversational interaction, which is Initiation-Response (I-R) (Sacks, Schegloff, & Jefferson, 1974), not only because of the evaluation of the response but also because of the initiating question. Unlike a real question that initiates normal conversation, in classrooms the initiation is usually an academic question to which the teacher already has an answer and which is asked only to elicit a display of knowledge.

One result of the pervasiveness of the IRE interaction pattern in educational settings is that the teacher is almost always in control of the topic. Students have limited opportunities to ask questions or to add to the interaction in such a pattern. Therefore, bilingual students' opportunities for output are limited in such situations. Additionally, such interactions allow for little negotiation of meaning. As Wells (1981) notes, "These are the conditions that foster language development: when one has something important to say and other people are interested in hearing it" (p. 107). Unfortunately, this does not describe most classrooms in which the IRE pattern predominates. Cummins (1986) states that the IRE or "transmission" pedagogical model "contravenes central principles of language and literacy acquisition" (p. 28). In terms of second language learning, opportunities to use the target language in "meaningful contexts" (McLaughlin, 1985, p. 162) are also limited in IRE classrooms. Children (Britton, 1990; Dewey, 1916/1944; Moffett, 1981/1988) and adults (Fingeret, 1989; Knowles, 1973/1978; Soifer, Irwin, Crumrine, Honzaki, Simmons, & Young, 1990) alike, whether in L1 or L2 learning situations need to have their educational goals and interests central to the learning experience if it is to be meaningful for them.

When examining multicultural classroom interaction, gender as well as ethnicity is an important sociolinguistic variable to consider (Shuy, 1969). As West and Zimmerman (1991) note, gender is constituted through interaction and "doing gender is unavoidable" (p. 24). Like research on Mexican American bilinguals, a common finding of research on gender and classroom interaction is silence on the part of female students (Coates, 1986; Stanley, 1986). In some cases, it even appears that young women do not want to participate in class (Davies, 1983; Swann, 1988; Whyte, 1984). At the same time it has been found that male students receive significantly more attention from teachers than female students—whether the teacher is male or female (Eccles & Blumenfeld, 1985; Morse & Handley, 1985; Swann, 1988; Whyte, 1984). Few studies, however, have examined both ethnicity and gender in a comparative study of classroom interaction and none have looked at bilingual Mexican American interaction and gender. But as bell hooks (1989) correctly points out, "sex, race and class, and not sex alone, determine the nature of any female's identity, status and circumstance, the degree to which she will or will not be dominated, the extent to which she will have the power to dominate" (p. 22).

Both Cummins (1986) and Freire (1970) have noted that the IRE interactional model (the "banking" model, according to Freire) serves to "mirror oppressive society as a whole" (Freire, 1970, p. 59). Analyses of classroom interaction must also consider that "institutional machinery is embedded in social interaction" (Cicourel & Mehan, 1985, p. 20). Schooling cannot be considered in isolation from the society at large and the interests of those in power. Interaction in the classroom is indicative not only of the immediate social situation but also the larger societal situation. According to Giroux (1983), in the study of literacy and schooling "we must recognize how ideologies are constituted and inscribed in the discourse and social practices of daily classroom life" (p. 208).

This article will describe the interactional differences in classroom discourse across ethnicity and gender between bilingual Mexican American adults and monolingual Anglo American adults by exploring how variations occurred across these factors in the classroom talk of community college students and their teacher. Further, it will investigate how the interaction of Mexican American students varied when the context changed from whole class, teacher-fronted discussion to one-to-one tutorials to unofficial peer talk, and it will explore the implications of these findings in the larger societal context. This analysis will reveal the importance of gender as well as ethnicity in understanding interactional differences observed in the classroom, tutorials, and peer talk. Because the development of oral language skills requires student output as well as appropriate input, these findings are important for understanding how to create classroom environments that will help develop the oral language skills of bilingual adults.

THE STUDY

Site

The site for this study was a community college outreach program in the primarily agricultural community of Appleton, California.[1] 1990 census figures show that 61% of the the town's population was Hispanic, 33% of it was Anglo, 4% was Asian or Pacific Islander, and less than 1% was Black (Zabin, 1991). Held at the Appleton Center, the program was located in a relatively new downtown shopping center where several stores had been rented and set up as three classrooms, a reception area, and an administrative office.

English 10 was a mainstream, basic writing course required for completion of the Associate of Arts or AA degree and for promotion to English 15, university transfer level English. Students were in English 10 either because they had been placed in the class as a result of a holistically scored direct assessment of their writing or because they were former English 5 students who had been promoted into English 10. Students called English

---

[1]The names of the people, places, and publications have been changed as necessary to protect the anonymity of the participants.

10 "bonehead English," although the instructor of English 10 in Appleton insisted that the community college faculty did not consider it a remedial course.

Participants

Key informants in this study included students from four semesters of English classes held at the Appleton Center, their teacher, and the tutors at the Center. The students ranged in age from approximately 18 to 60 years old. Over 55% percent of students in each English 10 class studied were bilingual Mexican American, with a variety of levels of proficiency in English. A number of these students had recently completed the series of ESL courses offered by the community college and were still working on their English writing, reading, and speaking skills. For example, one student, a seasonal strawberry picker, announced that her primary goal for the class was to learn to speak English more fluently to get a job that was not in the fields. I observed these students during classes, worked with them in one-to-one tutorials during class (as directed by the teacher), and chatted with them before and after class and during breaks.

Five students were selected as focal students for this project. These were students who asked for help from me outside of class, as well as in class, and who volunteered to be a part of my study. I worked extensively with these students on their writing, tutoring them both in and out of class. The focal students included two males and three females who ranged in age at the time of data collection from 18 to 37 years. All were bilingual Mexican Americans who had been schooled from at least the 6th grade in the U.S. All had varying degrees of proficiency in English, however, because of their individual life circumstances (e.g., educational experiences, work experiences, general exposure to English and Spanish). (See Table 6.1.)

The teacher in the class, an Anglo American woman who had taught 17 years at the community college, was also a key informant. A tenured faculty member, Carol had served in a variety of administrative posts including chair of the English department and chair of Women's Studies. She made efforts to stay abreast of current research, theory, and practice in composition by taking sabbaticals to teach in a nationally acclaimed writing program and to take graduate courses in language and literacy education.

Data Collection and Analysis

Data collection methods included, first and foremost, participant observation during 2 years as a tutor at the site. I also conducted informal interviews with key informants (the focal students, the teacher, the tutors, and other school personnel), collected audiotapes of classroom and tutorial interaction, and gathered relevant archival data related to the current and

TABLE 6.1
Focal Student Attributes

Student	*Age*	*Employment*	*Educational Background*
Amado	27	industrial laundry worker volunteer youth minister	1st grade in Mexico 3rd grade-diploma in U.S. attended bilingual classes
Federico	30	sewage treatment plant employee waiter	1st grade in Mexico 2nd grade-diploma in U.S.
Isaura	37	seasonal strawberry picker	1st–6th grade in Mexico 7th–8th grade in U.S. passed high school equivalency in Spanish
Juanita	22	bilingual classroom aide	K-diploma in U.S.
Mónica	18	drug store clerk	K-diploma in U.S.

historical social and political situation of the outreach program, the school, and the community of Appleton. The data discussed in this paper are from the last semester I observed English 10 and were analyzed to discover the sociolinguistic and interactional environment of the classroom. This analysis was completed for three different types of interaction that regularly occurred in the classroom: official whole class discussions, official one-to-one interaction with a tutor, and unofficial interaction among peers during tutoring sessions. Transcriptions were made as accurate as possible at the lexical level.

For the analysis of whole class discussions, transcriptions from three "typical" class meetings from the beginning to the end of the semester were analyzed. After 2 years of experience observing the class, it became easy to identify a typical lesson or tutorial. The subject of such a lesson was either students' assigned reading, workbook exercises, or a composition assignment. The lesson did not involve a guest speaker nor was it interrupted by unforeseen circumstances. In terms of structure and content, these typical lessons and tutorials began to appear quite similar over time—they had patterned opening, middle, and closing sections.

One-to-one tutorials occurred both in and out of class. This analysis is based on 18 tutorials ranging from 1–2 hours each held outside class. One-to-one tutorials outside of class usually began with a specific question from a student or with a general request for comments on a draft. The unofficial peer talk analyzed was also typical in that it could be about either class-related topics or personal topics. It usually began with a comment by one student that was picked up and developed by one or more peers.

The transcripts were analyzed to discover the "participant structures" or "structural arrangements of interaction" during classroom lessons

(Philips, 1972/1985, p. 377). The basic unit of analysis for this work was the "speech event . . . activities, or aspects of activities, that are directly governed by rules or norms for the use of speech" (Hymes, 1974, p. 52). The participant structures were then analyzed quantitatively to determine differences in frequency of turns and turn types (e.g., initiation, response) for different ethnic and gender-based groupings in the various interactional contexts of this study. Participant structures were also analyzed qualitatively to identify and describe the types of interaction strategies used in varying contexts. (For more details regarding turns and turn types, see Losey, in press.)

In addition, the whole class discussions were analyzed thematically, to gain insights into the topics of concern to the teacher and the students, using the episode, a series of turns on the same theme or topic, as the unit of analysis. Themes were found to recur in the talk of the teacher and students that served to elucidate how the teacher and the students understood and responded to particular interactive situations in the classroom. I call these explanatory themes *key themes* as they became key in understanding the interaction in the classroom. For all participants, these themes were inextricably tied to their personal histories and past educational experiences as well as to the larger sociocultural milieu in which the outreach program existed.

The next section describes the results of these analyses which revealed important differences between the interaction of bilingual students and monolingual students as well as gendered differences in the interaction of bilingual Mexican Americans.

STRUCTURE OF INTERACTION

Whole Class Discussions

Carol's class was characterized by the pervasive use of the IRE exchange. In an analysis of 310 exchanges from three typical whole class discussions, 79% of the exchanges were teacher initiated, and 57% were based on the IRE format. Only 21% of the exchanges were initiated by students. Control of classroom talk by the teacher during these whole class discussions served to limit the amount of output that any student in the class could produce. It also limited the topics to those favored by the teacher, usually known information or academic questions rather than the real questions one might find in ordinary interaction.

Another characteristic of this classroom found in other classrooms as well was the minilecture (Hull, Rose, Fraser, & Castellano, 1991). Usually added onto evaluations of student responses after a series of IRE episodes on a single topic, the minilecture was used to tie the questions and answers that immediately preceded it to the larger point of the lesson. It also served structurally to interrupt the flow of interaction and revert attention to the teacher and her topic.

The rules of participation during the whole class discussions in Carol's class generally required that the teacher provide an evaluation of student responses, but this evaluation did not necessarily come after each student spoke; it was often postponed for a few turns. In addition, the teacher rarely called on students (unless they raised their hands), but raising one's hand and waiting to be called upon was unusual in this class. Instead students just spoke out, often at the same time, in response to a teacher initiation. These factors combined to create very fast-paced classroom talk. At least two students independently characterized the fast-paced interaction in the class as "rolling." The rolling character of the discourse led to frequent interruptions in the classroom, and because the teacher did not usually call on students, there was little support from the teacher for students to take or keep the floor. The interactional structures and the restrictions on content I have described are important for understanding the interactional patterns described in the next section.

The Silence of Mexican American Women

An examination of the interaction patterns during whole class discussions in English 10 found that they varied according to ethnicity and gender. Anglo American students participated in class discussions in much greater percentages than their numbers in the class would suggest. Although 55% of Carol's class was Mexican American and 45% was Anglo American during the semester described here, 81% of student initiations were made by Anglo American students. Only 19% of initiations were made by Mexican American students. This general trend held in all classes I observed. Of the student responses to the teacher, 82% were made by Anglo American students and 18% were made by Mexican American students (see Table 6.2). Put another way, the Mexican American students initiated and responded to the teacher at approximately one third the rate expected given their representation in the classroom, if gender and ethnicity had no effect on interaction. An analysis of gender differences within and across groups shows that the relative silence of Mexican Americans in whole class discussions was largely the result of silence on the part of the Mexican American women.

The Mexican American women represented a majority in the class (47% of all students), yet they contributed only 12.5% of the initiations and 8% of the responses. Expressed in interaction ratios, the Mexican American women contributed only one fourth of the expected initiations and one fifth of the expected responses (see initiation and response ratios Table 6.2). The Mexican American men (comprising only 8% of the class) initi-

TABLE 6.2
Whole Class Interaction By Ethnicity and Gender

	Mexican American Total	*Anglo American Total*	*Mexican American*		*Anglo American*	
			Women	*Men*	*Women*	*Men*
Representation of Students in class (%)	55	45	47	8	32	13
Student Initiations (%)	19	81	12.5	6.5	53	28
Student Responses (%)	18	82	8	10	52	30
Student Initiation Ratio	0.35	1.80	0.26	0.83	1.65	2.15
Student Response Ratio	0.33	1.80	0.20	1.30	1.63	2.30

Note. Student Initiation Ratio = the ratio of student initiations in comparison to representation. Student Response Ratio = the ratio of student responses in comparison to representation.

ated interactions at a rate much closer to that expected and contributed more responses than expected. So whereas the Mexican Americans as a group appeared to speak relatively little in whole class discussions, an analysis by ethnicity alone would mask the effect of gender on the interaction in the classroom.

Anglo American women also spoke relatively less than Anglo American men, but between the Anglo American men and the Anglo American women, the differences were not as great as between the Mexican Americans. The Anglo American men interacted only about 1.3 times more than the Anglo American women in comparison to Mexican American men who initiated three times more interactions and responded six times more often than Mexican American women. Males, overall, regardless of ethnic background, interacted at rates higher than expected for their representation in the classroom. These figures indicate both ethnic differences and gender differences. The ethnic differences suggest an ethnic disadvantage for Mexican Americans in the Anglo American dominant culture and classroom, whereas the gender differences reveal the prevalence of traditional gender roles in both ethnic groups but with greater effects for Mexican Americans suggesting a stronger patriarchal hierarchy among Mexican Americans than among Anglo Americans. Also, these data show that gender and ethnicity have a cumulative effect, creating a hierarchy of interaction frequency with Mexican American women at the bottom and Anglo American men at the top.

Although these numbers provide some insight into the interaction of the bilingual Mexican Americans in the classroom observed, clearly revealing the silence of the Mexican American women, the upcoming qualitative analysis of the talk reveals the characteristics of talk and silence in the classroom that help explain the interactional differences observed.

The next section will present patterns of interaction that helped create and break the differential output found for bilingual Mexican American women.

The Voices of Mexican American Focal Women

Like other Mexican American women in their class, the classroom discourse of the Mexican American focal women in whole class discussions was also characterized by pervasive silence. Each of the focal women volunteered to speak only twice the entire semester, whereas the men took as many as 24 turns in a single class session. Unfortunately, it is impossible to effectively present examples of silence. Instead this section will present examples of typical interactional strategies the women used in an attempt to break the silence, thereby revealing how the structure and content of interaction may have contributed to their silence. The strategies that these women used to interact in this context suggest how classroom contexts might be changed to allow for more student interaction which will help develop the verbal skills of bilingual students in the class.

Finding an Opening: Minilectures and Elicitations. The combination of classroom interaction tightly controlled by the teacher and fast-paced interaction between the students and the teacher—the rolling effect described earlier in this article—played an important part in the silence of the Mexican American focal women. In order to find an opening during these rolling exchanges, the women waited until interaction slowed. On each occasion when the focal women spoke, the teacher had just completed a minilecture. This served to slow the pace of interaction between the students and the teacher, thereby allowing the women to find an opening for interaction. The following example is the first of two whole class discussions in which one student, Isaura, volunteered to speak during the semester. The interaction followed a rather lengthy minilecture in which the teacher discussed the importance of students using concrete language in their essays. I will provide only the end of the mini-lecture here as it is too long to include in its entirety.[2]

---

[2] Transcription conventions used in this study are as follows:

<table>
<tr><td>( )</td><td>Unintelligible on tape</td></tr>
<tr><td>(laughs)</td><td>Nonverbal cues and actions</td></tr>
<tr><td>[ ]</td><td>Contains information added by researcher to help the reader interpret the manuscript</td></tr>
<tr><td>Student: But-
Teacher: Yes</td><td>Overlapping speech</td></tr>
<tr><td>|Amy
|Stevie</td><td>Amy and Stevie talk simultaneously</td></tr>
<tr><td>. . .</td><td>Pause in the discourse</td></tr>
</table>

1. Teacher: We need details. It's just like at the bottom of [Lesson] 32 when they give you the sentences and ask you to elaborate. All right. Let's take a break. How 'bout, ah, any other questions? Did I miss anyone?
   Isaura: How 'bout labor?
   Teacher: Pardon?
   Isaura: Labor.
   Teacher: L-a-b-e-l? What do you think?
   |John: No.
   |Amy: No, Labor, O-R.
   Teacher: Labor. L-a-b-o-r. What do you think?

In this exchange Isaura chose to talk only after the teacher had given a rather lengthy minilecture and specifically asked for student input. The same strategy can be found in her only other attempt to speak in whole class discussions during the semester.

This slowing of the interaction during the minilecture appears to have provided Isaura, a relatively unpracticed speaker of English, the time she needed to produce her responses. She once explained to me in a tutorial that she tended to "think in Spanish," which caused a time lag because she had to "translate in[to] English . . . all that grammar."

The minilecture also usually led to a direct request by the teacher for students questions, such as "How 'bout, ah, any other questions" in this example, which provided a particularly inviting moment for students to speak up.

Interruptions: Keeping the Floor. Another characteristic of the exchanges in the class was frequent interruption. All of the bilingual Mexican American focal women experienced interruptions as a result of the interactional structure of this classroom. In the example above, Isaura was interrupted when other students attempted to clarify what she had said ("Labor"). Unlike Isaura, both Mónica and Juanita, who were also interrupted when they spoke in class, maintained their turns by interrupting their interrupters in return. In the following example, Mónica repeatedly used this interactional strategy, speaking up throughout the teacher's attempts to answer her.

2. Teacher: Mónica?
   Mónica: Do we give our own personal opinion after-
   Teacher: (emphatically) Yes-
   Mónica: each-
   Teacher: That's why-
   Mónica: After-

Teacher: That's why what I was saying before-
Mónica: But after each one?

Although it took her four turns to complete her question, Mónica persevered, interrupting the teacher as the teacher had interrupted her. Despite her persistence, Mónica did not get the information that she sought in this interaction. A few moments later she leaned over to me and asked, "So are we suppose' to give our personal view in the middle or after all three summaries?" Ultimately, even though she tried to ask her question, the pattern of interaction left her silenced in this situation.

Social Support. Mónica, Juanita, and Isaura all chose to speak when there were clear sources of support for their interaction in the classroom, that is, when someone encouraged them to interact. Both times Mónica interacted in whole class discussions, she received direct encouragement from her tutor—me. This apparent need of encouragement was not surprising considering her understanding of how others responded to her.

3. Mónica: You know, sometimes I feel like speaking out. Because, you know, I know things that I can say, but then I'm all like, nahh, they don't want to hear it (laughs).
Tutor: I think they do. . . .
Mónica: 'Cause you know, that was one of my fears, speaking out in classes. I've always been bad, until I know the whole class, then I feel free, a little. You know, I don't say anything. That was my fear always in high school. Then when I took the introduction into business and the supervision [in college], that was my fear too.

Mónica knew that she should have talked in class more, but felt that the class was not interested in her ideas. Furthermore, she felt that she did not know the class well enough. The fact that she was interrupted when she tried to talk would certainly serve to reinforce her belief that people were not listening to her or interested in her. In this classroom it was not only the structure of the lessons that contributed to the silence but also the lack of confidence of the women, either in their ideas, as in the case of Mónica, or in their language abilities, as in the case of Isaura, who at the end of the course described herself as "the worst of everybody" in the class.

These three women employed interactional strategies such as speaking after minilectures and elicitations to attempt to overcome the particular structure of this classroom and to attempt to give output. The focal men, however, used interactional strategies in whole class discussions that were quite different from those used by the women.

The Voices of Mexican American Focal Men

Unlike the Mexican American focal women, the interaction of the Mexican American men in whole class discussions was characterized by more talk than would be expected considering their scarcity in numbers in the class. Although they faced the same limited interaction structure as a result of the IRE format, they employed differing strategies for interacting within that structure. The men initiated unsolicited questions and comments, sometimes even disagreeing with statements made by the teacher. They effectively broke the normal pattern of teacher-student interaction in this classroom through the use of these strategies. The Mexican American focal men employed these strategies in a much greater ratio to their numbers in class than their Anglo American counterparts of either gender.

Requests: Creating an Opening. Amado and Federico asked questions in whole class discussions to request information about a particular essay assignment or more general course information. A typical question from Amado asked Carol about the content of an upcoming essay, "But what if you just focus on their [the author's] goal? One similarity?" Or a more general question of this nature asked, "What's our final exam gonna be like?"

Questions were also used to clarify points in class discussion. For example when Carol was discussing abstract and concrete words, Federico asked for a clarification:

4. Federico: You say it's subjective?
   Teacher: Yeah, it's very subjective.
   Federico: It's not objective?
   Teacher: Yeah, it's not objective. . . .

Requests such as these were rare among the Mexican American focal women.

Comments: Making Oneself Heard. Federico and Amado also initiated by making unsolicited comments during whole class discussions. These comments were generally a recognition of problems in their writing or about writing in general. For example, when Carol was discussing the proper development of the "interview" essay, she made the point that one should not put too much detail into the essay:

5. Teacher: The motto for this paper should be "Don't write a book."
   Amado: I have a tendency to do the opposite: I generalize.

Teacher: The second motto for this paper is "The reader does not know my grandmother [the subject of many interview papers]."

In responding to the comment, Carol did not interrupt the student. On the contrary, she developed his comment by making the point that students like Amado have to give enough details (as opposed to generalizing) so that the reader will get to "know" the subjects of their papers.

Challenges: Making Points. Federico and Amado asked questions and made comments that sometimes seemed to disagree with the teacher's stated opinion. In the following transcript, Federico openly disagreed with the teacher's description of one aspect of the writing process:

6. Teacher: You know how if you've ever kept a journal or a diary and you want to remember something that happened to you, you just jot down phrases really quickly, and as soon as you read those phrases, the whole memory of the experience can come back to you . . . everything comes back to you, all the details come back to you. . . .
   Federico: But they don't suddenly come rushing in.
   Teacher: I see.
   Federico: I'm not flooded with them.
   Teacher: Yeah, everyone is different in that way, how their memories work. . . .

Although there were no obvious signs of social support for the Mexican American focal men as there were with the women, the teacher did not appear to respond negatively to Federico or Amado's interaction strategies; rather, their interaction contributed to a positive evaluation of the men, as evidenced by the teacher's comments in interviews about their classroom interaction and her decision to recommend all of the Mexican American focal men for the next level of English.

Mexican American Focal Women: One-to-One Tutorial Interaction

In tutorials, the Mexican American focal women used the same strategies that the Mexican American focal men were seen to use in whole class interaction—requests, comments and challenges—taking control of the interaction as they did not in whole class discussion. The Mexican American focal women initiated frequently in tutorials, asking for advice on writing assignments, for clarification of concepts, and for information about the course. Requests for advice on writing assignments took two forms: general requests for help and specific questions. The Mexican American focal women also made frequent comments about themselves generally and as writers during one-to-one tutorials. The women disagreed with me frequently as we discussed how their essays might be improved, with such comments as "Well, didn't I write before how I felt?"

These patterns were identical to those found for the Mexican American focal men in whole class discussion. Unfortunately there is not space to provide examples of the interaction of the Mexican American focal men in tutorial or in peer interaction. However, in these contexts, their interaction fell into the same patterns that have been described for their interaction in whole class discussions.

The women asked so many questions in one-to-one interaction that it seemed they were making up for their lack of questioning in whole class discussions. Numerous questions pertained specifically to the content covered in the previous whole class discussion. At last, the women got their questions answered and in the process produced much output, in part because there were changes in the interactional context—changes in the number of interlocutors, their relationships between the interlocutors, and other aspects of the situation that affected the interaction pattern. The Mexican American focal women also learned about the content of the course through unofficial peer interaction.

Mexican American Focal Women: Unofficial Peer Interaction

Although the teacher forbade it, some students chatted during tutorial time while they waited for a tutor to reach them. This unofficial talk allowed the Mexican American focal women to gather information about the class content that they did not get from whole class interaction and provided an opportunity for them to discuss strategies for success in the course. In many ways the women taught each other; and as they explained what they understood to each other, they had opportunities to demonstrate and practice their oral English skills as well as their skills in the subject matter.

The following discussion, held informally during one-to-one tutorial time, shows the kind of talk and the kind of learning that occurred with neither a teacher nor tutor actively involved. Although I was present during the interaction, I was primarily an auditor rather than an active participant in this interaction.

7. Mónica: You know, you know what I didn't do on mine? I didn't describe.
   Marisa: That's what I forgot, too.
   Tutor: Oooh.

Marisa: But I was going to turn it in like that and when she returns it to us, I'm going to re-submit it.
Mónica: So then, there's no way-
Juanita: Re-submit, re-submit. (Juanita laughs)
Tutor: That sounds very professional, doesn't it? Yes, I'm listening.
Marisa: Well, I'm going to turn it in again. (laughs)
Mónica: Mine, like there's no way, you know, like I can put it in here, like maybe like, um,
Juanita: Well, mine has a part-
Marisa: At the beginning?
Juanita: At the beginning.
Marisa: Or at the end?
Juanita: ( ) at the beginning because it would be more
Marisa: Appropriate.

During these unofficial exchanges, the women were able to identify problems and solve them together, without any help from experts. In addition, they took part in a full range of interactional moves, asking questions, answering them, interrupting each other, even teasing. Moreover they displayed an expertise in the area of writing that was rarely revealed in either of the other interactional contexts. It was in this context, with other bilingual women, that the women produced the greatest amount and variety of output and learned much of the content of the course. Bilingual Mexican American men and monolingual Anglo Americans of both sexes rarely took part in such unofficial talk. They interacted with the teacher or the tutors or they worked silently at their seats, as they were supposed to during these times.

CONTENT OF INTERACTIONS

"Real" Versus "Academic": Finding a Purpose

Both the Mexican American focal men and women interacted with the content of classroom talk similarly. The patterns that I will report were the necessary conditions for interaction among the focal women—they would not talk without them—whereas the men, although they, too, preferred these conditions, would talk under other circumstances. Because these patterns were necessary conditions for the women, I will use examples from the women only to illustrate this section.

The teacher rarely asked students to discuss topics of personal interest in whole class discussions; instead her questions were academic in that they asked students for a display of knowledge about the text or a writing assignment. But both the Mexican American men and the Mexican American women preferred to talk about topics that were real rather than academic. A real topic, like a real question, was one that both the interlocutors had a genuine interest in. It was often of a personal nature rather than one for display of knowledge. Focal students, male and female, asked real questions for which they did not have answers, questions about how to complete an assignment, what was on the final exam, what a concept meant. These questions were qualitatively different than the type of known information questions initiated by the teacher.

Likewise, the questions that the Mexican American women responded to were in all cases real questions as opposed to academic, or known information questions. When Isaura asked about the word *labor*, the teacher had asked if students had any more questions. Similarly, Juanita's initial response came after a real question about whether anyone had felt discrimination in their educational careers, a question to which the teacher could not know the answer. Students were most likely to become involved in an interaction when real topics coincided with their key themes, often trying to relate other topics to their key themes through their talk.

Key Themes: Making Meaning

As noted above, key themes were students' personal interests or concerns that were revealed in an analysis of their talk in and out of the classroom. Those rare occasions when the topics under discussion were related to students' key themes were the times the focal women chose to speak. As mentioned above, Carol asked a highly unusual question eliciting Juanita's first voluntary comment in class after 3 months of silence. She asked if any of the students had ever felt discriminated against. Juanita responded to a question that allowed her to talk about a theme of importance to her: the education of Spanish-speaking students. Later in the class, the same discussion turned to the use of English and Spanish in the education of local youth, a topic clearly related to Juanita's interests and again she spoke up. The topic under discussion during this lesson was central to her personal interests and to her decision to pursue a bilingual teaching credential. In these ways content as well as structure influenced the classroom talk of Mexican American focal students. Other focal students' key themes were: the maintenance of traditional Mexican American values, the economic and educational oppression of Mexican Americans, the use of religion to save Mexican American youth, and the social and political situation of Mexican Americans in the community.

Important to note, however, was the ability of these students—male and female—to write on academic as well as real topics. Most writing assignments in the course were academic and focused on texts unrelated to students' key themes. Nevertheless, students wrote on these topics with reasonable success. (All focal students received a grade of C or above in the class.) But these topics did not elicit much interest in class discussions nor did they evoke the kind of interaction necessary to develop verbal skills. Mexican American women only spoke in class when the topics were real and related to their key themes.

DISCUSSION AND IMPLICATIONS

The most important finding of this study is not the silence of bilingual Mexican American adults in basic writing classes. That was predictable considering the findings of previous research on Mexican Americans in the classroom (Ortiz, 1988; Parsons, 1965; U.S. Commission on Civil Rights, 1973). By taking the analysis further to include gender, however, this study revealed that in the classroom under study only Mexican American women were silent—they responded to the teacher one fifth as often as expected—whereas the Mexican American men responded one third more often than expected, given their numbers in the classroom. With respect to the development of oral skills in the classroom, this finding suggests that the structure and content of classroom interaction during traditional whole class interactions differentially limited the output of bilingual Mexican American women.

Swain (1985) has noted that "comprehensible output is, unfortunately, generally missing in typical classroom settings" (p. 252). This conclusion holds for the class I studied, but only for a portion of the bilingual students—the women—and only in one interactional context—the traditional whole class discussion. This study found that in one-to-one tutorials and unofficial peer talk, the women took part in interaction using the same strategies as the bilingual Mexican American men and, to a lesser extent, the monolingual Anglo Americans, in whole class discussions.

The degree to which the interaction observed may be related to the mix of monolingual and bilingual students is worthy of consideration. It seems reasonable that the focal women in this study may have felt more self-conscious in this mixed situation that in a wholly bilingual class. This explanation does not help us understand, however, the focal men's willingness to speak up in this situation.

The women's preference for social support in whole class discussions, for interaction in unofficial peer groups and in one-to-one interaction coincides well with the findings of classroom research that suggested Mexican Americans may prefer cooperative, collaborative classroom structures over the more competitive structure of whole class discussions (Díaz, Moll, & Mehan, 1986; Trueba, 1987). But the Mexican American men did not seem to need this type of interaction to support their talk. In addition, the preference of both male and female students for topics that were related to their own interests rather than academic topics was also an important finding. This finding also is corroborated by previous research on younger bilingual Mexican American students (Díaz, Moll, & Mehan, 1986; Moll, 1988; Trueba, 1987). But again topics of personal interest related to students' key themes were a necessary requirement for interaction from the women only, not the men.

The findings of this study call into question many of the generalizations made about Mexican American interaction in the past. Previous research suggests that Mexican Americans—male and female—prefer an interaction-style of the type observed only in Mexican American women in this study. Analyzing for gender makes an important contribution to understanding how Mexican American interaction occurs.

The silence of women found in this study is well-supported by previous research on gender in the classroom which has found silence a common characteristic of classroom interaction among young women (Davies, 1983; Stanley, 1986). But unlike the studies of Whyte (1984) and Swann (1988) which indicated that young women did not seem to want to talk in class, this study revealed that the Mexican American focal women wanted to interact in whole class, teacher-fronted discussions, but aspects of the interaction such as interruptions and the fast pace of the talk limited their interaction as did self-perceptions, as suggested by Mónica's comment that she had nothing of interest to say and Isaura's concern that she was the worst speaker of English in the class. Furthermore, the teacher's choice of topic—whether it was real or academic and its relationship to the women's key themes—also had an impact on their silence.

According to Fine (1991), "in the odd study of what's not said in school, it is crucial to investigate 1) whom silencing protects; 2) the practices by which silencing is institutionalized; and 3) how the muting of students and their communities undermines a project of educational empowerment" (p. 32). Freire (1970) and Giroux (1983) find the type of interaction described in this classroom—its IRE structure and its content—indicative of a pedagogy that protects those in power by keeping all classroom power in the hands of the teacher and by preventing critical or dialogical interaction. The teacher, representing the interests of power in society, selects material and teaches in a way that maintains the status quo. Therefore, the pedagogical approach reproduces race, class, and gender-based oppression. Giroux would find the silence of women in this classroom a form of resistance against an attempt to oppress them educationally. Viewed as an unwillingness to participate, their silence would indicate a refusal to comply with the structure and content of the teacher's lesson which requires student response in the IRE exchange. And he would find the women's attempts to speak indicative of their desire to have a dialogical interaction based upon their educational goals and interests.

Low self-esteem or negative self-perceptions also played a role in the silence of these women. Shor (1980/1987) explains that silence can be "defensive" in the classroom, in that even monolingual students "know that they will betray their inferior class-background by simply speaking" and wonder "Why should they open themselves to judgment in front of a college-educated, articulate teacher?" (p. 74). They perceive an "alienation of their language from power" (p. 74). Language minority students, such as those in this study, experience even more directly the lack of status, given their native language is not the medium of instruction, is not the dominant language of the society, and is not provided with status in the curriculum choices made by the teacher (Cummins, 1986; Skutnabb-Kangas, 1981).

Although theories of minority oppression and lack of status certainly help explain why Mexican Americans would be more silent than Anglo American students in this classroom, they do not adequately explain why Mexican American women were more silent than expected or why the men spoke up so much more than expected. To what extent might being a double minority—Mexican American and female—explain the silence observed?

For many Chicano social scientists, a cultural explanation for the silence of these women is obvious: They were oppressed not only in Anglo American society at large, as women and as Mexican Americans, but also within the immediate contexts of their homes and culture (Nieto-Gómez, 1973; Mirandé & Enríquez, 1979; Valdés-Fallis, 1974). Although many social scientists are rightly arguing against old notions of the Chicano culture as dysfunctional, they nearly all agree that women have low status in the culture and men are generally seen as superior (Blea, 1992; Mirandé & Enríquez, 1979).

In the classroom, cultural expectations can lead to a self-imposed silence on the part of Mexican American women. Nieto-Gómez (1973) calls the "quiet Chicana" one response to the conflict between the Chicana's "traditional role in relation to men" and the role of the "independently minded student" expected in the classroom (p. 49). According to Nieto-Gómez, the "traditional role" requires a show of loyalty in public that "represses any open disagreement that she may feel in order not to disrupt the public image of the male authority be it her father, her brother, her boyfriend, or her husband," whereas the "independently minded student" requires "independent motivation," which Nieto-Gómez considers opposed to the traditional role. The "quiet Chicana" may feel unqualified to speak or simply realize that class participation will be defined as "aggressive" and "undesirable" (p. 50). Mirandé and Enríquez (1979) hypothesize that Chicanas "are probably even more adversely affected than Chicanos by the differential treatment of Chicano and Anglo students" (p. 137). Moreover, they conclude that "given the cultural norm that women should be seen and not heard, one would expect Chicanas to be very inhibited in their classroom participation, especially if the contributions which they make are neither acknowledged nor praised" (p. 137).

Couple being a double minority with a feeling of insecurity and low status as a result of language and an oppressive educational environment, and it is a wonder that students like Isaura attempted to speak at all in class, given the interactional context. However, she did try to speak. She wanted her voice to be heard. In the classroom described in this article, one can see a multitude of outside factors also at work in creating the silence of Mexican American women: societal oppression of Mexican Americans and women, oppression of women within the Mexican American culture, and language status. Considering social factors outside as well as within the classroom helps explain why Mexican American classroom interaction occurs as it does and the differential responses of the Mexican American men and women. It also reveals how a variety of factors can meet in the classroom to prevent interaction appropriate for the development of second language proficiency in adult students.

Although the generalizability of most qualitative studies is limited to those situations with similar circumstances, this study provides data consistent with other findings, suggesting that it reflects the reality of many classrooms. Therefore practical implications for the teaching of monolingual and bilingual students can be derived from it. If the goal is to increase the amount of output bilingual Mexican American women produce, we need to either reduce the number of whole-class teacher-fronted activities that occur, vary their structure, or change their topics.

When teachers select the content for a class without consulting their students or even considering their interests and backgrounds, they create a situation in which students feel alienated from the class and are less likely to participate. This study suggests that teachers should attempt to cover the required material in a way that is flexible enough to allow for student interests and key themes to be discussed and developed. In a writing class, students can be given a choice of topics or asked to move from a personal approach to a topic to a more academic approach in order to meet teachers' goals without completely eliminating student interest.

If whole class discussions are to occur, the findings suggest the need to slow down the interaction more frequently, the way the minilecture effectively slowed interaction in the class studied. We need to allow bilingual students time to formulate questions and responses in their second language. Increasing the wait time between when initiations are made and either repeated, answered by the teacher, or made to another student are all helpful practices. An increase in minilectures would not be the preferred way to slow interaction, however, because this would undermine the goal of increasing students' talk in the classroom with more teacher talk. There also must be an increase in social support for interaction. In addition to positive, individual praise and encouragement, teachers need to help ward off students who would interrupt bilingual students and refrain from interrupting bilingual students themselves.

This study also suggests that allowing for alternative forms of classroom organization will lead to differing structures in classroom interaction and increased participation and output. Although the Mexican American focal men did not take part in much peer talk, no findings suggest that they would not do well in such an environment and previous research on classrooms with such arrangements suggests that both male and female bilingual Mexican Americans interact well in such classrooms. Cummins (1986) recommends using "reciprocal interaction," which "requires a genuine dialogue between students and teacher in both oral and written modalities, guidance and facilitation rather than control of students' learning by the teacher, and the encouragement of student/student talk in a collaborative learning context" to enhance minority student learning (p. 28).

One-to-one tutorials were particularly successful in eliciting response in the classroom studied. Although these tutorials were with more advanced bilingual students at the community college, it seems peer tutors would also be effective, particularly in a mixed monolingual/bilingual classroom where monolingual students were paired with bilingual ones. Having monolingual tutors come into a bilingual class as part of their coursework could also be successful. As Wong Fillmore and Valadez (1986) have noted, "The ideal situation is one in which there is . . . balance between language learners and classmates who know the target language well enough to help in its learning, and there are many reasons for them to talk with one another" (p. 688).

This study also suggests allowing for small group interaction between bilingual peers. With more advanced speakers, like the ones in this study, the content need not be tightly controlled to ensure all students will become involved in the conversation. With less advanced speakers of the TL, teachers may need to require an information exchange as part of a structured activity to guarantee that students are required to provide output during their time in small groups (Pica & Dougherty, 1988).

These suggestions are important for all types of classrooms whether one is using an experiential approach or a more analytical approach. Stern (1990) makes the point that while social interaction is correctly considered a necessity for experiential classrooms "the analytic could also benefit from a flexible social organization" (p. 105). In this way, teachers can create a social environment in the classroom that supports second language acquisition by allowing all student voices to be heard, even if those voices are rarely listened to outside the classroom.

REFERENCES

Blea, I. (1992). *La Chicana and the intersection of race, class and gender.* Westport, CT: Praeger.

Britton, J. (1990). Talking to learn. In D. Barnes, J. Britton, & M. Torbe (Eds.), *Language, the learner, and the school* (pp. 91–130). Portsmouth, NH: Boynton/Cook.

Cazden, C. (1988). *Classroom discourse: The language of teaching and learning.* Portsmouth, NH: Heinemann.

Cicourel, A., & Mehan, H. (1985). Universal development, stratifying practices, and status attainment. In D. J. Treiman & R. V. Robinson (Eds.), *Research in social stratification and mobility, Vol. 4* (pp. 3–27). Greenwich, CT: JAI Press.

Coates, J. (1986). *Women, men, and language: A sociolinguistic account of sex differences in language.* London: Longman.

Cummins, J. (1986). Empowering minority students: A framework for intervention. *Harvard Educational Review, 56,* 18–36.

Davies, L. (1983). Gender, resistance, and power. In S. Walker & L. Barton (Eds.), *Gender, class, and education* (pp. 39–52). London: Falmer Press.

Delgado-Gaitan, C. (1987). Traditions and transitions in the learning process of Mexican children: An ethnographic view. In G. Spindler & E. Spindler (Eds.), *Interpretive ethnography of education at home and abroad* (pp. 333–359). Hillsdale, NJ: Lawrence Erlbaum.

Dewey, J. (1916/1944). *Democracy and education.* New York: The Free Press/Macmillan.

Díaz, S., Moll, L. C., & Mehan, H. (1986). Sociocultural resources in instruction: A context specific approach. In *Beyond language: Social and cultural factors in schooling language minority students* (pp. 187–230). Los Angeles, CA: Evaluation, Dissemination and Assessment Center, California State University, Los Angeles.

Eccles, J. S., & Blumenfeld, P. (1985). Classroom experiences and student gender: Are there differences and do they matter? In L. C. Wilkinson & C. B. Marrett (Eds.), *Gender influences in classroom interaction* (pp. 79–114). Orlando, FL: Academic Press.

Elsasser, N., & John-Steiner, V. P. (1977). An interactionist approach to advancing literacy. *Harvard Educational Review, 47,* 355–369.

Fine, M. (1991). *Framing dropouts: Notes on the politics of an urban high school.* Albany, NY: State University of New York Press.

Fingeret, A. (1989). The social and historical context of participatory literacy education. In A. Fingeret & R. Jurmo (Eds.), *Participatory literacy education* (pp. 5–15). San Francisco, CA: Jossey-Bass.

Freire, P. (1970). *Pedagogy of the oppressed.* New York: The Seabury Press.

Giroux, H. (1983). *Theory and resistance in education: A pedagogy for the opposition.* South Hadley, MA: Bergin & Garvey.

Gumbiner, J., Knight, G. P., & Kagan, S. (1981). Relations of classroom structures and teacher behaviors to social orientation, self-esteem, and classroom climate among Anglo American and Mexican American children. *Hispanic Journal of the Behavioral Sciences, 3*, 19–40.

hooks, b. (1989). *Talking back: Thinking feminist, thinking black.* Boston, MA: South End Press.

Hull, G., Rose, M., Fraser, K. L., & Castellano, M. (1991). Remediation as social construct: Perspectives from an analysis of classroom discourse. *College Composition and Communication, 42*, 299–329.

Hymes, D. H. (1972). Models of the interaction of language and social life. In J. J. Gumperz & D.H. Hymes (Eds.), *Directions in sociolinguistics* (pp. 35–71). New York: Holt, Rinehart & Winston.

Hymes, D. H. (1974). *Foundations in sociolinguistics: an ethnographic approach.* Philadelphia, PA: University of Pennsylvania Press.

Knowles, M. (1973/1978). *The adult learner: A neglected species.* (2nd ed.). Houston, TX: Gulf.

Krashen, S. D. (1976). Formal and informal linguistic environments in language acquisition and language learning. *TESOL Quarterly, 10*, 157–168.

Krashen, S. D. (1985). *The input hypothesis: Issues and implications.* London: Longman.

Laosa, L. M. (1977). Inequality in the classroom: Observational research on teacher-student interactions. *Aztlán: The International Journal of Chicano Studies Research, 8*, 51–67.

Lave, J. (1988, May). *The culture of acquisition and the pratice of understanding.* (IRL Report No. 88-0007). Palo Alto, CA: Institute for Research on Learning.

LeCompte, M. D. (1981). The Procrustean bed: Public schools, management systems, and minority students. In H. T. Trueba, G. P. Guthrie, & K. H. Au (Eds.), *Culture and the bilingual classroom* (pp. 178–195). Rowley, MA: Newbury House.

Losey, K. M. (in press). *"Listen to the silences": Mexican American interaction in the composition classroom and the community.* Norwood, NJ: Ablex.

McLaughlin, B. (1985). *Second-language acquisition in childhood: Vol. 2. School-age children.* (2nd ed.). Hillsdale, NJ: Lawrence Erlbaum.

Mehan, H. (1979). *Learning lessons.* Cambridge: Cambridge University Press.

Mirandé, A., & Enríquez, E. (1979). *La Chicana: The Mexican-American woman.* Chicago, IL: University of Chicago Press.

Moffett, J. (1981/1988). *Coming on center: Essays in English education.* Portsmouth, NH: Boynton/Cook.

Moll, L. C. (1988). Some key issues in teaching Latino students. *Language Arts, 65*, 465–472.

Morse, L. W., & Handley, H. M. (1985). Listening to adolescents: Gender differences in science classroom interaction. In L. C. Wilkinson & C. B. Marrett (Eds.), *Gender influences in classroom interaction* (pp. 37–56). Orlando, FL: Academic Press.

Nieto-Gómez, A. (1973). The Chicana—Perspectives for education. *Encuentro Femenil, 1*, 34–61.

Ortiz, F. I. (1977). Bilingual education program practices and their effect upon students' performance and self-identity. *Aztlán: International Journal of Chicano Studies Research, 8*, 157–174.

Ortiz, F. I. (1988). Hispanic-American children's experiences in classrooms: A comparison between Hispanic and non-Hispanic children. In L. Weis (Ed.), *Class, race, and gender in American education* (pp. 63–86). New York: State University of New York Press.

Parsons, Jr., T. W. (1965). *Ethnic cleavage in a California school.* Unpublished doctoral dissertation, Stanford University, Palo Alto, CA.

Philips, S. U. (1972/1985). Participant structures and communicative competence: Warm Springs children in community and classroom. In C. B. Cazden, V. P. John, & D. Hymes

(Eds.), *Functions of language in the classroom* (pp. 370–394). Prospect Heights, IL: Waveland Press.

Pica, T., & Doughty, C. (1988). Variations in classroom interaction as a function of participation pattern and task. In J. Fine (Ed.), *Second language discourse: A textbook of current research* (pp. 41–55). Norwood, NJ: Ablex.

Sacks, H., Schegloff, E. A., & Jefferson, G. (1974). A simplest systematics for the organization of turn-taking in conversation. *Language, 50*, 696–735.

Schumann, J. H. (1978). The acculturation model for second language acquisition. In R. Gingrass (Ed.), *Second language acquisition and foreign language teaching*. Washington, DC: Center for Applied Linguistics.

Shor, I. (1980/1987). *Critical teaching and everyday life*. Chicago, IL: University of Chicago Press.

Shuy, R. (1969, February). *Sex as a factor in sociolinguistic research*. Paper presented at the Anthropological Society of Washington, Washington, DC. (ERIC Document Reproduction Service No. ED 027 522)

Skutnabb-Kangas, T. (1981). *Bilingualism or not: The education of minorities*. Clevedon, England: Multilingual Matters.

Soifer, R., Irwin, M., Crumrine, B., Honzaki, E., Simmons, B., & Young, D. (1990). *The complete theory-to-practice handbook of adult literacy: Curriculum design and teaching approaches*. New York: Teachers College Press.

Stanley, J. (1986). Sex and the quiet schoolgirl. *British Journal of Sociology of Education, 7*, 275–286.

Stern, H. H. (1990). Analysis and experience as variables in second language pedagogy. In B. Harley, P. Allen, J. Cummins, & M. Swain (Eds.), *The development of second language proficiency* (pp. 93–109). Cambridge: Cambridge University Press.

Swacker, M. (1975). The sex of the speaker as a sociolinguistic variable. In B. Thorne & N. Henley (Eds.), *Language and sex: Difference and dominance* (pp. 76–83). Rowley, MA: Newbury House.

Swain, M. (1985). Communicative competence: Some roles of comprehensible input and comprehensible output in its development. In S. M. Gass & C. G. Madden (Eds.), *Input in second language acquisition* (pp. 235–252). Rowley, MA: Newbury House.

Swann, J. (1988). Talk control: An illustration from the classroom of problems analysing male dominance in conversation. In J. Coates & D. Cameron, (Eds.), *Women in their speech communities: New perspectives on language and sex* (pp. 122–140). New York: Longman.

Townsend, D. R., & Zamora, G. L. (1975). Differing interaction patterns in bilingual classrooms. *Contemporary Education, 46*, 196–202.

Trueba, H. T. (1987). Organizing classroom instruction in specific sociocultural contexts: Teaching Mexican youth to write in English. In S. R. Goldman & H. T. Trueba (Eds.), *Becoming literate in English as a second language* (pp. 235–252). Norwood, NJ: Ablex.

U.S. Commission on Civil Rights. (1973). *Teachers and students: Differences in teacher interaction with Mexican American and Anglo students. Report V: Mexican American Education Study*. Washington, DC: U.S. Government Printing Office.

Valdés-Fallis, G. (1974). The liberated Chicana: A struggle against tradition. *Women: A journal of liberation, 3*, 20–21.

Vygotsky, L. (1978). *Mind in society*. Cambridge, MA: Harvard University Press.

Wells, G. (1981). *Learning through interaction: The study of language development*. Cambridge: Cambridge University Press.

Wertsch, J. V., Minick, N., & Arns, F. J. (1985). The creation of context in joint problem-solving. In B. Rogoff & J. Lave (Eds.), *Everyday cognition* (pp. 151–171). Cambridge, MA: Harvard University Press.

West, C., & Zimmerman, D. H. (1991). Doing gender. In J. Lorber & S.A. Farrell (Eds.), *The social construction of gender* (pp. 13–37). Newbury Park, CA: Sage Publications.

Whyte, J. (1984). Observing sex stereotypes and interactions in the school lab and workshop. *Educational Review, 36*, 75–86.

Wong Fillmore, L. (1982). Instructional language as linguistic input: Second language learning in classrooms. In L. C. Wilkinson (Ed.), *Communicating in the classroom* (pp. 283–296). New York: Academic Press.

Wong Fillmore, L., & Valadez, C. (1986). Teaching bilingual learners. In M. C. Wittrock (Ed.), *Handbook of research on teaching* (3rd ed.) (pp. 648–684). New York: Macmillan.

Zabin, C. (1991, March 4). Latinos now 61 percent of population. *Appleton Daily News*, pp. 1, 9.

Chapter 7

ESL Versus Mainstream Classes: Contrasting L2 Learning Environments

Linda Harklau

Language minority students are often placed in mainstream, English-medium classrooms long before they develop the degree of language proficiency necessary to compete on an equal footing with native speakers of the school language. With the ever-increasing presence of such students in U.S. schools, ESL and content-area educators are working to better integrate their respective curricula and instructional roles. In order to accomplish this integration, significant instructional differences in these two contexts must be identified, and systematic comparisons must detail how L2 learners fare in each of these instructional environments. What do students lose and gain in their transition from ESL to the mainstream? This question was addressed in a 3½ year ethnography of the L2 learning experiences of newcomer students attending a high school in northern California. The study, which followed 4 Chinese ethnic immigrant students as they made the transition from ESL to mainstream classes, contrasted patterns of spoken and written language use in classrooms, identified significant differences in the content and goals of the ESL versus mainstream curricula, and documented language instruction and feedback in both contexts. Both contexts were also evaluated in terms of the socializing features of schooling, such as counseling and peer networks. As in many other U.S. public schools, the isolated and marginalized position of the ESL program in an institution that otherwise made no adjustment for nonnative speakers produced a makeshift system in which there was no appropriate instructional environment for learners of the school language.

Students in the U.S. who are in the lengthy process of acquiring English as an additional language are frequently found in mainstream English-medium classes alongside native speakers (O'Malley & Waggoner, 1984; Penfield, 1987). In some cases, students or their families may refuse special help because of a perceived remedial stigma, or students slip through screening systems set up by school districts to identify students who need special language instruction. More typically, however, schools do not have funding or administrative support to offer more than 2 or 3 years of special instruction to learners of the school language.

Bilingual education and ESL classes are often viewed as an extra burden on already overtaxed school resources. Equally significant in shaping educational policy for linguistic minority students is a pervasive folk belief that children will learn English faster if they are in regular classes with native speakers of English. Although evidence for this notion is far from conclusive (Wong Fillmore with Valadez, 1986), it nevertheless dominates practice. Newcomers are often placed in mainstream classes immediately upon arrival, concurrent with ESL or classes in their home language, and they are exited from special programs quite rapidly. Thus, even though language minority students may take up to 7 years to develop the level of language proficiency necessary to compete on an equal footing with native speakers of the school language (Collier, 1987; Cummins, 1982), they are likely to be in mainstream classes long before then.

This demographic reality has led educators to seek ways in which they might better articulate ESL and mainstream instruction and thus ensure a smooth transition. One approach to this issue has been to develop "sheltered" or content-area curricula for ESL classrooms (see Chamot & O'Malley, 1987; Crandall, 1987; Mohan, 1986). Another has been to provide practical pedagogical advice on educating language minority students to regular classroom teachers who are untrained in ESL (see Hamayan & Perlman, 1990; Richard-Amato & Snow, 1992; Riddlemoser, 1987; Rigg & Allen, 1989; Scarcella, 1990). Researchers, however, have noted the paucity of closely detailed ethnographic descriptions comparing these two contexts which might serve as the basis for such approaches and facilitate the articulation and transition between ESL and the mainstream (Crandall, 1993; Freeman, 1993). How do ESL and mainstream classrooms differ instructionally and linguistically as L2 learning environments? How do students experience the differences between ESL and mainstream classes, and what do they lose and gain on their transition from ESL to the mainstream? These questions were addressed in a 3½-year (Spring 1987 to Spring 1990) ethnographic study of the L2 learning experiences of newcomer students attending a high school in the San Francisco Bay area. The study represented a unique opportunity to compare the same students' language learning experiences and behavior across ESL and mainstream contexts and to trace each student's high school career each year as they were making the transition from ESL into mainstream classes. This article documents differences in the goals and organization of instruction of mainstream and ESL classrooms in one school context. The article also contrasts the functions of ESL and mainstream classes in terms of their role in socializing students into U.S. schools and society.

METHOD

Gateview High School (a pseudonym), where the study took place, was marked by the ethnic and social diversity typical of many urban high schools in the San Francisco Bay area, drawing its student population from both affluent hill areas and the poorer, industrial "flats" closer to the bay. The school population of approximately 1,600 students averaged 50% African American, 30% Asian American, 20% White, and 2–3% Hispanic. Nevertheless, its limited English proficient (LEP) population was relatively small, consisting of fewer than 100 students. One veteran teacher, Maureen Carson (a pseudonym), oversaw the ESL program serving these students. She established her classroom as the ESL homeroom for the school and was the language minority students' advocate and unofficial counselor at the school. Her formal training was in English and social studies, and she had taught ESL alongside these subject areas for some 20 of her 30 years in teaching. Although she was not formally certified in ESL, she had rich and lengthy experience working with ESL students and evidenced a commitment to continuing professional development on a number of fronts, including the local teachers' union, a university program for gifted students, a national College Board committee on preparing high school students for college, and a school-university partnership program.

Carson taught the majority of ESL classes at Gateview, including ESL 1, 2, and 3; a reading course for ESL 1 and 2 students; ESL sheltered U.S. and world history; and sheltered (but required) citizenship and first aid courses for seniors. Because she could not cover all of these courses by herself, however, the school assigned a mainstream teacher, untrained in ESL, to teach one or two of the courses on a yearly basis. Carson was often skeptical of the administration's motives in selecting teachers for these courses, and experiences over the course of the study showed her suspicions to be well founded. In two cases, an English and Spanish teacher exhibited difficulty in keeping ESL students in their classes on task, suggesting that they had similar or even greater difficulties with mainstream students. In another case, Carson believed that a mainstream social studies teacher volunteered to teach sheltered social studies courses because he saw them as an "easy out," with small class sizes and docile students. It was not until the final year of the study, in anticipation of Carson's retirement, that the school acquired another experienced ESL teacher, Pat Malone (a pseudonym). Because she had no background in content areas other than Spanish, however, Malone was not prepared to employ the sheltered subject matter approach that Carson used in higher proficiency levels of ESL and in social studies courses, and she thus took on the lower proficiency classes (ESL 1, ESL 2, and ESL reading) in the program.

The assignment of mainstream teachers to ESL classes was symptomatic of the relationship between the ESL program and the rest of the school. At best, the school administration tolerated the program as a necessary nuisance. As steadily increasing enrollments over the course of the study required more resources devoted to the program, administrators applied pressure to either increase class sizes to levels that exceeded those stipulated in the union contract and district regulations, or to decrease enrollment by encouraging some students to exit the program before they had reached the level of English proficiency legally required for reclassification. As a result, Carson was frequently embroiled in conflicts that resulted in time-consuming appeals to the union and district bilingual education office. Furthermore, the administration provided little leadership or encouragement of mainstream teacher involvement in language minority education at the school, fostering a widespread attitude that the ESL program and its students were Carson's exclusive concern. Mainstream teachers were untrained in working with language learners, and ESL and mainstream curricula were not coordinated. A survey of mainstream teachers done as part of an accreditation process showed many misunderstandings about the nature and purpose of ESL instruction.

Carson was my initial contact at the school, and her classroom served as my base of operations over the course of the study. Because the ESL classroom was the main gathering place for immigrant students at the school, I was quickly able to establish myself as a participant observer in a role similar to that of the two aides who worked in the program. Like the aides, I was accessible to students at lunchtime to help with homework, to provide information about negotiating the schooling system, or just to socialize. I was an observer and sometimes a participant in ESL classes at Gateview throughout the study. I frequently consulted with Carson to inform her about the progress of the study and to ask for additional information and insights.

Although there were more than a dozen linguistic and ethnic groups represented at any one time in ESL classes at Gateview, Chinese ethnic students were selected as the sample group for the study because of their predominance in the ESL program, in which they constituted one third of the student population. They also had conspicuous, well-formed intragroup peer networks and tended to take leadership roles in the mixed ethnic group peer networks among ESL and former ESL students. With the assistance of Carson, 4 students from this group were selected as case studies. The sample was "purposive" (Merriam, 1988), meaning that criteria for subject selection were predetermined on the basis of typical background characteristics of Chinese American ESL students at the school. Most of these students, for example, had several years of schooling and a strong literacy foundation in their native language. Most were planning to remain in the U.S., and most were planning to attend a U.S. college or university. Of the 4 case study students selected, 3 were Taiwanese immigrants, and 1 was from Hong Kong. They had arrived in the U.S. between sixth and tenth grade. (Figure 7.1 contains background information regarding individual focal students.)

Each of these students was followed over a period of four to seven semesters in the transition from ESL into mainstream classes. This transition followed a similar pattern for most students. Students at the ESL 1 (beginner) level were also enrolled in an ESL reading class and usually a sheltered social studies class as well. For the remaining two to three periods of instruction, students were enrolled in a math course, a science course, physical education, or an elective such as typing, music, or art. As students progressed through the program, their ESL course load was re-

Anne[a]:	
Native country:	Taiwan
Began school in U.S.:	enrolled in eighth grade in Fall 1985 (attended junior high school in the same school district as Gateview)
Participation in study:	seven semesters (Spring 1987–Spring 1990; Grades 9–12)
Eddie:	
Native country:	Taiwan
Began school in U.S.:	enrolled in sixth grade in Fall 1984 (attended one year of elementary school and junior high school in the same school district as Gateview)
Participation in study:	six semesters (Fall 1987–Spring 1990; Grades 9–11)
Gary:	
Native country:	Taiwan
Began school in U.S.:	enrolled in ninth grade in 1985
Participation in study:	five semesters (Spring 1987–Spring 1989; Grades 10–12)
Mei Li:	
Native country:	Hong Kong
Began school in U.S.:	enrolled in tenth grade in Fall 1986 (attended high school in the neighboring district for one semester)
Participation in study:	four semesters (Fall 1987–Spring 1989; Grades 11–12)

[a]Students' names are pseudonyms.

FIG. 7.1. Focal student background data.

duced to one class (ESL 2, intermediate, or ESL 3, advanced) and in some cases a second sheltered social studies course. Mainstream English and social studies courses were usually added at this point. All of the focal students joined the study at this stage, when they had been enrolled in ESL for at least 1 year and were taking ESL 2 or ESL 3. Within 1–2 years, all of them except Mei Li, who graduated, completed ESL 3 and were mainstreamed completely. (Each focal student's courses over the duration of the study are detailed in Fig. 7.2).

Each of the focal students was observed through full school days, in most cases on 2 consecutive days, in both ESL and mainstream classes. Samples of schoolwork and homework, and school records were collected. Much of my contact with students occurred in informal conversation at lunchtime, allowing students' emic perspective on their experiences to unfold, while providing opportunities to guide the conversation, clarify, or raise a new subject when necessary. Between two and seven formal interviews up to 1 hour long were conducted with each student at less frequent intervals, when informal contact did not suffice. In general, they took place when a student joined the study, at the end of school year, or following classroom observations.

Focal students' mainstream teachers were all interviewed briefly before or after class. Teachers were asked to comment on the student's performance in their class and if they had had other experiences with ESL students in their classes. Many teachers scheduled an extra 10 or 15 min to talk with me when their schedules permitted. For the most part, they seemed eager to share their reflections about ESL students in their classes. Formal 45-min interviews were conducted with two of the students' English teachers and two of their social studies teachers because these were the mainstream subject areas in which linguistic demands made of learners appeared greatest.

Student	*Grade 9*	*Grade 10*	*Grade 11*	*Grade 12*
Anne	ESL 2	ESL 3		
	Biology	Chemistry	Physics	Biology (advanced placement)
	Geometry	Algebra II	Math analysis	Calculus
	World history	Economics (1 semester)	American experience	American experience
		English	English	English
	Computer science (elective)	Computer science (elective)	Japanese (elective)	Japanese II (elective)
		Electronics (elective)	Photography (elective)	Band (elective)

FIG. 7.2. Focal student courses.[a]

Student	*Grade 9*	*Grade 10*	*Grade 11*	*Grade 12*
		Shakespeare (elective, 1 semester)	Computer science (elective)	Piano (elective)
			Band (elective)	
Eddie	ESL 2	ESL 3		
	Natural science	Biology	Chemistry	
	Algebra	Geometry	Algebra II	
	World history	Economics (1 semester)	American experience	
		English	English	
	Phsysical education	Physical education		
	Typing (elective)	Art (elective, 1 semester)	French (elective)	
		Japanese (elective)	Computer science (elective)	
			Japanese II (elective)	
Gary		ESL 3		
		English	English	English
		Chemistry	Chemistry (advanced placement)	Biology (advanced placement)
		Algebra II	Calculus	
		Math analysis		
			American experience	American experience
			Economics (1 semester)	
		Physical education		
			Piano (elective, 1 semester)	Computer science (elective)
			Computer science (elective)	
			Japanese (elective)	
				Piano (elective)
Mei Li			ESL 2	ESL 3
			ESL sheltered U.S. history	ESL sheltered American government (1 semester)
			English	English
			Math analysis	Calculus
			Biology	Physics
			Economics (1 semester)	
				Calligraphy (elective, 1 semester)
				Ceramics (elective, 1 semester

[a]All courses, with the exception of the first aid course, were credit bearing.

FIG. 7.2. *(continued)*

In the final year of the study, ongoing efforts to supplement case study observations and interviews were extended and formalized. A broad sample of Taiwanese and Hong Kong immigrants at the school was interviewed. Additional Chinese-ethnic students were observed in mainstream English and social studies classes, and two class discussion sessions were organized with immigrant students regarding their experiences in school. These data served to assess the representativeness of focal student experiences and to gain additional insight into immigrant student experiences at Gateview. All told, 315 hours of observations (165 hours in 56 mainstream classes, and 150 hours in ESL classes) and 38 formal interviews were conducted in addition to innumerable informal encounters that took place with students and school personnel during the 3½ years of the study.

The following discussion explores two significant ways in which ESL and mainstream instruction were found to differ. The first is in the organization and goals of instruction, such as how spoken and written language were used in classroom activities, how teachers' perceived goals affected course curriculum and content, and the degree to which explicit language instruction and feedback were reflected in the curriculum. It also explores what might be called the socializing functions of a U.S. high school, illustrating contrasts in opportunities for peer interaction and activities, as well as counseling.

ORGANIZATION OF INSTRUCTION AND LANGUAGE USE

Interactional Routines

Spoken Language Use in the Mainstream

One important contrast in the instructional and linguistic environment of ESL and mainstream classes was found in interactional routines, or the way spoken and written language were used in the course of classroom activities. Traditionally, the dynamics of spoken discourse patterns have received the most attention in both L1 and L2 classroom research (see Cazden, 1988; Green & Wallat, 1981; and Mehan, 1979 for mainstream classrooms; and van Lier, 1988; and Chaudron, 1988, for L2 classrooms), and thus it is a logical starting point for comparison. The nature of spoken interaction in high school classroom activities has been documented (see Applebee with Auten, 1981; Boyer, 1983), although the implications of these activities for L2 learning have not been explicitly addressed.

The predominant activity in mainstream classrooms at Gateview was what Applebee (1981) has termed *teacher-led discussion*. Discussion may be a misnomer for this activity because teachers overwhelmingly dominate the talk, initiating three quarters of the questions asked according to Applebee's findings. Thus, the value of these activities to L2 learners like those at Gateview rested mainly in the copious spoken input received from the teacher. Research has suggested, however, that the utility of input is not solely a function of quantity. Rather, effective input also has an authentic communicative purpose, emphasizing the content of the message rather than its grammatical form (Krashen, 1981; Lambert, 1984; Tikunoff, 1985; Widdowson, 1978; Wong Fillmore, 1985). Mainstream classrooms at Gateview fit this criterion for "good" input extremely well. Because the majority of students were native speakers of the language, the target language served an authentic communicative need, as the medium through which concepts needed to perform school tasks were communicated.

Nevertheless, input received by learners in mainstream classrooms had at least one major failing. Because they primarily were addressing native speakers of English, mainstream high school classroom teachers seldom adjusted input in order to make it comprehensible to L2 learners. Adjustments such as reducing the speed and complexity of speech; increasing repetition, pausing, and comprehension checks; and contextualizing abstract concepts through the use of realia such as maps or photos, graphs, or graphic organizers such as webbing have been identified as necessary in order to make input useful as raw material for language learning (Cantoni-Harvey, 1987; Krashen, 1981; Short, 1991; Wong Fillmore, 1985). Learners had particular difficulty understanding teacher talk which contained puns or was sarcastic or ironic. This talk provoked rejoinders or groans from native speakers but was received with blank, slightly puzzled looks from ESL students. Learners were also frustrated with teachers who habitually spoke very fast, who used frequent asides, or who were prone to sudden departures from the instructional topic at hand. One teacher, for example, was known for suddenly departing from lessons in order to tell tales about his days in the navy, much to the consternation of L2 learners in his class. Immigrant students expressed exasperation about such talk, like Mei Li, who commented,

1. I don't want to spend my time to listen to something I don't understand. . . . When my words come through my brain, and I couldn't, like, have time for me to understand? And then, when I take the time to understand, then he [the teacher] is speaking another stuff.

The evaluation of mainstream classrooms as spoken language acquisition environments rests not only on input received but also on opportunities for output and the entire process of interaction. The productive use of an L2 and feedback from native speakers is also a major component in the process of second language acquisition (SLA) (Hatch, 1983; Swain, 1985). Because Asian American immigrant students at Gateview reported that they communicated in their native language almost exclusively outside the classroom, interaction at school was learners' greatest potential opportunity to interact with native speakers. Opportunities for interaction in mainstream classrooms varied as a function of the instructional activity structures typically employed in various subject areas. Math classes, for example, relied almost exclusively on teacher-led discussion, while English and social studies classes were somewhat more likely to include group work or student presentations. Tracking also led to different curricula, activity structures, and language learning opportunities in classes deemed "high" and "low" in academic ability (see Harklau, in press a, b). Although case study students varied in their track placements, recently mainstreamed students typically were placed in low-track classes, on the assumption that such classes would be easier for them. However, high-track classes were most likely to employ interaction-fostering activities such as student-led group work, whereas low-track classes often relied heavily on teacher-directed activities and individual seat work. While acknowledging such variation among classrooms, one could say that overall opportunities to engage in extended interactions with mainstream teachers during classroom instruction were rare. Classes of up to 35 students were large and unwieldy to facilitate such interactions, and the demands that teachers faced to cover the material often made classroom discussion a luxury. As a result, teacher-led discussions featuring the similar initiation-reply-evaluation (IRE) sequence (Mehan, 1979) were the prevalent mode of instruction at Gateview. In an average class, all other things being equal, individual students had only a 1:25 or 1:30 chance of being allocated a turn by the teacher during these activities. Even more significant for L2 learners, student participation in teacher-led discussion using the IRE format was usually limited to a single word or phrase. Thus, learners had little occasion to practice the communicative strategies that they would employ in building interaction over several turns, such as negotiating turns, joint construction and maintenance of topics, and comprehension checks and repairs. Nor did they have the opportunity to produce extended, coherent discourse within a single turn, in which they might manipulate features such as tense usage, pronominal forms, or the arrangement of information through manipulation of clause structure, conjunctions, and subordinators.

Lacking specific training in strategies for teaching ESL students, teachers varied considerably in whether their instructional style facilitated interaction with the nonnative speakers in their classrooms. Many teachers had learned through experience to place ESL students in desks close to the front of the room so that they could scan students' faces for signs of comprehension, confusion, or responses to questions. However, there were also many teachers who seemed to face the board for most of the class. Although some teachers made a point of talking one-to-one with their students, including ESL students, others could not recall the names of students without reference to seating charts. Some teachers preferred to structure discussions so that every student was specifically invited to share opinions or information over the course of the class. In general, however, mainstream teachers were less likely to elicit output from ESL students than the native speakers in their classes. (Previous studies at the elementary and college levels have reported similar phenomena. See Schinke-Llano, 1983; Sato, 1982.) Many elicited student response by addressing questions to the entire class. This format favored the students who could most loudly or confidently bid for the floor and allowed more reticent students, such as English learners, to simply not respond. Some teachers noted that they wanted to spare nonnative speakers from being put on the spot. Learners often preferred to remain silent as well and rarely volunteered for turns. One explained,

2. I don't like to talk very much because of a lack of confident and I don't know what to say most of the times. Also kind of lazy in talking.

Gary also explained reticence as a cultural value, by referring to a Chinese saying,

3. "Being quiet is gold and vigorously debating is silver." Being quiet is considered polite and intelligent because only the insecure ones need to prove themselves smart by talking loud. For that reason, the school [in Taiwan] wanted the students to keep quiet in the classroom.

In total effect, the lack of interaction between L2 learners and their mainstream teachers at Gateview was quite striking. Observations recorded a total of only 8 instances of learners talking in class discussions over the course of 12 days of classes, and 10 dyadic exchanges with teachers over the same 12 days. In other words, students were on the average likely to engage in any form of interaction with teachers only once or twice during any given day of mainstream classes. One of Mei Li's teachers observed that he was not even certain that he would recognize her voice. Although there were no doubt native speakers for whom interaction with teachers was similarly limited, for L2 learners, this pattern assumed special significance, negating a potentially important source of output and interaction with native speakers.

Because they were seldom required to participate in classroom interactions, L2 learners were able to tune out many mainstream instructional interactions entirely. Students often sat, heads bent over desks, engrossed in their books and papers, paying little attention to teacher or peer talk going on in the class. Because it was an effort to understand spoken language used in a mainstream class, Mei Li commented that,

4. Like, sometimes I . . . just don't listen to him [the teacher]. So I do my own work.

Tuning out was partially a function of input that students found incomprehensible, and partially a function of their preferences for interaction with written materials. The net result was that students were often withdrawn and noninteractive in mainstream classes. They were not even paying particular attention to the input, much less engaging in interaction.

Spoken Language Use in ESL Classes

Teacher-led discussion was also the predominant activity conducted through the spoken channel in ESL classes. However, qualitative differences existed in how discussion was organized and framed, differences which resulted in qualitatively superior input and richer, more frequent opportunities for interaction and spoken language output. As one might expect, as an ESL teacher Carson was adept at adjusting input in order to make it comprehensible. For example, she used extremely explicit directives and transitions, such as "Look at me. Now, I'm going to point to you and give you a number. 1, 2, 3 . . . ." She scanned the faces of students as she spoke, looking for signs of comprehension or confusion. She kept a small blackboard by her side as she spoke, ready to draw pictures or write down unfamiliar words when needed. Such adjustments have been shown to be integral to creating an effective instructional environment for LEP students and in ensuring input that is comprehensible to nonnative speakers (Tikunoff, 1985; Wong Fillmore, 1989).

Besides making input more comprehensible than in mainstream classrooms, Carson also created extended opportunities for students to interact and participate. Students agreed that they talked the most in ESL classes. As one student commented,

5. And here [ESL class], I dare to talk more, and gradually I will rather ask more question.

Carson was able to create smaller classes by dividing classes between herself and aides. Unlike most mainstream classes, which were arranged in the traditional rows of desks facing the front, Carson arranged her classroom so that she and the students were seated close together in a circle in the middle of the room in order to facilitate communication. During instruction, she called on every student in the room several times. She frequently asked open-ended questions, modeling extended responses and then asking students to do the same, such as "If you had to think of one picture from the 80s that you would remember, what would it be? Mine would be . . . ." She then called on every student in the class to share his/her opinion. The overall effect of these differences was to stress participation and to encourage self-expression in class. In fact, although tuning out was common in mainstream classes, students were usually active participants in ESL class activities. They even bid for turns, a phenomenon rarely observed in mainstream classes.

Written Language Use in the Mainstream

Investigation of classroom language, particularly in L2 contexts, has tended to direct attention to spoken discourse processes in the classroom. It is only when one examines contexts such as mainstream high school classrooms, with a deep and pervasive bias towards the written mode, that one perceives the equally pervasive bias towards the spoken language often implicit in classroom SLA research and pedagogy. Indeed, it sometimes seems that classroom language is construed as synonymous with spoken language (see Chaudron, 1988; Ellis, 1984; Long, 1989; Mitchell, 1985; van Lier, 1988). Nevertheless, in the context of the U.S. high school classrooms examined in this study, spoken language was regarded by students and teachers alike as a relatively insignificant mode. Of course, communication—input and interaction—certainly occurs through the written channel as well, and some SLA researchers have explicitly linked the written mode to the particular linguistic demands of academic contexts (Adamson, 1993; Cummins, 1982; Saville-Troike, 1984). By high school, U.S. educators assume that native speakers of English are capable of conducting most of the linguistic transactions that take place in classrooms through reading and writing. It is not only the most efficient means of conveying content-area concepts, but it is also more highly valued as the mode through which the most important information is communicated and through which students' progress is measured. If we are to truly understand the differences between ESL and mainstream classrooms, then, it is critical that we explore the demands placed on students in linguistic transactions occurring in the written mode.

Reading, for example, is potentially an excellent source of input for L2 learners because, unlike spoken input, learners can adjust their interactions with texts according to proficiency level. In mainstream classes at Gateview, students read copiously. Although input in the form of reading was plentiful, however, it was also somewhat lacking in variety. Textbooks were the predominant source of reading matter for most students. Students in high-track classes were also assigned supplementary materials, such as magazine articles in social studies and science, and literature and poetry in English. For students in low-track classes, however, textbooks were likely to be the exclusive source of assigned reading. Although activities surrounding reading material varied by track as well (see Harklau, in press b; Oakes, 1985), comprehension exercises or tests requiring students to memorize factual information were most typical, along with problem sets based on math or science chapters.

Reading activities in mainstream classroom activities required an academically oriented, technical lexicon spanning several subject areas. Because literacy and language learning become symbiotic processes by the time individuals reach the secondary level of schooling (see Nippold, 1988), it stands to reason that L2 learners, just like their native-speaker peers, were developing the majority of their vocabulary through a process of contextual abstraction while reading. Students confirmed that their vocabulary came primarily from written sources. Eddie noted that his class studied the words that,

> 6. appear in the book. And if [you just saw] some kind of word is difficult, and all those stuff, and she [the teacher] will, like, write it down and tell us to memorize it.

Just as spoken output is hypothesized to be essential in developing L2 speaking proficiency, writing output—the process of composing and producing written texts—is viewed as necessary in order to develop proficiency in the written mode (Edelsky, 1986; Farr & Daniels, 1986). In mainstream classroom activities, students had occasion to produce extended discourse in written form much more frequently than they had to speak. Teachers reported that they had more opportunities to interact with students in written work, where they could respond and individualize according to learner needs. Nevertheless, the amount and quality of writing experiences offered to students were not consistent across mainstream classrooms. Although virtually all writing activities entailed the transfer of information from textbooks, literary texts, or other written sources to schoolwork, there was considerable variation across classes in the frequency and extent of composing and in the degree of original thought required by assignments. Although some students learned to produce academically valued genres, such as offering a personal opinion supported by a synthesis of information, in other classrooms, students did nothing more than locate and repeat verbatim information from textbooks. Assignments also varied considerably in length, ranging from a single sentence or phrase to three- or four-page essays, depending on students' track level and subject matter.

Like the spoken language activities in mainstream classrooms, many writing activities were limited to a single word or phrase, in the format of fill-in-the-blank, multiple choice, and short answer exercises. L2 learners in mainstream classes were proficient in bluffing their way through such mechanical writing exercises without a clear idea of what they were talking about. Eddie, for example, used his bilingual dictionary to generate "original" sentence contexts for vocabulary words, transforming the activity into a copying exercise. In other instances, students recast what teachers hoped were meaningful note-taking exercises into measures of how accurately they could copy what the teacher wrote on the board. Activities such as textbook or novel-reading summaries might elicit texts of up to a paragraph in length, but nevertheless limited, in that the text served only to recount learned facts. In response to such activities, ESL students became extremely adept at locating information in texts and repeating it in answer to factual questions, often with a marginal understanding of the information they were copying or memorizing.

Written Language Use in ESL Classes

As in mainstream classes, students were exposed to a great deal of reading material in ESL classes. Carson's selection of materials was, of course, also influenced by her students' limited language proficiency. In response to these needs, she often selected texts which had been written for younger students or abridged texts adapted especially for L2 readers. She realized, however, that these texts had shortcomings. She observed, for example, that abridged literary texts were often stripped of metaphoric language. She therefore supplemented these materials with authentic reading, such as newspaper stories about current events, particularly in students' home countries; political cartoons; and original works of short fiction. Carson also fostered extensive reading outside of ESL by using class time to distribute catalogues and take orders for a mail order paperback club for teenagers.

ESL learners had two somewhat distinct sets of lexical gaps or needs—(a) the vocabulary used in negotiating everyday U.S. culture and social interactions, and (b) the technical and academic vocabulary needed to perform academic tasks across subject areas. Perhaps because students faced such a need for content-area vocabulary in their mainstream classes, and perhaps because of learning preferences brought from previous schooling experiences, students favored academic and, to Carson's view, "esoteric" vocabulary. At the same time, they were sometimes unfamiliar with what native speakers would consider more basic or common vocabulary. One ESL student, for example, volunteered the word *silhouette* in a class discussion, even though later in the same discussion he had to ask the meaning of *sleeve*, and look up the word *snake* in the dictionary. Because Carson attempted to address both needs, one of the students' main complaints about ESL was that the vocabulary of everyday life and interaction they sometimes studied was too easy. As Eddie commented,

7. they [ESL] used vocabulary words very lower level.

Although writing opportunities in mainstream classrooms were inconsistent in frequency and quality, every student in ESL classes at Gateview received rich and plentiful experiences with written output. This was in large part due to Carson's own individual vision of the goals of ESL. Because of her emphasis on academic preparation, she made a point of including extended composition projects in every ESL class. Students wrote in a variety of genres. Every student, from beginning to advanced, wrote descriptive and narrative compositions inspired by the Bay Area Writing Project teaching philosophy and techniques (see Caplan & Keech, 1980). Every class level had unique projects as well. Students in the ESL government class were required to write their own legislative bills. Each year, the ESL 2 (intermediate-level) class wrote and illustrated storybooks based on folk tales from their native countries, which they then read for children at a local elementary school. Students in ESL 3 (the most advanced level) were required to do a library research project using outside sources. They chose topics such as the reunification of Germany or the enforcement of child abuse laws.

In contrast to most mainstream teachers, Carson was mindful of students' penchant for covering a lack of understanding by memorizing and repeating back language used in instruction and was vigilant in working against it. She was likely to call students' bluff when they incorporated language from source materials into their work without a clear understanding of its meaning. For example, when one student copied sentences from the book verbatim onto her homework and then read them aloud in class, Carson told her,

8. Jane, you're new to this class, but what we do is, we never write down words we don't understand.

In countering this propensity, Carson emphasized the ability to think critically and to support opinions. One of the school counselors at Gateview observed,

9. She [Carson] makes them—she makes a situation a seed bed, where opinionation can grow. That's what she likes to foster.

Structure and Goals of Instruction

ESL classes also differed significantly from mainstream classes in terms of the assumptions that guided teachers in planning instructional goals and in the institutional constraints and freedoms that impinged upon these goals. The content and course objectives of high school subject-area instruction presumed a relatively stable student population with a uniform knowledge base shaped by 8 or 9 years of previous instruction in U.S. elementary and middle schools. Thus, curriculum in subject areas depended on continuity, with content in any one course built upon a knowledge base that students were assumed to possess from previous courses in the sequence. In mathematics, for example, students were expected to follow a sequence from algebra to geometry to advanced algebra to math analysis to calculus. Even though there might be several algebra courses offered in any given year, each course had to be similar enough so that the following year's geometry teachers could assume a uniform knowledge base. Thus, all teachers at a given level followed the same course text and aimed to cover the same material. Mathematics courses followed the strictest uniformity in content and sequencing, while English and social studies teachers appeared to have the most latitude of subject-area teachers. Even in these areas, however, teachers worked together to ensure that whatever material was used at one grade level would not be repeated by another teacher in subsequent grades.

Curriculum in mainstream subject areas was also constrained by many forces outside the classroom, including state curriculum guidelines, district guidelines, the curriculum set by each subject-area department at Gateview, and the requirements of standardized measures such as Advanced Placement tests. For example, the social studies curriculum was shaped by a state directive that students receive at least 1 year of world history, 1 year of U.S. history, and 1 semester each of economics and of U.S. government while in high school. Less formal constraints also acted to routinize the curriculum. Because subject-area teachers worked as a group within their respective departments, curricula were mutually negotiated and predetermined by the department as a whole. For example, the syllabus for Advanced Placement English classes was set by a mandatory summer reading list for incoming students. Curriculum was also established by custom, as colleagues worked together over the years to develop and share resources for teaching a given unit.

In contrast to the relatively static curriculum and student population of mainstream classes, one of the most salient ways in which the ESL program at Gateview differed was that it was constantly changing. Over the years, Carson had dealt with a succession of students from widely varying cultural and linguistic groups, socioeconomic levels, and educational backgrounds ranging from refugee camps to exclusive private schools. Every September, the number of students entering the program was different, and new students suddenly appeared at random intervals throughout the school year. The constantly shifting needs of the population in ESL classes can exercise a profound effect on course curriculum and planning. Like many other ESL teachers, Carson had looser guidelines and considerably more autonomy in setting course curriculum than most mainstream teachers. However, she also faced challenges stemming from constant change which mainstream teachers did not face. Carson's response to these challenges was a spiral syllabus and unit-based approach to curriculum that followed a similar format and routine for all classes. It could easily be adjusted up or down or supplemented, depending on the needs of the class. She had built a repertoire of units based on abridged versions of classic U.S. and British literary works which she drew upon and adapted for each ESL 2, ESL 3, and reading class. However, because the class format was similar at all levels, students sometimes experienced a feeling of deja vu, contributing to an impression that ESL was an easy class. Eddie complained that,

> 10. ESL is kind of like re—I mean, every time is review. I mean, every year is exactly the same thing.

Students therefore tended to devalue ESL instruction compared to mainstream classes.

The latitude allowed ESL teachers also made it possible for different teachers to create very different instructional environments based on their own interpretations and beliefs about appropriate ESL curriculum and goals. Recall that there were two sometimes competing goals for ESL instruction. One goal was to equip newcomers with the background knowledge and skills commensurate with native speaker academic preparation for high school graduation and possibly higher education. The other goal, which is perhaps unique to ESL, was to make students more comfortable with the language of their new home, and to make them familiar with the language used in everyday life and interaction.

Carson emphasized the first goal, of preparing students to compete academically with native speakers of English. This is how she described her agenda:

> 11. My philosophy is that I want to prepare the students as soon as possible to get into the mainstream of the school. And since most of them are college bound, it tends to be more academic.

The teaching agenda of Malone, the new ESL teacher at Gateview in the final year of the study, contrasted considerably with that of Carson.

She focused on the other goal, of making everyday language more familiar to students. She believed that,

> 12. ESL should be a comfortable, safe environment for the students to explore and discover the language, and use it and experiment with it, so they can learn how to be comfortable with it, and not afraid of it.

and

> 13. In ESL they should have a lot of drama, and a lot of, uh, situations they can act out, so they can feel the language. And, my goal is that they can get some—soul into the—some, some, some soul of the language into them. And once it's in there, then they'll feel more comfortable with being in this country.

Malone emphasized activities such as role playing, information gap exercises using everyday vocabulary (e.g., giving directions), and expressive writing.

It turned out, however, that the Chinese American immigrants at Gateview High School did not particularly value instruction on the largely spoken, fluency-building content in ESL classes. Mei Li, for example, noted somewhat critically that

> 14. we have fun in this [ESL] class.

She evidently devalued ESL activities emphasizing everyday, communicative spoken language proficiency, and did not regard them as "real" learning. Anne complained,

> 15. . . . in this class [ESL], it's going very slow, and the language seems kind of like emergency things. If you don't learn it, you can't—you have to be stupid.

She felt that ESL included instruction in language that learners should pick up naturally in the course of living in an English-speaking society and therefore felt that it was unsuitable and unnecessary to give formal instruction in it.

Some of the content in Carson's class was devalued by students for this very reason. Because she construed this content as her main subject matter, Malone encountered more pronounced resistance. Taiwanese and Hong Kong immigrant students in her classes were often disruptive, bored, or unresponsive. It was not that Malone was a poor teacher. On the contrary, in both Carson's estimation and my own, she was quite skillful. She employed a variety of classroom activities which emphasized student participation and worked to elicit language through authentic communication and student experience in her classes. Many of the activities she employed, such as publishing students' poetry and personal reflections in a book at the end of the year, and using drama and role plays to facilitate spoken interaction, were exactly what one would find advocated in current ESL methods texts. However, her agenda did not match that of her students, and therefore increased their sense that ESL was stigmatized and remedial.

Explicit Language Instruction

Despite students' perception that classes were too easy, ESL nevertheless provided students with essential forms of language instruction not provided in the mainstream and activities which met students' particular linguistic needs. On students' written work, Carson provided explicit feedback which drew students' attention to language form in a way that has been found beneficial to learners (see Bialystok, 1981; Chaudron, 1988; Ellis, 1984; Schmidt, 1990; Sharwood-Smith, 1981; Swain, 1985; Wong Fillmore, 1985). She noted grammatical and mechanical errors such as incorrect use of articles, prepositions, verb tenses, and faulty spelling, and supplemented subject matter instruction when necessary with explicit grammar instruction targeting students' current weaknesses. Students learned to identify their own most frequent errors through proof reading exercises, as well as working with peers to identify and correct errors. Carson also incorporated language as a criterion in subject matter instruction. For example, worksheets and tests asked students to "Write five good sentences telling . . ." or "Use your own words and write about . . . ."

In contrast, out of all the mainstream classes at Gateview, explicit grammar instruction took place exclusively in English classes. Typically, activities focused on formalizing and labeling native speakers' intuitive understandings about English usage, rather than on articulating principles or rules that nonnative speakers could apply in lieu of these intuitions. For example, students in one English class learned to differentiate possessive nouns (e.g., brother's shoes, neighbor's dog), contractions (it's, they're), and possessive pronouns (ours, mine) so that they would be aware of correct apostrophe placement. No explanation was offered in the lesson as to how these items differed in grammatical function, and their use was explained only through a few sentence examples. Another English class exercise focused on errors in sentence run-ons and fragments, errors which native speakers have been found to make with far greater frequency than nonnative speakers (Fein, 1980; Raimes, 1979), and in yet another class, students labeled individual sentences in a textbook exercise as simple, compound, or complex. This exercise did not instruct nonnative writers on producing a compound or complex sentence but simply put labels on what native writers already recognize as grammatical options for building a sentence.

Mainstream teachers often seemed to be at a loss in dealing with the particular sorts of grammatical errors made by nonnative language writers, such as verb tense and preposition errors. They lacked the linguistics background necessary to explain to students why their language was wrong. As a result, schoolwork returned by teachers showed that they often chose to ignore errors entirely. For example, on one student's paper, the teacher left all errors unmarked, and simply wrote, "Syntax needs work—you lose clarity because of your expression." Another student reported that his teacher had told him, "Just don't write too long, in one sentence." These global comments would not be particularly useful to most writers, but they are particularly unproductive for nonnative language writers. More significant, however, is that such feedback indicates that many mainstream teachers were abdicating responsibility for instructing nonnative speakers on issues of language form.

Marking every error that nonnative writers make would, of course, be impractical as well as undesirable for students' self-esteem. However, when mainstream teachers at Gateview did mark errors, they did it inconsistently, selecting a random mixture of stylistic, grammatical, and word choice errors which they corrected or circled without comment. For example, one teacher corrected an error of number ("a property") in one line, while leaving a similar error in the next line ("different opinion") untouched:

16\. . . . every man has the right to own a property and it is up to the government to protect that right. However, they have different opinion about . . . .

Lacking a native speaker's intuitions about usage and learning primarily through vocabulary exercises and from academic sources, students made frequent errors in word choice and usage. Nevertheless, teachers tended to assume that students could alter such errors by ear. For example, one student wrote, "I wish you hadn't spared my birth" (i.e., I wish you had not allowed me to be born), and "the founding fathers were a discontented faction of the British regiment," (*regiment* meaning empire or citizenry). The student's teacher simply wrote question marks next to sentences such as these, or circled a word with the comment *Usage*, evidently not realizing how cryptic nonnative speakers would find such feedback.

As a result of learning English largely through mainstream instruction, students said that they edited their written work by ear, while at the same time noting that their intuition about what sounded right was faulty. When I asked Eddie how he edited his compositions—by using grammar rules or by asking how it sounds—he replied,

17. By sound, or how it sounds. But I need the rule. Mostly I just, [hear by sound], but not the rule. Sometime, like, the rule is kind of important, but I don't know much of the rule.

Feedback to learners regarding their pronunciation or spoken language errors was particularly problematic in a mainstream context. In a room filled with native speakers, teachers risked embarrassing learners who were extremely timid about speaking and who were subject to teasing or mockery from other students. Accordingly, mainstream teachers never discussed correct pronunciation, corrected student performance, or even rephrased what an ESL students said in class. However understandable or necessary, mainstream instruction nevertheless failed students in this respect.

In ESL, on the other hand, Carson was able to organize instruction so that students not only spoke frequently but were also evaluated on how they spoke. Learners were coached explicitly on speaking louder, more clearly, and maintaining eye contact while speaking; their pronunciation was corrected or rephrased when it impeded communication. ESL classes also included dictations to hone listening skills, which sometimes included homonyms or contrasting vowel sounds. Poetry was utilized to develop pronunciation and rhythm. Carson and the aides also audio- or videotaped some ESL class activities so that students could look at and evaluate their own language performance. Although students were not always particularly enthusiastic about hearing themselves on tape (an aide reported that they winced sometimes when they heard themselves speaking), such activities were useful in helping students towards a greater awareness of their articulation.

Socializing Functions of Schooling

The goals and organization of classroom instruction are the most obvious ways in which mainstream and ESL contexts differ in what they provide to L2 learners. There is another, less explicit but equally important function of schooling, however. Public schools, particularly high schools, are not simply vehicles for the transmission of academic knowledge. Most in the U.S. view them as having an important socializing function as well, as centers of teenage friendship networks and sources of extracurricular activities, and as sources of information about future schooling and career opportunities. The socializing function of schooling has been extremely important historically in assimilating new immigrants into U.S. society. In fact, accompanying the folk belief that immigrants should be mainstreamed as rapidly as possible is the implicit assumption that newcomers will inevitably be drawn into the social life of the school during this process. Thus, the folk belief dictates they will not only be motivated to learn

English but also will come to share the same social outlook as their U.S.-born peers. In terms of peer interaction, the social aspect of Gateview High School provided a number of potentially rich opportunities for L2 learners to learn language through interaction with their native-English-speaking peers. Simply because these interactional opportunities existed, however, does not necessarily mean that the English learners in this study had the ability or the inclination to take advantage of them.

Perhaps the single most salient aspect of observations of ESL students in mainstream classes was their reticence and lack of interaction with native-speaking peers. Students were intimidated by the sociolinguistic environment of mainstream classes where, they complained, "the kids talk too much." For example, in one instance, when a U.S.-born student tried to strike up a casual conversation with Eddie about one of the classes they shared, Eddie looked startled and even flinched a bit. Like most of the immigrant students, his response to the native speaker's conversational initiatives was shyly uttered monosyllables. Interactions between native and nonnative speakers often appeared awkward and uncomfortable, and they were unlikely to persist beyond two or three turns.

While U.S.-born high school students seized any teacher-sanctioned opportunity for classroom interaction such as group work, Asian American immigrant students showed a preference for working independently in silence at their desks. Even when they were asked to work with other students, they were likely to be reserved and uncommunicative, allowing or forcing other students to take over their role in the group. In one group work exercise, for example, a student from Hong Kong (Douglas) remained completely silent, even though he had a specific contribution that he was expected to make to the group, and even though he had the information he had prepared on a piece of paper sitting on his desk in front of him. Over the course of the discussion, a native speaker in his group began to grab the paper off his desk and read items from it to the rest of the group, while Douglas remained quiet and sometimes withdrawn from the work of the group. Learners were often observed retreating from group activities after a few minutes in order to work alone.

The lack of interaction between U.S.-born and immigrant students had several sources. Learners expressed frustration and embarrassment at their spoken English ability, which made even the most casual interactions with native speakers an effort. Furthermore, as Mei Li observed, immigrant students did not usually share native speakers' background in U.S. popular culture.

18. . . . it's very hard for a newcomer, especially, you know, you don't know English, not very well. And then you don't know about, the society very much, you know, they talk about singer or movie star. You couldn't know anything, right?

Thus, conversation was likely to be limited to the school-related concerns that they held in common. Racial and ethnic tensions between Asian American immigrants and the African American, European American, and Latino students at the school further complicated interactions.

Mainstream teachers at Gateview tended to play a very minor role in immigrant students' acclimatization to U.S. schooling. They seldom acknowledged the diversity of ethnic and cultural backgrounds found in their students, and many seemed to feel that it was not their business or responsibility. Furthermore, each teacher typically saw 150 to 175 students daily, leaving little time to pay attention to the backgrounds of students other than those who were having serious problems in their classes. It is not surprising, then, that a survey of mainstream teachers conducted by Carson one year showed that many of them did not even know who the English learners in their classes were, despite the fact that Carson circulated yearly memos with that information. Some teachers at Gateview incorporated ethnic perspectives into their curricula; for example, one English teacher did a unit annually on multicultural poetry featuring Asian American, African American, Latino, and Native American writers. Such activities, however, were the exception rather than the rule. For the most part, immigrant students' ethnic background and adjustment to U.S. society were likely to come to mainstream teachers' attention in only one of two ways. One, mainstream teachers were likely to talk with Carson about English learners who had just been placed in their classes or who were having difficulty. Two, students were likely to write about their background in journals or essay assignments exploring personal experience. In fact, both Anne and Gary learned that writing poignant essays about the immigrant experience was an excellent strategy for winning mainstream English teachers' attention and approval.

Outside of class, students seldom participated in Gateview-sponsored extracurricular activities. Students commented that their parents tended to place an emphasis on academic achievement to the exclusion of extracurricular and recreational activities that are typical for U.S.-born high school students. Comparing U.S.-born families' attitudes towards extracurricular activities to her own family's, Anne reflected,

> 19. They [U.S.-born families] have different values. They think if their kids are healthy, and they're having fun, it's more important than, you know, studying all day. And then, Chinese parents [are not] like that. Say if you don't study, it's the end of your life.

Gateview provided little in the way of role models for Chinese American students interested in extracurricular participation. There were never more than a handful of Asian American teachers at the school, for example, and none of them were from the local Chinese American community.

Although the school had a Chinese American Student Society, immigrant students reported that U.S.-born students of Chinese ancestry held a monopoly on its leadership.

Furthermore, immigrant students did not always find U.S.-born students' recreational pastimes particularly interesting or enjoyable. David, a student from Hong Kong, reported that he had engaged in the venerable U.S. teenage pastime of cruising with some U.S.-born Chinese acquaintances. He found it difficult to understand how anyone could enjoy pointlessly driving around with the radio blaring, calling his experience "frustrating" and "too loud." Most of these students' social activities and associations, such as extended family get-togethers or church socials, occurred within the Chinese American community. Venturing outside of the community was not a comfortable, natural, or easy process, and students who desired to do so generally had to work at it. Students perceived so real a distance between themselves and U.S.-born peers that they referred to it as the "wall" or the "barrier." Anne commented,

> 20. Because of the language barrier, they're [ESL students] often separated from the society, they don't feel they're a part of it by themselves. . . . That's why I think that friends that can speak your language are quite important while you are learning English in an English-speaking environment.

Thus, even though students at Gateview often spoke of ESL as though it were just another school subject, the program also played a facilitative role in the formation of peer networks and adjustment to U.S. school and society. In most of their school experience, students faced an overwhelmingly monolingual environment, where expressions of their native language and culture, if not actively discouraged, were certainly not encouraged. By opening up her classroom to ESL students at lunchtime and free periods, Carson provided students with a retreat from the English-medium mainstream, where students could be among others who valued and respected Chinese language and culture. In fact, Chinese-born students who had not been in ESL for years often came to spend their lunch hour among more recent immigrants. The importance of these associations to students was voiced by Anne, who wrote,

> 21. . . . having no friends speaking your language forces you to be cut off from your past.

The ESL program was also instrumental in the development of peer relationships among immigrants from various linguistic and cultural backgrounds at the school. Although the majority of the case study students' friends and acquaintances were ethnic Chinese, each of them had friends from other countries as well, including Japan (Anne), Korea (Mei Li), the Philippines (Eddie), and Iran (Gary). The importance of ESL to students' social life and interaction at school was evident in observations, where long hours of silence and impassivity in mainstream classes suddenly turned to noisy animation in ESL. ESL was where recent immigrants first formed their peer networks, and those associations endured long after students went into mainstream classes. As Anne put it,

20. I have been with my close friends for years. And . . . most of my close friends, I know them before I knew how to speak English well.

Only these students understood what the immigrant experience was like, knew what students had left behind, and what they were going through at school, at home, and in U.S. society.

The ESL program also provided students with assistance in adjusting to U.S. life and society which was unavailable in the mainstream. Carson and her aides went well beyond the usual realm of teacher responsibilities, providing students with assistance including lunch time tutoring, course placement changes, college application counseling, and coping with family problems. Over the course of the study, they dealt with everything from an illegal chain letter circulating among students, to a young man's failure to register for the draft, to student harassment in mainstream classes, to a swindling scheme in which a student gave $3,000 for luck charms to someone who told him he had a dangerous aura. Carson also worked, although with limited success, to get students involved in school activities such as the senior picnic or prom.

In sum, ESL performed a different and valuable role in students' education in terms of socializing students into U.S. society. It also facilitated the development of a supportive peer group while they made the transition. Although students were undoubtedly isolated socially from native speakers of English when they were in ESL, the formidable impediments that students perceived to social interaction with native speakers made them equally isolated in mainstream classes. In the complex social world of high school adolescents, one could not simply assume that proximity would ensure interaction. In this context, then, the special emphasis on spoken language skills and the social opportunities afforded by ESL classes took on extra significance, creating one place in the school where students regularly interacted in English, albeit with fellow nonnative speakers.

CONCLUSION

What were relative advantages and disadvantages of learning English in mainstream versus ESL classes at Gateview? The main advantage of mainstream classes was plentiful, authentic input that served a genuine communicative purpose—to transmit the content of school subject matter. The mainstream curriculum also provided students with rich and plentiful linguistic interactions through the written mode. However, the structure of mainstream instruction allowed few opportunities for extended interaction. Furthermore, L2 learners seldom received explicit feedback or instruction on the target language, leaving them to depend on somewhat faulty intuitions about language form. Finally, although the mainstream offered many social opportunities for language use and interaction with native speakers on the face of it, closer examination revealed that newcomers to U.S. society were seldom able to take advantage of such opportunities and perceived a barrier between themselves and U.S.-born peers.

ESL classes at Gateview, on the other hand, provided students with language instruction and experiences not commonly available in the mainstream. Instruction emphasized productive use of both spoken and written language. Students were given explicit feedback on their linguistic production and were given appropriate instruction on linguistic principles and rules which could help them monitor their own production. The ESL program also offered students readily available opportunities for counseling and peer social interaction. Nevertheless, ESL was not a panacea for these students. Students stigmatized ESL as easy and remedial because instruction not only addressed their need for academic language that would facilitate transition to mainstream instruction but also instructed them on the language used in everyday life and interaction. The fact is that there was no truly appropriate educational environment for L2 learners at Gateview. Rather, students' educational experience was a makeshift response of a system fundamentally geared towards the instruction of native speakers of the language.

This article depicts the experiences of ESL students within a single school. Nevertheless, Gateview High School's response to the challenge of educating its language minority students is probably not atypical. Many schools initially respond to this challenge by superimposing a layer of ESL or bilingual education on an unchanged mainstream curriculum. Increasingly, however, educators are going beyond this arrangement, acknowledging that special language instruction that is isolated from and unintegrated with the mainstream curriculum is not sufficient to develop the language proficiency required to succeed in academic contexts and that mainstream instruction must be more responsive to these students' needs. As van Lier (1988) has observed,

> We increasingly find classrooms in which only a few, or maybe just one, of the learners speak a native language which is different from the language of instruction. For these learners every classroom is an L2 classroom, and unless they are left to sink or swim, every teacher in such a classroom is at least a part-time L2 teacher. (p. 7)

By highlighting the strengths and weaknesses of each environment, detailed ethnographic examinations such as this one contribute to a long-term effort by educators in a variety of contexts to develop approaches that integrate language and content-area instruction.

How might mainstream instruction become more responsive to ESL student needs? At Gateview, perhaps the most pressing concern was to increase mainstream practitioners' and administrators' awareness of and sensitivity to learner needs. There were, in fact, many mainstream teachers with learners already in their classrooms who expressed interest in learning more about effective instructional approaches. These teachers' concerns could be built upon in developing a collaborative dialogue with ESL teachers and in-service professional development. At Gateview, discussion might center on issues such as how ESL instruction is organized and what ESL teachers do; how input can be adjusted for nonnative speakers; how instructional activities can be organized so that they foster student-teacher interaction and student-student interaction; how written assignments might be organized in order to foster extended synthesis and analysis; how appropriate, explicit, and consistent language instruction for ESL students might be incorporated into mainstream instruction; and what sorts of special help in counseling and social adjustment ESL students are likely to require.

How might ESL instruction become more responsive to the needs of students who will learn most of their English in mainstream classes? At Gateview, Carson prepared students to take on mainstream academic and linguistic demands by adopting a content-area approach to instruction. A survey of integrated language and content-area programs in U.S. schools now being completed at the Center for Applied Linguistics (1993) indicates that thousands of program across the country already have adopted similar approaches to linguistic minority student instruction. Such approaches necessitate a change in the disciplinary isolation of ESL educators from teachers in academic subject areas. The development of a curriculum that reflects both mainstream content objectives and the particular needs of ESL students requires that ESL teachers work closely with colleagues who have expertise in subject areas. At Gateview, some of the factors that Carson considered in implementing a content-ESL curriculum included the constantly changing population of ESL students and their diverse levels of English proficiency and academic preparedness; school curriculum guidelines for subject areas; opportunities in the content-area curriculum to interweave rich opportunities for language input and output in both speaking and writing; and students' need for preparation in the vocabulary and register of mainstream subject areas.

Although efforts such as these can enhance ESL and mainstream educators' understandings of their mutual roles, they nonetheless preserve a separation between them. More fundamental changes, leading to a systematic integration of content and language, might well serve students best. ESL and mainstream teachers might, for example, work collaboratively to develop a curriculum for language minority students that parallels the regular curriculum. In some programs, collaboration might lead to the formation of interdisciplinary teams of ESL and content-area teachers who instruct both learners and native speakers of English. Such a realignment of instructional roles is no doubt easier to accomplish at the elementary level than it is at the secondary level, where disciplinary boundaries are firmly established. At the same time, however, the increased linguistic and academic demands made of older learners make integrated content-area programs, if anything, more crucial for them. Collaboration between ESL and mainstream educators should also go beyond the classroom. The exclusion of language minority students' native languages and cultures in the mainstream at Gateview, and resulting barriers students perceived to interaction and to participation, confirm the notion that students need a schoolwide atmosphere in which diversity is respected and valued. Changes such as these often begin with individual educators who examine their own instructional context and include the means and the colleagues to initiate a collaborative dialogue. Although the form that these collaborations take will vary by context, they all begin with a comparative understanding of and sensitivity to the strengths and weaknesses of each of these contexts as language learning environments.

REFERENCES

Adamson, H. D. (1993). *Academic competence: Theory and classroom practice: Preparing ESL students for content courses*. White Plains, NY: Longman.

Applebee, A. N., with Auten, A. (1981). *Writing in the secondary school: English and the content areas*. Urbana, IL: National Council of Teachers of English.

Bialystok, E. (1981). The role of linguistic knowledge in second language use. *Studies in Second Language Acquisition, 4*, 31–45.

Boyer, E. L. (1983). *High school: A report on secondary education in America*. New York: Harper & Row.

Cantoni-Harvey, G. (1987). *Teaching ESL in the content areas*. Reading, MA: Addison-Wesley.

Caplan, R., & Keech, C. (1980). *Showing-writing: A training program to help students be specific*. Berkeley, CA: University of California, Bay Area Writing Project.

Cazden, C. B. (1988). *Classroom discourse*. Portsmouth, NH: Heinemann.

Center for Applied Linguistics. (1993). *A descriptive study of content-ESL practices. Final data analysis report*. Washington, DC: Center for Applied Linguistics.

Chamot, A. U., & O'Malley, J. M. (1987). The cognitive academic language learning approach: A bridge to the mainstream. *TESOL Quarterly, 21*, 227–249.

Chaudron, C. (1988). *Second language classrooms: Research on teaching and learning*. New York: Cambridge University Press.

Collier, V. (1987). Age and rate of acquisition of second language for academic purposes. *TESOL Quarterly, 21*, 617–641.

Crandall, J. (1987). *ESL through content-area instruction: Mathematics, science, and social studies.* New York: Prentice Hall.

Crandall, J. (1993). Current directions in curriculum development and materials preparation for culturally and linguistically diverse children. In G. R. Tucker (Ed.), *Policy and practice in the education of culturally and linguistically diverse students: View from language educators* (pp. 13–15). Alexandria, VA: TESOL.

Cummins, J. (1982). The role of primary language development in promoting educational success for language minority students. In California State Department of Education, Office of Bilingual Bicultural Education, (Ed.), *Schooling and language minority students: A theoretical framework* (pp. 3–49). Los Angeles: California State University; Evaluation, Dissemination, and Assessment Center.

Edelsky, C. (1986). *Writing in a bilingual program: Había una vez.* Norwood, NJ: Ablex.

Ellis, R. (1984). *Classroom second language development.* Oxford: Pergamon Press.

Farr, M., & Daniels, H. (1986). *Language diversity and writing instruction.* New York: ERIC Clearinghouse on Urban Education.

Fein, D. M. (1980). *A comparison of English and ESL compositions.* Unpublished master's thesis, University of California, Los Angeles.

Freeman, D. (1993). Preparing tomorrow's teachers for culturally and linguistically diverse children. In G. R. Tucker (Ed.), *Policy and practice in the education of culturally and linguistically diverse students: View from language educators* (pp. 13–15). Alexandria, VA: TESOL.

Green, J. L., & Wallat, C. (Eds.). (1981). *Ethnography and language in educational settings.* Norwood, NJ: Ablex.

Harklau, L. (in press a). "Jumping tracks": How language minority students negotiate evaluations of ability. *Anthropology and Education Quarterly.*

Harklau, L. (in press b). Tracking and linguistic minority students: Consequences of ability grouping for second language learners. *Linguistics and Education.*

Hatch, E. M. (1983). *Psycholinguistics: A second language perspective.* Rowley, MA: Newbury House.

Hamayan, E. V., & Perlman, R. (1990). *Helping language minority students after they exit from bilingual/ESL programs. A handbook for teachers.* National Clearinghouse for Bilingual Education. (ERIC Document Reproduction Service No. ED 321 583)

Krashen, S. (1981). *Second language acquisition and second language learning.* Oxford: Pergamon Press.

Lambert, W. E. (1984). An overview of issues in bilingual education. In California State Department of Education, Office of Bilingual Bicultural Education (Ed.), *Studies in immersion education: A collection for United States educators* (pp. 8–30). Sacramento, CA: California State Department of Education.

Long, M. H. (1989). Instructed interlanguage development. In L. Beebe (Ed.), *Issues in second language acquisition: Multiple perspectives* (pp. 115–141). Rowley, MA: Newbury House.

Mehan, H. (1979). *Learning lessons.* Cambridge, MA: Harvard University Press.

Mohan, B. (1986). *Language and content.* Reading, MA: Addison-Wesley.

Mitchell, R. (1985). Process research in second-language classrooms. *Language Teaching, 18*, 330–352.

Nippold, M. A. (1988). The literate lexicon. In M. A. Nippold (Ed.), *Later language development: Ages nine through nineteen* (pp. 29–48). Boston: College-Hill Press.

O'Malley, J. M., & Waggoner, D. (1984, June). Public school teacher preparation and the teaching of ESL. *TESOL Newsletter*, pp. 1, 18–22.

Oakes, J. (1985). *Keeping track: How schools structure inequality.* New Haven: Yale University Press.

Penfield, J. (1987). ESL: The regular classroom teacher's perspective. *TESOL Quarterly, 21*, 21–39.

Raimes, A. (1979). *Problems and teaching strategies in ESL composition (If Johnny has problems, what about Juan, Jean, and Ywe-Han?)*. Washington, DC: Center for Applied Linguistics.

Richard-Amato, P. A., & Snow, M. A. (Eds.). (1992). *The Multicultural classroom: Readings for content-area teachers*. New York: Longman.

Riddlemoser, N. (1987). *Working with limited-English-proficient students in the regular classroom. ERIC Q & A*. ERIC Clearinghouse on Languages and Linguistics. (ERIC Document Reproduction Service No. ED 289 368)

Rigg, P., & Allen, V. G. (Ed.). (1989). *When they don't all speak English: Integrating the ESL student into the regular classroom*. Urbana, IL: National Council of Teachers of English.

Sato, C. (1982). Ethnic styles in classroom discourse. In M. Hines & W. Rutherford (Eds.), *On TESOL '81* (pp. 326–327). Washington, DC: Teachers of English to Speakers of Other Languages.

Saville-Troike, M. (1984). What *really* matters in second language learning for academic achievement? *TESOL Quarterly, 18*, 199–219.

Scarcella, R. (1990). *Teaching language minority students in the multicultural classroom*. Englewood Cliffs, NJ: Regents/Prentice Hall.

Schinke-Llano, L. (1983). Foreigner talk in content classrooms. In H. W. Seliger & M. H. Long (Eds.), *Classroom-oriented research in second language acquisition* (pp. 146–165). Rowley, MA: Newbury House.

Schmidt, R. (1990). The role of consciousness in language learning. *Applied Linguistics, 11*, 129–158.

Sharwood-Smith, M. (1981). Consciousness-raising and the second language learner. *Applied Linguistics, 2*, 159–168.

Short, D. J. (1991). *How to integrate language and content instruction: A training manual*. Washington, DC: Center for Applied Linguistics. (ERIC Document Reproduction Service No. ED 359 780)

Swain, M. (1985). Communicative competence: Some roles of comprehensible input and comprehensible output in its development. In S. M. Gass & C. G. Madden (Eds.), *Input in second language acquisition* (pp. 235–253). Rowley, MA: Newbury House.

Tikunoff, W. J. (1985). *Applying significant bilingual instructional features in the classroom. Part C Bilingual Education Research Series*. National Clearinghouse for Bilingual Education. (ERIC Document Reproduction Service No. ED 338 108)

van Lier, L. (1988). *The classroom and the language learner: Ethnography and second-language classroom research*. New York: Longman.

Widdowson, H. G. (1978). *Teaching language as communication*. Oxford: Oxford University Press.

Wong Fillmore, L. (1985). When does teacher talk work as input? In S. M. Gass & C. G. Madden (Eds.), *Input in second language acquisition* (pp. 17–50). Rowley, MA: Newbury House.

Wong Fillmore, L. (1989). Teaching English through content: Instructional reform in programs for language minority students. In J. Esling (Ed.), *Multicultural education and policy: ESL in the 1990's* (pp. 125–143). Toronto, Canada: OISE Press.

Wong Fillmore, L., with Valadez, C. (1986). Teaching bilingual learners. In M. Wittrock (Eds.), *Handbook of research on teaching* (pp. 648–685). New York: Macmillan.

Chapter 8

Remediation as Social Construct: Perspectives from an Analysis of Classroom Discourse

Glynda Hull
Mike Rose
Kay Losey Fraser
Marisa Castellano

In this paper, we examine remediation as a social construct, as the product of perceptions and beliefs about literacy and learning, and we illustrate some ways in which inaccurate and limiting notions of learners as being somehow cognitively defective and in need of "remedy" can be created and played out in the classroom. We will look closely at one student in one lesson and detail the interactional processes that contribute to her being defined as remedial—this specific case, however, is also representative of common kinds of classroom practices and widespread cultural assumptions, ones we've seen at work in our other studies (Hull and Rose, "Rethinking"). In order to better understand these cultural assumptions and the ways they can affect classroom practices, we will attempt to combine an empirical, fine-grained analysis of classroom discourse with broader historical and cultural analyses. We want to place a teacher's instructional and evaluative language in the contexts that we believe influence it, that contribute to the practice of defining students as remedial.

We write this paper believing that, however great the distance our profession has come in understanding the students and the writing we call "remedial," we have not yet come far enough in critically examining our assumptions about our students' abilities—assumptions which both shape the organization of remedial programs and orient daily life in remedial classrooms. Engaging in such an examination is not so easy, perhaps because as teachers of remedial writing, we have good intentions: we look forward to our students' growth and development as writers; we want to teach our students to be literate in ways sanctioned by the academy and the community beyond. And, knowing our intentions, we can forget to examine our assumptions about remediation—assumptions that are deeply held and so ingrained as to be tacit, that can, without much conscious choice on our part, drive the way we structure a course and circumscribe the learning that students will do in it. Our hope, then, is that this paper will be an occasion to reflect on the ways we, as teachers, can inadvertently participate in the social construction of attitudes and beliefs about remediation which may limit the learning that takes place in our classrooms, and to consider some ways in which we can begin to examine these basic assumptions, building from a different ground our notions about our students' abilities and the nature of literacy learning.

ANALYZING CLASSROOM DISCOURSE

The centerpiece of our discussion—a fifty-minute classroom lesson on writing conducted in a remedial classroom at an urban college[1]—was one of several that we videotaped across a semester. As regular observers in the class, we also collected field notes and records of reading and writing assignments and homework and essays. We conducted interviews with students and teachers as well, sometimes asking them to comment on the videotapes we had recently made of classroom lessons. Outside of class, we served as tutors and thereby were able to audiotape our conferences with students and to elicit additional writing and reading performances.

In our studies, we have worked only with teachers rated highly by their departments and students. The teacher in this study was June, a recent and respected graduate of a long-standing composition program and a candidate for an advanced degree in literature. Our work with June confirmed her commitment to teaching. She spent a great deal of time responding to papers at home and meeting with students in conferences, and she was interested in discussing composition research and finding ways to apply it in her classroom. In fact, she volunteered to participate in our study because she saw it as an occasion to be reflective about her own teaching and to improve instruction for students in remedial classes.

The composition program in which June had studied was also a part of the college and included reading on and discussion of new composition theory and practice. The size of the class she taught was reasonable (approximately 15 students), though June taught three sections requiring two different preparations while completing graduate school. A remedial writing course and a complementary reading course were required for entering students depending on their scores on entrance tests. In the writing course, students kept a journal, made summaries of short reading passages, and wrote essays on assignments common to the program. Most of these assignments asked students to read short passages as background material and to use them as the basis for writing an essay on a specified topic related to the reading. One of these assignments gave rise to the classroom talk that we will analyze.

In this lesson, which took place the fourth week of the semester, June held a discussion to prepare students to write an essay on music videos and their appropriateness for viewers. The essay assignment consisted of a set of brief readings: a magazine article describing recently released and acclaimed rock videos; an editorial from a local newspaper on censorship; a review of the music video, *Thriller*; a list of recent music videos with brief descriptions. The assignment then asked students to take part in current debates about the regulation of music videos, developing a position on the issue perhaps by arguing that videos ought to be banned from television, or that there should be no censorship, or that some kind of rating system should be developed. The assignment emphasized that students should justify their arguments and make clear their reasoning.

In the class, June introduced the topic of music videos and, in preparation for the writing assignment, led a class discussion on accessibility and censorship issues. The discussion was, then, a kind of "pre-writing" activity, an attempt, June told us, to help students access their own knowledge and experiences and to draw upon them when writing an academic essay. "Many of these students don't have a lot to bring with them in terms of academic experience," she explained, "but they do have some life experiences to bring with them." What we want to do in our analysis of this lesson is to look closely at the conversation June had with her class, characterizing it in terms of its interactional patterns and the kinds of classroom discourse such patterns allow, and to consider the relationship between one student's pattern of talk and the teacher's perception of her cognitive abilities.

Let us explain why we have chosen to examine talk as a way to study this writing class. In *The Social Construction of Literacy*, Jenny Cook-Gumperz reminds us that literacy learning consists of more than the acquisition of cognitive skills; it also involves the "social process of demonstrating knowledgeability" (3). In other words, competence in classrooms means interactional competence as well as competence with written language: knowing when and how and with whom to speak and act in order to create and display knowledge. In the same way, then, that there are cultural "rules" for how to have conversations in particular contexts—the kinds of replies that are appropriate, the points at which it is acceptable to interrupt, the ways one might indicate attentiveness and interest—so there are rules for the talk that goes on in classrooms, rules students will need to know, at least tacitly.[2] From a significant amount of research on Western schooling, it is clear that a great deal of classroom talk is led by the teacher, and that a particular kind of participant structure—or way of arranging verbal interaction (Philips)—dominates classroom conversations.

This structure consists of a tripartite series of turns in which a teacher *initiates*, a student *replies*, and the teacher *evaluates* the student's response—the IRE sequence (Cazden; Mehan, *Learning*; Sinclair and Coulthard).[3] In the initiation, or opening turn, the teacher can inform, direct, or ask students for information. The student's reply to this initiation can be non-verbal, such as raising a hand or carrying out an action, or it can be a verbal response. In the evaluation turn, the teacher comments on the student's reply.

Here is an example of an IRE sequence in which June asks about music videos that students have seen lately. We first provide a plain transcript of this brief stretch of talk between teacher and students, and then we follow it with a second transcript (Figure 8.1) in which we attempt to capture some of the elements of speech that are lost when talk is written down—pauses, stress, and tempo, for instance—elements which suggest a speaker's communicative intentions. Such features, known as contextualization cues (Gumperz, "Contextualization," *Discourse*), signal how an utterance is to be understood, including how it relates to what precedes or follows. According to this system, speakers' turns are segmented into idea or information units[4] on the basis of both semantics and intonation (rising or falling contours). Other features are also represented: lexical prosody, such as vowel elongation or fluctuation, and overlapping speech, where more than one person talks at a time. We think this method enhances the understanding of classroom interaction, and we will incorporate it into our discussion accordingly.[5]

Transcript #1

Initiation	*Reply*	*Evaluation*
1. Teacher: How 'bout *I Want Your Sex*, Matt? What would [you rate] that?		
	2. Matt: R.	
		3. Teacher: R. All right. The title of it might indicate right off the bat that it should be an R rated video. Okay.
4. Teacher: How 'bout some of the rest of you?		
	5. Maria: I, I, just seen *Like A Prayer*.	
		6. Teacher: Okay, *Like a Prayer*, all right, good.
7. Teacher: What, do you know what the rating would be on that one?		

Here is the same segment of classroom talk, this time with contextualization cues marked. The most prominent symbols in this segment are slash marks (/ and //), which signal a drop in voice tone and the end of a speaker's turn; double equal signs (= =), which indicate overlap (that more than one person is speaking at once—e.g., lines g, h, and i in Figure 8.1) or latching (that they are speaking in rapid succession—e.g., lines a and b in Figure 8.1); asterisks (*), which label words that speakers are stressing; and indications of volume, pitch, and tempo in brackets—e.g., [p] means quieter speech, [f] means louder speech, [hi] means high-pitched speech.

---

a Teacher: how about i want your sex matt what would you rate that?
b Matt: = =r/
c Teacher: r// alright//
d the *title of it might-
e Maria: = =[laughs]= =
f Teacher: = =indicate right
off the bat that it should be . . an r rated video, okay/
g how 'bout some of the rest= =of you?
h Unidentified Speaker: = =(all last= =summer)
i Maria: = ={[f] uh
uh} . . i i just seen like a pray {[laugh]er}/
j Teacher: = = okay like *a prayer alright, {[hi] *good}/
k what-, do you know what the rating would be {[p] on that one}?

Selected Contextualization Cues

Symbol	Significance
//	turn-final falling intonation
/	slight falling intonation suggesting more to come
. .	pauses of less than .5 seconds
<2>	pauses timed precisely (= 2 second pause)
= =	overlapping or latching speech
m~	fluctuating intonation
*	accent, normal prominence
CAPS	accent, extra prominence
( )	unintelligible speech
(xxx)	unclear word, each "x" = one syllable
[ ]	non-lexical phenomena which interrupts the lexical stretch
{[ ]}	non-lexical phenomena which overlays the lexical stretch, such as:
	[p] quieter speech
	[f] louder speech
	[hi] high pitch
	[lo] low pitch
	[ac] accelerated speech

FIG. 8.1. Transcript with Contextualization Cues Marked

In this exchange, we see a series of initiations in the form of teacher questions, student replies, and teacher evaluations of those replies—these evaluations often signalled by the word "okay." Throughout the semester, we noticed that "okay" was June's most frequent evaluation token—whether or not a student's response was acceptable—but early on we learned to differentiate her positive "okays" from negative ones by means of intonation patterns. Here the first "okay" was pronounced with a slight falling intonation—a signal that the student's response had been appropriate. (Contrast this positive or at least neutral intonation pattern with the negative one for "okay" found below in line e of Figure 8.2.) Also apparent from Figure 8.1, but not from Transcript 1, is that there is a fair amount of simultaneous talk going on. Note that Maria overlaps her teacher's talk with a laugh in line e and then again in line i, but more loudly the second time, as she attempts to gain the floor. Paying attention to these kinds of contextualization cues helped us more confidently understand and interpret the dynamics of talk and interaction that characterized this particular lesson.

The majority of the conversational turns which occurred in this lesson—some 52 percent—followed the IRE pattern. There were portions of the class time, however, which did not strictly fit this pattern—such as teacher lectures, student initiations, and teacher responses to student initiations. One particularly salient participant structure we call the "mini-lecture." Teacher evaluations often led into these pieces of extended discourse, which served either to elaborate on information already provided or discussed, or to introduce new material. A noticeable feature of mini-lectures was that during them June did not acknowledge interruptions or entertain questions. Students who attempted to interrupt were not given the floor. Of the six attempts to interrupt her lectures during this particular class, June gave only one of these any attention, and that one just enough to work the topic into the mini-lecture.

The predominance of IRE sequences and mini-lectures suggests a discourse that is very much teacher-led. And, in fact, of all the exchanges that occurred during this lesson, 83 percent were directed by June. Two of the twelve students in the class, Andrea and Maria, made the majority of student initiations and responses—19 percent and 16 percent respectively—and also the majority of student responses to teacher initiations—24 percent and 20.5 percent. For the most part, the rest of the class sat quietly—at times they whispered or laughed to each other—but they answered few of June's questions, and they asked fewer questions still. In other words, they adhered to the participant structures that normally characterized interaction in this classroom.

Except, that is, for Maria. We now want to look closely at the talk of one student whose discourse patterns stood out, who did not always abide by the tacit rules that governed talk in this classroom. In fact, she often and obviously pressed at the boundaries of what was permissible conversationally. Of Spanish and Italian descent, Maria was born in El Salvador and moved to the United States with her parents when she was almost two years old. Although all her schooling had taken place in the United States, her first language was Spanish, and through a bilingual program in elementary school she had learned to read and write Spanish before she learned English. Maria told us that her parents don't speak English very well today, although they have been in the United States since 1971, and Spanish continues to be the language of their home, except between Maria and her thirteen-year-old sister.

What Maria told us about her experiences in school prior to college suggests that there she had been a successful student, particularly in English and foreign language classes. She claimed to enjoy writing and said that she had written a romance novel in high school. Her worst subject in high school, she reported, was math, in which she improved from a C to a B (suggesting that she was at least a B student in her other subjects). Maria told us that she had traveled with her high-school speech team and had won a $1000 scholarship to college. As a college freshman, she still enjoyed writing, especially short stories, and she also kept a journal regularly, writing in it about once a week.

Maria sat in the front row of her remedial writing class. She attended every class and turned in all of her homework on time. She also chose to get tutoring when it was offered. In many respects, then—her scholastic history, her engagement in the course, her goals for the future—she seemed very much the dutiful student, dedicated to schooling and willing to work hard. But as we will illustrate with examples of talk from this lesson, her rules for classroom discourse did not map well onto the norm for this class, particularly her strategies for gaining the floor. And this mismatch, this small but noticeable discontinuity, was to work to her disadvantage.

The difficulty was with turn-taking. In ordinary conversation, the potential exists for the speaker to change after every speaker's turn. That is, once a person has concluded her turn, unless she designates the next speaker, then anyone can take a turn (Sacks, Schegloff, and Jefferson). There are differences, of course, in conversational style: "high involvement" speakers tend to take more turns, talk more, and overlap their speech more than other speakers (Tannen). Generally, though, in an ordinary conversation, a speaker has the opportunity to talk after the current speaker finishes. But this state of affairs does not, as we illustrated above, exist in certain kinds of classroom conversations. When a teacher initiates, he takes the floor, his students reply, and then the teacher takes the floor back as he evaluates the reply. This IRE structure, this set of interactions, constitutes an integral unit. The appropriate time for students to gain access to the floor is after an IRE sequence. It's not appropriate in an IRE classroom for students to speak after any speaker's turn except the teacher's initiation, and certainly not during a turn. But this is what Maria does.

Maria not only speaks before an IRE sequence has been completed, interjecting between an initiation and a directed response, she also, on occasion, interrupts during a mini-lecture—an extended piece of teacher discourse which is supposedly non-interruptable—with an "Ohhh!" or "Huh Hmmm!" loud enough to be picked up by the audio recorder. Here is an example of such an interruption. Following a lively discussion of a potential rating system for music videos, June begins an explanation of the writing assignment:

Transcript #2

1. Teacher: Yeah, all right. Very frightening, traumatic, (kind of) blood and gore. [Laughter from the class.] Okay, yeah. All right, yeah. And they, yeah, there's a problem with the accessibility of music videos on television right now, and that's really what we're going to be dealing with in this essay, is the issue of music videos that is being considered right now, and you're going to have a chance to . . .
2. Maria: Oh.
3. Teacher: . . . try to convince your audience of your position. Okay?

When we analyzed this excerpt—in the manner of Figure 8.1—it was clear that June/the teacher intends this explanation of a new writing assignment to be non-interruptable: she completes the sentence she had begun as if Maria had not spoken. While Maria's "Oh" is not a lengthy interruption, it is a loud one, and we can also note that she is the only student to interrupt mini-lectures during this lesson.

In addition to interrupting the IRE sequence and mini-lectures inappropriately, Maria sometimes pursued topics for a longer time than June seemed to prefer, continuing to initiate statements about a topic after June was ready to move on. In fact, in the example above, when Maria interrupts the beginning of the mini-lecture with her "Oh," she seems to do so because she is still pursuing a topic that she had initiated moments earlier. Here is the larger context for that interruption, several turns both preceding and following it:

Transcript #3

1. Teacher: Any other music videos that you feel should have been rated in some way or another? [6 second pause]
2. Maria: How about those scary ones like, um, *Thriller*?
3. Teacher: Okay. All right. How could-, well, how could you rate those?
4. Maria: Uh, R. But they're, the, the, they're very, very—I don't like them 'cause they're very scary.
5. Teacher: Okay.
6. Andrea: That's why we should create another rating between R and X, 'cause it would-

7. Maria: No, because it's not only about, um, sex, about that, but it's those, those, those, those traumatic-

8. Teacher: Okay.

9. Maria: You hear about blood and-[Laugh]

10. Teacher: Yeah, all right. Very frightening, traumatic, (kind of blood and gore.
[Laughter from the class.]
Okay, yeah. All right, yeah.
And they, yeah, there's a problem with the accessibility of music videos on television right now, and that's really what we're going to be dealing with in this essay, is the issue of music videos that is being considered right now, and you're going to have a chance to . . .

11. Maria: Oh.

12. Teacher: . . . try to convince your audience of your position. Okay?

13. Maria: When I saw the first part of *Thriller* and that, that part when the first part about that corpse?

14. Teacher: Mmhmm.

15. Maria: And, and, he jumped up with blood and that was, I, I haven't seen a scene like that in a video before. (It was) scary. Very scary!

[Laughter]

16. Teacher: Yeah, I can tell just from the publicity which videos I'm gonna avoid just because of those kinds of scenes. So, okay. Wh-, tell me a little about whether you think music videos that you have seen should be allowed on TV. What kinds of things . . um . . should determine whether they can be on TV?

17. Andrea: Language.

18. Teacher: Okay, language . . .

The contextualization cues at the opening of the transcript suggest that something may be amiss conversationally right from the start. Note the overlap between June's and Maria's speech in lines b, c, and d, and the fluctuating intonation of June's "okay" and "all right" in line e, the intonation indicating that, in this teacher's repertoire, these are not affirmative responses.

---

a Teacher: {[f] any other music videos that you felt should . . be rated, that should have been rated in some way or another?}
<6>

b Maria: = =how about= =those scary ones-

c Teacher: = =(xxx)= =

d Maria: = =like um, thriller?

e Teacher: ok~ay, all r~ight/ {[hi] how could, well how could you rate those?}

FIG. 8.2. Section of Transcript with Contextualization Cues Marked

We can see from the extended portion of classroom talk in Transcript 3 that Maria interrupts the mini-lecture apparently to continue talking about a topic that she had brought up just moments earlier—the frightening violence in the video *Thriller*—but that June had discouraged. In fact, Maria pursues this topic quite persistently: she ignores June's question in turn 3 about how such movies are rated to comment further on their frightfulness in turn 4; she heads off Andrea's comment about a new rating proposal in turn 6 to argue for the salience of trauma over sex in turn 7; and she interrupts June's mini-lecture (which starts in line 10) to describe a particularly scary incident from *Thriller* in turn 13. We can see June responding to Maria's initiations with brief or disapproving responses (see turn 3/line e; see also turn 16) and finally taking hold of the discourse once again.

We think June's response in this instance is understandable: Maria appears to be reintroducing a topic that had been completed; June had shifted from discussion of specific videos to the essay question of whether or not music videos should be regulated. It is interesting to note, though, that the question June asks to bring the discourse round again to the essay topic—what kinds of things should determine whether a video could be aired on television?—was answered implicitly by Maria in her discussion of the violence in *Thriller*, but her contribution wasn't explicitly acknowledged.

In fact, June didn't appear to value what seemed to us appropriate responses from Maria, even when those responses did fit the pattern of classroom talk. Toward the end of Transcript 3 (turn 16), June asked what might determine how a movie video would be rated. In response to her question, students suggested "language," "sex," and "violence," and there were brief discussions of each in turn. June then asked the question again, for the fourth time, and when there was no response for several seconds, she explained that nudity might be another factor and explained how it's not to be confused with sexual scenes. Then, again, she asks the "what else" question; there's a long pause, and Maria replies:

Transcript #4

1. Teacher: Okay, can you think of anything else that might, they might consider when they're trying to decide how to rate a music video? (pause)
2. Maria: Um, is it like . .( ). . something to do with somebody that criticizes somebody else, like political issues, something like that?
3. Teacher: Um, I don't know, um, that-
4. Maria: Seems like, um yeah-
5. Teacher: That's not a widely recognized one but it might be one that is sort of subtle that's-

6. Maria: Yeah. Like talking about like if you ( ) somebody, like race or something like that, ( ) video ( ) something like that.
7. Teacher: Um, I don't know. Um, who would that kind of a video appeal to?
8. Maria: Um, I don't know, um.
9. Teacher: Would that appeal to children?
10. Matt: What music video is this?
11. Teacher: If, a music video about some kind of a political issue.
12. Maria: Yeah.
13. Matt: Oh, you mean like *Graceland* or something by U2?
14. Teacher: Yeah, something like that. Now is that the kind of video that would really appeal to children?
15. Andrea: No.
16. Teacher: Or who would that appeal to?

In the following analysis of turns 1–7, notice that after line a, there is a long pause—one that perhaps gives Maria and the rest of the class enough time to provide thoughtful responses. It's also noteworthy that in line b we see some indications—from her pauses, soft voice, and tentative questions—that Maria is struggling to articulate a partly-formed idea. Notice, though, that in line f Maria takes on steam as she thinks of race as a possible example and speeds up her talk.

---

a Teacher: . . . okay, {[hi] can you think of anything else that might}-, they might consider when they're trying to decide how to rate a music video? <5>
b Maria: Uhhm, is it like <4> {[p] ( ) uh <3> something to do with . . somebody that criticizes somebody else}, like . . political issues? something like that?
c Teacher: uh [sigh] <2.5> i don't know/ um= =that-
d Maria: = =seems like um, yeah-
e Teacher: = ={[f] that's not a widely recog}nized one but . . it might be one that is sort of subtle that's-
f Maria: y~eah like {[ac] [p] talking about like if you ( ) somebody, like race or something like that ( ) video ( ) something like that}
g Teacher {[p] mm hmm/} uhhm, {[hi] i don't know}/
h um, WHO would that kind of video appeal to?

FIG. 8.3. Section of Transcript with Contextualization Cues Marked

In this exchange, it seems to us that Maria brings up a new way to think about what influences ratings: a video with political overtones certainly could arouse concern or anger. Maria's comment, then, could have been an occasion for a discussion of censorship. For such a discussion to happen, however, June would need to provide some assistance, some verbal scaffolding, for Maria is struggling to express a partly formed idea about the importance of political contexts for music videos. But June does not assist this potential contribution; in fact, she disallows Maria's answer by undercutting it. (Notice June's use of "I don't know" in the evaluation slot in contrast to her usual, more ostensibly neutral, "Okay.") June shifts the discussion away from political censorship and toward the issue of age by asking an unexpected question: "Who would that kind of a video appeal to?" (In line h this shift is signaled by June's intonation, a specific use of a contextualization cue that we observed at other places in the lesson.) This question departs from the pattern she had earlier established—the repeated question of "what else" might determine how a video gets rated—and it has a silencing effect on Maria. The conversation gets short-circuited, and Maria's moment for contributing a piece of knowledge is lost, and so is an opportunity for the class to consider an important issue.

Soon after the lesson, June viewed the videotape we had made of it, and she commented on Maria's classroom talk:

> Maria is becoming to me the Queen of the Non Sequirurs. You know, she really is just not quite. . . . That's, that's why I'm sort of amazed at times at, at her writing level, which is not really too bad. . . . Because her thinking level seems to be so scattered that I would expect that her writing would be a lot more disorganized and disjointed.

June was amazed at the level of Maria's writing, which was "not really too bad," given the scattered cognition she surmised from Maria's oral performance in class. In fact, June actually awarded Maria's written logic and organization with steadily improving grades and positive comments on her essays: "I like the way you made distinctions between facts and opinions." "You are very thorough and your thinking about the advice is very clear and logical." But, in spite of such evidence, June seemed to be greatly influenced in her assessment of Maria's abilities by her talk in the classroom, using "talking" as a barometer for "thinking," labeling Maria the "Queen of the Non Sequiturs." At the end of the semester, when summing up her evaluations of students, June confided that Maria "was a sweet girl, but she drove me crazy." She accounted for the improvement Maria had made in her writing by surmising that she had probably gotten help from her parents. (This was unlikely, however, since Maria's parents spoke little English.) June then made a final comment about her thinking: "Maria has thinking continuity problems." She predicted Maria wouldn't pass the next writing class the first time through "because it requires coherent thinking."

We think we can outline the process by which June constructed her view of Maria. When we looked over our field notes and our videotapes, there was abundant evidence that Maria did violate some of this classroom's rules for talk. Over the course of the semester, Maria made twenty-eight statements that were recorded in our fieldnotes. Ten of these were responses that fit the IRE question/answer structure; the remaining eighteen were initiations in the form of questions, and of these questions, six were procedural—how long does our essay have to be? must we type or can we write by hand? what page did you say the exercises are on?—a type of question that may be bothersome, particularly if its timing is a little off and it occurs after the conversation has turned to other matters. And, in fact, June did notice Maria's questioning patterns, and commented at the end of the semester that Maria asked a lot of questions in class but didn't answer many that June had posed to her.

Maria did, then, seem to initiate more than she responded—asking questions, taking the floor, diverting the course of classroom talk—and hers was not exactly the expected posture for a student in an IRE classroom. There were times when her interjections did suggest that she was not paying attention or was involved in something else related to the class, like reading over the assignment sheet while June was talking. This, we would argue, led to June's construction of Maria as the "Queen of the Non Sequiturs," the student who could be trusted to make a comment that was inappropriate or off-target. Given the way Maria's conversational habits stood out, it seems likely that June's view of Maria as an inappropriate talker would eventually become salient enough to affect her perception of Maria even when she interjects in a way that is appropriate. Join this perception of a particular student with this teacher's strong predilection for an IRE participant structure, and you won't be surprised that Maria's chances to be heard would be undercut. The cycle continues as Maria's interactional patterns in class become not just an annoying conversational style, but the barometer by which to measure her cognitive abilities. Her bothersome conversational habits become evidence of a thinking problem—evidence that is so salient that it goes unqualified even in the face of counter-evidence that Maria, in fact, wrote rather well.

But though we can explain at least some of the steps in the construction of Maria as a scattered thinker, we are left with a troubling question: how is it that annoying conversational style can become a measure of intellectual ability? What we have seen here is a relatively minor disjunction between teacher expectation and student behavior, an irritating mismatch of styles that, perhaps, chafes at a teacher's sense of authority. But given that irritations with students can lead to a range of outcomes, what made June's judgment of cognitive deficiency possible? To answer this question, we believe we need to consider the broader educational and cultural context in which this teacher lives—the received language and frames of mind she works within. Put another way, we need to consider the ways our schools have historically judged mental ability from performance that is somehow problematic and the sanctioned paths of inference from behavior to cognition that emerge from such judgments. We will begin by describing what we think of as this larger context for remedial writing instruction with a brief history of "low achievers" in American education.

THE CULTURAL CONTEXT OF SCHOOL FAILURE

There is a long, troubling history in American education of perceiving and treating low-achieving children as if they were lesser in character and fundamental ability. Larry Cuban and David Tyack, citing work by Stanley Zehm, trace this history by examining the labels that have been attached to students who are low-achievers, for "contained in a name, either explicitly or implicitly, is both an explanation and a prescription" (4). In the first half of the nineteenth century the poor performer was a "dunce," "shirker," "loafer," "reprobate," or "wrong-doer" who was "stupid," "vicious," "depraved," "wayward," or "incorrigible." Some of these labels imply that students lacked intelligence, but the majority suggest a flawed character. Such assessments, note Cuban and Tyack, reveal "a set of religious and moral convictions that placed responsibility for behavior and achievement in the sovereign individual" (4). During the last half of the nineteenth century, the labels shifted somewhat toward intelligence rather than character, though with a developmental or organic cast: students were "born late," "sleepy-minded," "overgrown," "immature," "slow," or "dull." "The condemnatory, religious language used earlier was diminishing," note Cuban and Tyack, "but the notion that academic failure came from defects of character or disposition continued" (4). As we moved into the twentieth century, notions of developmental and intellectual normalcy—evident in the abnormalcy of labels like "born late" and "sleepy-minded"—continued to evolve and were applied, in a negative way, to poor performers. And with the advent of the IQ movement, the assessment of intelligence, as Stephen Jay Gould has observed, was pseudo-scientifically reified into a unitary measure of cognitive—and human—worth. Class and race prejudice, xenophobia, and the social engineering of Social Darwinists and Eugenicists absorbed the new technology of mental measurement, and the deficiency of those who performed poorly in school could, it was said, be precisely and scientifically assessed.

Though the ways of thinking about thinking generated by the IQ movement are still very much with us, we have changed perspectives somewhat since the heyday of the Eugenicists. The social reform movements of the 50s and 60s shifted the discussion of school failure from the character and ability of the individual toward the society that produces "alienated" and "socially maladjusted" youth and, as well, toward the economic conditions that have a negative impact on a lower-class child's readiness for school. Yet such social theories often reflected the influence of the theories that preceded them. Cuban and Tyack point out that along with the sociologically oriented analyses of the 50s—with their discussions of "social maladjustment" and "dropping out"—came designations of students as "immature learners," "unwilling learners," and "dullards." And many of the economic analyses of the 60s discussed minority and working-class culture in terms of deficit and pathology. A number of linguistic, psychological, and social psychological studies—focused, to a great extent, on African Americans—were designed and interpreted in such a way as to demonstrate impoverishment of language, maladaptive mother-child interaction, inadequate environmental stimuli for the development of cognition, and so on. (See Mitchell for a good overview.) Education tried to move beyond the moralistic, characterologic, deficit orientation of a previous era only to enshrine such orientations in a seemingly reform-minded social science research—and to continue to fault children for educational failure.

Through the 70s and 80s, two other perspectives on school failure have emerged: the effect cultural differences can have on communication and learning in the classroom (see, e.g., Au; Heath; Philips), and the effect class- and race-based resistance to socialization into the mainstream can have on school performance (see, e.g., Chase; Everhart; Giroux; Ogbu and Matute-Bianchi; Willis). We see these perspectives as powerful advances and—like many researchers of our generation—have been deeply influenced by them. But what concerns us is the ease with which older deficit-oriened explanations for failure can exist side by side with these newer theories, and, for that fact, can narrow the way such theories are represented and applied, turning differences into deficits, reducing the rich variability of human thought, language, and motive (Rose, "Language"; "Narrowing").

We think here of another teacher at another school in our study—a very good teacher, respected by colleagues and warmly regarded by students—a teacher who, upon receiving an assignment to teach his institution's most "remedial" course, dutifully sought out the program's expert in applied linguistics and schooling. The expert told the teacher, among other things, about research on differences in socialization for schooling. Our teacher later told a colleague that he was "in despair," fearful that he "may not be able to help these kids." Given their early socialization patterns "they barely have a chance. They're doomed by the time they enter school." There may be a harsh truth in the teacher's despair—poor kids do fail in disproportionate numbers—but note how variability disappears as rich differences in background and style become reduced to a success-failure binary and the "problem"—as has been the tendency in our history—shifts from the complex intersection of cognition and culture and continues to be interpreted as a deficiency located within families and students. In this perspective, school performance, as Ronald Edmonds once put it, "derives from family background instead of school response to family background" (23).

It is difficult to demonstrate causal relationships across the level of individual functioning and the levels of social, cultural, and historical contexts, what Erickson calls "system levels" or "levels of organization" (166–67). It is difficult to demonstrate, in our case, that pervasive, shared assumptions about ability and remediation influenced a teacher's interaction with and assessment of a student. One way to gain some reasonable evidence of influence, however, is to look closely at the language the teacher uses, and we have done that. Another way is to find institutional mechanisms that might serve to instantiate influential cultural assumptions. One such mechanism seemed to be the college's training program in which this teacher participated. In such programs, readings on topics like the composing process, the social context of schooling, and error analysis are sometimes combined, we have observed, with skills-and-drills materials and deficit-oriented theories and assessments. From what we could tell from the teacher's discussion of the program with us, this mix seemed to obtain. In addressing it, we can treat more fully a point we made earlier: the lasting power of deficit notions in our society and the way they can blend with and subvert more forward-looking notions about language and cognition. This blend is evident in two excerpts from June's commentary on the videotapes of the previous lesson and a present one.

In the first, June and the interviewer have been talking about the difficulty her students have with academic writing, particularly papers requiring categorization and comparison:

Teacher: They don't have those skills. Many of them don't. And many don't have an attention to detail that's necessary for some kinds of things; for instance, for classification, uh, exercises there's a need to look at, at specifics and at detail at times in order to be thorough, you know, to deal with that. They just, don't have the practice in doing that. Uh, I think what I'm trying to do is, um, make sure that I tie as much as I possibly can into their own experience. Um, because many of these students don't have a lot to bring with them in terms of academic experience, but they do have some life experience to bring with them so. . . .

Interviewer: Okay.

Teacher: So, for instance, what I did in class about, um, having them write about what they think the educational system should do. Uh, ideally I would have liked them to do that before they ever read the article on, uh, Wednesday, just to get them thinking about what they're, what they already know about it, what, you know, what experience has already shown them about the things or what they've heard somewhere. . . . A lot of these kids have prob-

> lems with connections between things. They, they don't see the connection between what goes on in their lives and what happens in the classroom, what happens, uh, at home. . . .

June notes, accurately we think, that many of her students haven't had sufficient practice in writing academic papers in which they must classify phenomena and attend closely to detail. She then observes that while her students may not have had a certain kind of privileged education, they certainly do have life experience and a history of schooling—both of which can be tapped and reflected upon, activating background knowledge that can help them with college assignments. But then look at the interesting thing that happens—a move that we witnessed in a number of our studies—the leap is made from an accurate description of particular difficulties (students have trouble writing certain kinds of papers) to a judgment about a general cognitive capacity: "A lot of these kids have problems with connections between things." Note, as well, the acknowledgment of a problem with the educational system—the segmentation of home and school knowledge—but the locating of it within the individual's cognition ("They don't see the connection") rather than within the system.

Now to the second excerpt:

Interviewer: Maria said something real interesting today. I asked them . . . to tell me what they think good writing or good reading is, and . . . she just immediately said "Good writing is creative writing."

Teacher: She's written a novel—incredible!

Interviewer: Yes, she told me that (both laugh).

Teacher: She's written about it in her journal and I, I, you know I thought that was neat. . . .

Interviewer: You know I asked her . . . if she tried to apply creativity in her writing, and she said, "Oh, Yes!"

Teacher: Well, she doesn't. . . . (laughs) She doesn't understand the difference between creative writing and expository prose.

Interviewer: I'm not sure.

Teacher: Yet.

Interviewer: I'm not sure.

Teacher: Well, that's not really something they get until, um, English 20A anyway. We don't really start talking about those distinctions until then. . . .

June wants to "tie as much as [she] possibly can into [her students'] own experience"; she also thinks it's a good thing that Maria wrote about her novel in her journal. But almost in the same breath she devalues Maria's extra-institutional literary activity and negates the possibility that she could learn things about literacy from it. The closing remark about English 20A is telling, we think, for with it June suggests that it is only through a lockstepped, carefully segmented curriculum that students like Maria can eventually develop the ability to understand the characteristics of different literacies and make distinctions between them. Perhaps because this teacher views fundamental cognitive abilities as deficient—thinking continuity problems, problems seeing connections—she suggests that it is only through the remedial therapy of a series of self-contained, carefully sequenced treatments that literacy knowledge can be developed. In a different guise, this is a skills-and-drills philosophy in which instructional scaffolding is replaced by curricular prostheses.

The point we want to make is that June is not alone in her judgments. For almost two centuries the dominant way to think about underachieving students has been to focus on defects in intellect or character or differences in culture or situation that lead to failure, and to locate the causes within the mind and language of the individual.[6] We are primed by this history, by our backgrounds and our educations, to speak of students as deficient,[7] even as we attempt to devise curricula we call forward-looking,[8] and this is true despite the great awakening that has occurred since the publication of Shaughnessy's *Errors and Expectations* in 1977. To be sure, we have found ways to understand our students' writing and promote its development, even when that writing differs markedly from the academic standard; we have come to see our courses as entry points to the academy, safe ground where students who have not had sufficient experience with academic reading and writing can make up for lost time, and do so without censure. Often, however, these new understandings come mixed with deeply held, unarticulated assumptions about remediation and remedial students, deficit assumptions that have been part of educational thought for a long time. Our unexamined cultural biases about difference, our national habits of mind for sorting and labeling individuals who perform poorly, our legacy of racism and class bias—these are the frames of mind which make it possible, even unremarkable, to assume that talk that is occasionally non-synchronous with the talk in a classroom indicates some fundamental problem in thought, to assume "thinking continuity problems" from a difference in conversational style. In examining June's ways of assessing cognition, then, we hope to set the foundation for ongoing self-examination, for we are all enmeshed in culture, and, even as we resist them, we are shaped by its forces.

EXAMINING ASSUMPTIONS

How can we as teachers and researchers examine our assumptions about remediation and remedial writing and remedial students? How can we be alert to deficit explanations for the difficulties that students experience in our classrooms? We have four suggestions: remembering teacher development, attending to classroom discourse, making macro-micro connections, and rethinking the language of cultural difference.

Remembering Teacher Development

When basic writing was just emerging as a course worth a teacher's serious attention and commitment, Mina Shaughnessy pointed out that most work was focusing on what was wrong with students rather than with teacher development. The effect of this tendency was the erroneous notion "that students, not teachers, are the people in education who must do the changing" ("Diving In" 234). Shaughnessy reminded us that students aren't the only people in a classroom who develop and grow, and she proposed a kind of impressionistic developmental scale for teachers of basic writing, each stage of which she named with a common metaphor: "Guarding the Tower," "Converting the Natives," "Sounding the Depths," and "Diving In." The significant thing to us about these metaphors is that they focus on teachers' attitudes about students' abilities. Teachers who guard the tower are so stunned by fractured writing that they believe the students who produced it have no place in the academy, for they will never be able to live up to the ideal of academic prose. Once this shock abates, and teachers begin to believe that students are educable, they proceed with conversion by offering them a steady flow of "truth" without thinking too much about the skills and habits students bring with them, often unconsciously, to their interactions with texts. The third stage involves the recognition that the writing behavior these students display has a logic that merits careful observation. At this point, then, a teacher is moving away from deficit notions and towards an appreciation of students' abilities. The last stage takes place when a teacher is willing to "remediate himself, to become a student of new disciplines and of his students themselves in order to perceive both their difficulties and their incipient excellence" (239). It is not at all easy, cautioned Shaughnessy, for a college teacher to assume that the students in a class, already labeled "remedial," possess this incipient excellence.

We want to argue that the situation Shaughnessy described is still with us. Granted, we have made much progress in learning about the writing process, in conducting interdisciplinary research, in imagining liberatory pedagogies, even in establishing composition programs which include some kind of training for teachers.[9] But what we have been much less successful in doing is promoting teacher development of the sort Shaughnessy described. We have assumed, as a best-case scenario, that if new teachers are introduced to writing theory and research as a part of their graduate training, and if they have the chance to prepare and develop curricular materials for their classes (conditions that are all too rare), then they will necessarily acquire whatever it is they need to know about remedial students. Maybe we have also assumed that teachers automatically move from "guarding the tower" to "diving in" just as a function of experience. Our studies make us question these assumptions. Because deficit notions of abilities are so deeply ingrained in most of us, it seems very unlikely that most teachers, pressed as they are by constraints of time and curricula, will discover serendipitously more productive ways to view students' abilities.

And how we view students' abilities, we have tried to illustrate in this paper, can have profound effects. A great deal of research has shown that students whose teachers expect them to do well, tend to do well, while students whose teachers expect them to do poorly, do poorly. These findings hold firm, even in cases of mistaken placement or misinformation. That is, "bright" students who are mistakenly expected to perform poorly in the classroom will often do poorly, while students labeled "average" will often excel if their teacher believes that this is what they are supposed to do (Brophy). We have illustrated that Maria's discourse style did not fit well with the IRE participant structure of her remedial writing class. It also occurred to us that Maria's conversational patterns more closely resembled the talk that is allowed in classrooms geared to the honors student. Perhaps Maria, who placed in non-remedial classes in high school and was on the speech team, was accustomed to speaking up with her own opinion, which she expected to be acknowledged by her teachers and to be of some import to the lesson. She displays an eagerness to be involved, to interact with her teacher.[10] By the end of the semester, the mismatch between Maria's discourse style and that of the classroom seemed to be taking a toll. Maria told us in her last tutoring session that she now "had some problems with . . . English," that her writing had gotten "longer" but not necessarily better, and that she was "not a very good speaker." Perhaps it is also noteworthy that she expressed interest at the end of the semester in teaching students who were poor performers in the classroom. In any case, her negative self-assessments are very different from the successful Maria we saw at the beginning of the semester—the student who loved writing and who'd been a member of the speech team—and suggest that she had perhaps begun to internalize her teacher's opinions of her abilities.

Research on expectancy theory thus supports Shaughnessy's claims about teacher development: the beliefs we construct of our students' abilities can influence their lives in our classrooms and beyond in profound ways. We want to suggest that it would be unwise just to rely on process pedagogy and experience in the classroom to foster the development of non-deficit attitudes among teachers and teacher-trainees. We need to spend some time thinking about teacher development—not just what knowledge to impart about writing, but how to develop the ability to question received assumptions about abilities and performance, how to examine the thinking behind the curricula we develop and the assessments we make.[11]

We might, for a start, look closely at writing instruction to identify moments when teachers transcend deficit attitudes, when teaching serves to invite rather than to deny. Roger Simon has written about "the contradictory character of the work of teaching" (246), illustrating that "what teachers choose to signify at any particular moment in time may present meanings which are ideologically inconsistent with meanings present at other times" (248). He locates the origin of these contradictions not in the individual but in the larger social and institutional context, and he sees contradictory moments as potentially liberatory, for they make possible the inclusion of oppositional knowledge in educational practice. In a related way, we might think of teaching as an ongoing flow of moments of invitation and moments of denial. The better, the more effective the teaching, the richer and more frequent the moments of invitation, encouragement, and assistance (though no extended period of teaching will be free of constraint, limit, even rejection). What has interested us in this paper is the way in which culturally sanctioned, deficit-oriented assumptions about learning and cognition can tip the scale. But what we need to do as well is identify, understand, and learn to foster those moments in which teachers encourage rather than restrict their students' potential.

Attending to Classroom Discourse

One of the things we have learned in doing this paper is the value of looking closely at the talk that transpires in classrooms. We have been interested particularly in conversational patterns—rules for turn-taking and the special participant structure that characterizes so much of talk in school, the IRE sequence. But this work on turn-taking, interesting and revealing though it can be, was a means to another end. In the classroom, it is through talk that learning gets done, that knowledge gets made. Using conversational turns as a unit of analysis gave us a window on knowledge-making.

In the analysis reported in this paper, we focused on a moment when Maria didn't get to make knowledge, when her chance to contribute a special piece of information, one that would have deepened the discourse at hand, was denied. We have argued that the reason her contribution was denied had to do with her teacher's construction of her as a particular kind of remedial student, a scattered thinker, and that such a construction likely had its origin in long-standing, widespread beliefs about low-achieving students, beliefs that such students are deficient and that the locus of any academic difficulty they have lies within them. In this instance, then, we saw faulty notions about cognition being played out and reinforced within a certain participant structure, the IRE sequence.

This finding raised for us the possibility that the IRE sequence could be the vehicle for a discourse of remediation, a discourse where most questions have "known" answers, where the teacher maintains tight control over conversation, where students are not allowed to participate in free-ranging talk. In the literature on classroom talk, many objections have been raised about the IRE participant structure in terms of the role that more free-ranging talk can play in knowledge construction (see, e.g., Applebee; Barnes; Cazden; Dillon; Edwards and Furlong; Moffett; Tharp and Gallimore). We too see a place for free-ranging, student-led discussion (Hull and Rose, "This Wooden").[12] But we would also suggest that the IRE participant structure does not itself circumvent knowledge-making and engagement; the kinds of questions that teachers ask and the kinds of evaluations that they give to students' responses will more often affect what knowledge gets made and who makes it. Questions that are genuine questions, that don't have pre-specified answers, and evaluations that validate students' contributions are going to create a different kind of classroom discourse and a different level of engagement.[13]

Let us look at some bits of conversation from our classroom lesson which do just that.

Teacher: Well, tell me a little bit about what would go into determining how the music videos that you have seen might be rated. What kinds of things, um, would be used to determine how, what, how a movie gets rated?

Student: Language.

Teacher: Okay, language (writes it on the board). Like what, tell me, give examples. I mean . . . You don't have to swear but. . . .

In this IRE sequence, June asks a follow-up question, incorporating the student's answer into her next question in order to elicit an elaboration on the student's answer. She considers the student's answer important enough to spend time on it, to work it into the exchange, to allow it to modify the subsequent discussion. And in so doing, she bestows value on it.

Teacher: Or who would that appeal to?

Matt: I don't think that—

Susan: ( ) over 18.

Matt: Children of what age level?

Teacher: Okay, that's a good question: children of what age?

Here June accepts a student's initiation and sanctions it as the topic of the next series of questions. This move shows, again, a willingness to accept students' ideas and to value them.

Teacher: What, what are some of the music videos you've seen recently?
Andrea: *Thriller.*
Teacher: *Thriller.*
Matt: *Graceland.*
Teacher: Okay, *Thriller* . . . and *Graceland.* I'll, I'll come back to that one, but *Thriller*, what's the rating on *Thriller*?

Here June acknowledges that a student's comment, although it cannot immediately be responded to is nevertheless important and will eventually be discussed.

And those moments when June was able to shift out of the IRE pattern—mixing conversation styles, encouraging other modes of participation—gave rise to yet other opportunities for fruitful talk. For example, when one student proposes that music videos could be rated by a quantitative tally of objectionable language, June responds:

Teacher: Okay. Now that's something I had not heard before, but that kind of makes sense.

Here, then, is an admission from June that a student knows something that she doesn't—an admission that might lessen the power differential in the classroom and make authentic discourse more possible. Another such moment occurred when a student points out that the same kind of violence that would result in a restrictive rating for a music video regularly occurs as part of on-the-scene reporting in newscasts—an assertion, by the way, that challenged the position June had adopted. The student then goes on to give an example of a murder shown recently on a local television news program:

Matt: I saw the shooting.
Andrea: Yeah, I've seen the shooting.
Jason: Yeah, ( ) They shot 'im like from, from where I'm at to where you're at. . . .

Following the above excerpt, the conversation takes off and continues for another two pages in our transcript. June does evaluate a few times during this conversation, but she sees that it is clearly a topic of concern for the students—a number of different students initiate during this discussion—

and she lets it go longer than any other student conversation in the lesson. She also becomes an "equal" participant at times, no longer evaluating but asking questions for which she doesn't have a particular answer in mind. These are not remarkable exchanges, but they were rare in the lessons we analyzed, and they do illustrate a capacity to engage in kinds of classroom conversation other than those we saw with Maria.

We want to recommend that attention be paid to the talk that goes on in our writing classrooms—analyses of the participant structures, whether they be IRE sequences or other patterns of interaction—with an eye for determining the kind of talk those structures allow. We have seen that discourse structures direct talk in particular ways and that certain moves within those structures can instantiate assumptions about cognition and undercut creative thinking and engagement. If we look closely at the talk we allow, we may also get a new sense of our own assumptions about our students' capabilities.

Making Macro-Micro Connections

What has frequently happened in the study of reading and writing is that researchers have conducted either fine-grained analyses of texts or of the cognitive processes involved in text comprehension and production *or* have produced studies of wider focus of the social and political contexts of reading, writing, and schooling. Such a separation isn't peculiar to literacy research, but characterizes as well divisions among disciplines. As anthropologist Frederick Erickson has pointed out, "Individual cognitive functioning has been largely the purview of cognitive psychologists who have often attempted to study thinking apart from the naturally occurring social and cultural circumstances of its use," while "the anthropology of education often has studied *anything but* deliberately taught cognitive learning" (173). Erickson goes on to suggest that "some rapprochement is needed, from the direction of the (more cognitively sophisticated) psychology of learning to the (more contextually sophisticated) anthropology of learning" (173).

Such calls to systematically integrate social and cognitive perspectives are increasing (Freedman, Dyson, Flower, and Chafe; Michaels; Rose, "Complexity"). Sociologist Aaron Cirourel argues that "the study of discourse and the larger context of social interaction requires explicit references to a broader organizational setting and aspects of cultural beliefs often ignored by students of discourse and conversational analysis" (qtd. in Corsaro 22). At the same time, educational anthropologist Henry Trueba reminds us, "the strength of ethnographic research [on school achievement] and its contribution to theory building . . . will depend on the strength of each of the microanalytical links of the inferential chains that form our macrotheoretical statements" (283). To adequately study language in society, then, one has to take into account "interrelationships among linguistic, cognitive, and sociocultural elements" (Cirourel quoted in Corsaro 23).

Moving between micro-level, close examination of oral or written discourse and macro-level investigations of society and culture—seeking connections between language, cognition, and context—is, we feel, particularly important in the case of students designated remedial and for our efforts to examine our assumptions about these students' abilities (Hull and Rose, "Rethinking"). Without the microperspective, one runs the risk of losing sight of the particulars of behavior; without the macroperspective, one runs the risk of missing the social and cultural logic of that behavior. In the case of Maria, micro-level analyses enabled us to examine closely the conversational processes by which a student was defined as a scattered thinker and the ways her opportunities to participate in and contribute to knowledge production were narrowed. Macro-level analyses can encourage a consideration of Maria's discourse processes in contexts other than the individual cognitive one provided by her teacher and, as well, encourage reflection on the very language June uses in making her assessment. So, let us now play out some macro-level considerations of Maria's conversational style.

Reproduction-resistance theorists and cultural-difference theorists, both mentioned earlier, would raise questions about the broader political and cultural contexts of Maria's behavior. The former group would wonder if Maria's conversational style was an attempt to resist an educational system that does not serve her well, while the latter group would wonder if Maria's conversational style reflected communication patterns shaped by her cultural inheritance and/or her family background. The focus of the "problem" of Maria's conversational style wouldn't automatically be on the isolated processes of her own cognition, but on the possible role played by other political or cultural influences. A somewhat related perspective would focus on Maria's history in classrooms—wondering what prior socializing experiences in school might have influenced her interactional style. A further perspective would tighten the contextual focus to the immediate psychosocial context of Maria's current instruction. Was there something about the way Maria expressed her need to be involved in the class and her teacher's conscious or unconscious reaction to it that affected Maria's conversational style?

In posing these perspectives, we do not want to suggest that each has equal explanatory power for Maria's case. For example, our data don't seem to support reproduction-resistance theory. Maria was an eager participant in the classroom community, taking part dutifully in virtually every aspect of her course. Her interruptions of classroom talk did not appear to us to be interruptions for the sake of disruption; rather she seemed to want to take part in class, to make a contribution, or to keep track of assignment information she may have missed. (The value of this perspective in Maria's case may be more general, however, in that it can lead one to examine the political context of schooling and the inequities of class in American educational history.) The applicability of the cultural-differences perspective is a more complicated issue. There may well be home/school differences at work in Maria's conversational style; unfortunately we were not able to visit Maria's home or collect information from other sources that could shed light on this hypothesis directly. One could argue, though, against the applicability of the cultural-differences hypothesis here in any strong way. While Maria may have operated with different cultural assumptions about communication when she first began elementary school in the United States, it seems unlikely that she would not have become aware of the dominant discourse of schooling, the IRE participant structure, by the time she entered college. Still, there is real value, it seems to us, in speculating on the possible conversational dynamics within Maria's family that might influence what she does in the classroom, especially under the pressure to articulate an idea. We have very limited data on the third perspective offered above—Maria's history of interaction with teachers—though this seems a good possibility to pursue, especially given her participation on a speech team, where somewhat more interactive conversational patterns could have existed. We think the fourth perspective—the psychosocial context of Maria and her teacher—is also promising, especially when we consider the less excitable Maria observed in our tutorial sessions.

Our best, and cautious, guess about the context of Maria's conversational style in this classroom, then, would be that three possible influences are at work: (a) Maria's previous experience in classrooms or other school contexts that were less teacher-centered, (b) characteristics of her nonclassroom conversational style, possibly shaped by family dynamics, and (c) Maria's eagerness—perhaps tinged with anxiety—to do well and be part of things and the growing number of disapproving cues she picks up from her teacher, which could lead to further uncertainty and anxiety, and with that, further communicative missteps.

Attempting to link micro-level with macro-level analysis—shuttling in a systematic way between close linguistic and cognitive study and studies of broader contexts—can, we think, provide a richer understanding of the history and logic of particular behaviors. It might provide, as well, checks and balances on the assessments we make about ability, and perhaps it can lead us to raise to conscious examination our assumptions about the nature and cause of performance that strikes us as inadequate or unusual. But even as we use this micro-macro metaphor, we are unhappy with it, for we recognize that it still separates cognitive behaviors and social contexts into different domains. In fact, one reason for much recent interest in Vygotsky and the extension of his work called "activity theory" (Wertsch, Minick) is that his sociocultural theory of mind provides an alternative to the division of cognition from context, mind from culture, knowing from acting. We see a need to work toward holistic conceptions of the study of schooling and students' performance which take as a given that linguistic and cognitive behaviors occur within, and can best be understood within, their particular institutional, cultural, and historical milieus.

Rethinking the Language of Cultural Difference

Our last suggestion for examining our assumptions about remediation and remedial students is to work toward a conceptualization of discourse that undercuts easy thinking about difference. This call is difficult, for it requires an engagement of the very language currently available to us to discuss school failure in a progressive way.

Research on cultural and class differences in communication and learning styles has revealed the coherence, purposiveness, and richness of behavior that has puzzled mainstream educators and resulted in harmful explanations and assessments of poor performance. Such research has moved us significantly toward a more democratic vision of learning and schooling and, in some cases, has helped us successfully tailor instruction to fit students' needs (e.g., Au; Heath). But our time spent in remedial programs—reviewing curricula, talking to teachers and administrators, catching our own disturbing reactions to the literacy performances we saw—has made us uncomfortable with much of the research that focuses on differences, whether such difference grows out of the recognition that communication styles at school aren't like those at home or that people come to intellectual tasks in different ways. The problem is that all American educational research—ours and everyone else's—emerges from a culture in the grips of deficit thinking, and any analysis that delineates differences will run the risk of being converted to a deficit theory (Rose, "Narrowing"). We believe that a focus on differences, while potentially democratic and certainly instructive, can lead us to forget two things: (1) in fundamental ways, we all possess the means to use language to make meaning; we all participate in fundamental linguistic and cognitive processes by virtue of our common humanity and (2) human beings, given the right social conditions, are astoundingly adaptive, and to determine what works against this adaptability, we need to look at the social and instructional conditions in the classroom rather than assume the problem is to be found in the cultural characteristics students bring with them. Two research-based observations are pertinent here. The first is from Asa Hilliard, and the second comes from Luis Moll and Stephen Diaz:

> I do believe that greater sensitivity to [learning] style issues will make meaningful contributions to pedagogy in the future. Yet I remain unconvinced that the explanation for the low performance of culturally different "minority" group students will be found by pursuing questions of behavioral style. Since students are adaptable, the stylistic difference explanation does not answer the question of why "minority" groups perform at a low level. . . . [C]hildren . . . are failing primarily because of systematic inequalities in the delivery of whatever pedagogical approach the teachers claim to master—not because students cannot learn from teachers whose styles do not match their own. (Hilliard, 68)

> Although student characteristics certainly matter, when the same children are shown to succeed under modified instructional arrangements it becomes clear that the problems . . . working-class children face in school must be viewed primarily as a consequence of institutional arrangements that constrain children *and* teachers by not capitalizing fully on their talents, resources, and skills. (Moll and Diaz, 302)

It is useful here to recall Ray McDermott s discussion of the way our society "keep(s) arranging for school failure to be so visible." "We might do better," he continues,

> to ask how it is a part of the situation of every minority group that it has had to be explained, or about the degradation every minority group has had to suffer from our explanations. . . . By making believe that failure is something that kids do, as different from how it is something that is done to them, and then by explaining their failure in terms of other things they do, we likely contribute to the maintenance of school failure. (McDermott 362–63)

McDermott takes us all to task for our manufacture of failure, our entrapment in a way of thinking and of organizing society that virtually assures failure. We struggle within a discourse that yearns for difference, and difference, in our culture, slides readily toward judgment of better-or-worse, dominance, otherness.

Yet the moment we express our concerns about a focus on difference, we must stop short. Without such a focus one can easily forget that "intellectual development is socially and culturally based, and that what happens in the home, school, and local community . . . is crucial to understanding the learning processes and academic achievement of all children, including minority children" (Trueba 279). Such a perspective can lead to a greater appreciation of the richness of background, language, and gesture that comprise America. In fact, a focus on cognitive and linguistic *similarity* can shift readily to a leveling vision that not only reduces the variability that should be a cause for celebration, but, in its way, can also blind us to the political and economic consequences of difference. As Linda

Brodkey puts it, a focus on similarity can distract us "from noticing the consequences of difference, namely, inequity" (599). Given a history of diminishment, of a devaluation and ridicule of difference, it is not surprising that some members of historically subjugated groups want to move beyond an embrace of cognitive and linguistic similarity to an elevation of difference. Within French feminism and African-American cultural studies, for example, some writers are arguing for the existence of distinctive female and Afrocentric epistemologies. Their move is to turn otherness on its head, to celebrate ways of knowing that have been reduced and marginalized.

Given the culturally received ways we have to think about school failure in America, it seems that we have to keep these two perspectives in dynamic tension, see them as elements in a complex dialectic, a dialectic that can lead us to be alert to the ease with which we can make limiting, harmful judgments about linguistic and cognitive ability, the ease with which rich differences can be ignored or converted to deficits, but the ease, as well, with which differences can be represented in essentialistic and deterministic ways that reduce human variability and adaptability. For that fact, we need to be vigilant that the very dialectic we want to honor does not degenerate into the kind of bipolar, better-worse scheme that has been so characteristic of our thinking about language use. To focus on the possible cultural or class differences of a student like Maria can both reveal the logic of her behavior and—given the ways we carry with us to react to difference—blind us to the shared cognitive and linguistic processes she displays. But to focus on the shared nature of Maria's cognitive and linguistic processes can blind us to the specifics of her background, and, further, can lead us to downplay variability and the way difference has been historically embedded in inequity. To talk about difference in America, given our legacy of racism and class prejudice, requires us to talk, as well, about the many reductive, harmful ways difference has historically been represented. What we need to develop are conceptual frameworks that *simultaneously* assert shared cognitive and linguistic competence while celebrating in a non-hierarchical way the play of human difference.[14]

NOTES

1. The work reported here is part of a larger study, "Literacy, Underpreparation, and the Cognition of Composing." We gratefully acknowledge the support of the James S. McDonnell Foundation's Program in Cognitive Studies for Educational Practice, the Spencer Foundation, the National Center for the Study of Writing, and the National Council of Teachers of English Research Foundation.
2. For other discussions of interactional classroom competence and reviews of previous work in this area, see Mehan ("Competent") and Corno.

3. We should point out, however, that most of the research identifying the IRE sequence has been done with classrooms in the elementary grades. For an exception to this, and an example of how the IRE participant structure can be used to analyze writing conferences, see Freedman and Katz.
4. The transcription conventions were developed by John Gumperz, with help from Wallace Chafe and Noreen Barantz. Gumperz has stressed that the system is more interpretive than descriptive, and that the key to its proper usage is consistency.
5. In the interest of saving space, we haven't provided transcripts with contextualization cues for every stretch of classroom talk. Readers interested in seeing such transcripts can request a copy of Technical Report #44 from the National Center for the Study of Writing at the University of California, Berkeley.
6. For another account of this history, see Robert Sinclair and Ward Ghory's *Reaching Marginal Students.*
7. British researchers Michael Golby and John R. Gulliver make a related point in their critical review of remedial education in England and Wales: "In order to understand what exists, we must see remedial education firstly in its historical context, and secondly as a manifestation of ideologies obtaining not only within education but also having corelative applications within wider social policy" (11). See also Michael Cole and Peg Griffin.
8. For a related argument, see Sandra Schecter and Tamara Lucas's position paper on "Literacy Education and Diversity."
9. A special issue of the *Journal of Basic Writing* (1981) was devoted to discussions of the kinds of programs that would best prepare basic writing teachers.
10. This explanation of Maria's interactional patterns is developed more fully by Kay Losey Fraser in a paper delivered at the 1989 Conference on College Composition and Communication.
11. To this end, with our colleague Cynthia Greenleaf, we are creating a set of cases and an interpretation of remedial education in America that we hope can be used to engage teachers in the kind of inquiry that leads one to trace the connections between the mind of the student and the classroom and the community beyond.
12. We aren't, however, offering student-led discussion, collaborative groups, or peer conferencing as a panacea. Thomas Fox has illustrated that conversation between peers can be dramatically and negatively affected by gender and race relations. See also Trimbur.
13. Martin Nystrand and Adam Gamoran at the University of Wisconsin–Madison are currently engaged in studies of classroom lessons aimed at characterizing high-quality instructional discourse.
14. We would like to thank Carmen Colon Montes de Oca for helpful conversation and Cynthia Greenleaf, Kris Gutierrez, Rebekah Kaplan, Jacqueline Jones Royster, and Gloria Zarabozo for reading and commenting on the manuscript. We also benefitted from the comments of three anonymous reviewers for *CCC*. We appreciate Susan Thompson's assistance throughout the research project.

WORKS CITED

Applebee, Arthur N. *Writing in the Secondary School: English and the Content Areas*. NCTE Research Report 21. Urbana: NCTE, 1981.

Au, K. "Participation Structures in a Reading Lesson with Hawaiian Children." *Anthropology and Education Quarterly* 11 (June 1980): 91–115.

Barnes, D. *From Communication to Curriculum*. London: Penguin, 1976.

Brodkey, Linda. "Transvaluing Difference." *College English 51* (Oct. 1989): 597–601.

Brophy, Jere E. "Research on the Self-Fulfilling Prophecy." *Journal of Educational Psychology* 75 (Oct. 1983): 631–61.

Cazden, Courtney B. *Classroom Discourse: The Language of Teaching and Learning*. Portsmouth, NJ: Heinemann, 1988.

Chase, Geoffrey. "Accommodation, Resistance and the Politics of Student Writing." *College Composition and Communication* 39 (Feb. 1988): 13–22.

Cole, Michael, and Peg Griffin. "A Sociohistorical Approach to Remediation." *Literacy, Society, and Schooling: A Reader*. Ed. S. de Castell, A. Luke, and K. Egan. Cambridge: Cambridge UP, 1986. 110–31.

Cook-Gumperz, Jenny. "Introduction: The Social Construction of Literacy." *The Social Construction of Literacy*. Ed. Jenny Cook-Gumperz. Cambridge: Cambridge UP, 1986. 1–15.

Corno, Lyn. "What It Means to be Literate about Classrooms." *Classrooms and Literacy*. Ed. David Bloome. Norwood, NJ: Ablex, 1989. 29–52.

Corsaro, William A. "Communicative Processes in Studies of Social Organization: Sociological Approaches to Discourse Analysis." *Text* 1 (1981): 5–63.

Cuban, Larry, and David Tyack. " 'Dunces,' 'Shirkers,' and 'Forgotten Children': Historical Descriptions and Cures for Low Achievers." Conference for Accelerating the Education of At Risk Students. Stanford U, 1988.

Dillon, J. T. ed. *Questioning and Discussion: Multidisciplinary Study*. Norwood, NJ: Ablex, 1988.

Edmonds, Ronald. "Effective Schools for the Urban Poor." *Educational Leadership* 37 (Oct. 1979): 15–24.

Edwards, A. D., and V. J. Furlong. *The Language of Teaching: Meaning in Classroom Interaction*. London: Heinemann, 1978.

Erickson, Frederick. "Taught Cognitive Learning in Its Immediate Environments: A Neglected Topic in the Anthropology of Education." *Anthropology and Education Quarterly* 13 (1982): 149–80.

Everhart, R. B. *Reading, Writing, and Resistance: Adolescence and Labor in a Junior High School*. Boston: Routledge, 1983.

Fox, Thomas. "Collaborative Learning, Literacy, and Conversational Analysis." Unpublished paper. Chico State U, 1989.

Fraser, Kay Losey. "Classroom Discourse and Perceptions of Cognitive Ability: An Analysis of Interaction in a Basic Writing Class." Conference on College Composition and Communication Convention. Seattle, 1989.

Freedman, Sarah Warshauer, Anne Haas Dyson, Linda Flower, and Wallace Chafe. *Research in Writing: Past, Present, and Future*. Technical Report 1. Center for the Study of Writing, U of California, Berkeley, and Carnegie Mellon U, Pittsburgh, 1987.

Freedman, Sarah Warshauer, and Anne Marie Katz. "Pedagogical Interaction During the Composing Process: The Writing Conference." *Writing in Real Time: Modeling Production Processes*. Ed. Ann Matsuhashi. Norwood: Ablex, 1987. 58–107.

Giroux, Henry. *Theory and Resistance in Education*. South Hadley: Bergin, 1983.

Golby, Michael, and John R. Gulliver. "Whose Remedies, Whose Ills? A Critical Review of Remedial Education." *New Directions in Remedial Education*. Ed. Colin J. Smith. London: Falmer Press, 1985. 7–19.

Gould, Stephen Jay. *The Mismeasure of Man*. New York: Norton, 1981.

Gumperz, John. "Contextualization and Understanding." *Rethinking Context*. Ed. A. Duranti. Cambridge: Cambridge UP, in press.

—. *Discourse Strategies*. Cambridge: Cambridge UP, 1982.

Heath, Shirley Brice. *Ways with Words: Language, Life, and Work in Communities and Classrooms*. Cambridge: Cambridge UP, 1983.

Hilliard, Asa G. "Teachers and Cultural Styles in a Pluralistic Society." *NEA Today* 7 (Jan. 1989): 65–69.

Hull, Glynda, and Mike Rose. "Rethinking Remediation: Toward a Social-Cognitive Understanding of Problematic Reading and Writing." *Written Communication* 8 (April 1989): 139–54.

—. " 'This Wooden Shack Place': The Logic of an Unconventional Reading." *College Composition and Communication* 41 (Oct. 1990): 287–98.

McDermott, R. P. "The Explanation of Minority School Failure, Again." *Anthropology and Education Quarterly* 18 (Dec. 1987): 361–64.

Mehan, Hugh. "The Competent Student." *Anthropology and Education Quarterly* 11 (June 1980): 131–52.

—. *Learning Lessons: Social Organization in the Classroom*. Cambridge: Harvard UP, 1979.

Michaels, Sarah. *The Literacies Institute: Technical Proposal*. Newton, MA: Education Development Center, 1989.

Minick, Norris. *L. S. Vygotsky and Soviet Activity Theory: Perspectives on the Relationship between Mind and Society*. Technical Reports Special Monograph 1. Newton, MA: The Literacies Institute, 1989.

Mitchell, Jacquelyn. "Reflections of a Black Social Scientist: Some Struggles, Some Doubts, Some Hopes." *Harvard Educational Review* 52 (Feb. 1982): 27–44.

Moffett, James. *Teaching the Universe of Discourse*. Boston: Houghton, 1968.

Moll, Luis C., and Stephen Diaz. "Change as the Goal of Educational Research." *Anthropology and Education Quarterly* 18 (Dec. 1987): 300–11.

Nystrand, Martin, and Adam Gamoran. *Instructional Discourse and Student Engagement*. Madison: National Center on Effective Secondary Schools and the Wisconsin Center for Education Research, 1989.

—. *A Study of Instruction as Discourse*. Madison: National Center on Effective Secondary Schools and the Wisconsin Center for Education Research, 1988.

Ogbu, John U., and Maria Eugenia Matute-Bianchi. "Understanding Sociocultural Factors: Knowledge, Identity, and School Adjustment." *Beyond Language: Social and Cultural Factors in Schooling Language Minority Students*. Los Angeles: Evaluation, Dissemination and Assessment Center of California State U, 1986. 73–142.

Philips, Susan U. *The Invisible Culture: Communication in Classroom and Community on the Warm Springs Indian Reservation*. New York: Longman, 1983.

Rose, Mike. "Complexity, Rigor, Evolving Method, and the Puzzle of Writer's Block: Thoughts on Composing Process Research," *When a Writer Can't Write: Studies in Writer's Block and Other Composing Process Problems*. Ed. Mike Rose. New York: Guilford, 1985. 227–60.

—. "The Language of Exclusion: Writing Instruction at the University." *College English* 47 (April 1985): 341–59.

—. "Narrowing the Mind and Page: Remedial Writers and Cognitive Reductionism." *College Composition and Communication* 39 (Oct. 1988): 267–302.

Sacks, H., E. A. Schegloff, and G. Jefferson. "A Simplest Systematics for the Organization of Turn-taking in Conversation." *Language* 50 (Dec. 1974): 696–735.

Schecter, Sandra R., and Tamara Lucas. "Literacy Education and Diversity. A Position Paper." Unpublished manuscript, U of California, Berkeley, 1989.

Shaughnessy, Mina. "Diving In: An Introduction to Basic Writing." *College Composition and Communication* 27 (Oct. 1976): 234–39.

—. *Errors and Expectations*. New York: Oxford UP, 1977.

Simon, Roger I. "But Who Will Let You Do It? Counter-Hegemonic Possibilities for Work Education." *Journal of Education* 165 (Summer 1983): 235–56.

Sinclair, J. M., and R. M. Coulthard. *Toward an Analysis of Discourse*. New York: Oxford UP, 1977.

Sinclair, Robert L., and Ward J. Ghory. *Reaching Marginal Students: A Primary Concern for School Renewal*. Berkeley: McCutchan, 1987.

Tannen, Deborah. *Conversational Style: Analyzing Talk among Friends.* Norwood: Ablex, 1984.

Tharp, Roland G., and Ronald Gallimore. *Rousing Minds to Life: Teaching, Learning, and Schooling in Social Context.* Cambridge: Cambridge UP, 1989.

Training Teachers of Basic Writing. Special Issue of the *Journal of Basic Writing* 3.2 (Spring/Summer 1981).

Trimbur, John. "Consensus and Difference in Collaborative Learning." *College English* 51 (Oct. 1989): 602–15.

Trueba, Henry T. "Culturally Based Explanations of Minority Students' Academic Achievement." *Anthropology and Education Quarterly* 19 (Dec. 1988): 270–87.

Wertsch, James V. *Vygotsky and the Social Formation of Mind*. Cambridge: Harvard UP, 1985.

Willis, Paul. *Learning to Labor: How Working Class Kids Get Working Class Jobs.* New York: Columbia UP, 1977.

Zehm, Stanley J. "Educational Misfits: A Study of Poor Performers in the English Class 1825–1925." Diss., Stanford U, 1973.

Chapter 9

Observing the Second Language Learner: An Example of Teachers' Learning

Celia Genishi

Watch "the habits of the moon" and record what you see in a journal: this was Eleanor Duckworth's (1986) out-of-the-ordinary assignment to her university students. She wanted to engage them with a phenomenon, something of interest to observe that would provide the foundation for discussions about the nature of learning and teaching. The students, who were also teachers, reacted to the assignment as any class would: some found it puzzling, others found it irritating, others became quickly engrossed in it. Those who at first resisted it often had a change of attitude later, as this journal entry shows:

> Then, questions began to arise from this "casual watching." . . . The questions led to new questions, to new curiosities and, also, to new surprises. I'm still a beginner as a moon-watcher and I have thousands of questions: How do changes in shape occur? Why do I see it sometimes "here" and sometimes "there"? Does it move always at the same pace? Where does it go when I don't see it? (p. 485)

Observing the second language (L2) learner is far more engaging than observing the moon, of course. L2 learners are participants in your own classroom, and you have a personal interest in any changes in their behavior and learning. Like moon watching, though, watching L2 learners may raise more questions than it answers: How do changes in language competence occur? Why does the child look competent in one setting and not another? How can I match my teaching pace with his learning? How much English does he use outside of school? We may ask some of these questions about all students, but L2 learners present a special challenge because they have less knowledge than their classmates of the primary tool for learning in classrooms in this country: the English language.

What assumptions can we make about L2 learners in elementary classrooms as we try to answer our questions? Some are:

1. They have considerable knowledge about *language* as a result of learning the one they speak at home.
2. Although it would be ideal to build on what children know and to offer classroom instruction in their home language, most teachers are prepared to instruct only in English (and believe it is to the child's advantage to learn English quickly).
3. Typically we know *very little* about their knowledge of English when they enter our classrooms.
4. Although all language learners need opportunities to use language in situations they find meaningful, L2 learners vary widely in their inclinations and abilities to take advantage of those opportunities. In other words, each child approaches L2 learning in her or his own way.

In this article the focus is on the third and fourth assumptions. Observation is presented as the key to discovering *what L2 learners already know about English* and to discovering *what their inclinations and abilities are when they enter our classrooms, or what kind of L2 learners they are*. Thus, the first questions we ask in "L2 learner watching" are, how much English does she or he already know, and what kind of L2 learner does she or he seem to be?

Observing the L2 Learner's Language Use

In the classroom where language, spoken and written, permeates every part of the curriculum, there are many opportunities to assess, or document informally, children's progress in using language. Listening to interactions and reading written products in a variety of activities gives us evidence about what kind of language users children are becoming. With L2 learners, though, there may at first be little language to hear and see; and an initial assessment about their language use seems impossible. In your class you may have a non-English-speaker who has said nothing, for weeks. Writers tell poignant stories about their own experiences that document this period of silence. Novelist Maxine Hong Kingston (1976), for example, remembers her kindergarten year in a California school:

> During the first silent year I spoke to no one at school, did not ask before going to the lavatory, and flunked kindergarten. My sister also said nothing for three years, silent in the playground and silent at lunch. There were other Chinese girls not of our family, but most of them got over it sooner than we did. I enjoyed the silence. At first it did not occur to me I was supposed to talk or to pass kindergarten. I talked at home and to one or two of the Chinese kids in class. . . . It was when I found out I had to talk that school became a misery, that the silence became a misery. I did not speak and felt bad each time that I did not speak. (pp. 192–193)

Author Richard Rodriguez tells of how he felt as he became an English speaker, also in a California school, in his book *Hunger of Memory*:

> Fortunately, my teachers were unsentimental about their responsibility. What they understood was that I needed to speak a public language. So their voices would search me out, asking me questions. Each time I'd hear them, I'd look up in surprise to see a nun's face frowning at me. I'd mumble, not really meaning to answer. The nun would persist, "Richard, stand up. Don't look at the floor. Speak up. Speak to the entire class, not just to me!" But I couldn't believe that the English language was mine to use. (In part, I did not want to believe it.) I continued to mumble. I resisted the teacher's demands. . . . Silent, waiting for the bell to sound, I remained dazed, diffident, afraid. (pp. 19–20)

The misery of not being able to communicate in the public language of schooling is hardly unique to these gifted writers—two people whose English voices eventually developed with eloquence. That misery is felt by increasing numbers of non-English-speakers in our schools, who may lack the verbal gifts of Hong Kingston and Rodriguez. If our task is to follow—and motivate—the progress of these children, what is there to follow or hear or assess?

At first there may be nothing to hear; instead there are signs to see, signs that we are barely aware of. We wait for a look in the eyes that indicates interest. To illustrate, a preschool teacher who had six L2 learners in her group watched as they listened to the class's own version of the predictable book, *A Dark, Dark Tale* (Brown 1981): "In a dark, dark house, was a dark, dark attic. In the dark, dark attic, was a dark, dark, box. In the dark, dark box, was a ghost!" The teacher observed that the two silent children in the group of six were enchanted as she read the repetitive story, and, in her words, "their eyes lit up like the sun." These nonverbal clues, which all children send, are especially noted in L2 learners. They are the substance of our observations until the learner is able (or willing) to speak in L2.

During this silent period we need a sharper than usual eye and more than the usual amount of patience, as we wait for L2 learners to demonstrate their English-using abilities. And we need empathy, the ability to see classroom experiences from the L2 learner's point of view. Sensing their embarrassment or, sometimes, their misery bolsters our ability both to be patient and to see the anticipated subtle changes.

One Teacher's Learning through Observation

Beth Level, a fifth-year teacher of kindergarten and first grade in the Columbus City Schools, tells a story of frustration and success about her first experiences with L2 learners. In her kindergarten class of twenty-nine children, four are L2 learners. On the first day of school, Beth feels panicky since she has not encountered this situation before; in her words, "we sort of muddled through, and everyone smiled a lot." but unconsciously she has started to do what all concerned teachers do, observe the L2 learners carefully, looking for signs of understanding or confusion and making guesses about what they know and don't know. Beth decides that the school district's guidelines for kindergarteners are "unfair" for these L2 learners: at this point they should not be expected to know their names, addresses, birthdays, and colors as other children might, for example.

In fact, the four children vary in what they do know and in their approaches to learning English in the classroom. Dan, who is Chinese, experiences a silent period of about three weeks, so that while Beth has started to write down what the other children say during that time, she has no examples of speech from Dan. He depends first on nonverbal behavior, taking a firm hold on the teacher's arm, to get adult attention. He also occasionally holds up both hands, clawlike, and makes a face as if imitating some creature he's seen on television. Beth is unsure that he understands any English until he takes a trip to the zoo where he is able to name the camels, fish, and turtles. (The class has been talking about animals to prepare for the trip.) In less than a month, Dan has made some progress and can now also say his name and address in English.

Lee and James are Korean, come to school together, and, according to Beth, "she sticks to him like glue." Lee seems to be an observer who is quiet but aware of her surroundings. Her parents have told Beth that Lee simply doesn't like to speak English. This may explain why she sometimes whispers to James, who then says something to Beth in English. Lee has already discovered that her own talking may not be necessary, and an interpreter is a useful thing. On rare occasions, she says a few words; for example, on the day that she notices Beth's fingernail polish, she makes it clear with very little language that she thinks it is wonderful.

James, by contrast, is the most talkative and outgoing of the four L2 learners and has even taught the class a song in English. His most memorable utterance during his first few days was "tyrannosaurus rex," a demonstration that a passion for dinosaurs is not restricted to native English speakers. Both he and Lee are intent on making sense of the classroom. As Beth puts it, "I can tell by just watching their faces. They concentrate more than anyone else."

In her notes Beth has written that James has this to say about a Fourth of July fireworks display, "I saw (shakes head up and down) big yellow one that went like dis (moves arms and spreads them out), and little drops fell down!" Lee, by contrast, just smiles and nods her head up and down when asked whether she saw the fireworks. On the same day James says, "Teacher, Lee is going to fly up in the air!" (holding hands up). Lee again smiles and nods her head. The conversation then sounds like this:

Beth: Are you going on a trip?
Lee: *(shakes head and smiles)*
James: She going to Korea.
Beth: Do Grandma and Grandpa live in Korea?
Lee: *(shakes head, twists fingers together, and smiles)*

Lee is clearly a "comprehender," attentive and cheerful—and willing to let James be the "talker." She thus manages to say little for four weeks, yet gives the impression that she has missed nothing. James is not only rapidly becoming an English speaker, he is also on his way to becoming a reader/writer. After about a month in the classroom, he dictates to Beth this caption for his drawing: "Today good day. He's doing a picnic. In the sky gots sun. He eating a sandwich." As with other children's dictation, Beth writes down exactly what James says, documenting how much he has already learned and respecting his ways of expressing himself in English.

Ben who is from Morocco has said very little for two weeks or so, giving one-word responses when questioned. Beth remembers feeling frustrated at being unable to understand some of his responses. She does not want to embarrass Ben by repeating, "What?" so many times. Like the other L2 learners Ben demonstrates his budding knowledge of English the day the class goes to the zoo. He starts talking animatedly—and loudly—on the school bus and continues until he falls asleep on the ride back to school. He busily describes what he saw (helicopters, trucks, cars) and "read" in the out-of-school environment (McDonald's, Kroger's, where his mother shops). In her notes, Beth has recorded some of Ben's utterances: "Teacher, look (points to sky) helicopter, helicopter !!" And:

Ben: Kroger.
Beth: Does you mommy shop at Kroger?
Ben: No.
Beth: Your mommy doesn't buy food at Kroger?

Ben: No, not dis Kroger, uh, Kroger on High Street.

Despite his silence in the classroom, Ben demonstrates quite an ability to communicate when his surroundings are familiar. Beth's impression is that all four children have been more talkative since that trip. The class theme had been "animals," so their ability to name what they saw at the zoo was not surprising; but the experience of going to see the animals initiated more prolonged and sophisticated expression than she anticipated.

As a result of her observations over a period of about a month, Beth's panic has eased; the progress of these young L2 learners has been remarkable. Even the one silent child has begun to enter the world of English speakers. Beth tracked their individual paths by two principal means: observation and interaction. Whenever she could she engaged these children in conversation, even when their responses were nonverbal. She then helped herself to see patterns within each child's language learning story by taking notes on what she heard and saw. She also had the sense and sensitivity to modify her expectations for these four children and not rigidly follow school district guidelines about what they should already know. In other words, she allowed herself to follow the children's lead.

Conclusions

When Eleanor Duckworth (1986) asked her students to observe the moon, she knew that a vital part of teaching is learning. Through observation we learn about things we might teach (for example, the habits of the moon), about ourselves as learners, and most importantly about the children we teach (see Genishi and Dyson 1984 and Jaggar and Smith-Burke 1985 for extended looks at observation). We have been engaged in observing the phenomenon, not of moon watching, but of learning a second language, through the eyes of adults who have either learned a second language well or who are helping children become speakers of English.

Teachers who use their sensitivity and observational skills to engage themselves in the story of L2 learning may lack firm answers to their questions. They may not know exactly what triggers changes in competence in the L2, or how best to match their talk with the individual child's pace and style of learning. Like moon watchers, teachers observing L2 learners find new questions to ask as soon as they find answers to earlier ones, for change is part of learning (and teaching). It is observation that enables teachers to notice change and try out conversational topics and activities that move children farther in L2 learning.

Beth's story, that of a monolingual kindergarten teacher with no special training in L2 teaching, is only one person's story. But it illustrates critical points about the process of language learning and effective teaching in general. The work reported in Rigg and Allen (in press), Wong Fillmore (1983), and Wong Fillmore and Valadez (1986) has demonstrated the complicated relationship between the process of second language learning and individual differences. In Wong Fillmore's (1983) two-year study of a group of Chinese and a group of Spanish-speaking children learning English, for example, she found no clear language learning "types." Children who learned English were not all highly sociable, and those who did not learn were not all quiet. Neither did the Chinese or Hispanic students as a group have a "typical" approach. Unlike the moon, each child followed his or her own unique timetable and an unpredictable path toward L2 learning.

Similarly, the four L2 learners in Beth's class displayed their own approaches and styles. Dan was not timid about interacting with others, but he used nonverbal behavior to communicate at first. Ben seemed not to be concerned with communication until the trip to the zoo, where his whole style became that of a "talker." Lee seemed to view English as a language others spoke (sometimes *for* her). James seized upon it as a welcome tool for communication, to use whenever possible. Our first conclusion can only be that each child does have her or his own individual approach to the process of L2 learning, and this approach might change over time or in different situations. As teachers we accept each child's approach or style while we encourage all attempts to communicate.

As sociolinguists (along with our four L2 learners) tell us, all language users demonstrate their linguistic abilities differently in different situations. Thus, Ben enthusiastically displayed a vocabulary and knowledge of English that Beth was unaware of until a new situation, an exciting field trip, prompted him to demonstrate his knowledge. Further, people within the language learning situation make a difference. Each of the four L2 learners was not alone; she or he was one of four. Of course we can't know how they would have progressed if they were alone, but these four were part of a peer group that was a potential source of support. Because it's hard to predict how any situation will affect language use, our second conclusion is that classrooms with a variety of activities and people—or lots of potential situations for talk—have the best chance of supporting the L2 learner.

Her L2 learners' responses to different situations were the object of Beth's sharp eye and ear. To be effective in encouraging talk, she provided a sensitive social support system that allowed the four to try out their new language. Beth herself played a complex role, trying to take the perspective of the L2 learner, seeing when the children looked confused or interested, responding to nonverbal cues, allowing friends James and Lee to stay together, keeping conversations alive with any of the four as long as possible, recording in her notes signs of the children's learning. Our third conclusion, then, is that in the classroom the teacher is at the heart of the L2 learner's support system. Observant teachers build on what they notice to aid the child's progress. Their watchfulness is heightened for the L2 learner who works to enter a linguistic world that classmates already know.

REFERENCES

Brown, R. *A Dark, Dark Tale.* New York: Dial Books for Young Readers, 1981.

Duckworth, E. "Teaching as Research." *Harvard Educational Review*, 56 (1986): 481–495.

Genishi, C., and A. Haas Dyson. *Language Assessment in the Early Years.* Norwood, NJ: Ablex, 1984.

Hong Kingston, M. *The Woman Warrior*. New York: Vintage Books, 1977.

Jaggar, A., and T. Smith-Burke (Eds.). *Observing the Language Learner.* Newark, DE/Urbana, IL: International Reading Association/National Council of Teachers of English, 1985.

Rigg, P., and V. Allen (Eds.) *English for Everyone.* Urbana, IL: National Council of Teachers of English, in press.

Rodriguez, R. *Hunger of Memory*. Boston: David R. Godine, 1981.

Wong Fillmore, L. "The Language Learner as an Individual: Implications of Research on Individual Differences for the ESL Teacher." In *Pacific Persectives on Language Learning*, edited by M. A. Clarke and J. Handscombe. Washington, DC: Teachers of English to Speakers of Other Languages, 1983.

Wong Fillmore, L., and C. Valadez. "Teaching Bilingual Learners." In *Handbook of Research on Teaching*. 3rd ed., edited by M. C. Wittrock. New York: Macmillan, 1986.

Reflection and Inquiry

REFLECTING ON THE READINGS

Respond to one or more of the following:

1. At the beginning of this unit, there are three suggestions for reflecting on classroom observation. How do any of the chapters in this unit expand your understanding of what to look for in a classroom setting? For example, how might John Fanselow's categories for seeing the classroom (chapter 5) inform your own observations?
2. How do these readings on seeing the classroom (chapters 5–9) build on the notion of questioning the nature of methods (chapters 1–4)? How, for example, do the findings of one of the classroom studies in Unit Two support a position articulated in Unit One?
3. Think about a time you were observed and evaluated as a teacher or student. How would you characterize the conversation that ensued between you and the observer? What do you feel was helpful? What was problematic? To what extent does this recollected experience confirm Fanselow's notion that prescriptive advice can lead to resentment or learned helplessness on the part of the person observed (chapter 5)?
4. Think of a classroom in which you are currently a teacher or student. Drawing on the readings in this unit, what specific factors would you like to change? Why would you want to make these changes? Is there a way for you to make any of these changes possible?

5. Harklau notes that ESOL courses often function independently of other courses in schools (chapter 7). Her research further demonstrates that students have divergent experiences in these two kinds of courses. Does your own experience confirm her findings? What do you see as the strengths and/or limitations of her recommendations for bringing these curricular programs together?

6. To what extent do the ethnographic experiences described in this unit point to classroom issues or factors that you have observed or experienced? For example, has gender, ethnicity, or first language background contributed to the way you or another student or a student whom you have taught behaved or performed in a classroom? Has a particular teacher's expectations or assumptions affected the way you or another student has been "read" by the teacher?

7. On the basis of their study of classroom discourse, Hull, Rose, Fraser, and Castellano conclude that we need to rethink the ways in which we research and talk about "cultural difference" (chapter 8). They argue that "we need to look at the social and instructional conditions in the classroom rather than assume the problem is to be found in the cultural circumstances students bring with them." How do assumptions about "cultural difference" help teachers address students' needs? How do such assumptions limit teachers' understanding?

8. Chapters 6 through 8 are classroom ethnographic studies that examine the "culture" of particular classrooms. Select one of these studies and identify what the researcher was looking for, how issues were explored, and what was found. Did anything surprise or intrigue you? Did the study suggest some aspect of teaching or learning that you would like to explore further? Why do you think these issues resonate for you?

9. The chapters in this unit demonstrate a variety of strategies for studying the classroom. What strategies in the readings appeal to you and why? Which of these strategies might you try to use in order to explore an issue either in your own classroom or a classroom in which you observe? What advantages and disadvantages do you see in each of them?

10. Select a passage (one sentence or several sentences) from one of the readings in Unit Two that struck you in some way. For example, it may be a passage that resonates with your own experience, that reminds of you something else you've read or seen, or that makes an important point. Highlight or copy the passage and then reflect on why you chose it.

READING FOR FURTHER REFLECTION

Respond to one or more of the following:

1. Read the following excerpt from M. Elaine Mar's *Paper Daughter: A Memoir*, in which she recounts her experience in first grade, five months

after she emigrated from Hong Kong to the United States. What strikes you? How might your understanding of this experience inform your own teaching?

> "Elaine?" Mrs. Tate repeated. . . . I immediately knew the answer, but I couldn't think of the word for "seven" in English. . . .
>
> *I'll write it on the board*, I thought. I slid out of my seat.
>
> Misunderstanding my action, Mrs. Tate said, "No, no, you can't go to the bathroom now." The class exploded with laughter. San translated the sentence for me. "I want to write the answer," I told him.
>
> Too late. Mrs. Tate decided to solve the problem herself: "All together class, one, two, three—"she tapped at the lines she'd drawn"—four, five, six, seven. The answer's seven!"
>
> The experience was repeated several times a day. Mother's friends and my teachers in Hong Kong had always praised my intelligence. Now Mrs. Tate needed to shush my classmates' giggles and give me extra time whenever I tried to speak. I began to wish that I *were* stupid—then at least they'd be picking on me for the right reasons. There was nothing worse than knowing the answers and not being able to say them.
>
> I felt trapped inside my body. Language seemed a purely physical limitation. Thoughts existed inside my head, but I wasn't able to make them into words. As a consequence, I was forced to observe my classmates from a place inside myself. And the kids just laughed, not able to see beyond my physical shell. They had no idea who I was beyond the mute, lifeless form in the classroom.

2. Read the following interview with a teacher from Earl Stevick's *Teaching Languages: A Way and Ways*. How does the observational experience recollected in the interview give you insight into teaching? What alternatives might there be for the ways in which the observed teacher behaved? If you were to discuss your observation with this teacher, how might you proceed?

> One day I had an opportunity to observe a teacher in an adult Basic English class. . . . I believe that this teacher entered the class with a set image of herself to be presented to the students: she was the teacher whose goal was to teach the completing of the simplest income tax form. As she began explaining how to fill in the different blanks on the form, it was apparent that the students were not understanding much. . . . For one thing, she did more talking and the talk became louder, perhaps with the notion that in this way the material would sink into the students' heads. Second, the teacher (in rapid English) told the students to write down what she said in the appropriate blanks without the students really knowing why. Finally, after the students filled in the blanks with figures they did not understand, the teacher praised them with the classic "very good."

3. Read the following excerpt from Patrick Chamoiseau's memoir, *School Days*, in which he recounts his experiences as a Creole-speaking child who was required to use French in school. What strikes you? What might a teacher do to explore a learner's "mindful of mysteries"?

> Sometimes the teacher tried to winkle sentences out of the children, but. . . . they all sat mum. The little boy had arrived with a mindful of mysteries—things seen, the bizarre habits of insects, how to understand night-blooming flowers or becoming one with the wind toying with the mere dust on the windowsill—and he could sense the souls of motionless beings that haunted abandoned temples, the secret sighs that drifted out of tiny chinks in the world. In an effort to spark discussion the Teacher sometimes showed them pictures, anyone of which the little boy could have turned into a thousand words, but the Teacher had reduced him to a silence that only deepened each time he heard the now constant lament: *Oh, this Crreole brrood has nothing to say!*

4. Read the following excerpt from Maxine Hong Kingston's *Woman Warrior: Memories of a Girlhood Among Ghosts*. Do you in any way identify with the experiences Kingston describes? Contrast the experiences of the Chinese students in the English-language classroom to their experiences in the Chinese school. What strikes you? How do you account for the differences?

> When I went to kindergarten and had to speak English for the first time, I became silent. A dumbness—a shame—still cracks my voice in two, even when I want to say "hello" casually, or ask an easy question in front of the check-out counter, or ask directions of a bus driver. I stand frozen, or I hold up the line with the complete grammatical sentence that comes squeaking out at impossible length. "What did you say?" says the cab driver, or "Speak up," so I have to perform again, only weaker the second time. A telephone call makes my throat bleed and takes up that day's courage. It spoils my day with self-disgust when I hear my broken voice come skittering out into the open. It makes people wince to hear it. I'm getting better, though. Recently I asked the postman for special-issue stamps; I've waited since childhood for postmen to give me some of their own accord. I am making progress, a little every day. . . .
>
> During the first silent year I spoke to no one at school, did not ask before going to the lavatory, and flunked kindergarten. My sister also said nothing for three years, silent in the playground and silent at lunch. There were other quiet Chinese girls not of our family, but most of them got over it sooner than we did. I enjoyed the silence. At first it did not occur to me I was supposed to talk or to pass kindergarten. I talked at home and to one or two of the Chinese kids in class. I made motions and even made some jokes. . . .
>
> It was when I found out I had to talk that school became a misery, that the silence became a misery. I did not speak and felt bad each time that I did not

speak. I read aloud in first grade, though, and heard the barest whisper with little squeaks come out of my throat. "Louder," said the teacher, who scared the voice away again. The other Chinese girls did not talk either, so I knew the silence had to do with being a Chinese girl. . . .

After American school, we picked up our cigar boxes, in which we had arranged books, brushes, and an inkbox neatly, and went to Chinese school, from 5:00 to 7:30 P.M. There we chanted together, voices rising and falling, loud and soft, some boys shouting, everybody reading together, reciting together and not alone with one voice. When we had a memorization test, the teacher let each of us come to his desk and say the lesson to him privately, while the rest of the class practiced copying or tracing. Most of the teachers were men. The boys who were so well behaved in the American school played tricks on them and talked back to them. The girls were not mute. They screamed and yelled during recess, when there were no rules; they had fistfights. . . .

SUGGESTED PROJECTS FOR INQUIRY

Select a project that you would like to pursue:

1. Undertake one of the following three observational studies.

a. Observe a classroom in which you are a teacher, student, or outside observer. Drawing on the readings in this unit, select a particular observational strategy and use it to record what you see. For example, you might
   - tape record and transcribe a segment of classroom interaction
   - take detailed observation notes and then later reflect in writing on what you saw
   - take detailed observation notes and later rearrange and categorize them.

   What are the benefits of using this strategy? What are the limitations?

b. Observe a particular classroom through different perspectives or circumstances. For example, you might
   - focus on the teacher during one set of observations and on the students during another
   - change where you sit from one observation to the next
   - observe on different days

   How does the change of focus, site, or day, etc. affect what you see in this classroom? Is there anything that intrigues, surprises, or puzzles you? What do your different observations teach you about the teaching and learning experience in this classroom? What do your different observations teach you about the nature of observing and understanding classrooms?

c. Focusing on one factor, observe a class over time. For example, you might focus on the following:
   - nonverbal communication such as eye contact, gestures, movements of teachers and/or students
   - the kinds of questions the teacher asks (e.g., questions to which the teacher already knows the answer or questions that are genuine)
   - the kinds of responses or contributions the students make (e.g., answers to the teacher's questions, answers to other students' questions, unsolicited comments, silence)
   - the teacher's responses to students' errors, mispronunciations, unintelligibility, etc.
   - the use of the blackboard or any other visual media materials
   - the use of classroom materials: texts, textbooks, handouts, etc.

   What patterns, if any, do you see as you focus on this factor? What does the pattern suggest to you about the teaching and learning experience in this classroom? How does focusing on one factor enlarge or limit your understanding?

2. Interview several teachers about their experiences with being observed and evaluated. Then explore what these recollected experiences reveal about the nature of classroom observation. What experiences, according to these teachers, were helpful? What do the teachers feel was problematic? What suggestions do these teachers have for making classroom observation a positive and productive process?

3. Undertake a case study of one or more students. Observe each student across different instructional contexts. For example, you might
   - shift from whole class to small group discussion
   - shift from students' before-class interactions to their in-class interactions
   - shift from an ESOL class to another class

Note how the student's performance, behavior, and interactions change in these different settings. What changes do you notice as a student moves from one context to another? What factors do you think contribute to these changes? If possible, interview the student(s) and teacher(s) to gain insight into their perspectives. What do your findings reveal about the relationship between context and students' behavior and language use?

4. Undertake an ongoing case study of one student in the same classroom. Keep notes about the student's behavior, interactions, and performance, and, as much as possible, make copies of that student's work. If

this is a student in your own classroom, record reflections about your assessment and expectations. If this is a student in someone else's classroom, interview the teacher about his or her assessment of and expectations for this student. What does your case study reveal about this student's experiences and progress? What does it reveal to you about the relationship between assessment and expectations?

5. If you are a teacher in a classroom, experiment by changing one factor in your teaching (e.g., changing the seating arrangement of students and/or teacher, assigning students to different groups, asking students to freewrite about an issue before engaging them in class discussion, waiting longer for students' responses after posing a question, asking students to call on or speak directly to one another). Keep notes about what happens as you make these kinds of changes. What happens as these changes are enacted?

Unit **III**

THEORIES INTO PRACTICE: PROMOTING LANGUAGE ACQUISITION

BEFORE READING

Respond to one or more of the following:

- Think of a language learning experience of your own. Where did it take place? Were you successful at learning the language? Why or why not?
- Recall a teacher who had a strong influence on you, either positively or negatively. Explain why this teacher is so memorable. To what extent might your experience with this teacher guide your own teaching?
- Read the following quotation from Peter Elbow's Embracing Contraries. Drawing on your own experiences, what principles do you believe need to be satisfied in order to produce good teaching and learning?

> . . . surely there cannot be only *one* right way to learn and teach: looking around we see too many diverse forms of success. Yet, surely this issue cannot also be hopelessly relative: there must be *principles* that we must satisfy to produce good learning and teaching—however diverse the ways in which people satisfy them.

Chapter 10

Theory Versus Practice in Language Training

Stephen Krashen

Given two methods of language teaching, method A and method B, suppose we want to know which is the more effective method. I will approach this question of "best method" in several ways. To give the punch line in advance, what I will conclude is that revolutions in language teaching will not be new ways of analyzing grammar, expensive laboratories, exotic methods, or the like, but the proper utilization of what we already have: speakers of the language. I will also suggest that the better methods are also the ones that are the most pleasant. (The converse is of course not necessarily true: just because a method is pleasant does not mean it is effective.)

I will begin by describing three areas that can influence us in our quest for the best method, suggesting how these areas can influence and help each other, and then what each of them has to say about method. The areas are: theory, applied linguistic research, and intuition. My contention is that each of the three ways we will consider arrives at basically the same conclusions.

Area 1: Theory of Second Language Acquisition. This consists of a set of related hypotheses put forth to account for observed phenomena in second language acquisition. Its generalizations are supported by empirical evidence, experiments, research done with theory in mind. They cannot be proved or definitively verified, but they are subject to disconfirmation.

They can be disproved by counterexamples, unless some deeper generalization or better theory emerges that can account for the counterexamples. At the moment each of the hypotheses I will give you is without serious counterexample. Moreover they are interrelated; evidence for one will count as evidence for another. Let me add that theory is not intended to be practical or even applied to anything, but in the long run there may be nothing more practical than sound theory.

Area 2: Applied Linguistics Research. Applied linguistics research may or may not be done with theory in mind. It is aimed at problem solving. For example, applied linguistics research may engage in comparing language-teaching methods, or research the question whether bilingual education is beneficial or harmful to the full development of L1.

Area 3: Intuition. This is the world of intuitions that do not belong to any theory but come from experience, reflection, introspection, informal observations. It is ideas that work in the classroom, practice not derived from theory.

The three different areas can and should influence teaching practice, all three at once, and they should influence each other. That is, theoretical researchers should be students of applied research, and vice versa. Knowing theory will give applied linguistics researchers some idea of where to look, even if they are not interested in testing a given theory. Similarly applied linguistics researchers as well as theoretical researchers would benefit by experience in area 3, by teaching a language in the classroom and/or attempting to acquire second languages.

In reality, there is very little interaction among the three domains. And the consequences of this are evident. We have seen theory appealed to in the past all by itself. But theory by itself is inadequate. [This is what happened with audiolingualism. We had basically a theory (behaviorist psychology)—not about language acquisition, but about something else—applied whole-hog to the language classroom.] Transformational-generative grammar was tried, but all it did was make teachers feel bad they did not know Chomsky's theory very well. (Neither behaviorist psychology nor grammar theories are theories of language acquisition. Both are based on analysis of product, not of process.)

As a result of the failure of interaction among the three domains, the third domain, that of intuition and ideas, is currently the primary input into practice. This is due to the failure of linguistic theory and the lack of substantial applied linguistic research. What we see now are texts and materials based pretty much on classroom experience alone.

How are we to know what direction to go in? I think we can safely adopt an approach when all three sources of knowledge support it.

THEORY

First, then, I will present a theory, a set of hypotheses about adult second language acquisition. I will say here again that these hypotheses are supported by empirical evidence and by research done with theory in mind. The hypotheses are interrelated and they are without significant counterexample. I will conclude by looking at pedagogical implications of these hypotheses and show that these implications are consistent in all cases with applied linguistic research and with our intuitions about language acquisition.

Let me now go through the hypotheses. I will try to give you a feeling for what the evidence is for each of them. I will give you nine of them:

1. The acquisition-learning distinction hypothesis
2. The natural order of acquisition hypothesis
3. The monitor hypothesis
4. The input hypothesis
5. The affective hypothesis
6. The aptitude hypothesis
7. The filter hypothesis
8. The L1 hypothesis
9. Individual variation in monitor use

Hypothesis 1: The Acquisition-Learning Distinction

The first is the most central and has been the most useful to me in understanding the literature and understanding second language acquisition. We think that for adults approaching a second language with the intent to "learn" it there are two ways: (1) they can "acquire," which is the way children "get" their first language, subconsciously, through informal, implicit learning. Once you have acquired something you're not always aware you have done it. It just feels natural; it feels as if it has always been there. Quite distinct from acquisition is (2) conscious language learning. This is knowing about language, explicit, formal linguistic knowledge of the language. We generally see this in language classrooms.

To make a long story short, our conclusion after a few years of research is that the first way, acquisition, is central, far more important than we ever thought it was, and that the second one, learning, is in fact peripheral.

Hypothesis 2: The Natural Order of Acquisition Hypothesis

Two years ago this was the central concern of our research. It is still quite interesting, but other things now are more exciting. What this says is that in acquisition people acquire items in a predictable order. Certain things come first, certain things come in the middle, certain things come late. Given the average language acquirer, we can make a pretty safe bet as to what will come first and what will come later. If we do correlation statistics, we get orders that nearly always come out significant. (This applies to acquisition, of course, not necessarily to learning.)

The main research here was begun by Roger Brown in first language acquisition and carried on by Dulay and Burt and others in second language acquisition. And what has been found applies to a fairly wide variety of phenomena. Let me take a moment here to illustrate this.

With English as a first language and English as a second language some morphemes come early. The progressive marker and the plural marker are very early for some reason. (The order of acquisition of some morphemes is not the same in first and second language acquisition; these happen to be the same; so it is a good example.) Others are late. The third person singular on verbs: (*He goes to the store*) is late. Also the possessive marker in English, *John's hat*, is late. In first language acquisition you might see from 6 months to a year separating those two groups of markers. In adult second language acquisition, you might see 10 years. Or you might not see the later ones come at all.

Some children will have plural before *-ing*, some will have *-ing* before plural. The same goes for second language acquisition. But you can talk about a statistical average. Practically no one is going to have plural way at the end. Practically no one is going to have third person singular at the very beginning.

Hypothesis 3: The Monitor Hypothesis

This hypothesis tells us what the interrelationship is between the conscious and the subconscious processes. What it says is this: when we get our fluency in a second language, when we can use it easily for communication, it comes from acquisition, not from learning. That is very important. Let me illustrate it with a diagram.

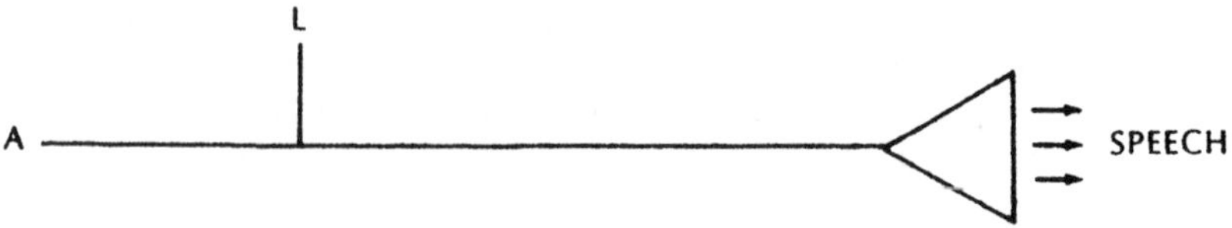

The L stands for conscious learning. The A stands for acquisition. When we talk, the speech is initiated or "driven" by the acquired system. In other words, your fluency in Spanish or French comes from what you have acquired, not from what you have learned. All those grammatical rules you have do not make you fluent. I did not believe this years ago, unfortunately, when I studied French, but the data have borne it out, linguistic research supports it, and what is going on today in teaching backs it up.

Learning, we think, has a limited function in language performance, It can only function as a monitor, as an editor. We apply learning after the utterance has already been generated, or sometimes after we say it, by way of self-correction. So we use learning to make corrections, in fact only to make small corrections. We can use learning only for very simple rules, the ones that are easy to teach, easy to remember. Also we hypothesize that the things we can consciously monitor are not very important for communication. They are the fine tuning, the things that give speech a more finished look. We apply learning to our output, sometimes before we speak, sometimes after we speak. It is only a corrector. It does not make things go. It is an afterthought, a polisher, an autocorrector. Learning then plays a fairly limited function here.

This brings us to the subject of error correction. People ask me whether error correction is good. As a first attempt at trying to answer that question, I give a subhypothesis of the acquisition-learning hypothesis: error correction is aimed at learning. When you make a mistake, if your teacher corrects it, what he is trying to get you to do is change or recall your conscious mental representation of the rule.

An ESL student says: "I goes to school every day," and the teacher says: "No, I go to school every day." The student is supposed to think, Oh yes, that is third person, not first person. That is what is supposed to happen. So theoretically, error correction is aimed at learning, not at acquisition.

So conscious learning (L) does have some function, but it turns out to be quite a small function, relatively small with respect to acquisition. As our research proceeds, that function seems to be getting smaller and smaller.

We now hypothesize, and this is a subhypothesis of the monitor hypothesis, that if you want to monitor successfully, many conditions have to be met, and these are necessary conditions.

1. Time. You have to have time if you want to use conscious rules. If you are involved in a conversation, you do not have time to think of the rule for the subjunctive. It's your turn to talk. You'd better come out with a sentence.

Do you know what I do in the languages I'm intermediate at? I plan my next sentence. Do you do this? I note whether the verb is subjunctive or not, whether I've got the subject-verb agreement and whether I've done all the contractions. But while I'm doing all this, my conversational partner is not waiting. He is talking. I'm not listening. I'm busy planning. So I rapidly lose touch with the conversation. That is what happens when you overuse the monitor in conversation. You get in trouble. So you have to have time.

2. Focus on Form. You have to be thinking about rules if you are going to monitor. You have to be thinking about correctness. But if what you are talking or writing about is very interesting, even if you have all the time in the world you may not think about conscious rules. You're in a conversation in your second language and you are talking about things that are very dear to your heart. You do not care about subject-verb agreement any more. You do not care if you have the relative clause just right. You're thinking about what you are saying, not how you are saying it.

3. Knowing the Rule. You have to know the rule if you want to monitor. Do this. Draw a circle about the size of a quarter. The circle represents all the rules of a language, let's say English. Now draw a proper subset, a circle within that circle, that represents all the rules of English you think the best linguists have actually described, let's say all the rules that Chomsky knows.

Now think of what the best applied linguists know. Represent the rules that these people know by a circle within the other circles.

Now take all the rules that the best teachers have learned. Then all the rules presented in class. Then all the rules that the best students actually learn. Then all the rules that the best students remember. Then all the rules that the best students carry around in their heads as mental baggage that they can apply to their output. That is what the monitor can do. No more.

I have not told you why we think the monitor hypothesis is valid. I'll just tell you this in a nutshell. We find that second language performers, when we put them in positions where they cannot monitor, display the same error patterns that children make. I'm oversimplifying it grossly, but that is the thrust. Under these conditions we see the acquisition laid bare. We see the same natural order in adults as in children.

In a test we have given to ESL students on several occasions where time was not allowed for them to use the monitor, we have found that they have the same order children do when they learn English as a second language: *-ing* and the plural will be up there; third person and possessive will be way down. Take the same subjects and give them a paper and pencil grammar test and you no longer see the same error pattern that children have. It changes. We get an unnatural order. What is happening? They are bringing in the conscious grammar. This is the intrusion of the monitor. In adults that third person singular jumps up. It is an easy rule to learn.

My study of German with its complicated case endings is a good example. We used to bring our monitors to class with us. Remember your German tests? As you are walking up the stairs to class you're thinking: der die das, des, der des, dem, den, dem. . . . And then you sit down and you immediately write those at the side of the page! No one acquires the morphology of German articles in first year German. But that is a major focus of the course, right?

Hypothesis 4: The Input Hypothesis

This hypothesis is, in my opinion, the most interesting in second language research today. To my mind it is crucially important because it attempts to answer a question of great theoretical and practical importance: How do people acquire language? It states simply that the way we acquire language (not learn it) is through comprehensible input: focus on the message, not the form. The input hypothesis goes for child language acquisition as well as for adult language acquisition. It claims that listening comprehension is of primary importance in language acquisition, and that speaking will emerge with time.

Let me say it a little more formally for you. Acquisition is brought about when you talk to acquirers so that they understand the message, and when the input includes a little language that is somewhat beyond them. So if you want to teach someone to talk, do not teach them to talk, give them comprehensible input! That is what research is saying to us now. Their ability to talk will emerge with time. It is not my idea, but this is screaming out from all I have seen. This is where our research is going.

Let me expand on that a bit. The input hypothesis says that if a student is at a certain stage in language acquisition (i.e., some stage along the natural acquisition order) and he understands something which includes a structure at the next stage, this helps him acquire that structure. Let's say you are at stage 3; the question becomes how do you move to stage 4? More technically, you are at stage i and you want to move to the next stage, $i + 1$. You want to pick up the next structure or group of structures.

But how do you understand something beyond you? The answer is probably context—extralinguistic information. When caretakers talk to very young children, they talk so that the children will understand. Caretaker speech, which we used to call "motherese," is not designed to teach language. It winds up doing so, but that is not what it is meant for. It is designed to communicate. Caretakers speak in a simplified register or code to get children to understand. They talk about the "here and now." They talk about what is going on in the room at the moment in front of the child. They do not say, "what do you think happened upstairs yesterday?" They talk about the "here and now," because that is the sphere of mutual interest. But look what that does to comprehension. Look how it makes it possible for the child to figure out subconsciously what the linguistic system is.

As the child gets older and grows more linguistically mature, the input from the caretakers will get a little more complicated. If you look at the correlation coefficients between complexity of input and linguistic maturity, however, you will find that they are not really high. It is *not* the case that the caretaker exactly tunes the input to the child. The input is not finely tuned; it is roughly tuned. Caretaker speech contains input that covers the $i + 1$.

What I think is going on is this: the child talks, and from that output the caretaker gets a rough idea of how to talk to the child so it will understand. In doing this the caretaker will generally include structures that are next up in the child's built-in syllabus for language acquisition. The caretaker does not *exclusively* provide those structures, however. That makes sense. It would really be unusual if it were any different. Caretakers would have to be incredibly sensitive to language to finely tune input.

Think about this. Think about how in some ways fine tuning is less practical than rough tuning. If we did finely tune, we would have to make a guess as to where the child is in his acquisition syllabus—which we might miss. And if we have more than one child in the room, one child might be getting good input, but the others aren't. In rough tuning a whole day-care class can be covered!

After reading Snow and Ferguson, Roger Brown stated that he finally knew what to say to mothers when they ask how to get their child to acquire language faster. (This is what Piaget calls the American disease: we always want to get there fast. Formal operations by age eight!) Brown's advice is simply this: Talk to your child so that he understands what you are saying. Bear in mind that he can understand more than he can say. Don't worry about consciously trying to do anything. There are more things you will subconsciously build in than you could possibly program for comprehensible input.

So children get simplified codes, speech in a reduced register, where the focus is on communication roughly tuned to their level, and they get comprehension help from extralinguistic context.

The next question is whether adults have the same simple codes available to them. I think they do. And I think that these simple codes are in fact not just helpful for language acquisition; practically, they are probably the way nearly all second language users make progress.

There are three potential simple codes we can talk about: "foreigner talk," "teacher talk," and "interlanguage talk." Foreigner talk is defined here as the adjustments native speakers make in talking to less competent speakers. Foreigner talk in the classroom is "teacher talk." This is the language of explanation in second language classes. When you take roll or explain how many points the midterm is worth or how an exercise works, that is teacher talk. And finally "interlanguage talk" is the speech of second language acquirers to each other.

Available studies tell us that foreigner talk is roughly tuned. So is teacher talk. All studies confirm that teacher talk is simpler than what goes on in the outside world. (Usually you find that more advanced students get somewhat more complicated input language.) All this, foreigner talk, teacher talk, and interlanguage talk is for communication. The goal is the message, not the form. It may be the case that these kinds of simple codes are analogous to caretaker speech in child language acquisition.

In a French IV class I was in last year the teacher walked into the class the first day and said in French: "I couldn't find a parking space, I'm sorry I'm late, this is such a complicated campus, I'm really sorry, this won't happen again." Then she switched into English and announced how many points the midterm was worth and how many points quizzes were worth. What a mistake! Nobody cared where she parked her car. Everybody was thrilled that she was late. But everybody wanted to know how many points were on the midterm. If that had been in French, that would have been real input. That is where she made the mistake.

In another French class I took two summers ago my teacher was trying to explain some phrase to us and none of us had any idea what she was talking about. This was a direct method class where the teacher used absolutely no English in class. She tried to explain with one anecdote that took about three minutes, and came to the last sentence, where she brilliantly used the phrase in a contextualized situation, thinking we could figure it out. Do you understand? she said. None of us did. So then she told another story, a longer one, and in the conclusion she used the phrase again, expectantly. Still no one understood. She thought she had blown ten minutes of class. Not true. We had ten minutes of comprehensible input where we were hanging on every word.

When foreign students speak to each other in ESL situations you get a great cohesive peer group built up, and this language is real communication. The focus is on the message. When I first went to Austria, I was terrified of native speakers. I had had three semesters of college German, but I could not understand a word. When I went to a German class for foreign students I heard teacher talk, which I understood. And when I met my fellow students from other countries in class, German became our lingua franca. And as time went on and I grew in competence I could then relate to native speakers who would talk down to me. (In the beginning even that was too much.) This, I think, was the bridge to real competence in the language.

There are problems with this. Teacher talk will take you only so far, because of the limited discourse domain of the classroom. After a while it won't include much of the $i + 1$. I could go to a French III class the rest of my life, even if they were all in French, and they wouldn't give me the input I need now.

Let's look now at the advantages and disadvantages of fine tuning versus rough tuning. Fine tuning is what is known as the lockstep approach. Today we do the present progressive; tomorrow we are going to do the future. And suddenly all the characters in this book switch tenses. Each structure gets five class periods, and if you haven't gotten it, too bad! Except that the second year you review it all over again. That is what they do in foreign language courses: the first year we go through the whole grammar and nobody has come close to mastering it; so the second year we review it all over again. What we are doing here is guessing at what our students' $i + 1$ is. We are guessing as to what comes next in the natural order. And we are also guessing that we know how much to give them. And that we know how to present it. Unfortunately, we usually guess wrong on all these things.

If we give people natural communication, there's no problem: if you don't get the future tense today, you are going to hear it again. And again. And again. Because natural communicative language is a rich source of grammar. All the structures are there. Especially all the frequent ones, all the ones you're going to need. So there is no guesswork as to where a structure is on the natural order. There is no guesswork as to how much. Comprehensible input at the $i + 1$ level has built-in review, built-in recycling all the time. And it handles individual variation. It is certainly the case in any class that the students are going to be at slightly different stages. So $i + 1$ for Johnny is not the same as $i + 1$ for Betty. With natural input everybody is covered as long as there is comprehension.

What this means is that the good teacher is the one who speaks so that all the students understand, not necessarily the teacher who presents things in a structured syllabus. The best syllabus may simply be the natural communication situation, simply talking to someone so that they understand.

How do good language teachers help someone understand something that contains grammar that is beyond them? Context. Situational context. They use things like pictures, visual aids, algebricks. It is good pedagogy. I did not understand why pictures and realia were important before, but I do now.

This to me then is the single most exciting subhypothesis of the single most exciting hypothesis in second language acquisition theory and practice today: that the language acquirer has a built-in syllabus in his head. So if I can talk to you and make you understand what I'm saying in a second language, I'm doing better than the best-planned syllabus in the world. It is that simple. The best input is the input we naturally give people when we talk to them so they understand.

I have referred to rough tuning in technical papers as the "net" which is cast by communication: when someone talks to you in another language so that you understand most of what is said, the speaker casts a net of structure around your current level; this net will usually include lots of instances of what is next for you, your $i + 1$. This means that when we talk to our students in the target language and they understand what we are saying, we are not only giving a language lesson, we might be giving the best possible language lesson. All we are trying to do in our teaching is aim a net at $i + 1$. It may be the most efficient thing we can do. (You could draw analogies to a fishing-line versus a net if you wanted, or to single-vitamin therapy and a well-balanced diet.)

How do students understand something that is beyond them? The answer, which is something all teachers know, is context, extralinguistic context. In other words, first we understand the message and that "teaches" us grammar, not vice versa. We do not get grammar first and then use grammar to understand. First we understand, and that helps us acquire.

How do we teach production then? We don't. Production will emerge over time. The best way to teach talking is to give people input. Talking will come all by itself.

I think that the input hypothesis is a very conservative theory. It is the most conservative one I can think of. And according to the way we do science, because this is the most parsimonious, this is the theory we should prefer. We should not add to it unless we have to—unless there is counterevidence. The input hypothesis happens to fit with everything we know about the reality of subconscious language acquisition.

Hypothesis 5: The Attitude Hypothesis

What the attitude hypothesis says is that people with certain personalities and certain motivations perform better in second language acquisition, and also that certain situations are more conducive to second language acquisition.

It comes as no surprise to us today to discover that low-anxiety situations are more conducive to language acquisition than high-anxiety situations, and that people with high self-confidence and self-esteem acquire faster than those without these characteristics.

Hypothesis 6: The Aptitude Hypothesis

There's also something called language aptitude, and we'll simply define it as how well you do on the Modern Language Aptitude Test. What is interesting is that the literature has said for many years that both attitude and aptitude are positively correlated with second language achievement, but they are not correlated with each other. You could be good in one, good in both, bad in one, bad in both. They're independent.

My interpretation of the literature is that attitude relates directly to acquisition, for the most part, and that aptitude relates directly to conscious learning. We think that aptitude relates to conscious learning for the following reasons. If you look at an aptitude test, you will see that the tasks are learning tasks. They involve conscious linguistic knowledge, induction of rules. In fact one of the authors of the MLAT, John Carroll, points out explicitly that this is what the test does.

Second, we see high correlations between how well people do on aptitude tests and how well they do in foreign language classes in grammar tests. Aptitude measures how fast you learn; so it probably relates to learning and not acquisition.

Hypothesis 7: The Filter Hypothesis

Dulay and Burt suggested that a filter, an affective filter, can keep input from getting in. We used to speak of a mental block, a block against language learning. Filter is another word for mental block. You have to let the input in. There can't be a filter keeping the input out, which is what we think the effect of attitude motivation is. With acquirers who do not have self-confidence, where the situation is tense, where (in Stevick's terms) they are on the defensive, the filter goes up. Even when the input is there, even when it is understood, they do not acquire with full efficiency.

What the filter hypothesis says about pedagogy is that the more we do to lower the filter, i.e., the more our classes are low-anxiety, the better off our students will be.

So input is necessary but not sufficient. What you also need is a low filter. You need comprehensible input, a low filter, a low-anxiety situation where people can focus on the message and not on the form.

The newer methods, the more successful ones, are the ones that encourage a low filter. They provide a relaxed classroom where the student is not on the defensive. So good methods concentrate generally on getting comprehensible input in and/or getting the filter down. When we do both we're going to have real success.

Hypothesis 8: The L1 Hypothesis

The L1 hypothesis says that the first language is used as a substitute utterance initiator in situations where L2 acquired competence is not available. In picking up a second language, a child may have a prolonged silent period while he or she acquires by input. An adult, on the other hand, often initiates speaking very early, using his L1 as a substitute generator for L2 and repairing the product with his monitor, his conscious knowledge of L2.

In terms of the Monitor Model it looks like this. We substitute first language competence for second language competence because we have not acquired the second language yet. Let's say it is the first day of a German class. The students have been exposed to 15 to 20 vocabulary words and a couple of rules. Now what? It is time to talk German. They expect to talk the first day. They want to go home speaking German. What can they possibly do? The only thing they can do is to use English sentences, plug in German words, and use their monitor to make as many repairs as they can think of.

What we often do in second language classrooms is force people into using this mode. It is in fact a very limited mode. It will get you a short distance into the language quickly, but it won't take you very far. The reason it won't is that you are at the mercy of your monitor. You must have it turned on all the time. And what it does is correct the places where the first language does not fit with the second. You have to watch your sentence the whole way. You are about to make an adjective come before a word and you remember that in this language it is different, so you have to switch it around as you go. That is no way to speak a language, but that is what we do when we make people talk too soon. We get performance without competence.

Note how a method that pushes production early goes against the input hypothesis. If instead of pushing production we give them listening comprehension and interesting reading, the acquisition will come by itself.

What happens to children in second language situations at the beginning? What do they do? Do they talk very much? No they don't. Take an immigrant child six or seven years old, put her in the middle of an American community, and see what happens. Put her in a kindergarten . . . hardly a word for three or four or five months in many cases, except for a few memorized expressions.

What these children are doing during this silent period is building up acquired competence the natural way. When they're ready to talk they'll talk. One mistake adults make (because we push them into it) is to use the first language as the generating device for producing utterances in the second language. In fact we do not have to force people to use this mode. To do so is counterproductive, we now think. If you want to beat the system, to produce in a language right away, you can do it with L1 plus Monitor Mode. You can use conscious learning plus the surface structure of the first language, and you can talk right away. And that is what a lot of adults do. But this mode has limitations.

Hypothesis 9 (Individual Variation in Monitor Use)

This is a very illuminating one for me. This says that we can predict at least one kind of individual variation by how people monitor. Some people monitor a lot, some people monitor not at all, and some people do it just right.

Monitor overusers are people like you and me who do not trust acquisition but who are constantly thinking of rules. Every time you utter a sentence, you are checking it with that grammar up there to make sure you got it right.

What happens to an overuser? Hesitancy. Disability in following and participating in conversations. Pathological language output. And we help bring it about with the way we teach languages. We focus you on form, we focus you on correctness.

There are interesting case histories in the literature on overusers, people who are so concerned with grammar they can hardly get a word out. And I'm sure that at universities you see more overusers than anything else.

Another type that you see in adult education programs in ESL, but only occasionally in a college language class, are underusers. These are people who, for some reason or another, have no conscious grammar to speak of. These are people who rely totally on their acquired competence. What is very interesting about these people is that they often do quite well with the language. They often acquire substantial amounts of English syntax—not all of it, but a lot of it. If you think conscious learning has to come first, please explain those people to me. These are people who don't know a prepositional phrase from their elbow.

I think our pedagogical goal should be to produce optimal users. These are people who monitor, but it does not get in the way of communication, people who refer to conscious rules when they can, but do not get hung up on them. They use them in written language and in prepared speech. But in normal day-to-day conversation they may use them very little.

APPLIED LINGUISTIC RESEARCH

I think I have given you enough theory so we can talk about some of the implications, but let me give you a little evidence now from the area of applied linguistic research. If you look at the history of method comparison, comparing method A with method B, you will find that the results are rather striking in that there are very few differences between methods. The classic experiment is something like this: five classes are audiolingual or inductive method with pattern practice; five classes are grammar-translation or deductive method. It usually turns out that at the end of two years one method proves a little better than the other. The results generally show that with adults the deductive ones are slightly better. It is usually statistically significant, but not by a large margin. On a 60-point test maybe the deductive people will score 38 and the inductive people will score 33. The inductive ones still acquired language, they got something out of the course, and they weren't much worse than the deductive students.

So what is going on?

This question prompted Earl Stevick to ask his "riddle": if method A is based on one theory of the brain (that we are stimulus-response organisms), and method B is based on a totally different theory of the brain (that we are cognitive thinkers) and yet both methods give approximately the same results, how can this be accounted for? How can both theories of the brain coexist? My answer is that neither of these systems is much good; neither is really getting much comprehensible input. And the only reason either of them works is by accident: they happen to provide people with some comprehensible input, despite their best efforts to keep comprehensible language use away from the students. We will do much better, theory predicts, if we have methods that focus on the input.

There is a variety of new methods which we might call "input" methods. These are methods with the following things in common: (a) Focus on communicative input in the classroom—not listening-comprehension for form but listening for meaning—where the student is actively attending to the message. (b) There is very little emphasis on output. Output is allowed to develop on its own. (c) Something is usually done to keep the affect as good as possible.

One example, which has not received the attention it deserves, is Asher's approach called Total Physical Response. In Asher's system the instructor gives commands to the students such as stand up or sit down, and the students follow the commands as the instructor demonstrates the expected action. Not only are students who have been trained through total physical response better, they are apparently a lot better. In one study they did in 32 hours what the standard students did in 150 hours—that is, five times faster. They do about equally well in reading, writing, and speaking, and far better in listening comprehension. That is not just one study; many studies scattered through various journals report this since the mid-sixties.

INTUITION

We move to the third way of determining what kind of method we should have: anecdotal evidence, intuition, observations, what teachers are doing. This kind of evidence is difficult to gather and difficult to evaluate; so I will rely on my own biased observations of what I see going on.

If you go to ESL conferences and foreign language conferences, what you see is interesting. What kinds of papers are teachers presenting to each other? You no longer find people giving presentations of new pattern practice techniques, a new analysis of the relative clause using stratificational grammar, or the like. Instead what they talk about is: using the newspaper in the language class, how to get your students to understand TV, role-playing, socio-drama, etc. I see them focusing on what works, on affect, getting the students to get to know each other, and getting concrete spoken language input, real language use, helping them to survive on the outside so they get more language use.

Another source of evidence we can bring to bear on this is from language learning in other cultures. There is an interesting piece of reporting from Arthur Sorenson, who observed apparently successful language acquisition in adulthood among certain Indian tribes in the Amazon Basin in South America. He reports that about two dozen languages are spoken among these people. No member of any tribal group is allowed to marry anyone who speaks the language of his or her own group. (That would be incestuous.) You can only marry someone who speaks a different language. These people are constantly learning languages from the time they are little kids to the time they are old.

How do they do it? According to Sorenson, the Indians do not practice speaking a language they do not know well yet. Instead they passively learn words and phrases in it and familiarize themselves with its sounds. They may occasionally attempt to speak a new language in an appropriate situation, but if it does not come easily they do not force it. Input lets speaking emerge.

Let me tell you now about a method that takes into account all the theory we have talked about. It is not the only possible manifestation of it, but I think it is a good one, and it is one we're trying out at USC with some success. The method is called the Natural Method. Its inventor is Tracy Terrell of the Spanish Department of the University of California at Irvine, and this approach has been used there in teaching Spanish and German.

The classroom is for acquisition. Learning is done somewhere else. The function of the classroom is to provide students with comprehensible input. No grammar is presented in the classroom ever. The teacher uses the second language exclusively. His goal is to make students understand. The student can respond either in his L1 or in the L2. (This is not new. No single idea in the Natural Approach is new, but put together like this the approach is novel and it works.) If they choose to respond in the second language, the errors are not corrected unless there is a breakdown in communication.

The idea is that talk helps us get more input. That is it: get input. Comprehensible input. This allows speaking to emerge. Homework is grammar: standard, old-fashioned, discrete-point grammar to be used in monitoring. And it is given so that it can be used under appropriate conditions: when you have time, when you have the rule and occasions when the focus is on form.

The results of this approach have been quite encouraging. People understand fairly complex things right away. It handles individual variation. In a college class you may have a lot of homework. In adult education or a class for children you may not have any. In junior high school you may have some. In any case acquisition is central in the classroom and conscious learning is not the goal.

Children do this in picking up a second language. They are quiet for about three or four months before they say a word. They are building competence through listening. The new pedagogical strategy is to allow adult learners to have a silent period. Give them comprehensible input, and natural language will emerge on its own.

SOME PROBLEMS

Now let me list a few problems with all this.

1. Acquisition is slow and learning is fast. Using discrete-point grammar testing, learning appears to produce quick results. If you give a grammar test to the people who have been having acquisition only, they may not do well. Take a group of linguists and we can conquer the grammatical structure of a language very rapidly. We can do well in a discrete-point grammar test, yet not be able to speak a word of the language. On the other hand acquisition is applicable to any situation. It is slow, however, and needs time to emerge.
2. Learning feels good. Especially to monitor users like myself. Every time I use the subjunctive correctly in French I rekindle the thrill of having conquered it.
3. Who has control of the language teaching profession? People interested in the structure of language. Monitor overusers, many of us crazy about grammar. And we think our students are going to be just as crazy about it as we are.

So that leads us to problems of implementation if all this is correct. The students think that language is grammar. They have expectations of getting grammar. Administrators think that language is grammar.

SOLUTIONS

I can think of two solutions to this. In the long run we will have to educate the administrators and the masses. In the short run we can practice a little useful deception. We can teach vocabulary, situational routines, grammar, whatever we like, and as long as we fill it with acquisition opportunities, as long as we keep providing comprehensible input, we are contributing to natural language acquisition.

Chapter 11

Recent Language Research and Some Language Teaching Principles

Karl J. Krahnke
Mary Ann Christison

The underlying assumption of this article is that linguistic and communication research can support principles on which to base revisions in the content and method of language teaching. The article first reviews the results of research in language acquisition, interactional analysis, pragmatics, repair, error, and social and affective factors. Four general principles are then extracted from this research, principles relating to acquisition activities in the classroom, the importance of affective factors, the communicative capacity of learners, and the nature and treatment of error.

INTRODUCTION

Over the last ten to fifteen years, the language teaching profession has been provided with a wealth of new information on language and language use from several areas of linguistic and language-related research. As is usual, the problem for designers and providers of language instruction has been to determine how to assimilate, evaluate, and apply this new knowledge. The process of application really involves two questions: the effect of research on what aspects of language behavior we choose to teach and the effect of research on how we teach. Much recent work has focused on the former question, especially the work done for the European Unit/Credit system (van Ek 1975) and much of the work done in Britain on communicative language teaching. Methodological questions have been addressed in the work of Curran (1968, 1972, 1976, 1978), Gattegno (1972, 1976), Lozanov (1979), Asher (1977), Winitz and Reeds (1973), and Terrell (1977, 1982). None of these, however, has attempted to draw systematically on the results of broad-based research in developing their methodologies. Stevick (1976, 1980, 1982) has done so in a personal and practical way, but his recommendations are often more eclectic than systematic. Krashen (1981, 1982) has begun to address questions of methodology and approach, but his view is tied quite closely to the model of second language acquisition which he has developed.

All of this work is instructive and useful. The pedagogical recommendations of Krashen (1982) and Krashen and Terrell (1983), in particular, come closest to bridging the gap between theories of language and language acquisition and actual classroom techniques. This article does not attempt to address that same issue but rather focuses on how an examination of recent language-related research can suggest principles on which effective language teaching can be based, principles which relate to approach, design, and procedure in language teaching (Richards and Rodgers 1982). What this article consists of, therefore, is a review of research that relates to questions of instructional methodology and the suggestion of four principles which can be used to guide specific methodological decisions.

ACQUISITION AND LEARNING

A useful theoretical construct in language acquisition research is the now widely accepted distinction between learning and acquisition (Krashen 1978). Krashen's hypothesis is that adult language learners have two different means available to them to gain knowledge of a second language—*learning* and *acquisition*. In brief, *learning* results from deliberate, structured, and conscious attempts to learn the language, such as through drills and rule memorization. *Acquisition*, on the other hand, results from natural and meaningful interaction with other speakers in the target language. According to this hypothesis, learning is very different from acquisition in that it only functions to correct or "monitor" (Krashen 1978) the language being produced. These corrections or changes can take place before or after a sentence is actually spoken or written, but in order to make the correction the learner must recognize the error, know how to correct it, and have sufficient time to do so (see Krashen 1978 and 1982 for a more detailed consideration of this point). In immediate, face-to-face or pen-to-paper, communicative encounters, these conditions can rarely be met, so it is argued that learning may not be as important in developing the ability to communicate fluently, verbally or in writing, as we previously believed.

Rather, according to the hypothesis, fluency develops gradually as a result of communicative experience in the target language, with progress occurring when the learner is able to understand most of what is contained in the communication but when that communication also contains language material the learner needs and is ready to acquire. Krashen (1982:9) refers to this understandable language as *comprehensible input* and defines it as language that is comprehended by the learner but which still contains and, therefore, provides new structures or other language material that the learner has not yet acquired. That is, it is hypothesized that learners can acquire language when they have to use it to communicate their wants and needs, when the focus is on *what* they need to say rather than on *how* they should say it.

More research is being done to clarify the relationship between learning and acquisition, but our present understanding of the distinction seems sufficient to suggest an explanation for the evident lack of positive transfer to actual performance in communicative situations in the target language of much language instruction in which the emphasis is on drills and rule memorization. What the learning/acquisition hypothesis suggests is that activities which result in learning may have a limited role in an overall language instruction program, a role of assisting learners in developing learning- and monitoring-sensitive abilities in such areas as spelling, punctuating, and test taking, for example. But, the hypothesis suggests, if effective use of the language in realistic settings is the goal of the program, then learning-fostering activities should not dominate the language classroom to the exclusion of acquisition-fostering activities which help students develop spoken and written fluency in the target language.

LANGUAGE ACQUISITION

Research in language acquisition has focused on three different types of acquisition: 1) first language acquisition in children, 2) second language acquisition in children, and 3) second language acquisition in adults. Data have been collected in formal and in informal environments from all three types of subjects. From theories and research in first language acquisition we can draw conclusions for second language teaching and learning. There are, undoubtedly, important cognitive, affective, neurological, and physical differences between the acquisition of a first and a second language and between children and adults. At the same time, however, there are important similarities; essentially, both children and adults acquire languages from similar types of experiences and at essentially similar rates when conditions are optimal. Although it has been suggested that children are more likely to be able to take advantage of these experiences than adults (Asher and Garcia 1969), or at least have the advantage of receiving real intake while adults may not (Wagner-Gough and Hatch 1975), the question for language pedagogy is not the *degree* of similarity or difference between first and second language acquisition but rather the recognition of the similarities so that those similarities, and not just the differences, may be taken advantage of to increase effectiveness in second language instruction.

There are three basic ways in which first and second language acquisitions are similar. They are summarized as follows:

1. **Natural order.** One area of research which has received considerable attention in the past few years is the study of the order of acquisition of various morphemes. Brown (1973) first demonstrated that there was a natural order in which children acquired some of the morphemes of their first language. Brown's longitudinal findings were confirmed by de Villiers and de Villiers (1973). Studies of the sequence in which adults acquire grammatical morphemes in a second language began with the work of Bailey, Madden, and Krashen (1974), who confirmed that adults also showed a regular order in acquiring the eight morphemes studied. Dulay and Burt (1974), using the *Bilingual Syntax Measure* (Burt, Dulay, and Hernandez 1975), established a similar order for children learning a second language. Andersen (1976) and Krashen, Butler, Birnbaum, and Robertson (1978) reported natural orders in the written production of adults. Although there are some problems with these studies, specifically concerning the statistical procedures used, whether the natural ordering is an artifact of the *Bilingual Syntax Measure*, and whether or not morphemes in obligatory contexts reveal enough about the language acquisition process (Larsen-Freeman 1975, Porter 1977, Hakuta and Cancino 1977, and Rosansky 1976), there is no counter-evidence to the hypothesis that the existence of a natural order is part of the creative construction process in both adult and child language acquisition.

2. **Comprehension.** Children acquiring first languages learn to comprehend before they learn to speak. Winitz and Reeds (1973) claim that in first language acquisition, comprehension outpaces production by about a year. They claim that this sequence of development is a functional property of the brain and cannot be reversed or greatly modified. Recent studies support the hypothesis that delaying speech in second language instruction, while at the same time providing active listening, causes no delay in attaining proficiency in a second language (Gary 1975, Postovsky 1977). In fact, according to Gary (1974), early oral performance may not be profitable for children and adults studying second languages in formal settings. Terrell (1982) has also found strong evidence to support a preproduction phase for classroom instruction.

3. **Linguistic input.** Language acquirers in natural situations receive what we call *comprehensible input* (see above). In first language acquisition this type of input is called *caretaker speech*, and in second language acquisition it is sometimes called *foreigner talk*. Hatch (1979) summarizes some of the important characteristics of simplified input: reduced rate of speech (words and phrases are not stretched, but more frequent pauses are inserted at possible boundary points), shorter utterance length, greater use of redundancy (repetition and gesture), simplification of syntax, and more frequent use of specific discourse phenomena (e.g., *yes/no* questions and tag questions). All of these modifications to normal adult speech assist learners in making useful guesses about the language and in developing an internalized working grammar of it. Snow (1979) reports that children figure out underlying structures with the aid of simplified input. Rúbin (1975), Terrell (1982), and others have suggested that the same processes operate for adults.

From the point of view of research, the role of conscious learning in the language acquisition process remains unclear. Much of present language pedagogy is based on the assumption that language acquisition can be quantitatively and qualitatively improved through formal instruction in the language, especially instruction in the grammatical regularities of the language. Lee, McCune, and Patton (1970), however, have provided evidence that strongly suggests that students do not pay much attention to repetitive drills after a few repetitions, and Hendrickson (1976) has noted the lack of effect on student writing of explicit correction of formal errors. But, at the same time, it is obvious that many language learners have somehow benefited from being exposed to explicit grammatical instruction.

Krashen (1982) argues that the role of conscious learning in language acquisition is limited almost entirely to being a source of input for those learners who are open to it, and that there is little or no transfer from formal, conscious learning to communicative performance. Others (Bialystok 1978, Stevick 1982) have posited a greater role for conscious learning but with little evidence to support their views.

Given the strength of the acquisition hypothesis, it is difficult to support a view that calls for a central role for conscious learning in language instruction. Since the input which leads to language acquisition is ultimately not defined by the type of language available to the learner but rather by how the learner is able to utilize it, the acquisition hypothesis presents the stronger case that acquisition is an incidental outcome of instruction. Instruction may certainly serve as input for some learners, but it is an additional empirical question whether instruction intended to lead to conscious learning is the most direct route to a useful competence in a new language. Conscious learning may positively affect the learning of some routines and patterns (Krashen 1981:96–99) and limited aspects of language behavior, such as editing written work, but there is strong evidence that extensive communicative experience with a new language is necessary for communicative competence to develop (Carroll 1967, Saegert, Scott, Perkins, and Tucker 1974). What remains to be better determined is the nature of the relationship between learning and acquisition and the nature of classroom experiences that can foster communication and acquisition.

INTERACTIONAL ANALYSIS

Since acquisition is hypothesized to be a product of meaningful interaction, it would be useful at this point to review what has been discovered about the form and content of conversation and verbal interaction. The sociological perspective on which much of this work is based was set by Goffman (1967, 1971), but the formal or structural analysis of conversation is a relatively new topic of interest. Most of the work has been done by the late Harvey Sacks and his colleagues, Schegloff and Jefferson. Their work (especially Sacks, Schegloff, and Jefferson 1974) has established the *turn* as the basic unit of verbal interaction and has characterized conversations as being governed by a *turn-taking system*. Their analyses are purposely focused on the structural properties of this system, on what behavioral devices are used to establish and hold turns and to open and close conversations. They are less concerned with which linguistic forms are used to accomplish these ends. Their work has established that competent speakers of a language use a system for structuring verbal interaction which is somewhat independent of the form and meaning of the language used in the interaction. There are, in short, expectations and regularities that typically operate in conversation even when, through error, misunderstanding, or perversity, a speaker produces an utterance which does not seem to perform an appropriate function. Coulthard cites an extreme example of a doctor and schizophrenic patient maintaining the turn-taking system even though the patient does not fill his turn appropriately:

> A: What is your name?
> B: Well, let's say you might have thought you might have had something from before, but you haven't got it anymore.
> A: I'm going to call you Dean. (Coulthard 1977:63)

While this example is bizarre, the careful observation of turn-taking formalities in it demonstrates that conversation can be governed by structural constraints, at least at a basic level. Some details regarding how turn selection is done seem to differ from culture to culture, but the system of taking turns and the expectancy on the part of speakers to do so is universal enough that it constitutes a basis for verbal interaction by language learners in the new language well before they are competent enough to participate skillfully in that interaction (Conrad 1982). The learners come to the new language with the expectation that it will be organized into turns and that filling turns is a minimally adequate way of sustaining conversation. They also assume a system of openings and closings, the details of which must be learned or acquired.

The concept of turn taking has been elaborated with the notion of *adjacency pairs* (Sacks, cited by Coulthard 1977:70), a frequently occurring but specialized pair of turns that are related in that the nature of the second turn is predicted by the first. Question-answer is one obvious pair; greeting-greeting is another. A small list is given by Richards (1980:421), with the suggestion that language instruction address this phenomenon more directly. But the phenomenon is a discourse universal and, as such, constitutes pre-existing knowledge of the structure of discourse. Language instruction can use this pre-existing competence as a basis for instruction in the specific forms that are used in adjacency pairs in the language being learned.

Gordon and Lakoff (1975) and Grice (1975) have identified several principles or postulates that, they claim, govern the conduct of conversation. These principles are the *sincerity condition*, the *reasonableness condition*, and the *cooperative principle*. Taken together, these principles assert that participants in a conversation assume, unless there is evidence to the contrary, that their conversational partners will be sincere and reasonable in the conduct of their conversational behavior and that they will be clear and orderly in what they say. These are basic notions, to be sure, but their suspension predictably requires participants in interaction to use more complex interpretation strategies to process utterances in which the principles are violated. We may offer the following example:

A: How was your date last night?
B: I got a good night's sleep.

By not relating the answer directly to the question, A forces B to do more complex work to interpret the answer.

In most normal conversations, however, conversational principles are strictly observed, giving second language learners another set of tools to use in deciphering the language that is directed to them. If they assume that the interaction they are involved in is governed by universal principles of conversation, then they have a structured predisposition and set of expectations as to how to interpret the speech presented to them.

PRAGMATICS

To the familiar division of language analysis into phonology, syntax, and semantics, *pragmatics* has been added to account for the phenomena that relate a given utterance to its functions or meaning in a given instance of conversational interaction. *It's cold in here* may be used to inform, but it may also be used to get someone to close a door or window.

Pragmatics encompasses a wide range of contextual factors including, among others, social and physical circumstances, identities, attitudes and beliefs of participants, and the relations that exist among participants. Pragmatic competence gives speakers the ability to correctly interpret sentences such as *It's cold in here* in the way they are intended, to choose the appropriate form of address for another person in a given situation, and to fulfill many other interactional functions in between. When there are problems with the pragmatic system, misunderstandings can be quite serious, as in the case of the Japanese student who almost abandoned a new friendship because the new friend had remarked, in haste, "I'm in a hurry now—I'll call you sometime." The Japanese girl interpreted this as a permanent dismissal.

There has been considerable research into the pragmatics of English from the point of view of how the pragmatic system is used by competent speakers. In addition, Fraser, Rintell, and Walters (1980) have carried out some initial work into the acquisition of pragmatics by second language speakers and have presented a suggestion for how research should proceed. Their work is based on three assumptions (1980:78):

1. There is a basic set of speech acts common to all languages.
2. The same set of strategies for performing speech is available in all languages.
3. Between languages there is a significant difference between *when* a speech act is performed and *what* strategy is used to perform it.

Borkin and Reinhart (1978), Fraser (1981), Fraser and Nolen (1980), Manes and Wolfson (1981), and Schmidt and Richards (1980) are other examples of specific studies concerned with the acquisition of pragmatics in second languages. This area of research is still too new for well-founded conclusions to be drawn, but what is clear is that pragmatics is such an integral and universal part of language behavior that it must be addressed by language teachers from the beginning stages of classroom teaching and should not be left until later or for outside the classroom. The conventions of pragmatics vary greatly from one language to another and are of great subtlety and complexity, but since much of message design is pragmatically determined, and since setting and interaction provide much of the contextual basis for pragmatic interpretation, the need for specific interactional activities in language teaching programs is clear. Kramsch's handbook (1981) is useful and practical and provides an overview of pragmatics and other discourse phenomena as well as some excellent suggestions for classroom activities to aid learners in acquiring them.

Given the complexity and abstractness of pragmatic rules and the dialect and individual variation that accompany their use, it is doubtful that the recommendation of Taylor and Wolfson (1978) that pragmatic rules should simply be taught to students is of any value other than for Krashen's Monitor over-users (Krashen 1981:4). Of more value is the position taken by Coulthard that "the language teacher cannot hope to explain discoursal meaning in the traditionally regarded 'cut-and dried' way of teaching grammatical rules" (1977:xii) and that "ways of teaching should shift from teacher-telling to learner interpreting . . . Learners need to become analysts of discourse themselves" (Coulthard 1977:xiii)

REPAIR

Some of the most interesting work on verbal interaction has been conducted to determine how speakers *repair* problems that arise in conversation. The early work on repair by native speakers was done by Schegloff, Jefferson, and Sacks (1977), who defined repair as any conversational move which occurs because there is some real or perceived difficulty in the conversation. Repair is a more general phenomenon than correction, but errors in form or meaning are one kind of trouble, and correction is one type of repair. Schegloff, Jefferson, and Sacks refer to repair as a "self-righting mechanism for the organization of language use in social interaction" (1977:381). Repair in conversation between native or competent speakers is overwhelmingly *self-repair*, where it is the speaker who attempts to repair the conversational trouble, whether the trouble was self-perceived or perceived by another participant in the interaction (Schegloff, Jefferson, and Sacks 1977:376).

Gaskill (1980) has studied correction between native speakers and non-native speakers of English, and Schwartz (1980) has considered repair between pairs of non-native speakers of English. Both have concluded that self-repair and self-correction are far more frequent than *other-repair* (repair done by a participant other than the speaker), although in Schwartz's non-quantified analysis other-repair was also frequent. Conrad's still unpublished thesis (1982) is a detailed study of many of the factors involved in the interaction of native speakers of English with non-natives who are at different levels of language proficiency. Conrad demonstrated that initiation of repair, or calling attention to the need for repair, was done more frequently by the non-native member of a conversational dyad who was at a low level of language proficiency. The imbalance was reversed at higher levels of proficiency, where it was the native-speaker member who more frequently initiated repair. As for the accomplishment of the repair itself, however, self-repair was carried out by non-native speakers at all levels of ability and increased as ability increased. These facts, plus a number of other observations on context, the relationship of interactants, and the types of moves used in repair, paint a rich and detailed picture of the conversational interaction of native and non-native speakers. If there is a conclusion beyond the instructive ones reached by Conrad himself, it is that language learners have a demonstrated ability to utilize non-language-specific techniques of interaction maintenance which also facilitate their comprehension and, we can assume, their acquisition of the new language. Even relatively non-proficient learners have this ability, and it is most productively used in the context of extended and sincere personal relationships with native speakers.

ERROR

Probably no aspect of language pedagogy has been the subject of more interest and misunderstanding than that of learner error. Although a great deal of research has been done on the matter of error, basic questions remain as to:

1. the source of learner error
2. the characterization and classification of error
3. the effects or gravity of learner error
4. the treatment of error in the classroom

Source

Early work on error asserted that error in second languages resulted largely from differences between the learner's first language and the language being learned (i.e., from *transfer* or *interference*), or from inadequate or unmastered instruction. Recent studies (summarized in Dulay, Burt, and Krashen 1982, on which this review is based) have established that interference from the learner's first language accounts for much less of learner error than had previously been supposed. Until now, studies of the sources of learner error have focused on syntactic error. Phonological error is probably much more the result of first language influence (Dulay,

Burt, and Krashen 1982:97–98) as, possibly, are the relatively unstudied areas of semantic, pragmatic, and interactional error.

Studies of the sources of second language error (as summarized in Dulay, Burt, and Krashen 1982:163–172), have identified four types of error. The first of these are *developmental* errors, errors which are similar to the errors made by children learning the language as their first language. Developmental errors are assumed to be a natural product of gradually developing ability in the new language and, in the studies so far carried out, developmental errors make up the majority of errors exhibited by second language learners. *Interlingual* errors, or errors clearly attributable to first language influence, make up a maximum of 25% of learner error, with the percentage being higher for adults than for children. The third and fourth types of error are, first, errors that could be either developmental or interlingual (i.e., *ambiguous* errors) and, last, *other* errors, which are neither developmental nor interlingual.

While researchers have made some progress in identifying the source of learner error, the processes by which these errors are produced are still poorly understood. *Transfer* and *interference* are terms that are more metaphoric than empirical since very little is known about what actual linguistic or psychological processes learners are employing when errors are produced.

Classification

Classifying syntactic error according to linguistic type is a more familiar way of categorizing error and is possibly of more immediate use to classroom teachers. In this approach to error, the sources or effects of errors are ignored in favor of classifying the errors according to the part of the linguistic system which is ill-formed (e.g., the phoneme /o/, third person singular verb endings, article omission, inappropriate use of *excuse me*, and so on). There are several such classifications which have been done, the most useful being that of Burt and Kiparsky (1972). Classification by linguistic type can be a useful analytic procedure and can provide a useful basis for instructional intervention as long as the classification is not mistaken for a psychologically real analysis of the process by which the errors are produced or for a hierarchy of the communicative effect of errors.

Effect

It has long been recognized that not all errors have the same communicative effect, significance, weight, or gravity, but few studies have been done to measure that significance or to determine the factors affecting it. One study of error significance was done by Burt and Kiparsky (1972) in conjunction with their linguistic classification of syntactic errors. Although their methodology was not rigorous, they established the distinction between *global* and *local* error, the former interfering with communication more than the latter. Global errors, which affect overall sentence organization and "confuse the relations among the constituent clauses" (1972:6), include misordering of sentence elements, using connectors inappropriately, and regularizing exceptions to syntactic rules. Local errors include errors in noun and verb inflection, articles, and auxiliaries. For example, the globally erroneous sentence *Why like we each other?* was judged less comprehensible than the locally erroneous *Why we like each other?* (Dulay, Burt, and Krashen 1982:192).

Johansson (1978) has produced the most comprehensive study on error gravity, in which he points out that it is not possible to assign specific weights or values to specific errors because factors such as receiver (or listener) characteristics (age, experience, education, and so on), the context of the communication, and the social roles or status of the speakers all play a role in the success or failure of particular communicative acts. In the research reviewed and carried out by Johansson, several clear conclusions emerge, which are summarized in Fig. 11.1. Johansson makes two other important observations. One is that a learner's status as a non-native speaker contributes both to success and to failure in communication. The failure is accentuated by the faultier form of the message produced by the non-native, but because native-speaker interlocutors work harder to understand such faultier messages, the overall success of the communicative effort may be facilitated (1978:8). The second observation is that topic or content adequacy can override errors in form, and for most native-speaker

Most Interference
▲ *Phonological error*
  Prosodic error
  Segmental error
Semantic error
  System-free*
  System-bound*
Syntactic error
  System-free*/global
▼ System-bound*/local
Least Interference

Note: *These terms are the present authors' and refer to the degree to which the erroneous item is constrained within the linguistic system. *System-bound* items are members of small sets with many constraints on their occurrence (e.g., *He was swimming in the* ________. *Judy take* ___ *the bus every day.*). *System-free* items are members of large sets with few constraints (e.g., *He has a* _________. *Bill came here* ________.).

FIG. 11.1

interlocutors, comprehension of content is the overwhelming consideration (Johansson 1978:17).

This last consideration is strongly echoed by Ludwig in her review of research on error significance (1982), in which she examines research on irritation as well as on comprehensibility. The distinction is sometimes confusing, since the two are said to be covariant, but Ludwig says that irritation is "the result of the form of the message intruding on the interlocutor's perception of the communication" (275). In irritation studies, vocabulary errors or errors combining problems in vocabulary and syntax have been found to result in the most irritation (Ludwig 1982:276), but there is a wide range of difference in the results obtained by the studies Ludwig cites. She concludes her review with some implications for teaching, recommending, in general, a pedagogy which calls for a greater use of realistic language-use activities in the classroom.

Treatment

There have been few controlled studies of the treatment of learner errors in or out of the classroom. Allwright (1975) has demonstrated the inconsistency with which errors are generally treated in the classroom. Methodological recommendations have ranged from correction of all discernible errors to a relatively tolerant attitude toward learner errors. Learners themselves tend to state a preference for a great deal of overt correction (Cathcart and Olsen 1976, Conrad 1982). Hendrickson has done some research into the effectiveness of specific intervention techniques (1976, 1977) and has summarized his work and that of others (1978). He points out that communicatively interfering, stigmatizing, and high frequency errors are the most likely candidates for treatment (1978:342). Most direct methods of intervention, in which a teacher points out and explains or corrects the error, have been shown to have little or no effect on the production of error by learners (1978:393). At present, no methods of intervention have been demonstrated to have a significant effect in decreasing learner error, although both Hendrickson (1978:396) and Ludwig (1982:281–2) have made recommendations. Conrad's work, referred to earlier, demonstrates that even low-level learners are capable of using interactionally embedded repair techniques to correct both form and content.

In summary, error is inevitable in the process of language acquisition. Most of the errors that learners produce result from incomplete but gradually increasing control over a new linguistic system. Other errors probably result from some kind of interference from the learner's first language through processes not yet well understood. There are marked differences in the amount of interference that different errors and error types contribute to communication. Phonological errors are probably the most serious and syntactic the least (Johansson 1978:47 and 68), but context and the compounding of error play important roles in the communicative effect of error. While learners often request overt correction of most or all errors, there is evidence that such direct intervention is not very effective. Some feedback on formal adequacy is almost certainly required for acquisition to continue, and there is some evidence to suggest that learners are able to utilize meaning-based, interactionally modulated repair techniques, which acquisition theory suggests are the most useful form of feedback. Affective factors also play a significant role in the persistence of error (i.e., *fossilization*) and in the effectiveness of various intervention techniques.

SOCIAL AND AFFECTIVE FACTORS

Following the fundamental work of Gardner and Lambert (1972 and 1973) and Larsen and Smalley (1972), a good deal of speculation, and some research, has focused on the role of attitudes, motivation, and affective factors in language acquisition and learning. Gardner and Lambert established that learners' attitudes toward the society or culture connected with the language being learned can strongly affect success in learning the language. Motivation, which is difficult both to define and to measure, may play a role in the success of formal learning more than in informal acquisition (Krashen 1981:28). Gardner and Lambert's claim that *integrative* motivation (learning so as to become similar or closer to the new culture and society) would be a greater contributor to success in learning a second language than *instrumental* motivation (learning so as to achieve some goal through a possibly limited use of the new language) has been brought into question by Lukmani's (1972) research.

The work on social and affective factors in the last ten years can be viewed through the taxonomy developed by Schumann to categorize the many factors he has identified as playing a role in the success or failure of learners he has studied (J. Schumann 1976 and elsewhere). The categories relevant here are:

1. **social factors**, such as the relative size of language groups, and social attitudes between groups
2. **affective factors**, such as language and culture shock, and motivation
3. **personality factors**, such as self-esteem, and sensitivity to rejection.

While there are many other factors that affect language acquisition, it is generally agreed that the above three are the major ones. The problem has been to evaluate these factors quantitatively. Oller (1981) attempted to do this for one factor, motivation, and demonstrated that adequate measuring instruments are lacking. J. Schumann (1978) suggests a number of experimental studies, none of which, to our knowledge, has been undertaken.

Guiora and his colleagues (Guiora, Brannon, and Dull 1972, Guiora, Paluzny, Beit-Hallahmi, Catford, Cooley, and Dull 1975) have done work on empathy and what they call *ego boundaries*. They suggest that language teaching make a greater effort to reduce these boundaries to facilitate language learning, and Clarke (1978) provides a useful theoretical perspective on the relationship of language learning to culture shock.

There is general agreement within the field that social and affective factors have a major effect on who learns languages and how well they learn them. While the present authors have heard an anecdotal argument that educated learners can overcome attitudinal and affective barriers through the force of intellect, recent diary studies (F. Schumann 1980, F. Schumann and J. Schumann 1977) and the work of Stevick (1976, 1980, 1982) suggest that attitudinal and affective factors play a lesser role in formal learning than in informal acquisition but that, for all language learners, affective factors influence the ability to use new languages spontaneously and effectively.

Many recent developments in approach and methodology have been motivated by a recognition of the need to reduce affective barriers to language acquisition, what Krashen (1978) calls the "affective filter" after Dulay and Burt's "affective delimitor" (1977:99). These developments range from methods such as Suggestopedia (Lozanov 1979) and Counseling-Learning (Curran 1968, 1972, 1976, 1978) to many of the valuable techniques and materials produced by humanistic language teachers (Moskowitz 1978, for example), and to more general suggestions offered by Stevick (1976, 1980, 1982).

CONCLUSIONS

Historically, fashions in language teaching have often been based on the prevailing perspectives of linguistics and psychology. It is only recently that research in second language acquisition has developed as an independent field. Just as the oft-repeated mistake of the past was to rush into the classroom with the latest results of linguistic research, so it would be a mistake now to assume that all recent language-related research has a *direct* application in the classroom. However, evidence from empirical research and from informal observation strongly suggests that language instruction can be made more effective in the sense that learners can be led to an improved ability to use or apply knowledge of the new language and to an improved ability to continue learning on their own.

Rather than go directly to the classroom, we offer here a set of principles, based on the research reviewed above, that can help guide decisions regarding classroom practice.

Principle 1. Language instruction which has as its goal functional ability in the new language should give greater emphasis to activities which lead to language acquisition than to activities which lead to formal learning.

It is undeniable that instruction in the forms of a new language can result in language learning and, to some extent, language acquisition. But the shortcoming of formal instruction is its relative inefficiency in helping students become effective users of the language outside of instructional settings. If recent research is correctly interpreted, instructional activities and experiences that foster language acquisition can overcome much of this shortcoming. When complemented with formal learning activities, classroom activities leading to language acquisition, we are suggesting, can help learners become more competent users of a new language and more open to acquiring more of the language independently.

Traditional classroom learning activities have tended to have correct production and even conscious ability to describe particular language forms or structures as goals. Acquisition activities concentrate on input and interaction. Instructors who are attempting to foster language acquisition must concentrate on providing experiences for the students in which there is a great deal of language input, language which is both comprehensible and meaningful and which is presented in an activity context which encourages attention and involvement. Meaningfulness is facilitated by the reality of the subject matter (Taylor 1982) and by having "life" rather than "language learning" as its content (Fanselow 1977). Interaction allows students to modulate the input they receive to increase its comprehensibility and to test the hypothesis they are forming about the new language.

It is the opinion of the authors that the reason why more acquisition activities are not being used in instructional programs is that few well-structured activities have yet been developed. While there are many collections of activities that attempt to make instruction more active and student-centered, or that attempt to increase the quantity of learner production, few instructional materials have been produced which meet the criteria of providing comprehensible input and supporting it with meaningful interaction. Recent work by Krashen and Terrell (1983), Taylor (1983), and the collection of work edited by Johnson and Morrow (1981) is beginning to shape our understanding of what such materials should look like, but there remains a dearth of actual instructional material.

Principle 2. Because negative affect, in the form of the affective filter, seems to be a major impediment to success in language acquisition and learning, instruction should make the minimizing of such affective interference one of its primary goals.

Along with the goals of providing input and interaction, language instruction must attempt to lower students' affective resistance to acquiring the new language. There are two aspects to this problem—the methodology of instruction and the content of instruction. Stevick has addressed the methodological issue at length (1976, 1980, 1982), and a valuable review of the role that methodology can play in lowering affective resistance has been provided by Taylor (1983). Specific instructional activities have been developed by Moskowitz (1978), Christison and Bassano (1981), and others.

In general, an affectively positive or supportive classroom is one in which students are encouraged to initiate and sustain real communication and to take risks in using the new language in that communication. The encouragement is provided by carefully defining the instructional task or activity, preparing the students for it, and assisting and supporting the students in carrying out the activity by providing resources and feedback as they need them.

Principle 3. Language instruction must make greater use of the learners' own abilities to acquire language from natural interaction.

Language instructors have tended to mistrust or undervalue the role that natural, non-instructional interaction plays in the language acquisition process. Instructors may mistrust natural interaction because they feel it does not provide enough feedback on the accuracy of student production. Instructors may also believe that meaningful interaction is not possible in a second language until a sound basis in the forms of the language has been achieved. But meaningful interaction is crucial if students are to develop functional ability in the new language (Carroll 1967, Saegert, Scott, Perkins, and Tucker 1974), and there is considerable evidence that such experience is possible and beneficial, even at very low levels of second language ability.

What research into the structure of interaction, the turn-taking mechanism, and the techniques of repair supports is the view that learners have a predisposition to interact under the proper circumstances (usually not a traditional language classroom), that they are well aware of the general structure of interaction, and that they can make use of the repair mechanisms available to competent speakers to increase the comprehensibility of the input being provided to them and to improve the accuracy of their own production. By structuring interaction so that the settings, the purpose, and the participants' roles are as natural as possible, so that the informational content is the focus of the interaction, and so that the interactants are willing and able to provide feedback in the form of repair, natural interaction can be made a beneficial part of a language instruction program.

Principle 4. Error produced in the process of acquiring a second language should be viewed as a natural product of the acquisition process, as a source of information on learner strategies, and as a problem best addressed through more input and interaction rather than through correction and drill. To concentrate on developing students' abilities to monitor their production, or to enforce correction while students are engaged in interaction or production, should be regarded as counter-productive.

In any behavior, there is a balance between how much is done and how or how well it is done. Traditional language teaching has emphasized the latter at the expense of the former by equating success with accuracy or mastery of form. In language or in communication, success is determined just as much by how rich and flexible one's linguistic resources are. In language learning, there is increasing evidence that accuracy develops more efficiently when it is viewed as one element in a communicative effort, an overall effort which includes meaningfulness, appropriateness, creativity, and reality. To treat accuracy as usage, the socially approved choice of language forms, is less valuable to learners than teaching accuracy as instrumental to the successful accomplishment of a larger communicative task.

Some specific recommendations which we believe are called for in the treatment of error are:

1. Teachers should attempt to analyze students' behavior to determine which errors are signs of incorrect learning, which errors seriously interfere with comprehensibility, and which errors are inappropriate at the learners' stage of development. These errors should be distinguished from those errors which are simply signs of incomplete learning, those which do not interfere with communication, or those which are persistent for all learners. The first types are candidates for treatment, the second probably not.
2. Because language users' ability to monitor for formal accuracy is limited in scope and effect, teachers should expect conscious control only over those few features of the language that are subject to monitoring (i.e., a few salient surface features, generally only in the written mode).
3. Because direct methods of error correction (identification, explanation, correction) have not been shown to be effective, teachers should encourage more indirect methods of error improvement, possibly employing peers, and generally assisting and encouraging students to use communicatively and interactionally modulated repair and clarification techniques to improve accuracy.

4. Teachers should be aware that many aspects of error are affectively determined. Pronunciation errors especially, but many other errors as well, serve to mark the learner's identity as a non-native speaker, a status that is often psychologically reassuring and interactionally advantageous. Teachers must also realize that they are often unrealistically harsh judges of accuracy (Ludwig 1982:280) and that naive listeners tend to focus on content more than on form. One mistake should be avoided. In Ludwig's words, "Too often students and teachers mistakenly relate linguistic accuracy with increased social acceptance, thinking that if they could speak and write with fewer mistakes, then people would like them more . . . However, the data indicate that cultural stereotypes aside, each L2 user is regarded as an individual with his or her own personality and opinion, neither of which is judged on linguistic criteria in the mind of the native speaker" (1982:282).

5. Teachers can identify for learners those modes of language use in which formal accuracy is more important (e.g., academic writing, possibly) and teach editing skills and the use of reference works and feedback resources to assist the learners in achieving accuracy in those contexts.

The conclusion to be drawn from this consideration of error is that formal correctness should be accorded a place somewhat lower on the instructional scale than it has traditionally had—not abandoned, but viewed as secondary to instructional experiences which call for independence and risk taking on the part of students, and greater openness on their part to feedback from others.

In conclusion, practice in language teaching has characteristically developed from theory or from accumulated classroom experience. Both are excellent sources of direction. What we have attempted to do in this article is to emphasize a third basis for direction and evaluation in language teaching—empirical research into language acquisition and language use. In concluding, we return to the comment made earlier that not all of what is discovered about language and language learning is *directly* applicable to the classroom. By suggesting four general principles to guide language teaching, we hope that evolving practice will help determine and refine empirically sound and coherent teaching practice aimed at developing functional ability in second language learners.

REFERENCES

Allwright, Richard L. 1975. Problems in the study of the language teacher's treatment of student error. In On *TESOL '75*, Marina K. Burt and Heidi Dulay (Eds.), 96–109. Washington, D.C.: TESOL.

Andersen, Roger W. 1976. A functional acquisition hierarchy study in Puerto Rico. Paper presented at the 10th Annual TESOL Convention, New York, March, 1976.

Asher, James. 1977. *Learning another language, through actions: the complete teacher's guidebook*. Los Gatos, California: Sky Oaks.

Asher, James, and R. Garcia. 1969. The optimal age to learn a foreign language. *Modern Language Journal* 53 (5):334–341.

Bailey, Nathalie, Carolyn Madden, and Stephen Krashen. 1974. Is there a natural sequence in adult second language learning? *Language Learning* 24 (2):235–243.

Bialystok, Ellen. 1978. A theoretical model of second language learning. *Language Learning* 28 (1):69–83.

Borkin, Ann, and Susan Reinhart. 1978. Excuse me and I'm sorry. *TESOL Quarterly* 12 (1):57–70.

Brown, Roger. 1973. *A first language*. Cambridge, Massachusetts: Harvard University Press.

Burt, Marina, Heidi Dulay, and Eduardo Hernandez. 1975. *The bilingual syntax measure*. New York: Harcourt, Brace, Jovanovich.

Burt, Marina K., and Carol Kiparsky. 1972. *The gooficon: a repair manual for English*. Rowley, Massachusetts: Newbury House Publishers, Inc.

Carroll, John B. 1967. Foreign language proficiency levels attained by language majors near graduation from college. *Foreign Language Annals* 1 (2):131–151.

Cathcart, Ruth L., and Judy E.W.B. Olsen. 1976. Teachers' and students' preferences for correction of classroom conversation errors. In On *TESOL '76*, John F. Fanselow and Ruth Crymes (Eds.), 41–53. Washington, D.C.: TESOL.

Christison, Mary Ann, and Sharon Bassano. 1981. *Look who's talking*. San Francisco: Alemany Press.

Clarke, Mark. 1976. Second language acquisition as a clash of consciousness. *Language Learning* 26 (2):377–390.

Conrad, Timothy. 1982. Preference for correction in the interaction of native and non-native speakers of English. M.A. thesis, Utah State University.

Coulthard, Malcolm. 1977. *An introduction to discourse analysis*. London: Longman.

Curran, Charles. 1968. *Counseling and psychotherapy: the pursuit of values*. Apple River, Illinois: Apple River Press.

Curran, Charles. 1972. *Counseling-learning: a whole-person model for education*. New York: Grune and Stratton.

Curran, Charles. 1976. *Counseling-learning in second languages*. Apple River, Illinois: Apple River Press.

Curran, Charles. 1978. *Understanding: a necessary ingredient in human belonging*. Apple River, Illinois: Apple River Press.

de Villiers, Peter A., and Jill C. de Villiers. 1973. A cross-sectional study of the acquisition of grammatical morphemes in child speech. *Journal of Psycholinguistic Research* 2 (3):267–278.

Dulay, Heidi, and Marina Burt. 1974. Natural sequences in child second language acquisition. *Language Learning* 24 (1):37–53.

Dulay, Heidi, and Marina K. Burt. 1977. Remarks on creativity in language acquisition. In *Viewpoints on English as a second language*, Marina Burt, Heidi Dulay, and Mary Finocchiaro (Eds.), 95–126. New York: Regents Publishing Company, Inc.

Dulay, Heidi, Marina Burt, and Stephen Krashen. 1982. *Language two*. New York: Oxford University Press.

Fanselow, John. 1977. Beyond *Rashomon*—conceptualizing and describing the teaching act. *TESOL Quarterly* 11 (1):17–39.

Fraser, Bruce. 1981. On apologizing. In *Conversational routine*, Florian Coulmas (Ed.), 259–271. The Hague: Mouton.

Fraser, Bruce, and W. Nolen. 1980. The association of deference with linguistic form. *International Journal of the Sociology of Language* 27 (1):93–109.

Fraser, Bruce, Ellen Rintell, and Joel Walters. 1980. An approach to conducting research on the acquisition of pragmatic competence in a second language. In *Discourse analysis in second language research*, Diane Larsen-Freeman (Ed.), 75–91. Rowley, Massachusetts: Newbury House Publishers, Inc.

Gardner, Robert C., and Wallace Lambert. 1972. *Attitudes and motivation in second-language learning*. Rowley, Massachusetts: Newbury House Pubushers, Inc.

Gardner, Robert, and Wallace Lambert. 1973. Attitudes and motivation: their role in second language acquisition. In *Focus on the learner,* John Oller and Jack Richards (Eds.), 235–245. Rowley, Massachusetts: Newbury House Publishers, Inc.

Gary, Judith Olmstead. 1974. The effects on children of delayed oral practice in initial stages of second language learning. Ph.D. dissertation, University of California at Los Angeles.

Gary, Judith Olmstead. 1975. Delayed oral practice in initial stages of second language learning. In *On TESOL '75*, Marina Burt and Heidi Dulay (Eds.), 89–95. Washington, D.C.: TESOL.

Gaskill, William. 1980. Correction in native speaker—non-native speaker conversation. In *Discourse analysis in second language research,* Diane Larsen-Freeman (Ed.), 125–137. Rowley, Massachusetts: Newbury House Publishers, Inc.

Gattegno, Caleb. 1972. *Teaching foreign languages in schools: the silent way.* New York: Educational Solutions.

Gattegno, Caleb. 1976. *The common sense of teaching foreign languages.* New York: Educational Solutions.

Goffman, Erving. 1967. *Interaction ritual.* Garden City: Anchor Books.

Goffman, Erving. 1971. *Relations in public*. New York: Basic Books.

Gordon, David, and George Lakoff. 1975. Conversational postulates. In *Papers from the seventh regional meeting of the Chicago Linguistic Society*. Chicago: Chicago Linguistic Society.

Grice, H. Paul. 1975. Logic and conversation. In *Speech acts*, Peter Cole and Jerry Morgan (Eds.), 41–58. *Syntax and Semantics,* Volume 3. New York: Academic Press.

Guiora, Alexander, Robert C.L. Brannon, and Cecilia Dull. 1972. Empathy and second language learning. *Language Learning* 22 (1):111–130.

Guiora, Alexander, Maria Paluzny, Benjamin Beit-Hallahmi, J. C. Catford, Ralph Cooley, and Cecilia Dull. 1975. Language and person: studies in language behavior. *Language Learning* 25 (1):43–61.

Hakuta, Kenji, and H. Cancino. 1977. Trends in second language acquisition research. *Harvard Educational Review* 47: 294–316.

Hatch, Evelyn. 1979. Apply with caution. *Studies in Second Language Acquisition* 2 (2):123–143.

Hendrickson, James. 1976. The effects of error correction treatments upon adequate and accurate communication in the written compositions of adult learners of English as a second language. Ph.D. dissertation, The Ohio State University.

Hendrickson, James. 1977. Error analysis and selective correction in the adult ESL classroom: an experiment. Arlington, Virginia: ERIC, Center for Applied Linguistics.

Hendrickson, James. 1978. Error correction in foreign language teaching: recent theory, research, and practice. *Modern Language Journal* 62 (8):387–398.

Johnson, Keith, and Keith Morrow. 1981. *Communication in the classroom*. Essex, England: Longman Group Ltd.

Johansson, Stig. 1978. *Studies of error gravity*. Gotheborg, Sweden: Universitatis Gothoburgensis.

Kramsch, Claire. 1981. *Discourse analysis and second language teaching*. *Language in Education: Theory and Practice* 37. Washington, D.C.: Center for Applied Linguistics.

Krashen, Stephen. 1978. The monitor model for second language acquisition. In *Second language acquisition and foreign language teaching,* Rosario Gingras (Ed.), 1–26. Arlington, Virginia: Center for Applied Linguistics.

Krashen, Stephen. 1981. *Second language acquisition and second language learning*. Oxford: Pergamon Press.

Krashen, Stephen. 1982. *Principles and practice in second language acquisition.* Oxford: Pergamon Press.

Krashen, Stephen, James Butler, Robert Birnbaum, and Judith Robertson. 1978. Two studies in language acquisition and language learning. *ITL Review of Applied Linguistics* 39–40:73–92.

Krashen, Stephen, and Tracy Terrell. 1983. *The natural approach: language acquisition in the classroom.* San Francisco: Alemany Press.

Larsen, Donald, and William Smalley. 1972. *Becoming bilingual: a guide to language learning.* New Canaan, Connecticut: Practical Anthropology.

Larsen-Freeman, Diane. 1975. The acquisition of grammatical morphemes by adult ESL students. *TESOL Quarterly* 9 (4):409–420.

Lee, Richard, Linetta McCune, and Layne Patton. 1970. Physiological responses to different modes of feedback in pronunciation testing. *TESOL Quarterly* 4 (2):117–122.

Lozanov, Georgi. 1979. *Suggestology and outlines of suggestopedy*. New York: Gordon and Breach.

Ludwig, Jeanette. 1982. Native speaker judgments of second language learners' efforts at communication: a review. *Modern Language Journal* 66 (3):274–283.

Lukmani, Yasmeen. 1972. Motivation to learn and language proficiency. *Language Learning* 22 (2):261–274.

Manes, Joan, and Nessa Wolfson. 1981. The compliment formula. In *Conversational routine*, Florian Coulmas (Ed.), 115–132. The Hague: Mouton.

Moskowitz, Gertrude. 1978. *Caring and sharing in the foreign language class.* Rowley, Massachusetts: Newbury House Publishers, Inc.

Oller, John. 1981. Can affect he measured? *International Review of Applied Linguistics* 19 (3):227–235.

Porter, John II. 1977. A cross-sectional study of morpheme acquisition in first language learners. *Language Learning* 27 (1):47–61.

Postovsky, Valerian. 1977. Why not start speaking later? In *Viewpoints on English as a second language*, Marina Burt, Heidi Dulay, and Mary Finocchiaro (Eds.), 17–26. New York: Regents.

Richards, Jack S. 1980. Conversation. *TESOL Quarterly* 14 (4):413–432.

Richards, Jack C., and Ted Rodgers. 1982. Method: approach, design, and procedure. *TESOL Quarterly* 16 (2):153–168.

Rosansky, Ellen. 1976. Methods and morphemes in second language acquisition. *Language Learning* 26 (2):409–425.

Rubin, Joan. 1975. What the good language learner can teach us. *TESOL Quarterly* 9 (1):41–51.

Sacks, Harvey, Emanuel Schegloff, and Gail Jefferson. 1974. A simplest systematics for the organization of turn-taking for conversation. *Language* 50 (4):696–735.

Saegert, Joel, Margaret Sue Scott, John Perkins, and G. Richard Tucker. 1974. A note on the relationship between English proficiency, years of language study, and medium of instruction. *Language Learning* 24 (1):99 104.

Schmidt, Richard, and Jack C. Richards. 1980. Speech acts and second language learning. *Applied Linguistics* 1 (2):129–157.

Schegloff, Emanuel, Gail Jefferson, and Harvey Sacks. 1977. The preference for self-correction in the organization of repair in conversation. *Language* 53 (2):361–382.

Schumann, Francine. 1980. Diary of a language learner: a further analysis. In *Research in second language acquisition*, Robin Scarcella and Stephen Krashen (Eds.), 51–57. Rowley, Massachusetts: Newbury House Publishers, Inc.

Schumann, John. 1976. Social distance as a factor in second language acquisition. *Language Learning* 26 (1):135–144.

Schumann, John. 1978. *The pidginization process: a model for second language acquisition.* Rowley, Massachusetts: Newbury House Publishers, Inc.

Schumann, Francine, and John Schumann. 1977. Diary of a language learner: an introspective study of second language learning. In *On TESOL '77*, H. Douglas Brown, Carlos Yorio, and Ruth Crymes (Eds.), 241–249. Washington, D.C.: TESOL.

Schwartz, Joan. 1980. The negotiation for meaning: repair in conversations between second language learners of English. In *Discourse analysis in second language research*, Diane Larsen-Freeman (Ed.), 138–153. Rowley, Massachusetts:Newbury House Publishers, Inc.

Snow, Catherine E. 1979. Conversations with children. In *Language acquisition: studies in first language development*, Paul Fletcher and Michael Garman (Eds.), 363–375. Cambridge: Cambridge University Press.

Stevick, Earl. 1976. *Memory, meaning and method.* Rowley, Massachusetts: Newbury House Publishers, Inc.

Stevick, Earl. 1980. *Teaching languages: a way and ways*. Rowley, Massachusetts: Newbury House Publishers, Inc.

Stevick, Earl. 1982. *Teaching and learning languages*. Cambridge: Cambridge University Press.

Taylor, Barry P. 1982. In search of real reality. *TESOL Quarterly* 16 (1):29–42.

Taylor, Barry P. 1983. Teaching ESL: incorporating a communicative, student-centered component. *TESOL Quarterly* 17 (1):69–88.

Taylor, Barry, and Nessa Wolfson. 1978. Breaking down the free conversation myth. *TESOL Quarterly* 12 (1):31–39.

Terrell, Tracy. 1977. A natural approach to second language acquisition and learning. *Modern Language Journal* 61 (7):325–337.

Terrell, Tracy. 1982. The natural approach to language teaching: an update. *Modern Language Journal* 66 (2):121–132.

van Ek, J. A. 1975. *The threshold level for modern language learning in schools.* London: Longman.

Wagner-Gough, Judy, and Evelyn Hatch. 1975. The importance of input data in second language acquisition studies. *Language Learning* 25 (2):297–308.

Winitz, Harris, and James A. Reeds. 1973. Rapid acquisition of a foreign language (German) by the avoidance of speaking. *International Review of Applied Linguistics* 11 (4):296–317.

Chapter 12

On the Nature of Technique: What Do We Owe the Gurus?

Mark A. Clarke

Professionals constantly work back and forth between the insights of theory and the constraints of practice in an effort to construct a reasonably well-informed framework within which to conduct their day-to-day activities. One interesting aspect of the theory/practice dichotomy is the impact of acknowledged experts on the classroom behaviors of teachers. In this article I describe in detail one technique for teaching writing to ESL students and use this description as the basis for a discussion of the nature of technique. I then trace my teaching behaviors back to a number of individuals who have influenced my attitudes toward and approaches to the teaching of writing. Finally, I attempt to characterize the relationship between a successful classroom technique and the teachings of gurus.

All teachers who take their jobs seriously work back and forth between the insights of theory and the demands of practice. We try to keep up with the latest research, read what we can, evaluate emerging bandwagons, attend conventions and workshops, discuss issues and problems with mentors and colleagues, and so on—all in an effort to construct a reasonably well-informed theoretical framework within which to pursue our day-to-day teaching goals.

But, what *is* the relationship between research on the Monitor Model and the drills and exercises we use in our classes to teach vocabulary and grammar? And what *is* the relevance of Skinnerian psychology or Maslow's Hierarchy of Human Needs or Rogerian Principles of Active Listening to the daily grind? And how do we use the suggestions of the acknowledged experts in the field to meet the demands of our teaching day? It is my belief that the relationship between prescription and practice is more complex than generally acknowledged, and in the pages which follow I attempt to trace the connections between one classroom technique—the blackboard composition—and the teachings of several individuals whose advice I have tried to follow in my own work. This examination illuminates important characteristics of good teaching and produces insights which I believe are important for teachers, teacher trainers, and gurus.

THE BLACKBOARD COMPOSITION

My first attempts at using blackboard compositions date back to my early teaching days, when I first tried to show a roomful of students how to develop an idea in a series of reasonably well-constructed sentences. As with all teaching activities, some days went well and other days were miserable failures, but gradually, as I gained experience and added ideas acquired from colleagues, conventions, and journal articles, the technique became a regular part of my repertoire. It is not the best technique for teaching writing nor even, for that matter, my favorite, but over the years I have found it to work more often than not, and it demonstrates very clearly the influence of gurus on my teaching.

Briefly, the blackboard composition is a group effort at writing in which a topic is selected and developed in an energetic, loosely controlled jam session. The teacher (or one of the students) writes sentences on the board as they are suggested by members of the class. Each sentence is critiqued and refined as the work proceeds until a respectable composition results. This allows the teacher to focus on specific problems of vocabulary, syntax, and style while simultaneously demonstrating the process of composing a representative product, both of which (the process and the product) can then serve as models for students' future efforts. The following detailed description of a specific instance of the technique will provide a point of reference for the discussion which follows.

My upper-intermediate-level class is comprised of sixteen students (nine males and seven females) between the ages of 18 and 23: four Japanese, three Venezuelans, two Mexicans, four Arabs (two from Egypt, one from Lebanon, and one from Saudi Arabia), and one student each from Turkey, Taiwan, and Nigeria. All are attending an intensive English program (four hours a day, five days a week) in preparation for university-level work in the United States. The particular class session described below takes place on Monday morning of the seventh week of a 15-week semester. Because we have written blackboard compositions numerous times, the students are familiar with the goals and procedures of the technique.

After the business of the class (roll taken, graded papers returned, questions regarding the midterm exam answered) is taken care of, I announce that we are going to write a blackboard composition on "Love and Marriage in the United States." For several weeks we have been reading, talking, and writing about the mores and morals of Americans. The topic has generated a great deal of interest. At one point in the semester, the students even developed a questionnaire and conducted a survey of their English-speaking peers. As a result of the semester's efforts, everybody has accumulated a wealth of information, insight, and opinion on the topic.

I give the class precisely seven minutes to get organized. This is time that the students use according to their own inclinations: Some seem to meditate, eyes half-closed, chins resting on palms, pencils tapping lightly; others scratch notes furiously, apparently driven by inspiration which they fear will escape them; one student rifles through her book bag in search of the questionnaire and a previous paper (she is the one who always insists on examples and citations to support generalizations); two students talk quietly at the back of the room. Most seem gratifyingly engaged in the activity, although one student appears to be sleeping, and another arrives late and does not really get down to work before the time is up.

At the end of the seven minutes, I announce to the students that they are to compare notes and to discuss their musings in pairs and small groups. They know that the object of their discussion is to produce a list of main ideas around which we can build an essay. I do not indicate a time limit here but rather, circulate among the groups, eavesdropping on the discussions and commenting on the growing lists of main ideas. After about ten minutes, I call the class to order.

A student raises his hand. His group believes that the title of the composition should he changed to "Love and Courtship in the United States." Marriage, they contend, is less interesting than courtship, and besides, the topic needs to be narrowed. There is a murmur of assent, and I substitute *Courtship* for *Marriage* on the board. Another student suggests that we narrow the topic even further by discussing love and courtship in Ann Arbor, since that was the area covered by the survey. After a brief discussion, this suggestion is withdrawn; the group does not want to limit itself to a discussion of Ann Arbor. (Perhaps the students are thinking of juicy examples from California that they want to use.)

I ask for a sampling of main ideas, writing them on the board as students call them out. As we fall into the familiar rhythm of the activity, a pleasant hum of banter and discussion develops, providing a backdrop for the energy which is focused on the task. The main ideas are jotted down, in sentence fragments, on the long board which covers one side of the classroom. We hit a lull and pause to study the selection, which includes:

influence of leisure time	freedom
disintegration of family	women's liberation

changing values in society
goals of young people
sexual promiscuity
the importance of sports
role of parents
generation gap
advertisements
financial realities

One student points out that the ideas are not all equal, that some seem more important than others. I move to the side of the board and lean against the wall, not speaking, but nodding in agreement. One of the Arab students goes to the board, adds *the importance of religion* to the list, and sits down. Some of the students are copying down the main ideas, others are going through their notes, a few are scribbling diligently in their copybooks. I walk to the board at the front of the room. "Shall we start?" I ask. "What'll be our first sentence?"

There is a momentary silence, then one of the scribblers offers, " 'Today the American have too much freedom.' " I write it on the board and step away, looking at the sentence in a manner intended to convey thoughtful contemplation. After a brief pause, someone says, " 'Americans.' " I add the *s* and move to the window. The Nigerian, who sits near the front, gets up and erases the *the*. We now have, "Today Americans have too much freedom."

"It's very negative," one of the Japanese women quietly asserts. "How about, 'Today, American youth have much freedom'?"

" 'A great deal,' "says a voice from the back.

The Nigerian, still at the board, writes it out below the other sentence: "Today, American youth have a great deal of freedom."

"How do these relate to our title?" I ask. More murmurs and scribblings.

"Try this one," says one of the Venezuelans. " 'Today, because of too much freedom, American youth enjoy love and courtship.' "

" '. . . but their parents don't,' " adds the Nigerian. Amid the chuckles of the class, he writes the new sentence on the board. We now have three sentences:

Today, Americans have too much freedom.

Today, American youth have a great deal of freedom.

Today, because of too much freedom, American youth enjoy love and courtship, but their parents don't.

"What is the point we're trying to make?" I ask, and the discussion becomes a noisy exchange, developing into a debate in which one group of students maintains that Americans allow their children too much freedom, while the other group admits that there is a great deal of freedom in the United States but that this is not necessarily negative. After considerable give-and-take, during which we hear impassioned references to religious tenets and emphatic quoting of newspaper articles and survey results, we finally settle on an opening sentence:

> Today, because of the freedom enjoyed by American youth, love and courtship have become very complicated.

The group identifies two major points that can serve as the focus for the next sentence: "freedom" and "the complexity of love and courtship." They decide to produce a couple of sentences which elaborate on freedom before tackling the complexity issue. I put our topic sentence at the far end of the front blackboard, erase the trial sentences, and we begin the process again, building the first paragraph, sentence by sentence.

We are now in full swing. The board fills with sentences, each modified according to suggestions from me and from the students. An adjective or two are added to a noun phrase, two sentences are collapsed into one with a relative clause, a nonfinite verb phrase is suggested to serve as a sentence opener. A few sentences are rejected because they are too vague, while another sentence is erased because it is too wordy. I walk to the back of the room and sit in a student desk during one debate between two students who differ on the need for examples as opposed to explanation. The group decides both can be used. At several points I am at the board asking how to vary the types of sentences we are using, demanding a closer link between two sentences in the paragraph, or asking for details that give the reader a clearer picture of our point of view. Grammar errors are generally caught by the students. From time to time, I correct spelling and punctuation errors without comment. Word choice and stylistic options are areas where I am usually needed to point out a problem or to suggest an alternative. Several times we get caught up in differences of opinion about the content, about what we want to say. There are sporadic attempts at coercion, and from time to time, bursts of Arabic, Japanese, and Spanish signal that commitment to the debate has overtaxed the English proficiency of the debaters. We work to find out exactly what the disagreement is, and we produce sentences which reflect the different opinions. The issue is then decided by a vote, but the other sentences are there to be copied down by the students who championed them. At several points I look at the clock nervously, wrestling with my frustration at the snail's pace of the essay; with most of the hour gone, we only have half a dozen sentences. Once or twice I cut the debate short, modify the sentence under consideration, explain why my changes are necessary, and urge the class to pick up the tempo. From time to time I stroll down the aisles and position myself behind a student, who appears only marginally involved, hoping that my authoritarian proximity will spark a little energy.

Finally, with about ten minutes left in the hour, I call a halt and make the assignment for the end of the week: The students are to use the paragraph we have written as the beginning of a three-page essay with the same title. They are to use their peer review groups to work on the essays. I will give them 20 minutes on Wednesday to work on the papers, but I predict that they will need to meet in their groups outside of class during the week.[1] The students use the class time which remains to copy down the main ideas which have not been used, to meet with group members, or to get organized for the next class. The bell rings, and they disappear into the corridor.

This is a reasonably accurate description of a typical class session. Now, as it happens, this particular group, which included a number of talkative students, worked well together and enjoyed the technique. Even so, there were days when I spent the entire hour wheedling sentences out of them, days when my calm demeanor disguised my frustration and annoyance at their collective refusal to participate. I can also remember whole class sessions devoted to grammar explanations, discussions of the topic sentence, or debates over alternative ways to convey one idea. And there have been times when my studied attempts at nondirective teacher behavior blew up in my face; one semester I discovered, during a blackboard composition on Kissinger's shuttle diplomacy, that the class contained an Israeli and a Palestinian from the same side of the Jordan River but on different sides of the issue. I mention these points to anticipate criticism concerning the verisimilitude of my example. I do not pretend that the lesson always proceeds as smoothly or as productively as the session described, but I can claim that the class described is representative.

I like the technique because it reproduces, in a remarkably accurate way, the process of composing—the bursts of energy which produce several concise sentences, followed by the painful hills in creativity, when every word seems wrong, nothing fits together, and one's best efforts produce

---

[1]The peer review groups were established early in the semester. After I had seen a few writing samples from everyone, I ranked the students from best to worst and then assigned them all to groups of three, being careful to put individuals of different ability together: group 1—students #1, #16, #8; group 2—students #2, #15, #9; group 3—#3, #14, #7, and so on. I tinkered with the membership of the groups until I had a mixture of languages and a male/female balance in each one. I also paid some attention to personality differences, hoping to avoid groupings that were obviously destined to fail because of conflicts. The groups were used as an extra source of feedback and support. Approximately one in every three writing assignments required the groups to convene in order to read and critique each other's papers. On such occasions, the grade of the poorest composition was given to each student in the group.

only confusion. Another reason I like the technique is that it allows me to teach composing skills (and grammar and vocabulary and spelling) at the very moment when students are struggling to express an idea in writing. I am able to remind students of material covered in previous classes, thereby contextualizing principles of rhetoric or particular grammar rules which the students may not have completely understood when we studied them earlier.

The technique can be cumbersome and time-consuming, and I have colleagues who argue that similar results can be obtained in other, more efficient ways. However, my purpose here is not to promote a particular teaching activity but rather, to use this example as the basis for a discussion of the nature of technique and the relationship between gurus and classroom teachers.

THE NATURE OF TECHNIQUE

The term *technique* is merely a label for what we do as teachers, a sort of conversational shorthand which, among other things, allows us to negotiate professional discussions with a minimum of confusion—and at times, I suspect, with a minimum of communication. (How often, for example, are we committed enough to a discussion that we will push past the rhetoric, the jargon, and the posturing to find out what people *really* mean when they say they use *dictocomps*, for example, in their classes?) It is, however, a convenient label, and I think we can benefit from a careful examination of the behaviors which the label covers. We discover, for example, that a technique, like all behavior, is not some*thing*. It is not a static, formalized object or condition. Rather, it is an instance, a realization of potential, the particular manifestation of our ability to select, from a bundle of options, that piece of behavior which we believe will work, given our formal training, our experience, and the prevailing conditions (see Clarke 1983 for a detailed discussion of this point). The key, I think, is insisting on an examination of the behaviors and the context and how they interact. That is, if we are to understand how learning takes place in classrooms, we have to eschew formulaic prescription, generic description, abstract references. We have to look at the minute-by-minute interaction of people in real, or at least believable, classes. We have to adjust the frame of our vision so that we can examine a specific activity *as it is occurring*. For convenience, we will call that activity by a name. In a sense, then, we are back to where we started because that name will be the label of a particular technique. We will not stop there, however, since we realize that this examination has meaning and provides insight only so long as it focuses on something which is alive. This contention is based on the conviction that we should not reduce the complexity of reality as a first step toward attempting to understand it.[2]

What we are left with, then, is *technique* as a series of decisions that we make as we go, depending on our assessment of a large number of complex, interrelated variables: the size of the class; the ages, backgrounds, and interests of the students; the quality and availability of teaching materials; the material already covered and the content of future lessons; the nature of tests and assignments required by the curriculum; the personal and professional characteristics of our immediate superiors; the time of day, the day of the week, the quality of the spinach salad at lunch. This list is by no means exhaustive; the items listed are intended to suggest the virtually limitless number of factors which influence our behavior in the classroom. While I would not claim that all of the variables are of equal importance, I would not attempt to rank order them, either, since to do so would remove us from the particular to the general, and we would be back to the old game of labeling things rather than trying to understand them. Besides, it is relatively easy to conjure up a situation in which, for example, a spinach salad assumes far greater importance than the personality of one's immediate superior, so any ranking of variables becomes an academic exercise, which may be diverting, but which does not lead us closer to an understanding of the nature of technique.

I believe this perspective has a number of important implications for teachers and teacher trainers. First, from this point of view, there is no such thing as a "good" or "bad" technique, at least not at the level of labels. That is, we cannot evaluate *dictation* or *chain drills* or *small-group work* independent of the actual occurrence of the technique. Certainly we can reflect on a particular class session and proclaim the experience (and by inference, the technique) to be an unparalleled success or an unmitigated disaster. Presumably we would form a judgment concerning the technique which would influence our attitudes and future behavior, but this should not constitute a blanket endorsement or rejection of the technique. It is

[2]A detailed defense of this perspective is beyond the scope of this article, but a substantial body of scholarship can be cited as its source. Bateson's (1972a, 1972b, 1972c, 1979) discussion of cybernetic explanation, for example, provides a foundation for the argument that an accurate picture of reality must account for the complex interaction of organisms with their environment. Furthermore, recent discussions of language acquisition reflect Piaget's (1926) conviction that intelligence and language development are inextricably bound up in individuals' ongoing interaction with their surroundings (see, for example, Vetter and Howell 1971, Dore 1974, Wells 1974, Bruner 1975a, 1975b, Halliday 1975). For me, this perspective is compelling, whether we are considering infants' acquisition of a first language in the home or adults' mastering of a second language in the classroom.

entirely likely that a colleague could have radically different experiences with the same activities or that we could have more or less success on different days or with different students. As professionals, we are obliged to look beyond the labels, to examine specific occurrences of techniques and to work to understand their strengths and weaknesses. I do not argue that it is necessary for teachers to abandon their critical judgment of teaching practices, but I do contend that the profession's tendency to discuss the labels rather than the substance of techniques reduces most debates to name-calling sessions. I believe the above perspective on the "nature of technique" constitutes a first step toward an understanding of effective teaching.

A second implication is that any technique which I use becomes, by definition, uniquely mine. By virtue of my experience and understanding, my effort and energy during the exercise, my evaluation of what is required at any moment—all of these factors make the technique *my* slice of reality. The technique is, therefore, only secondarily (and somewhat irrelevantly) an example of the generic category indicated by the label which we typically use to refer to it.

The third implication follows from the first two: In a consideration of teaching techniques and materials, or of classroom practice, there can be no prescription—only description and suggestion. In other words, as a teacher, I have to decide what will work for me and how I will use it, and I make my decisions both before the class begins, as I prepare my lessons, and as the class unfolds, in the heat of the activity.

Even if I see myself as an orthodox follower of a particular approach, my day-to-day, hour-by-hour behavior will still exhibit the uniqueness that is characteristic of all teaching. However, in spite of the conviction that my teaching is largely idiosyncratic, I do not contend that my skills and insights were acquired by revelation. As I reflect on the above lesson, I can identify a virtually limitless number of people and experiences that could be cited as inspiration for the behaviors I have described. If I were to treat the transcript of this particular class session as a Talmudic exercise, I believe that I could in fact trace every behavior, every statement, question, inflection, and gesture back to a specific source. That source might be an article or textbook, a conversation with a professor, a hallway encounter with a colleague, or participation in a workshop at a convention. Or it might be a series of class sessions in which I experimented with the technique, gradually modifying it until I was satisfied with the results. Furthermore, in spite of all I have said about the independence and integrity of classroom teachers, I do acknowledge the importance of a number of gurus in my professional development in general and in my understanding and execution of the blackboard composition in particular.

WHAT DO WE OWE THE GURUS?

The dictionary definition of *guru* includes the following: "Hindi, from Sanskrit: heavy, weighty, honored; a Hindu spiritual guide or teacher." I would have preferred another word; *guru* is used a great deal these days in a sarcastic or derogatory sense, and I use it here as a term of respect for an individual whose work has influenced mine. What follows is a list, briefly annotated, of my gurus in the teaching of composition.

Robert B. Kaplan

Although I have always been interested in writing, I had not given much thought to the problem of teaching writing until I arrived at the American University in Cairo to work on my M.A. in TEFL. Composition was taught there in the manner that it is taught in many intensive English centers—as an extension of the grammar class. I was struggling with sentence combining, substitution frames, and a variety of other "controlled composition" techniques, feeling free-floating frustration at the complete lack of evidence that I was having any impact on students' writing, when I read Kaplan's 1966 article, "Cultural Thought Patterns in Inter-Cultural Education." Kaplan argues that because rhetorical principles are culture-specific, the teaching of writing must focus on discourse units larger than the sentence. From the moment that I read the article, I began working on ways to teach "above the sentence." The basis for this instruction was the presentation, explanation, and analysis of model paragraphs and essays, combined with attempts to get students to recognize the rhetorical requirements of English as distinct from those of their native languages. As a result of reading Kaplan's article, I began teaching writing in conjunction with reading, and I worked to reduce the emphasis on vocabulary choice and grammar. Influences of Kaplan in the blackboard composition can be seen in the heavy reading schedule which precedes the activity and in the fact that the predominant question throughout the lesson is, What are we trying to say?

Francis Christensen

A footnote in Kaplan's article refers to the work of Christensen, and on a visit to Ann Arbor one fall I managed to find a copy of his little yellow book, *Notes Toward a New Rhetoric* (1967), in a university bookshop. I practically memorized whole chapters of that book because here at last was something specific to guide me in teaching "rhetorical principles." Needless to say, my efforts at teaching "above the sentence" had not been altogether satisfying. As I slogged through swamps of grammatically correct but illogically placed sentences, I began to understand why ESL teachers had stuck with the time-honored *awk* written in the margins of students' papers and why they cranked out masses of dittoed worksheets on sentence connectors, nonrestrictive relative clauses, and topic sentences. It is easier to work on something manageable than to struggle with the real problem faced by all composition teachers, whether their students are native or non-native speakers of English: Good writing requires the author to anticipate the needs of the reader and to build an essay by adding ideas (expressed, of course, in wellformed sentences) to each other in a way which the reader finds logical and convincing. Christensen's book provides the framework for teaching such writing.

I experimented with Christensen's ideas until I developed "rules of thumb" which students could apply to their writing and which I could use as the framework for in-class critiques of student papers and native speaker models. These rules of thumb were three principles: 1) The Principle of the Main Idea, 2) The Principle of Addition, and 3) The Principle of Subordination and Coordination. My strategy was fairly simple. Rather than serve as the editor and proofreader for 40-odd students each semester, I attempted to teach them to consciously address a series of questions as they worked. The first question, to be asked again and again, was, What am I trying to say? The second question—What information does the reader need here?—allowed them to build on the main idea by adding details, focusing on a specific quality, or drawing a comparison. The third question, which required the writers to scrutinize each sentence as they produced it, was, How does this sentence fit? According to Christensen's scheme, every sentence is either subordinate (semantically and syntactically) to the sentence immediately preceding it or coordinate with a sentence somewhere above it.

Writers who follow these rules of thumb may not win literary awards, but they will be guaranteed a level of consciousness about their writing which increases the likelihood of comprehensibility. It is fairly easy to produce worksheets and models for focused classroom practice of the three principles, but the major advantage of this approach is that the principles provide a framework for the private and public critique of a piece of writing. In the blackboard composition my questions concerning the main idea, or my requests for clarity and focus, or my demands to know the function of a particular phrase or sentence all evoke countless previous lessons, worksheets, and homework assignments. In spite of the haphazard appearance of the lesson, the development of the paragraph on the board represents harnessed energy, an attempt to consciously apply a small number of rules in the development of an idea.

Daniel Fader

By the time I began working on ways to teach writing to ESL students, I had already spent two years studying the ideas of Daniel Fader, Professor of English at the University of Michigan, author, and school reformer. As an undergraduate, I had read his *Hooked on Books*, and in tutoring a group of inner-city Chicano children, I had experimented with his suggestions for promoting literacy. Like many leaders in education, Fader advocates a functional approach to the teaching of reading and writing. He believes that students should have to read and write in all segments of the curriculum and that drills and worksheets should be replaced by activities which match students' interests and accomplish goals important to the students.

I have incorporated a number of Fader's ideas into my teaching—journals to encourage writing, paperback books to lure students into reading, discussions with students to find out what *they* think is important in their education—but the idea which is most obvious in the blackboard composition is the use of peer teaching. Fader is a tireless foe of ability-grouping, and his respect for the teaching ability of learners is evident throughout his book. Class and small-group discussions of ideas in class are products of this respect, and the peer review group is his mechanism for promoting peer teaching. By reducing the importance of the teacher in the learning process and by organizing an experience which shows students how much they have to offer each other, the teacher increases the probability that learners will acquire the skills and attitudes of literate users of language.

Donald Murray

Donald Murray (1978, 1982a, 1982b) has a great deal to say to the writer-as-a-teacher about attitude, approach, and classroom technique, but the thrust of all of his work is that the writer must develop an appreciation for the process. Writing requires effort—we must work at a piece of writing until it satisfies us. But writing also produces insight into what we are trying to say. That is, in the process of trying to get our ideas down on paper, we begin to discover what it is that we want to express. Murray asserts that in order to write well, we must develop a certain amount of respectful self-consciousness about the process. We do not all write well under the same conditions or with the same tools, and if we are to be successful as writers, we must work to produce the conditions which promote success for us.

I have used Murray as justification for a great deal that I do as a composition teacher, especially the explicit discussion of strategies for producing good writing, but his influence is most obvious in the laborious working and reworking of sentences as we develop our blackboard composition. When we begin, we do not know exactly what we are going to say, much less how we are going to say it. As we struggle to identify ideas and opinions, as we bicker over words and phrases to express them, we come very close to the process which, Murray argues, is the key to good writing: revising. Aspects of the blackboard composition which make it unattractive for many teachers—it is time-consuming, painful, and plodding—are precisely those qualities which recommend it to me. It is as close as I have been able to come to modeling the process of composing while actively involving the learners in that process.

Earl W. Stevick

More than anyone else, Earl Stevick (1976, 1980, 1982, 1983) has influenced my work in teaching languages and in working with teachers. Because of this, it would be impossible to identify every aspect of the blackboard composition which can be traced to Stevick, but there are two important influences that are especially prominent.

The first concerns the general atmosphere of the class. Whatever success we have with the group composing process is due to the sense of security which students have and the freedom which that security promotes. That is, I have worked very hard to create an atmosphere which encourages student initiative and interaction. I am clear on what the limits are, and I try to provide enough guidance and encouragement to ensure the progress of the lesson; within those limits, however, students are free to do whatever is necessary to get the job done. The second obvious debt to Stevick is actually a specific manifestation of the first: In virtually every lesson, I work to produce experiences which 1) have something for the emotions, which get the students excited about and involved in what they are doing; 2) give the students a chance to interact; and 3) provide the opportunity for self-committing choices, choices which permit the students to assert and defend their own points of view (see Stevick 1980: 197–212).

In using the blackboard composition, I carefully describe the goals of the process to the students at the beginning of the term. Because many of them come from cultures which emphasize the authority of the teacher, I do not merely hand the class over to them the first day we use the technique. Rather, I gradually recede into the background over a number of weeks, explicitly stating my conviction that they must rely on their own judgment and exercise their prerogatives as they participate in class. I encourage them to suggest composition topics, I allow ample time for small-group interaction, and I demand that they respect everyone's right to an individual opinion. In other words, I do not relinquish control of the class, but I do attempt to establish conditions which encourage students to take the initiative, to use the language skills they are acquiring to accomplish tasks which are important to them.

And so, what exactly do I owe the gurus? A great deal, obviously, for insight and inspiration, as well as for specific techniques and classroom practices. In fact, I think it is impossible to adequately acknowledge their contributions to my professional development, to my perspective of my work, and to the teaching skills which I have acquired over the years. At the very least, I owe them a heartfelt "thank you."

And yet, without diminishing this tribute, I think it is important to point out that "thank you" is all that I owe them. If that blackboard composition worked at all, I can take the credit, without apology or protestations of modesty. It worked because I made the right decisions at (literally) every second during the lesson. The success of that technique was due to (among other things) my training and professional preparation; my planning; my effort and energy in the classroom; my insight into the students' strengths and weaknesses; my ability to select, from a limitless number of options, that specific action (or absence of action) which I believed would work.

CONCLUSION

I have delivered versions of this article a number of times over the past year in settings as diverse as can be imagined, and I have been surprised at the variety of reactions it has provoked. Some people have taken it as a methodology presentation, a detailed discussion of the teaching of writing. Others have commented on the narrative style and assumed that this is my personal credo, a sort of professional "Pilgrim's Progress." Discussions with colleagues and graduate students tend to focus on the gurus I have chosen to mention, which leads to comparisons of the impact that different individuals have had on our lives and on the field.

All of these impressions are valid, of course, but unless they are taken together, they do not convey the message I mean to convey. It was necessary to dwell in some detail on a particular teaching activity and to describe a specific instance of its use, because only then could we glimpse the complex, dynamic, variable nature of *technique*. And it was also important that I present the technique as I would use it so that the influence of my personal preferences and style could be discerned. After all, there is no such thing as a generic application of a technique; even in the most rigidly controlled curriculum, there exists a great deal of individual variation in teachers' attempts to implement syllabus mandates. And finally, it is undeniable that some individuals do have an important impact on the profession. It is a wonderful irony that in this era of narcissistic independence and bootstrap psychology, there should also be an unparalleled popularity of "guruism." But it is the simultaneous consideration of these three factors—the nature of technique, the personal stamp that each of us puts on any teaching activity, and the importance of gurus—that permits us to examine the context of second language teaching and to arrive at an understanding of one aspect of the theory/practice dichotomy: the relationship between the prescription of gurus and the classroom behaviors of teachers.

Typically, we have a mental image of the guru on stage looking down at an auditorium full of teachers who, pencils scratching furiously on precariously balanced notepads, strive to catch every phrase, every morsel of wisdom and insight. In fact, this may be an accurate picture of the physical setting, but if my perspective of teaching is at all correct, this image does not adequately represent the relationship between gurus and teachers. In fact, it is the teacher who is in the position of authority, because only the teacher can decide what to take and what to leave, whom to listen to and whom to ignore. In a very important sense, the success or failure of students, the future of the profession, and, just as certainly, the reputation of the gurus depend overwhelmingly on decisions made by teachers. I do not want to be understood as advocating a form of professional anarchy, a return to the "do-your-own-thing/anything goes" existentialism of the 1960s. I believe strongly in formal preparation, continual professional self-examination, and the need for teachers to develop and adhere to a consistent philosophical framework in their teaching. But, given the propensity of our profession to jump from one bandwagon to another (see Clarke 1982) and given the regular appearance (and the appeal) of charismatic leaders who offer important insights and helpful advice to the battle–weary, it is very easy to forget the pivotal role of the well-informed, sensitive, and decisive teacher. The teacher is the only person who is in a position to take advantage of the wealth of information available and to select the appropriate moment to apply it in the classroom.

The implications of this point of view are, I believe, of fundamental importance to the profession in general, and to teachers, teacher trainers, and gurus in particular, but that is certainly another story. Let me say, however, that writing this article has forced me to scrutinize a number of issues to which I had given only cursory attention in the past. In the process, I came to understand, for the first time, this adage: The only good advice is the advice you take.

REFERENCES

Bateson, Gregory. 1972a. Conscious purpose vs. nature. In *Steps to an ecology of mind*, Gregory Bateson (Ed.), 420–439. New York: Ballantine Books.

Bateson, Gregory. 1972b. Cybernetic explanation. In *Steps to an ecology of mind*, Gregory Bateson (Ed.), 399–410. New York: Ballantine Books.

Bateson, Gregory. 1972c. The logical categories of learning and communication. In *Steps to an ecology of mind*, Gregory Bateson (Ed.), 279–308. New York: Ballantine Books.

Bateson, Gregory. 1979. *Mind and nature*. New York: E. P. Dutton.

Bruner, Jerome. 1975a. From communication to language—a psychological perspective. *Cognition* 3(3): 255–287.

Bruner, Jerome. 1975b. The ontogenesis of speech acts. *Journal of Child Language* 2(1): 1–19.

Christensen, Francis. 1967. *Notes toward a new rhetoric*. New York: Harper and Row.

Clarke, Mark A. 1982. On bandwagons, tyranny and common sense. *TESOL Quarterly* 16(4): 437–448.

Clarke, Mark A. 1983. (The scope of) approach, (the importance of) method, and (the nature of) technique. In *Georgetown University Round Table on Languages and Linguistics, 1983*, James E. Alatis, H. H. Stern, and Peter Strevens (Eds.), 106–115. Washington, D.C.: Georgetown University Press.

Clarke, Mark A., and Bernard H. Seward. 1979. A model for training the non-traditional TESL student. In *On TESOL '79*, Carlos A. Yorio, Kyle Perkins, and Jacquelyn Schachter (Eds.), 250–266. Washington, D.C.: TESOL.

Clarke, Mark A., and Sandra Silberstein. In preparation. Problems, prescriptions and paradoxes in second language teaching.

Dore, John. 1974. A pragmatic description of early language development. *Journal of Psycholinguistic Research* 3(4): 343–350.

Fader, Daniel. 1976. *The new hooked on books*. New York: Medallion Books.

Halliday, M.A.K. 1975. *Learning how to mean: explorations in the development of language*. London: Edward Arnold, Ltd.

Kaplan, Robert B. 1966. Cultural thought patterns in inter-cultural education. *Language Learning* 16(1): 1–20.

Murray, Donald. 1978. Internal revision: a process of discovery. In *Research on composing: points of departure*, Charles Cooper and Lee Odell (Eds.), 85–104. Urbana, Illinois: National Council of Teachers of English.

Murray, Donald. 1982a. The listening eye: reflections on the writing conference. In *Learning by teaching*, Donald Murray (Ed.), 157–162. Montclair, New Jersey: Boynton.

Murray, Donald. 1982b. Teaching the other self: the writer's first reader. *College Composition and Communication* 33(2): 140–147.

Piaget, Jean. 1926. *The language and thought of the child*. New York: Meridian.

Stevick, Earl W. 1976. *Memory, meaning and method*. Rowley, Massachusetts: Newbury House Publishers.

Stevick, Earl W. 1980. *Teaching languages: a way and ways*. Rowley, Massachusetts: Newbury House Publishers.

Stevick, Earl W. 1982. *Teaching and learning languages*. London: Cambridge.

Stevick, Earl W. 1983. My understanding of *Teaching languages: a way and ways*. In *On TESOL '82*, Mark A. Clarke and Jean Handscombe (Eds.), 63–76. Washington, D.C.: TESOL.

Vetter, Harold J., and Richard W. Howell. 1971. Theories of language acquisition. *Journal of Psycholinguistic Research* 1(1): 31–64.

Wells, Gordon. 1974. Learning to code experience through language. *Journal of Child Language* 1(2): 243–269.

Chapter 13

What Is a Participatory Approach to Curriculum Development?

Elsa Roberts Auerbach

As curriculum theorists point out, every approach to curriculum development reflects a certain view of learners and learning. Very often, these views are implicit in the way curriculum is developed and structured, in the choices about curriculum content and goals, and in the patterning of social relations in the classroom.

We started our own work in the Family Literacy Project by trying to get a sense of the range of approaches and models that others had developed for similar programs. While we brought a wealth of experience teaching adult ESL and literacy in a variety of contexts (from refugee camps to workplace and community-based programs), none of us had worked in a family literacy program before. Thus, we felt that it would be important to situate our work within the broader framework of existing research and conceptualizations of family literacy, to understand on the one hand what the research had to say about how families contribute to literacy development and, on the other, how programs were designed to promote this development. We wanted to examine the range of answers to questions like those posed above, looking not just at program designs but at the assumptions they were based on and the rationale that informed them. This led us to step back and ask a set of questions about the social context of family literacy programming itself:

- Why is family literacy becoming such a popular trend now?
- What models are now being used to involve English and language minority families in children's literacy development?

- What assumptions are these models based on?
- What does the research say about how families contribute to the literacy development of children?
- How do the families' contributions vary according to class and culture?
- What alternatives are there to the predominant models?

We embarked on this investigation process by doing three things:

1. reviewing studies of home literacy contexts and family contributions to literacy development of children from different classes and cultures (ethnographic research);
2. looking at existing family literacy program models; and, perhaps most importantly,
3. learning from our students, investigating with them their own family literacy contexts.

While this is not the place to present an in-depth analysis of our findings, there are several points that are critical for understanding our rationale in pursuing a participatory approach to curriculum development. (See Auerbach, 1989, for a fuller analysis of these questions).

Most importantly, what we found was that existing programs were often not informed by research findings. The evidence about family contributions to literacy acquisition and implications for practice pointed in one direction while the predominant approach to program design pointed in another.

On the one hand, programs are often based on the assumption that the homes of low-income, minority, and ESL students are "literacy impoverished," with limited reading material, parents who don't read, don't value literacy, and don't provide support for their children's literacy development. Based on this notion of family deficit, program goals are often framed in terms of transforming home contexts into sites for mainstream literacy interactions; parents are taught to do specific school-like literacy tasks with their children and to interact with the schools on the schools' terms. Curricula focus on giving parents instruction in becoming home tutors, training in "effective parenting," and information on the culture of American schooling. In this "transmission of school practices" model, the direction is from the schools to the families.

On the other hand, studies of low-income, minority, and immigrant families show that they often use literacy for a wide variety of purposes, have homes filled with print, and not only value literacy, but see it as the key to mobility. Even parents with little education and limited literacy support their children's literacy development in a variety of ways (Chall & Snow, 1982; Delgado-Gaitan, 1987; Taylor & Dorsey-Gaines, 1988). When we investigated family interactions around literacy with our students, we found a picture of mutual support and sharing of strengths as the following examples show.

I help my Kids.
I teach them good things.
I play with them. I protect
them. I correct them.
My Kids bring me things.
My Kids will teach me English.
My Kids make me happy.
Maybe they will take care of me.

Gebre Goso

I help my Kids by staying
together with them. By talking to
them. I help them by confronting
them and telling them whats wrong
or Right. Just as they do me.
I help them when they need a
favor or money just as they do me.
It's Just like you scratch my
back I scratch your back with
my family.

Maria Bento

Interestingly, the way the second piece was written itself exemplifies the "you scratch my back, I'll scratch yours" dynamic in this family: The mother is herself a beginning ESL student with minimal first language literacy skills. She collaborated with her daughter in a language experience process to produce this piece. The mother told the daughter what she wanted to say and the daughter helped the mother to write it.

Further, studies of the homes of successful readers found that interactions around print varied greatly. No specific school-like instructional practices accounted for literacy acquisition; rather, literacy was integrated in a socially significant way into many aspects of family life and developed to the extent that it was a tool for addressing needs and issues of importance for the family. Thus, Taylor (1983) concludes:

> The approach that has been taken in recent years has been to develop parent education programmes which very often provide parents with a battery of specific activities which are designed to teach reading, and yet very little available evidence suggests that parents with children who read without difficulty actually undertake such 'teaching' on a regular basis. The present study suggests that there are great variations in approaches the parents have evolved in working with their children and that the thread that unites the families is the recognition that learning to read takes place on a daily basis as part of everyday life. (p. 101)

The following piece, written by a student, Rosa, while she was in a primarily grammar-based classroom, is a response to the teacher's exasperated query about why no one had done their homework exercises:

Why I Didn't Do the Homework

Because the phone is ringing
the door is noking
the kid is yumping
the food is burning
time runs fast.

Implicit in this response is a plea for the teacher to understand the complex context of the student's life: She is more than a student—she is a parent, wife, cook, neighbor, and community member, trying to balance the demands of these many roles. Formal decontextualized homework becomes one more burden that seems in conflict with the demands of daily living. It doesn't always fit in or make sense. The following piece, written by the same student when she was in a family literacy class where the teacher invited students to explore and write about the dynamics of language choice in their families, uses the home context as content for writing, focusing on the issues that the student is involved with in her daily life.

At Home

I talk to my kids about school
I ask . . . ¿Como se portaron?
They say very good.
I continue in ask
about the food . . . and the homework.
they speak to me in english. . . .
I say I am sorry. . . .
Yo no entendí nada; por favor háblame

> en español . . . The older boy says OK . . . OK.
> You study english you are supposed to
> understand. They repeat again to me
> slowly and more *clearly*. Yo les digo . . .
> Muchas gracias. . . . I love you.
> They are 4, 6 and 10 years old.

Here literacy no longer seems in opposition to the student's concerns but is a tool for reflecting and acting on them. With these two pieces, Rosa's message here is clear: It is important to connect what happens inside the classroom with what happens outside the classroom so that literacy can become a tool for making changes in students' lives.

Taken together, this evidence suggested to us a very different model from the predominant transmission of school practices model: a model that acknowledges family strengths; investigates with students family contexts for literacy usage, attitudes and practices; and explores with students possibilities for change. Rather than proceeding from the schools to the families, the direction of this model is from the families and communities to the schools. Parents' roles, thus, are no longer defined in terms of implementing school goals or practices, but rather in terms of using literacy as a tool to deal with issues in their own daily reality. The premise here is that literacy will become socially significant in family life (and thus provide a context conducive to children's literacy acquisition) when participants in family literacy programs become critical readers of their own social contexts and authors of the changes they hope to make. The approach to curriculum development, thus, must be context-specific, grounded in the particular realities of each group of participants, and based on a collaborative investigation of critical issues in family and community life. As these issues emerge, they are explored and transformed into content-based literacy work so that literacy can, in turn, become a tool for making change in the conditions of students' lives. The two pieces on the previous page by Rosa illustrate the impact on student literacy development of these two differing approaches to literacy curriculum development.

While we arrived at our analysis within the context of a family literacy project, there are two lessons that are generalizable to other adult literacy contexts:

1. In order to develop a conceptual basis for any project, *it is important to understand the social context in which the project itself takes place*: why the project is being funded, what assumptions it rests on, whose interests it serves, whose agenda is driving it, how it views learners, etc.
2. The key to successful literacy acquisition is the extent to which literacy is rooted in and integrally related to issues of importance in learners' lives. It is this second claim that we will explore further in the rest of

this chapter. We will start by stepping back to get a broad picture of traditional and participatory approaches to curriculum development, going on to examine in more detail some of the characteristics of a traditional approach and the rationale for and characteristics of a participatory approach, and concluding with general principles of participatory curriculum development.

TWO APPROACHES TO CURRICULUM DEVELOPMENT: THE BIG PICTURE

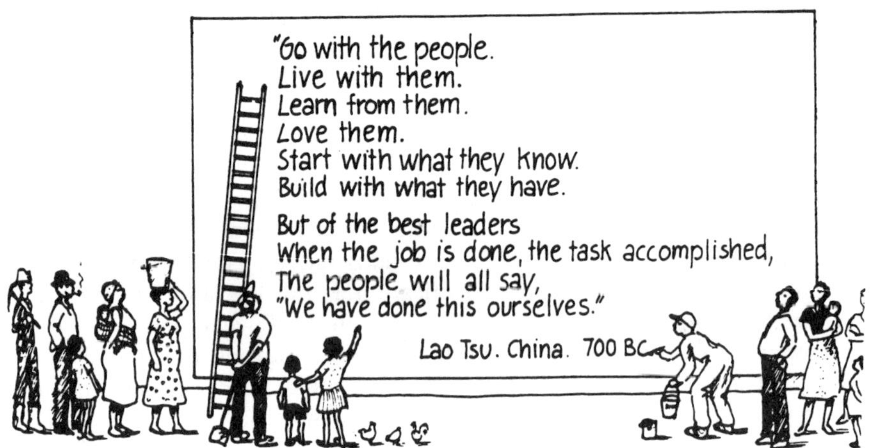

Reprinted by permission of SWAPO Literacy Campaign.

This graphic comes from the *Literacy Promoter's Handbook* (SWAPO Literacy Campaign, 1986, p. 6), a guide for Namibian literacy workers. Although the quote was originally written almost three thousand years ago, and is taken here from materials being used in a third world setting, the message is a universal one, fully relevant to our work with immigrants and refugees in a North American context. The message is a simple one: that people learn best when learning starts with what they already know, builds on their strengths, engages them in the learning process, and enables them to accomplish something they want to accomplish. This is the essence of a participatory approach. The only thing astounding about this approach is that it is not the norm; in fact, it is diametrically opposed to the way that many of us have been taught, and, as the following pages (excerpted from the same manual, pp. 3–4) indicate, differs from the "old" methods used in many adult literacy settings.

As you read the next few pages, think about how each of the methods presented relates to your own learning and teaching experiences. Which method is closest to the way you learned . . . ? Which is closest to teaching approaches you're familiar with?

Reprinted by permission of SWAPO Literacy Campaign.

Reprinted by permission of SWAPO Literacy Campaign.

What Characterizes a More Traditional, Ends–Means Approach?

One way to explain a participatory approach to ESL literacy is to contrast it with the more familiar ends–means approach in which experts identify a body of knowledge to be covered during a specified time period (ends) and provide a plan (means) for meeting predetermined objectives before instruction begins. Of course, the danger of setting up such a contrast is that it creates a kind of polarization that may not correspond to the lived experience of practitioners. Most programs are neither purely traditional nor purely participatory, but draw on elements of each and lie somewhere on a continuum between the two extremes. As such, the contrast oversimplifies reality. Nevertheless, it serves a function: It should be seen not so much as a system for categorizing or labeling programs, but rather as a tool for framing thinking about possibilities and situating programs along a continuum. Having said this, I now proceed with the oversimplified description of an ends–means approach!

The curriculum development process starts with experts identifying and describing a body of knowledge to be covered (as in the case of the Texas Adult Performance Level Study [APL] in which university-based researchers surveyed literacy usage in a wide variety of contexts, identifying 65 competencies that they claimed were necessary for "successful functioning in society"). Often this is done by consulting those in the mainstream society who will be interacting with the learner (e.g., employers or school personnel) in order to determine their expectations: what they need, hope, or expect the learner to be able to do as a result of instruction. The results of the investigation process then determine what gets taught (thus, the APL Study became the basis for competency-based ESL texts and curricula).

Content, in this view, derives from this externally defined body of knowledge (whether it be in the form of grammar, language use, cultural information, life skills, or competencies). This received content is broken down into parts according to topic, function, or form, with the resulting syllabus becoming a kind of blueprint or roadmap for instruction. The recent concern with accountability has led to very detailed specification of content, linguistic/behavioral tasks, outcomes, and performance standards.

Needs assessment very often follows the formulation of the syllabus. Thus, it is done a priori, as a *precondition* to instruction, to determine for the purposes of placement which skills students lack. In many cases, assessment is done by someone other than the teacher and results are presented to the teacher in quantified form, with no account of the assessment interaction itself. Often, assessment data inform instruction only to the extent that they serve as a baseline against which progress is measured. Sometimes (e.g., in competency-based ESL), teaching specifically targets weaknesses identified in pretesting and considers any teaching not related to these points to be deviations that don't count.

The teachers' role in this process is to transmit skills and knowledge; the ***students' role*** is to receive knowledge. Thus, the teacher is the knower and the student is the knowee. Because learning is defined as the acquisition of skills or knowledge, it is seen to be primarily an individual process, with each learner proceeding at his/her own pace, accumulating skills/knowledge with assistance from the teacher. Although there may be flexibility in terms of materials or methods for attaining the prespecified objectives, any classroom activity not directed at meeting these objectives is considered a deviation.

Outcomes are also measured against these predetermined objectives. Teachers are evaluated in terms of how well they cover the syllabus. Students are evaluated in terms of gains between pretesting and posttesting. Great stress is placed on quantification of progress and objectivity of assessment. Further, outcomes must be correlated with objectives; this means that predictability is valued. Funding is often contingent on meeting goals that have been specified before students have been admitted. Thus, to the program, projected *results* shape recruitment: Only those students who are likely to meet predetermined outcomes are accepted.

Thus, in this approach, the educator/expert does most of the work of naming the reality, determining the needs and objectives, developing the educational plan, providing the materials, and evaluating the outcomes. As a result, according to Freire (1981), the educator acts as a *problem-solver* for the student, "curing" the student by prescribing or transmitting educational medicine (in the form of skills, behaviors, or competencies), with the result that the student's voice is silenced.

Quite a literal example of this silencing took place in a factory-based ESL class that I observed several years ago. I arrived early and found the students, Portuguese women who had been in this country for many years, engaged in an animated and angry discussion of something that had happened to one of them that day: After eight years on the job, she had suddenly been shifted from an hourly rate job to a piece-rate job in violation of the union contract. The teacher, who herself was Portuguese, joined the discussion. Passionate debate ranged from why the boss had done this, to what the woman could do and how the others might help. Suddenly the teacher looked at her watch and said it was time to start class. She had prepared a lesson on calling in sick, after a careful needs assessment of the kinds of language the women needed for the workplace. What followed was a solid hour of silence, with the women alternately looking out the window, at their shoes, and at the clock.

This episode represents more than just missing a teachable moment; it represents a stance toward education. The teacher felt she had to stick to her lesson; it was what she was "supposed to do" and if she had allowed the students to keep talking about what had happened at work, she said she would have felt guilty. She was a committed person who had spent long hours doing a needs assessment and preparing detailed lesson plans on the skills her students needed to fit into the workplace. But by making the decision for her students, she assumed control of the situation, robbing them of the chance to participate in directing their own learning.

A Participatory Approach: the Emergent Curriculum

In contrast to the ends–means approach, a curriculum that aims to be centered on issues of importance to participants must be tailored to each group of students. It can't be developed before the educator ever comes in contact with the class, but rather has to be built on the particular conditions, concerns, and contributions of specific groups of participants at a particular point in time.

A host of factors must be taken into account: Are participants from the same language group or different ones? Are they working or on welfare? What are the ages of their children? Do they live in public housing? The list goes on, but the point is that educators can't know the specific concerns of any group until they come in contact with them. There may be a set of generic issues—issues that are common and predictable for most immigrants and refugees in this country—but it isn't possible to know which of these will be resonant issues for any given group at a given point in time. The only way to find out what a particular group is concerned about, how they already use literacy, and how they might use it to address these concerns, is to investigate the social context of their lives with them.

Clearly, this approach demands a fundamental reconceptualization of curriculum development. Whereas, in the traditional approach, the teacher walks into the classroom armed with a predetermined set of objectives or outcomes, syllabus, lesson plans, and texts, in a participatory approach the curriculum *emerges* as a result of an ongoing, collaborative investigation of critical themes in students' lives. But where does this leave the teacher? Contrary to some misconceptions, it doesn't mean that the teacher goes into the classroom empty-handed, waiting for issues to fall from the sky. *A participatory approach provides the teacher with a structured process for developing context-specific curricula, involving students at every step of the way*. To implement this process, the educator needs four things:

1. a clear *conceptualization* of the rationale for the approach (what this chapter hopes to provide);
2. an *overview of the process*;
3. a set of *tools and procedures* for finding and developing student themes into literacy work; and
4. a set of *resources* to draw on in implementing the approach, including materials and coworkers to talk to about the process as it develops.

Rationale for a Participatory Approach

The "why" for participatory literacy comes from adult learning theory, second language acquisition theory, and literacy theory, each of which is touched on only briefly here.

Adult Learning Theory. A central concept in adult learning theory is *self-directed learning*. As Knowles (1984) and others have pointed out, adult education is most effective when it is experience-centered, related to learners' real needs, and directed by learners themselves. Rather than abstract, decontextualized instruction focusing on isolated skills or generic topics, content must be contextualized in terms of student-determined interests and goals. It must be related in a meaningful way to the students' everyday reality and useful in enabling students to achieve their own purposes. Thus, adult learning theory supports the view that learners must be involved in determining both the content and direction of their education.

Second Language Acquisition (SLA) Theory. This concern with context and meaning are reflected in SLA theory. In the past twenty years, there has been a paradigm shift away from grammar-based and behavioral approaches (both of which are form-centered in orientation) toward *meaning-centered* approaches to English as a Second Language (ESL). Language is no longer seen only as a system of rules or behaviors that have an autonomous existence independent of their usage. The notion of *communicative competence* implies that it is not enough to know the grammar of a language; it is necessary also to know appropriate forms to use as the context changes. According to this view, both grammatical and sociolinguistic knowledge are acquired in the process of meaningful interaction in a range of settings, with a range of purposes, and participants. Real communication, accompanied by appropriate feedback that subordinates form to the elaboration of meaning, is key for language learning.

It is the teachers' task to create contexts for this type of communicative activity to take place. One of the means for creating such contexts is through *content-based* instruction: Contexts that focus on the exchange and creation of substantive information provide opportunities to link language acquisition with cognitive development. Further, *cooperative learning through peer interaction* provides students with greater opportunity to use language than teacher-centered participant structures; in addition, task- or problem-oriented activities provide a context for authentic dialogue and purposeful language use.

Literacy Theory. Central to recent developments in literacy theory is the notion that literacy practices, like language, are variable, context-dependent, and culture-specific. Until recently, literacy was seen as a monolithic set of neutral skills existing independently of how or where they're used. Literacy was seen to have certain inherent qualities that inevitably led to higher order cognitive processing (e.g., logical thinking) and economic advancement (see Gee, 1986, for a review of these perspectives).

However, studies of the real-world uses of literacy and literacy acquisition in different settings have revealed that the ways people read and write vary according to the task, the situation, the purpose, and the relationship between reader, writer, and setting. Further, the particular practices and beliefs about literacy for a given society depend on a range of cultural, social, and political factors. This research refutes claims made for literacy, showing that logical thinking is a consequence not of literacy per se but of how it is taught; economic advancement is determined more by race, ethnicity, and class than by literacy level (see Gee, 1986, for a comprehensive review of recent research supporting this analysis). Heath's (1983) work showed that although different communities use different literacy practices, those of middle-class communities are most like those of schools; and because authority is vested in those with mainstream ways (i.e., the ways of the school), children from middle-class communities had an advantage. This advantage has more to do with power relationships than with any inherent qualities of their particular literacy practices.

Street (1984) argues that it is no accident that literacy has traditionally been viewed as a unitary phenomenon, with inherent qualities and consequences. He argues that this view of literacy is a way of privileging one group's "ways with words" over others'. Recognizing only one culture-specific set of literacy practices, namely those taught and used in school (what Street calls "western essay-text literacy"), and elevating it to universal status, serves to maintain the dominance of those who use it. Its status comes not from its inherent features, but from its relation to the social order, because of who owns and has access to it. Street, Heath, and others argue that it must be explicitly acknowledged that each view of literacy reflects a particular ideological perspective. The traditional view justifies the status quo by valuing certain literacy practices over others; the socio-contextual view opens the door to changes in power relations by recognizing the legitimacy of diverse literacy practices.

A number of studies exploring the implications of this perspective for literacy instruction have appeared recently (again, see Gee, 1986 and Heath, 1983). Heath and Branscombe (1985), for example, suggest teaching students to become ethnographers of their own literacy communities, involving them in the process of investigating language and literacy usage. Their work with middle school students showed that when students become literacy researchers, exploring literacy beliefs and practices in their own families and communities, they make tremendous literacy gains. This study suggests that the process of observing, collecting, recording, and analyzing data about language and literacy use in itself facilitates literacy acquisition because *literacy is both the instrument and the object of study*. As we embarked on our project, we tried to identify features that characterized Heath and Branscombe's approach to literacy instruction, and came up with the following guidelines:

Guidelines for Literacy Instruction

1. Create a literate classroom environment.
- Permeate the atmosphere with talk about language and literacy use.
- Constantly link reading and writing to students' daily lives.
- Treat students as though they are avid readers and writers.

2. Make literacy classroom activities real, student-centered, and communicative.
- Start with personal writing: autobiographical, student-initiated topics.
- Use literacy for real purposes and audiences (e.g., set up letter-writing teams).

3. Connect content inside the the class to the community outside.
- Have students investigate language, literacy, and variability of usage.
- Identify contexts and purposes for literacy practices.

4. Develop literate practices through research in which students:
- collect data (participant observation, interviews, reading inventories);
- record data (field notes, taping, transcribing);
- analyze data (finding patterns, comparing);
- report on the analysis and present findings; and
- establish a community of researchers for responding, criticizing, refining, and producing a revised analysis.

The recent theoretical developments discussed above suggest that instruction must include explicit discussion of literacy learning itself. This means (a) involving learners in the investigation of their own literacy practices; (b) critically analyzing with learners how the educational system has shaped their development, self-image, and possibilities by devaluing their knowledge and promoting one culture-specific norm at the expense of others; and (c) involving students in determining their own purposes, rather than prescribing practices for them.

The work of Brazilian educator Paulo Freire is perhaps the most important inspiration for a participatory approach to ESL. His approach, developed in the 1950s during a literacy campaign among peasants and slum-dwellers in Brazil, involved engaging learners in dialogue about key words representing problematic issues in their lives in order to foster critical analysis of the issues. These dialogues became the basis for literacy development and action for change.

What was significant about Freire's work was his insistence on linking literacy to social change. As he says, "reading the word" and "reading the world" go hand in hand: Literacy education is meaningful to the extent that it engages learners in reflecting on their relationship to the world they live in and provides them a means to shape that world (Freire & Macedo, 1987). Freire claims that every curriculum reflects a particular view of the world, whether or not it is explicitly acknowledged. Thus, education is never neutral. It can either serve to perpetuate existing social relations or to challenge them.

> Education either functions as an instrument which is used to facilitate the integration . . . into the logic of the present system and bring about conformity to it, or it becomes the "practice of freedom," the means by which men and women deal critically and creatively with reality and discover how to participate in the transformation of their world. (Freire, 1970, p. 15)

Freire argues that both the content and the processes of traditional adult literacy perpetuate the marginalization of learners. When literacy is taught as a collection of decontextualized, meaningless skills, starting with letters and sounds divorced from any significance in learners' lives, they cannot use their minds or bring anything to the learning process, and therefore become objects of instruction. Students are seen as lacking the skills and behaviors needed to function in the society as it exists; the curriculum focuses on transferring knowledge that will help students fit in. Freire calls this the "banking model" of education: Learners are seen as empty vessels, devoid of any knowledge, and the educators' job is to fill the empty accounts by making deposits of knowledge. The learners thus become passive recipients of prepackaged and predetermined curriculum content. The classroom processes themselves are disempowering because they rehearse students for submissive roles in the social order outside the classroom. As Freire (1970) says, this kind of curriculum is domesticating in that it tames people into uncritical acceptance of things as they are, discouraging them from actively challenging the forces that keep them marginalized.

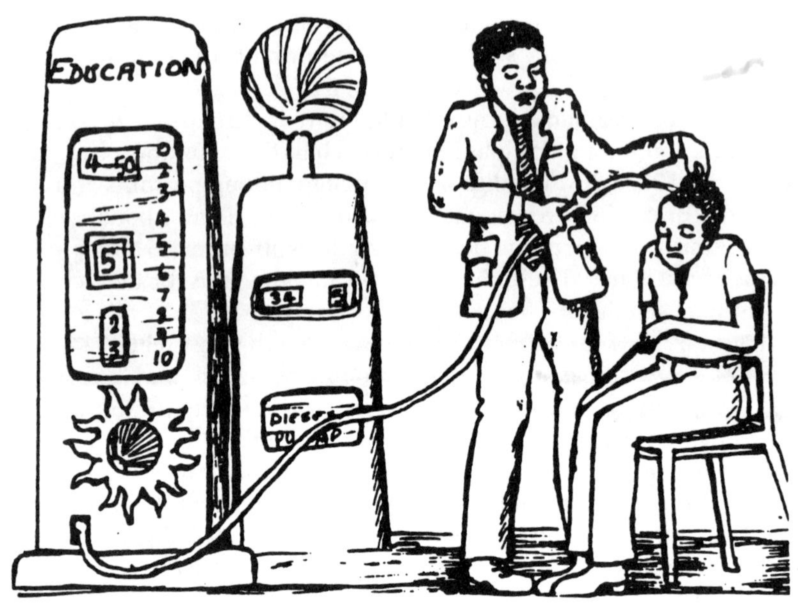

From *Training for Transformation, Book 1* (p. 103) by A. Hope and S. Timmel, 1984, Giveru, Zimbabwe: Mambo Press. Reprinted by permission.

In contrast to this domesticating education, Freire proposes a model whose goal is to enable learners to become active participants in shaping their own realities. Both the content and processes of this model invite learners to become the subjects of their own education. Content centers on problematic issues from their lives, so literacy is immediately relevant and engaging. Because this reality is problematized (presented in all its complexity, without predetermined solutions), participants become the creators rather than the recipients of knowledge. They engage in a process of reflection and dialogue, developing both an understanding of the root causes of the problem and generating their own alternatives for addressing it. Literacy learning becomes a context for thinking critically about social issues in a process that Freire calls "conscientization." "Learners enter into the process of learning not by acquiring facts [skills, competencies] but by constructing their reality in social exchange with others" (Auerbach & Wallerstein, 1987, p. 1). This radically transforms their relation to education, making them subjects of their own learning; at the same time, because literacy becomes a tool for addressing problems, it transforms their relation to the world, making them subjects of their own history. Education thus is part of a liberating process rather than a domesticating one. Freire's four-part process for putting this theory into practice can be characterized as follows:

Overview of Freire's Curriculum Development Process

1. The listening phase. During this time, the educator immerses him or herself in the community of the students, becoming intimately familiar with their daily reality. Through this investigation process, the educator identifies critical social issues from students' lives and selects a core group of shared issues that become the backbone of the literacy curriculum. Issues are selected on the basis of their evocative power—the extent to which they trigger strong emotional responses. The educator then distills these themes into codes or codifications—abstracted representations in graphic form of the issues, depicted so that they are depersonalized and objective but immediately recognizable. Problems are presented in a two-sided way so that no solution or predetermined interpretation is implied. For each theme, a generative (key) word is selected that both reflects the loaded issue and has a regular syllable structure.

2. The dialogue phase. Learners work together in dialogue circles, reflecting on the codes; the facilitator/teacher guides their dialogue through steps moving from literal interpretation of the code, to linking it to personal conditions and situations, to reflecting on its root causes and considering alternative ways of addressing the problem. Through this conscientization process, participants deepen their understanding of the conditions shaping their lives. The group nature of this process is critical: Participants each contribute their interpretations and collectively arrive at an analysis of the situation; they share experiences and ideas in order to generate their own alternatives for action.

3. The decoding and recoding phase. Once students have "read the world" of a generative word, they move on to "reading the word" itself, grappling with syllable structure. The process moves from analyzing the word in terms of its meaning in participants' lives, to analyzing it linguistically, breaking it into syllables that are then recombined to make new words, and new meanings.

4. The action phase. The final phase entails doing something in the real world as a result of the reflection and dialogue. In Freire's case, the literacy campaign led peasants and slum-dwellers to become active participants in the political process. On a more limited scale, the point of the action phase is to return to the problem that inspired the literacy work and work to change the conditions that gave rise to it.

Beyond Freire

For the past three decades, educators around the world have been working to put Freire's vision of "education for transformation" into practice. Early attempts often focused on struggling to transpose Freire's pedagogy into different contexts in a literal way; however, because his work grew out of specific conditions, took place in a third world country, was developed for a syllabically regular language, and was part of a movement for social change, this kind of literal translation was often not possible, causing some practitioners to become discouraged or to question its applicability to their situation. However, over time, it became clear that this kind of transposition of methodogy was neither the intention nor the spirit of Freire's approach. Rather, practitioners realized that they had to constantly reinvent Freire for their own contexts, taking from his work the underlying outlook but developing tools to implement it according to their own situations. Thus, over the past twenty years, Freire's vision has been adapted for second language, workplace, health, and peace education internationally. The popular education and participatory research movements have both been influenced by Freire. His ideas have been widely adapted for ESL with the development of Wallerstein's (1983) problem-posing approach and the participatory ESL movement in Canada.

The challenge for anyone trying to apply a Freirean perspective is to figure out what is and what isn't relevant to a given context. The brief summary outlined here is by no means a prescription for practice. As the body of Freire-inspired practice grows, there have been inevitable refinements, reformulations, and challenges to both the form and content of Freire's ideas. Key among these is expansion of the learners' role in the curriculum development process; specifically, where Freire suggested that the educator undertake a period of investigation and identification of themes before instruction begins, others have moved toward a process of identifying themes through dialogue with participants, as part of the instructional process. In addition, rather than focusing on a single method (moving from code to dialogue to generative word to syllabification to creating new words and moving toward action), others have expanded the range of tools and processes for exploring issues, with student involvement in the production of material. Further, many have questioned the notion that the teacher's role is to facilitate conscientization and analytical thinking because it implies that the teacher has a more developed understanding than the students. The process of trying to redefine roles in the classroom has been as much a learning process for teacher-learners as for student-learners. The following passage is an adult basic education (ABE) teacher's explanation of how her thinking developed on this issue.

> Up to a year and a half ago, I was a teacher because I thought people needed to think more critically about the social conditioning of their personal experience, to look underneath the myths that obscure our vision of what's going on in our lives and the world . . .
>
> But the problem this notion began to raise for me is that the women where I worked often did view reality with a critical consciousness; they quite often did see the social conditioning of their own lives. John Gwaltney, in *Drylongso: A Self Portrait of Black America*, said that "principled survival is a

> preeminently analytical process." A woman in one class once talked about how you have to lie to your caseworker to squeeze what you need out of welfare, but that having to lie in front of your children "takes away your freedom." Deciding which to trade off—your right to demonstrate your real integrity to your child, or getting her a decent looking coat so she doesn't feel humiliated at school—knowing that freedom is what hangs in the balance, is a "preeminently analytical process . . ."
>
> When I first wrote the paragraph above, I wondered if I should take it out. I shouldn't *have* to remind myself that the women I work with think analytically. But I have to painfully admit that sometimes my eyes aren't open to it. . . .
>
> I also began to realize that within the framework I'd used, there wasn't a place for me, as a teacher, with which I was comfortable. The role it left me was that of a facilitator whose consciousness was already raised, helping other people to raise theirs. I was beginning to see that I couldn't reconcile that role with the reality of who the women in my classes really were. I also started to see how that premise didn't fit with the fact that my own awareness of many things still needed raising, or that even when my awareness of an issue is high, my actions don't always match it. In sum, I couldn't reconcile this role with the view I wanted to have of myself as a co-learner . . ." (Martin, 1989, pp. 5–6.)
>
> *Reprinted by permission of the author.*

It is the accumulated body of practice based on Freire's work that is the real inspiration for a participatory approach. While Freire's work is a starting point, the broadened perspective that has emerged through teachers sharing experiences in conferences, in written accounts of their practice, and in informal networks is the essence of participatory education.

What Characterizes a Participatory Approach?

Going back to our comparison (polarization!) between an ends–means approach and a participatory approach, we can see how they differ in terms of essential features. Most importantly, in a participatory approach, teachers and students work together to decide what to focus on in class and how to proceed, rather than having educators/experts deciding for them.

The curriculum development process involves students at every step of the way, from needs assessment through evaluation. Students are assumed to be the experts on their own reality and very much involved in researching that reality with teachers. This collaborative investigation of what is important to students is at the heart of the instructional process, the direction of which is *from the students to the curriculum* rather than *from the curriculum to the students*. In place of a static body of knowledge defined by outside experts, students and teachers have a set of principles and processes to guide their own selection of content and production of knowledge. Not only are students involved in deciding *what* is to be done, they are involved in deciding *how* to do it; as they participate increasingly in creating and producing their own forms and materials (drawings, photos, drama, stories, music), they take more control of the learning process.

Learning is seen to be a collective process, where participants share and analyze experiences together in order to address concerns, relying on each others' strengths and resources rather than addressing problems individually or relying on outside experts to solve them.

Needs assessment is an ongoing process, integrated into classroom interaction rather than preceding instruction. Of course, students are grouped according to certain criteria (which may include literacy level, interests, native language, age of children, etc.). However, rather than serving as a baseline against which to assess progress in posttesting, ongoing needs analysis is used as the basis for curriculum development; analyzing needs, interests, strengths, and concerns is very much part of the process of acquiring control over one's own learning and is therefore an important part of the students' work. If, as we said earlier, family literacy is seen as a social process shaped by a host of factors inside and outside the family (family roles, housing conditions, work, childcare, etc.), one of the important functions of the needs analysis is to engage students in examining their own contexts, identifying factors and dynamics that shape their environment so they can begin to change it.

Content in this approach emerges through the ongoing classroom interaction. With no received body of knowledge to be covered or transmitted, an important part of participatory curriculum development is transferring the tools for the production of knowledge to the students. This means they have to be involved not only in determining content but in explicitly reflecting on what counts as knowledge, on how learning takes place, and on their own roles in the process. As Barndt (1986) says, students discover their own knowledge, create new knowledge and act on this knowledge. The bank from which content is drawn is the social reality of students' lives: It may range from the immediate context of the classroom itself to family or community contexts to broader political issues; it may include explicit discussion about literacy practices and literacy acquisition. This doesn't mean, however, that nothing can be prepared in advance. . . . [T]eachers can draw on prior experience in terms of familiarity with potential issues, catalysts to trigger exploration of issues with each group of students, tools to develop literacy around these themes, and resources to deepen the analysis of issues as they arise. Many centers, for example, compile files, with copies of all class materials around particular themes that teachers can draw from if and when those themes arise in class.

Choices about content are made collaboratively through "negotiated selection from these open-ended banks, guided by the curriculum principles" (Candlin, 1984). The syllabus, in this view, is more of a *retroactive account* than a blueprint or roadmap; it is a syllabus of *how* rather than a syllabus of *what* (Candlin, 1984). Again, this doesn't mean that the teacher walks into the class with no plan; rather, it means that the actual syllabus is an account of the interaction between the plan and the reality (what happened when the teacher tried to implement it). As Candlin (1984) says, "It is only from the tension between classroom action and curriculum guidelines . . . that we can expect innovation. It is this tension which can drive curricula forward, maintaining their relevance to the society of the classroom and that of the world outside."

The teacher's role is to act as a *problem-poser*, facilitating the process of uncovering important issues and reflecting on them. Because students are experts on their own reality, the teacher is a co-learner. The teacher's stance is one of asking questions rather than providing answers or transmitting knowledge or skills; when the teacher does answer questions it is in the spirit of sharing information as one member of a group, rather than as the expert. Because the learning process is seen to be a collective, group process, the teacher's job is to draw out the experience and perspective of participants so that they can use their collective knowledge to address issues. The teacher does this by creating a context where students feel comfortable in sharing what's important to them, by providing structures for getting at their concerns, by re-presenting issues in a form that will facilitate dialogue, by helping to structure exploration of the issues, by modeling and presenting choices for learning activities, and by sharing his or her own experiences, knowledge, ideas, and opinions.

Outcomes cannot be predicted if content and processes are genuinely student-centered. The *unpredictability* of outcomes is valued in that it indicates participants have genuinely been involved in determining their objectives for themselves. As L. Stenhouse (in Candlin, 1984) says, "Education as induction into knowledge is successful to the extent that it makes the behavioral outcomes of the students *unpredictable*." Thus, rather than feeling guilty about deviating from the plan when unexpected issues surface, the teacher welcomes precisely this kind of occurrence as the meat of a participatory process and is able to respond to it.

Further, in a participatory approach, *qualitative* change is given as much or more weight as *quantitative* change because the primary goal is that students move toward being able to address real life concerns and take action; this means that being able to describe and analyze changes is more important than being able to count them. Whereas measurable changes in skill or grade levels are valued in an ends–means approach, the diversification of uses of literacy and the ability to make literacy meaningful in everyday life are valued in a participatory approach. These changes are not easily measurable and may have no clearly observable behavioral manifestations.

This means that *subjective* as well as *objective* evidence of progress is valued in a participatory approach. Since many of the changes are internal and affective, students' own assessment of accomplishment is important. As a result, the notion of external objective evaluation is no longer sufficient; it is critical that students themselves be involved in the evaluation process both because of the valuable evidence they can provide and because their participation is part of the process of gaining control of their learning and their lives.

Finally, progress is seen to be *cumulative* and *cyclical* rather than occurring in discrete, linear steps. Evidence of learning may not show up within a prespecified time frame or at the moment it is being evaluated. It may take months after a class ends for its impact to manifest itself. Thus, in a participatory approach, there is no expectation that students will attain predetermined objectives within mandated time periods. Rather, both language and literacy acquisition are allowed to develop at their own pace, without the attempt to collapse into a short time frame a process that takes first language/literacy learners years to accomplish.

As in the ends–means approach, both the content and processes of a participatory classroom rehearse people for life roles; however, in this case, classroom relations prepare people for changing social relations outside the classroom, rather than for fitting into someone else's agenda. The transformation of student-teacher roles serves as a model for changes in roles outside the classroom. As participants become involved in directing their own education, they explore and rehearse active participation in other areas of their lives.

WHAT DO THESE APPROACHES LOOK LIKE IN PRACTICE?

In the context of family literacy work, these two approaches to curriculum development take very different forms. An assimilative, ends–means approach would instruct parents to conform to school expectations by extending school practices into the home, teaching about American school culture and modeling "appropriate" parental behavior. A critical, participatory approach, on the other hand, would explore existing parental concerns, expectations, and practices, evaluate and challenge school practices if necessary, and use literacy to influence these realities.

An example from one of Loren's classes illustrates the difference between how assimilative literacy and critical literacy model and prepare students for life roles. One day, a student brought to class a flyer from her daughter's school with a list of ways parents can help their children with homework. In an assimilative approach, the teacher might have gone over the flyer point by point, talking about what parents can do to help their kids. Instead, the teacher did something quite different. The class still read the flyer, but the reading was followed by questions like this: *Which of these things do you already do? Which would you like to do? Which do you think are ridiculous, impossible, or not useful?* and *What do you already do that's not listed in the flyer?* This way of framing the reading led to a discussion of cultural differences in perceptions of teachers' vs. parents' roles (some critical cultural analysis). In addition, the parents identified both their own strengths (what they already do to help their children) and new things that they would like to try. By relating the flyer to their own reality, looking at it in a broader social context, and exploring possibilities, they maintained a stance of independence and choice in the learning process. This simple prescriptive flyer became the basis for shaping some of their own alternatives.

SUMMING UP: PRINCIPLES FOR PARTICIPATORY CURRICULUM DEVELOPMENT

1. Students are engaged in curriculum development at every stage of the process. Ideally, this means that students participate in identifying issues, generating content, producing materials, determining outcomes, and evaluating learning. Realizing this ideal is a slow, gradual process that involves moving back and forth between old and new ways of doing things and making the approach to curriculum itself explicit. Students' increasing participation fosters motivation and self-confidence.

2. The classroom is a model; what happens inside the classroom shapes the possibilities outside the classroom. Both *what* is learned (content) and *how* it is learned (processes) shape students' perceptions of their own possibilities and prepare them for particular ways of acting in the outside world. Classroom social relations are a microcosm of social relations beyond the classroom. Making changes inside the classroom itself models a way of addressing issues and redefining roles outside the classroom.

3. The focus is on strengths, not inadequacies. Students are seen as experts on their own reality and, as such, are invited to believe in themselves. The content stresses their capacity to create new knowledge rather than reproduce or duplicate someone else's knowledge. This means investigating, validating and extending what participants can (and want to) do rather than stressing what they can't do or imposing what educators/experts think they should be doing.

4. ***The teacher's role is one of problem-poser rather than problem-solver.*** The teacher is not the one with answers, but the one who facilitates students' discovery of their own answers. The teacher catalyzes reflection on students' everyday reality. As concerns are identified, the teacher re-presents them to the class and guides students through an exploration process, contributing linguistic expertise while learning from the students' about their reality. "Everyone teaches, everyone learns." (Arnold, Barndt, & Burke, 1985, p. 16). The group generates its own ways of addressing concerns through collective dialogue.

5. ***The content comes from the social context.*** For literacy to be relevant, what goes on inside the classroom must relate to students' lives outside the classroom; thus, the starting point is the concrete experience of the learner. Students develop literacy by reading, writing, and talking about social factors (like housing, work, or neighborhood safety) in their family and community contexts and, most importantly, about ways that they can shape these conditions.

6. ***Language, literacy and culture are explored as part of the content because they are important aspects of the context.*** Through investigation of literacy use and cultural practices, learners develop metacognitive awareness of variations in form and function while also developing their own proficiency. Looking at who uses which language for what purposes, how literacy develops, and attitudes towards bilingualism promotes critical reflection on schooling and education.

7. ***Content also comes from the immediate context of the classroom.*** Because the students' primary shared context is their learning community, negotiating classroom dynamics and procedures is an important part of the content. By transforming these issues into content-based literacy activities, involving students in examining student-teacher roles, making decisions about curriculum content and processes, and resolving conflict, roles and social relations in the classroom can be redefined.

8. ***Individual experience is linked to social analysis.*** Participants look at their personal situations in light of each others' experiences and examine the root causes of problematic conditions. Thus, they talk not only about someone's difficulties finding an apartment, but about why there is a housing shortage, about why some landlords prefer to rent to immigrants and others prefer not to, and about strategies for finding housing. This collective reflection depersonalizes problems, provides support, and is the basis for action.

9. ***The content goes back to the social context.*** The goal is action outside the classroom to address participants' concerns; content is meaningful to the extent that it enables learners to make changes in their lives. This means that reality is not seen as static or immutable; learners can do more than adapt to it. Thus, literacy is not the end in itself, but rather a means for participants to shape reality, accomplishing their own goals. Skills are taught in service of action for change rather than as independent, isolated objectives.

REFERENCES

Arnold, R., Barndt, D., & Burke, B. (1985). *A new weave: Popular education in Canada and Central America*. Toronto: Canadian University Services Overseas and OISE Press.

Auerbach, E. (1989). Toward a social-contextual approach to family literacy. *Harvard Educational Review, 59*, 165–181.

Auerbach, E., & Wallerstein, N. (1987). *ESL for action: Problem-posing at work. Teachers' guide*. Reading, MA: Addison-Wesley.

Barndt, D. (1986). *English at work: A tool kit for teachers*. North York, Ontario: CORE Foundation. (OP. See Barndt, Belfiore, & Hanscombe, 1991, for revised edition.)

Candlin, C. (1984). Syllabus design as a critical process. In C. J. Brumfit (Ed.), *General English syllabus design* (pp. 29–46). Oxford: Pergamon Press.

Chall, J. S., & Snow, C. (1982). *Families and literacy: The contributions of out of school experiences to children's acquisition of literacy* [The Harvard Families and Literacy Project final report]. Washington, DC: National Institute of Education.

Delgado-Gaitan, C. (1987). Mexican adult literacy: New directions for immigrants. In S. R. Goldman & K. Trueba (Eds.), *Becoming literate in English as a second language* (pp. 9–32). Norwood, NJ: Ablex.

Freire, P. (1970). *Pedagogy of the oppressed*. New York: Seabury Press.

Freire, P. (1981). *Education for critical consciousness*. New York: Continuum.

Freire, P., & Macedo, D. (1987). *Literacy: Reading the word and the world*. South Hadley, MA: Bergin-Garvey.

Gee, J. (1986). Orality and literacy: From *The Savage Mind* to *Ways with Words*. *TESOL Quarterly, 20*, 719–746.

Heath, S. B. (1983). *Ways with words*. Cambridge: Cambridge University Press.

Heath, S. B., & Branscombe, A. (1985). "Intelligent writing" in an audience community: Teachers, students, and researcher. In S. W. Freedman (Ed.), *The acquisition of written language: Response and revision* (pp. 3–32). Norwood, NJ: Ablex.

Hope, A., & Timmel, S. (1984). *Training for transformation*. Giveru, Zimbabwe: Mambo Press.

Knowles, M. (1984). *Andragogy in action*. San Francisco: Jossey-Bass.

Martin, R. (1989). *Literacy from the inside out*. Watertown, MA: Author.

South West African People's Organization (SWAPO). (1986). *Literacy promoter's handbook*. Luanda: Author. (Distributed by Namibia Refugee Project, 22 Coleman Fields, London N1 7AF, England)

Street, B. V. (1984). *Literacy in theory and practice*. Cambridge: Cambridge University Press.

Taylor, D. (1983). *Family literacy: Young children learning to read and write*. Portsmouth, NH: Heinemann.

Taylor, D., & Dorsey-Gaines, C. (1988). *Growing up literate: Learning from inner-city families*. Portsmouth, NH: Heinemann.

Wallerstein, N. (1983). *Language and culture in conflict: Problem-posing in the ESL classroom*. Reading, MA: Addison-Wesley.

Reflection and Inquiry

REFLECTING ON THE READINGS

Respond to one or more of the following:

1. According to the first three readings in this unit, how is language acquired? Which of the theories and principles help you to make sense of your own language learning or teaching experiences?

2. Based on your understanding of the readings in Units One, Two, and Three, explore how using a method is different from embracing a set of principles.

3. Krashen presents a series of hypotheses to account for the way(s) language is acquired (chapter 10). Which of these hypotheses resonate with your own experience as a language learner or teacher? Do any of your experiences as language learner or teacher call into question any of Krashen's hypotheses?

4. Krashen discusses the limitations of grammar instruction, but he acknowledges that "students think that language is grammar. They have expectations of getting grammar. Administrators think that language is grammar" (chapter 10). On the basis of your own experiences in language classrooms as a student, teacher or observer, to what extent would you agree that an underlying assumption of these classrooms is that "language is grammar"? As a prospective or practicing (English) language teacher, what might you do to address students, colleagues, or administrators who embrace such an assumption?

5. Clarke describes what he owes his "gurus" (chapter 12). Whom might you identify as one of your gurus, and why? How might this person influence your teaching?

6. Although you cannot see the classroom in which the blackboard composition is generated (Clarke, chapter 12), how would you characterize the interaction, the turn-taking, the kinds of questions raised, the roles that the teacher and students play? To what extent does the IRE pattern (initiate-respond-evaluate) pattern seem to exist? Who responds? Who reacts to whom? How is knowledge constructed? What other observations or reactions do you have?

7. To what extent could the approach described by Auerbach (chapter 13) be implemented in a class you are attending, teaching, or observing? To what extent ought it to be implemented? What constraints might make this difficult? How might such constraints be addressed?

8. Apply the theories and principles discussed in this unit to any of the projects you have already undertaken (see *Suggested Projects for Inquiry* in Units One and Two). Consider how the readings in this unit help you make sense of the data you have already gathered through observations or interviews?

9. Given the theories and principles presented in this unit, consider one or more of the following. How might you proceed as a teacher of English to speakers of other languages (ESOL)? What would your teaching try to do? How would you determine what materials to use? What would you have students do with these materials? What would your role be? How would you address mechanical issues of language, e.g., structure, syntax, error? How would you assess the effects of this practice?

10. Imagine that you have just returned the first set of papers in which you responded to the students' ideas and pointed *selectively* to a number of recurring errors. After class, a student approaches you to ask why you didn't correct all of the errors. Drawing on the readings in this unit, how might you formulate a response to this student?

11. Select a passage (one sentence or several sentences) from one of the readings in Unit Three that struck you in some way. For example, it may be a passage that resonates with your own experience, that reminds of you something else you've read or seen, or that makes an important point. Highlight or copy the passage and then reflect on why you chose it.

READING FOR FURTHER REFLECTION

Respond to one or more of the following:

1. Read the following excerpt from John Dewey's *The School and Society*. Do you agree with his perspective? To what extent would Dewey's conviction about teaching language apply to teaching a second language?

> Think of the absurdity of having to teach language as a thing by itself. If there is anything the child will do before he goes to school, it is to talk of the things that interest him. But when there are not vital interests appealed to in the school, when language is used simply for the repetition of lessons, it is not surprising that one of the chief difficulties of schoolwork has come to be instruction in the mother tongue. Since the language taught is unnatural, not growing out of the real desire to communicate vital impressions and convictions, the freedom of children in its use gradually disappears, until finally the high-school teacher has to invent all kinds of devices to assist in getting any spontaneous and full use of speech. Moreover when the language instinct is appealed to in a social way, there is a continual contact with reality. The result is that the child always has something in his mind to talk about, he has something to say; he has a thought to express, and a thought is not a thought unless it is one's own. On the traditional method, the child must say something that he has merely learned. There is all the difference in the world between having to say something and having something to say.

2. Read the following excerpt from Ernest Hemingway's short story, "In Another Country." Can you identify with the narrator's experience? Drawing on principles of second language acquisition, can you explain the narrator's experience?

> The major, who had been the great fencer, did not believe in bravery, and spent much time while we sat in the machines correcting my grammar. He had complimented me on how I spoke Italian, and we talked together very easily. One day I had said that Italian seemed such an easy language to me that I could not take a great interest in it; everything was so easy to say. "Ah yes," the major said. "Why, then, do you not take up the use of grammar?" So we took up the use of grammar, and soon Italian was such a difficult language that I was afraid to talk to him until I had the grammar straight in my mind.

3. Read the following excerpt from Julia Alvarez's *Something to Declare*, in which she describes a teacher in the United States who nurtured her love of language. What strikes you? Do you in any way identify with her experience? What do you think promoted Alvarez's acquisition of English as a second language in school? You might want to contrast this experience with her earlier English classroom in the Dominican Republic (see Unit One, Reading for Further Reflection).

> Sister Maria Generosa did not make our class interminably diagram sentences from a work-book or learn a catechism of grammar rules. Instead, she asked us to write little stories imagining we were snowflakes, birds, pianos, a stone in the pavement, a star in the sky. What would it feel like to be a flower with roots in the ground? If the clouds could talk, what would they say? . . .
>
> . . . My mind would take off, soaring into possibilities, a flower with roots,

a star in the sky, a cloud full of sad, sad tears, a piano crying out each time its back was tapped, music only to our ears.

Sister Maria stood at the chalkboard. Her chalk was always snapping in two because she wrote with such energy. . . . "Here's a simple sentence: 'The snow fell.' " Sister pointed with her chalk. . . . "But watch what happens if we put an adverb at the beginning and a prepositional phrase at the end: 'Gently, the snow fell on the bare hills.' "

I thought about the snow. I saw how it might fall on the hills, tapping lightly on the bare branches of trees. Softly, it would fall on the cold, bare fields. On toys children had left out in the yard, and on cars and on little birds and on people out late walking on the streets. Sister Maria filled the chalk board with snowy print, on and on, handling and shaping and moving the language, scribbling all over the board until English, those verbal gadgets, those tricks and turns of phrases, those little fixed units and counters, became a charged, fluid mass that carried me in its great fluent waves, rolling and moving onward, to deposit me on the shores of my new homeland. I was no longer a foreigner with no ground to stand on. I had landed in the English language.

4. Read the following excerpts from journal entries written by two college students who participated in an ongoing study of students' experiences in courses across the curriculum. What generalities can you make about what promoted the learning of these students? What do their experiences suggest about the relationship between content and language acquisition?

Student Journal Entry on a History Course

I only heard dates and facts. Facts, dates. I reacted by sitting quiet and feeling very frustrated. I did not feel like sharing any of my opinions. . . . The lectures were missing the combination of creativity of my classmates' reflections. I started to lose the grounded self I carried with me from my ESL class experience. I tried several times to become visible during the lectures by letting out my voice. But I found myself lost because the lectures were without writing. . . . I remember that silent students in the classroom started to feel like a normal part of the lecture. Many times two or three words were my contributions in class. They were replacing the long and sometimes unclear sentences that previously in my ESL class were disentangled to reveal a powerful thought. . . . My writing started to experience a metamorphosis because I was copying dates and facts from the blackboard. There was not a drop of motivation to enjoy my journey of learning. I felt illiterate at the end of the semester. I did not learn a single new word.

Martha Muñoz

Student Journal Entry on a Philosophy Course

The first day of the course, the professor gave us an ungraded paper assignment: The subject was about our image toward philosophy. On the second day, he posed the same question to the class, and started to call on the students from the first row. Since I was sitting in the left corner of the front row, he called on me by verifying my first name. I was nervous to speak up in front of everybody whom I had not yet known, but because I already organized my idea and image toward philosophy last night in my assignment, though it was far from the fluent English, I somehow managed to bring myself to the end.

After I finished, the professor briefly summarized what I just said by using more sophisticated and philosophical sounding words. Then he raised two important issues from my statement and wrote down on the blackboard. I felt so delighted. I felt I was included. I felt my existence was affirmed. The reason why I was and still am hesitated to raise my voice in the classroom is because I am always intimidated by two big worries, which are "Will everybody be able to understand what I say?" and "Does my idea is important enough to be raised?" Most of the time, these two questions envelop my mind so that I cannot release my words; especially when I sense that the class circumstance is neither comfortable nor worthy enough to take the risk.

But this time, the professor displayed very warm and sensitive conduct before me. Perhaps that was a really trivial matter for other people, but because I was always worried about my English deficiency, even such a small matter became a big deal in my mind. A kind of hope was gradually growing in my mind, and I sensed that something urged me to take future chances in the class. I felt fortunate to take his course.

Motoko Kainose

5. Create a metaphor for teaching language. Create a metaphor for learning language. Complete the following sentences using these metaphors:

Teaching language ______________________________________.
Learning language ______________________________________.

Combine your sentences with those of other writers to create a class poem. Read and discuss the poem. What underlying themes are revealed in this class poem?

SUGGESTED PROJECTS FOR INQUIRY

Select a project that you would like to pursue:

1. Conduct a survey or series of interviews in which you explore several individuals' experiences learning an additional language. Create questions that explore the process through which they acquired (i.e., internalized) the language. Compare your findings with those of the researchers in this unit.

2. Interview several (English) language teachers about the theories and principles that inform their work. How did they come to have these theories and principles? How do these teachers draw on these theories and principles to determine their classroom practices? Do any factors constrain the implementation of these theories and principles? To what extent are these theories and principles congruent with those presented by the readings in this unit?

3. Observe a classroom or continue your ongoing observations of a classroom. In what ways, if any, do the theories and principles discussed in the readings in this unit get enacted in the classroom you are observing? Do the readings in this unit broaden your understanding of what seems to be "working" or not working in this classroom? How might specific instructional activities that you have observed be reframed or expanded on the basis of (any of) the theories and principles discussed in this unit?

4. Tape-record a segment of classroom interaction and transcribe a short section of this exchange. What is revealed about the dynamics in this classroom? Who asks the questions? Who responds? What kind of work is the classroom talk focused on? To what extent does the IRE pattern (the teacher initiates and questions, a student responds, the teacher evaluates) dominate classroom talk? If this pattern does not occur, how would you characterize the classroom interaction?

5. In a class in which you are a teacher, student or outside observer, ask students to share accounts in which they recollect particular teachers who influenced them, either positively or negatively. This information can be gathered through interviews or student writing. What do these accounts reveal about the teachers and how they influenced these students? Do these accounts confirm or reflect (any of) the theories and principles discussed in the readings in this unit? How do these accounts contribute to your understanding of teaching and learning?

6. In an ESOL class in which you are a teacher, tutor or outside observer, collect several students' papers to which teachers have responded in writing. Examine the comments, corrections, markings. Can you determine the purposes of these responses? If you have the opportunity, interview one or more of the student writers to determine the extent to which these students can make sense of the teacher's responses. What does this exploration teach you about responding to student writing? To what extent do the theories and principles presented in the readings help you make sense of your findings?

Unit IV

THEORIES INTO PRACTICE: KEEPING LANGUAGE MEANINGFUL

BEFORE READING

Respond to one or more of the following:

- Recall a time when you were interested in or excited about learning a particular subject in school (e.g., history or biology). Were you successful at learning this subject? Why or why not? What specifically facilitated or undermined your understanding (the teacher? the materials? the activities? the other students? etc.)?
- Have you ever been in a classroom in which students shaped the direction, goals, and/or content of the course? How did it affect the teaching/learning process? How did it affect the teacher–student relationship? How did it affect student and teacher roles?
- Recall a classroom in which you were studying a second or foreign language. Describe the materials (written or visual) and/or the activities that were used in that classroom as a basis for language study. To what extent did these materials or activities promote your second language acquisition?

Chapter **14**

The Classroom: A Good Environment for Language Learning

Judith Wells Lindfors

It's an interesting paradox that the more we find out about how language development differs from individual to individual and situation to situation, the more we find out about how it is similar for all. The specific differences shed light on and help us identify the deep general and unifying principles that operate across those specific differences of individual learners and situations. The first given is this: virtually all children effortlessly and naturally learn their native tongue, and many learn at least one more language as well. The second given is this: the specific situations in which this effortless learning occurs are very different one from another. The question, then, is this: how does it happen that the same result—the ability to communicate effectively in at least one language—is achieved through such diversity? The answer involves two parts: (1) what is *there*—the environment—for the child to use, and (2) the ways that the child uses it. Of course, these turn out to be the two most fundamental interests of the classroom teacher: providing a rich learning environment for children and supporting them in their effective use of it.

Though language development continues throughout life, it is most dramatic in the early years, before the child comes to school. An initial look at the environments in which young children develop their language reveals a great deal of variety. Children learn the language(s) of their social group, whatever the physical conditions, political systems, economic circumstances, cultural orientation, etc., of that group. And whatever the group's family structures, religious beliefs, moral values, educational practices, and social mores, the children learn the language(s). But even within the experience of any particular child the variation in language experience seems extraordinary: the child encounters language used for many different communication purposes (e.g., explaining, coaxing, promising, inviting, entertaining, deceiving), in many different types of events (conversations, rock songs, storybooks, scoldings, letters from grandma), involving many different participants and focusing on many different topics. The variety in every child's language world is quite remarkable.

However, a closer look reveals a crucial commonality: namely, that the specific language situations children in any society encounter are all real communication events. That is, people are engaging in the events in order to communicate with one another, *not* in order to "teach" the child his or her language. No, they're not "teaching" language, they're *doing* language—joking, informing, arguing, inquiring, comforting, challenging, and so on. The fact that the child learns language from the pervasive absence of explicit instruction has led some people to refer to language learning as "learning without teaching." The fact is that across an incredible array of specific environmental differences, there is one stunning commonality: it is *living* language that the child's environment is full of, language *in use*, communication.

It's quite incredible that, with people all around using language with her and with each other but not explicitly trying to teach her language, the child gets language figured out—language, that incredibly complex and abstract system for relating meanings (what we express) and expression (the ways we convey meanings). This brings us to our second question, the question of *how*: how does the child figure language out in this communication environment? What does the child *do* with what is *there*? We now know that the child does not try to take in and store specifics. Rather, he attends to the language around him in a selective way, tuning into it, noticing regularities and patterns that enable him to construct the organizational system that the talk and writing he encounters are examples of. The child—every child—is born to do this: to make *sense* of this mess of communication all around; to construct sense, order, design, organization. We do not hand a child our adult sense of language; the sense the child builds of language is his or her own, fashioned out of his or her own personal experience in the world. Many call the child's active sense-making "creative construction," "construction" in that it is the child's building of a system, and "creative" in that it is a system never explicitly given or described or taught, but rather a system fashioned by the child out of available, ever-present language material. It is a system gleaned, constructed, tried out, and confirmed in the many contexts of ongoing experience in the world, especially encounters with cognitive and social meanings and people's expression of them.

The child is well endowed for creatively constructing the language system that underlies the wide variety of bits and pieces she hears and sees. It is a human thing to do; it is, in fact, inevitable for a human to do this. Evolution has seen to this. Evolution has endowed our species, and no other, with unique anatomical and neurological mechanisms that we put to good use in figuring out how meaning and expression (signs, speech, written symbols) relate to one another and how to accomplish our many social purposes.

Yet it's easy to see that what is common for all in language learning—the child's creative construction process at work in her world of meaningful communication—is, at the same time, absolutely unique. For each human being, both the totality of personal experience (the "what is there") *and* his own active sense-making (his creative construction of language) will be his own, different from every other human's. The wonder of language! And of humans!

We see endless examples of children creatively constructing language out of their experience, if we know to look at children's language behavior—their talk and writing and reading—in this way. Here are some examples.[1]

- A five-year-old monolingual child is telling her mother a story for the wordless book *Hiccup*.

> The drink accidently got on her, and she was mad at him. But she forgived him . . . The girl, the girl hippopotamus was eating a sandwich and the boy was eating a ham—uh—a apple. And they were both hiccuping. And they both hiccuping and hiccuping and hiccuping and they thought it was alicious. And they hollered at each other and they keeped on hiccuping . . . And she kicked him into the water. And she was alaughin' at him, and sticked her tongue out at him.

- A teacher asked a four-year-old monolingual child who was sweeping the nursery school floor, "Are you mopping?" The child replied, "No, I'm brooming."
- A four-year-old monolingual child had found one shoe and asked his father, "Where's the other shoe that rhymes with this one?"
- A Spanish-dominant kindergarten child "reads" *The Little Engine That Could* aloud: "El choo-choo train think I can. Once a choo-choo train so happy. Oso, [bear] and elephant, two dolly and own-uh-own [orange], apple, milk, candy. Said, 'Why you stop?' 'Wait, wait . . .' 'Wha happen?' 'You help us?' 'No, I tired for that. I too tired for that.' 'Stop! Stop! Stop!'

  'Stop!' 'Wha happen?' 'The engine broke. Can you help us?' 'I, I, no, I too little. I think . . . all right, I can. Think I can, think I can, think I can, think I can, and then I can, and then I can, can, caaaaaaaan, (child is singing softly). 'I think I can, can, can. Now.' The end" (Seawell 1985, 127–28).

- A Spanish-dominant child, in second grade, starts her five-page story as seen in Fig. 14.1.
- Monolingual Julia, five years old, is asked to write a letter and a song. Her work is reproduced in Fig. 14.2.

You can see that these expressions are not the result of instruction or of imitation, because adult speakers of English would not have expressed themselves in these ways or taught anyone else to. You can also see that the children in these examples have figured out a great deal about how language works, and they are using that knowledge to guide their expression of their meanings as they communicate with others. Notice that these examples come from first- and second-language children, and they involve oral expression and written, but they all tell the same story: the tale of an active and creative sense-maker building an organizational system for communication even as she participates actively in communication, the very phenomenon she is figuring out.

No one is more concerned than the classroom teacher with the "what is there" in the child's learning environment and with supporting the use the child makes of it. That's simply the business of being a teacher. It's comforting to know that, in terms of children's language development in classroom settings, what's good for the first-language learner is good for the second: Children develop language best by observing and engaging in

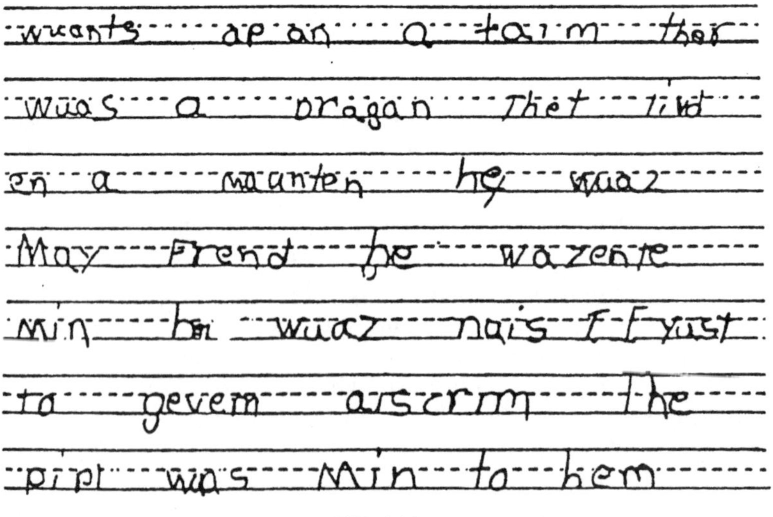

wuants ap an a taim ther
wuas a dragan thet livd
en a maunten he wuaz
May Frend he wazente
min he wuaz nais I Fyust
to gevem ascrm the
pipl was Min to hem

FIG. 14.1.

FIG. 14.2.

authentic communication—language used in situations that are meaningful and purposeful to participants. And so it is of crucial importance to recognize what is, and is not, authentic communication.

Interestingly, when we reflect on particular possible scenarios involving words outside of the classroom, we recognize quite easily which are authentic and which are not. Consider some examples.

- If you came into my kitchen at breakfast time, you would find each family member reading a different section of the morning paper while eating. And if one of us suddenly said, "Now *here's* a guy with a problem. 'Dear Abby . . .' " and continued to read the humorous letter aloud, this would not strike you as strange. But if you came in and found us all looking at our individual copies of the same page of the newspaper and taking turns reading paragraphs of the same article aloud, one by one around the breakfast table, while the others listened and read along silently, this would strike you as odd. This is not what people do with newspapers. What they do with newspapers is find out things—what their horoscope says, what the weather's going to be, what Snoopy's up to, how the Red Sox did, who's having a sale on summer sandals.
- If you were having dinner with your eight-year-old nephew and his mother asked the child, "Have you seen Jonathan yet and asked him to your party?" you'd hardly notice. But if his mother asked him, "What can you tell me about this salt shaker?" you'd wonder why she was doing this. Language is for telling people things they want to know or things you want them to know. Language isn't for performing your ability to list attributes of salt shakers. Nobody wants to know that, and anyway, they can see for themselves.

- If you and I were in my car on our way to my home and we got completely stuck in rush-hour traffic and, while sitting there, I nudged the car forward a little so I could read the bumper sticker on the car in front of me—"If you can read this you're too close"—you'd think my behavior perfectly normal. But if, as we sat there, I whipped a set of flashcards out of my purse and started reading each one in my announcement voice—*can, close, if, too, this*—you'd think me strange. (Stranger still if I started giving definitions for each one.) Bumper stickers and flashcards look alike, but bumper stickers are language and flashcards aren't. Bumper stickers tell people things: they make jokes or tell what causes the driver supports or who he's voting for or where his kids go to college. But why would I "read" words that don't have any message for me? Language is for messages.
- If you found me sitting at my desk filling in the blanks on a catalog order form, you'd hardly notice. But if you found me sitting there selecting words with short vowel sounds from a list and writing them in the blanks in a set of unrelated sentences, you'd think this peculiar. Language is for doing things, like ordering socks and underwear. Order forms do things. So do some other kinds of fill-in-the-blank forms: income tax forms and crossword puzzles and lottery tickets. But not vowel exercises.
- You might find me sitting at my desk writing a letter. "Whatcha doing?" you'd ask. "Just dropping my sister a line to let her know our exact arrival time, now that our flight arrangements are finally definite." Of course. But what if, instead of this, I answered your question by saying, "I'm just dropping my sister a line using this set of spelling words" (showing you a set of ten *ie / ei* words). You'd think me either joking or mad. We write letters to tell people things, not to use a particular set of words.

It's easy enough to see which of these examples are really language—meaningful and purposeful—and which are not; easy enough to see which are authentic.[2] But when we're in the classroom, the distinction isn't always so easy. So much that is *in*authentic—*non*language—has for so long been accepted as what-people-do-in-school that the *in*authentic has taken on a life of its own. And so it seems perfectly reasonable for a teacher to have children read aloud around the circle from the same basal text, or to ask students questions she already knows the answer to in order to elicit a series of attributes that are visible to all present, or to have students "read" words on flashcards or fill in blanks on worksheets or write text "using as many of this week's spelling words as you can." This isn't language outside of the classroom, and it isn't language inside the classroom either. Children develop language by doing language, not by doing something else.

MAKING THE CLASSROOM AUTHENTIC

The good news is that classrooms can be—and many are—authentic language environments for children to creatively construct their first and second languages in. I choose to demonstrate this with three examples, one which primarily involves reading, and one which primarily involves writing. I say "primarily" here because authentic communication usually involves more than one way of using language. For example, if you liked reading the book, you'll probably go see the movie; if your friend writes to you, you'll probably write back (or maybe call); I tend, while talking (listening) on the phone, to jot down topics I want to be sure my friend and I "cover" before we hang up. However much we talk about "speaking," "listening," "reading," and "writing" as if they were separate and distinct, they aren't, of course; they're all tangled up in our real experience, and so they should be. And so my "oral" example is only partly that: it begins as somebody's talk but immediately is somebody's listening, and who knows what writing and reading events it might lead to. And so with my "reading" and "writing" examples. They're really much more. I choose my examples from the only possible starting place: children and experiences I know they love, for these are bound to be authentic.

In the first class I ever taught, second grade, my children used to tell me what they liked and didn't like by using the phrases *get to* or *have to*, as in "Do we have to do *X* today?" (You can hear the different tones of voice, can't you?)

Show and Tell

One of the absolutely predictable daily "get to's" was "show and tell." I confess I never could understand why. What, I wondered, could be so compelling about telling or listening to others tell about an object or event that, from my perspective at least, was often minimally interesting at best. But we had show and tell almost daily, not because I understood why the children liked it, and not because I saw special value in it, but basically because there were twenty-four of them and only one of me. But now I'm glad they outnumbered me, and I see that they were right. The situation was authentic: they wanted to tell each other about the events and objects they lugged in; they wanted to have and to be audiences for one another. And I'm sure there were matters of social status and acceptance and such which were crucial here that I didn't even begin to recognize. But these are language, too—what language is about, what language is for. So show and tell was authentic for these children, and it was a "get to" *because* it was authentic for them. But besides this, it was the perfect opportunity for them to control,[3] to shape, to design—yes, to creatively construct both what to tell and how. And their response to classmates' tellings were of their own constructing, too.

I see now that the children and I could have carried this much further. We could have had the day's show-ers and tellers set themselves up in different areas of the classroom. Each would have needed enough space to demonstrate what his or her object could do and to allow other children to try it out. Classmates of the show-ers and tellers could have moved freely from one area to another according to their particular interests. Or we might have extended this display-type format into a "show-and-tell fair" and invited another class to come and visit. Or we might have sometimes broken into smaller groups so that each child could have had more opportunities to show/tell and so that the interaction could have been more conversational and less performance-like. "Author's chair" (Calkins 1986) seems a particularly rich variation of the basic show-and-tell idea: the child author reads aloud to his classmates what he has written and invites input and discussion from them. There were many possibilities, but I didn't see them then. Show and tell seemed to me so marginal, even trivial. I thought we had more important things to do. I was wrong.

I also see now the special value that this experience would hold for the ESL child. It would have provided the perfect situation for the child to participate in socially, the first concern of the second-language learner. It would have provided contextual support that could have helped the child to convey his or her meanings and to grasp those expressed by others. Above all, it would have provided a real reason for the child to interact with classmates and to shape his or her own message in his or her own way in the new language.

Story Time

Another good thing we had going, a "get to" for my second graders, was story time. Now this one is as old as humankind. We were never more engaged together—all of us—than when I read *Charlotte's Web* or some other favorite aloud. But if this was so good (and we all knew it was), more would have been even better. And, as I see it now, I could have done so much more. I could have varied the tales, the tellers, the audiences, and the ways of the tellings (the presentations) in many ways.

1. *The tales.* Besides favorite children's books to read aloud, I could have used:
   - wordless storybooks for which the children would have provided verbal texts.

- ongoing classroom events written in a classroom journal or in a class newspaper that would have circulated through the school and to the children's homes regularly.
- dramas created spontaneously in the sociodramatic area of the classroom.
- favorite stories played, or new ones created, in the puppet area of the classroom—real episodes from my own experience (I find that many children are fascinated with the personal incidents their teachers tell).
- comics read and sometimes created by the children.
- narrative songs and poems.
- the children's own written narratives on topics, real or imagined, that they had selected themselves.
- picture stories. I think immediately of Polaroid pictures the children might have taken while on a walk, to which they later could have added text to make a picture story. I also think of the ongoing pictures and text some kindergarten children provided over several weeks as they observed eggs and then newly hatched chicks and a caterpillar that finally became a butterfly.
- biography. Some fine published biographies are available, but autobiography also could have been an important type of writing and telling for the children. Older children could have been helpful scribe-partners for many students who could have told their life stories for the older children to write down for them. (See Tasseil 1983 for a description of such a partnering autobiographical project.)
- the child's own ongoing personal journal or diary (written or taped).
- plays to be read or written.
- oral histories. I think of some school children whose study of the Depression era included interviewing older people in their neighborhoods to gather oral histories of their experience during the Depression.

2. *The tellers.* Besides myself, I could have drawn on:
   - adults whom I and the children could have invited to come into the classroom to read aloud (e.g., school personnel, parents, community folks, children from upper grades, especially the children's heroes). My students could have decided whom they wanted and then invited them to come. Especially fascinating would have been readers with various voices and dialects and styles—a variety that

might have been interestingly demonstrated by having several different people read the same story to the children.
  - professionals on record or on tape.
  - the children themselves, reading their own narratives they had written, or choosing and reading favorite stories to classes of younger children.
3. *The audiences*. I tended to think always of the whole class listening together as I read aloud. But I could also have thought of:
  - an individual child at the listening center.
  - pairs of children in a quiet corner—classmates, perhaps, or maybe cross-grade partners—reading or telling stories to one another.
  - small groups at a listening center, following a taped story together in their accompanying books.
  - me as audience. Every time a child came to me with, "Know what?" and I answered, "No, what?" I had accepted the audience role, just as I did when I listened and responded to the child as she read something to me that she had written.
4. *The ways of telling*. I thought mainly of myself reading aloud, but I rarely thought of:
  - a telling instead of a reading.
  - the tape-recorded voice.
  - dramatization—the children using their own voices and bodies to express sequences of events.
  - dramatization through the use of puppets.
  - the professional's voice on tape or record.
  - the children's own dramatization recorded and presented on videotape.

And we musn't forget the most basic of all: the child sitting down with a book and as much time as he wants to read it. All these would have provided ways for the children to creatively construct meaning and expression in and through story, the most timelessly and universally authentic event of all.

Dialogue Journals

Dialogue journals are my third example.[4] People sometimes talk about dialogue journals as if they were new, but they're not. Only the label is new. The event itself is far older than we are: it's people who want to write to each other doing just that, and writing about what they want to write about and responding to each other's writing. That's surely a "get to."

Recently I did a month of dialogue-journal writing with a class of Zulu sixth grade students (ages twelve to sixteen) in South Africa. The students' writing gave me a new appreciation for creative construction in authentic communication contexts. At the beginning, one student wrote, "I'll write to you . . . I want to communicate." And that's what we did. The students expressed a wide range of communication purposes in their writing.

- They used the writing *to teach*. For example, several gave me lessons in Zulu—lists of Zulu words and sentences along with their English translations.
- They used their writing *to inquire*. One girl asked,

> Does American children at the age like me have a boyfriend? If they have them, does they show them to their parents like TV shows us?

- They used their writing *to joke*, as in

> Thabiso says to his teacher, Sir, would you beat a boy for something he did not do?
> Teacher: Of course not Thabiso.
> Thabiso: That's good sir, I don't do my homework.

- And they used their writing to *inform*. One student wrote,

> When you visit at Town most of people they go on Saturdays because haven't got no time because during the other days they worked.
>
> When we go to town let me say you go with boyfriend to visit somewhere at town when you finish to buy grocery we visit at byeskop or museum we walk very nice because we are free.

- They used written English *to scold* as in the following example, in which a student scolded me for not being quick enough in getting him a pen pal.

> Mrs. Lindfors you didn't answer me about a friend (girl) not a girlfriend. I want a person who will wrote for me and I wrote for her.

- And they used it *to offer*, as in:

> If is there any question that you do not understand send for me, I will be here to tell you.

- They used their journal writing *to request*. For example,

  If we finished to write on these journal can I take it from my home?

- They used this writing *to seek clarification*. I had asked one student to tell me about how teachers in South Africa help pupils to learn. He wrote back:

  I don't understand what do you mean about "What teachers here do to help the pupils."

- They also used it *to compliment*. One wrote,

  I told my patness [partners] about Miss professor Lindfors. She is a beautifull lady a short lady a funny lady. And I like him too, much. She is clever women. She is a lovely lady. My classmates love him.

- They used their writing *to apologize*. For example,

  I am very sorry to call you Judith because I don't no you surname. But I think you don't mind.

- They used written English *to explain*. One wrote,

  I like to explain what's a play mother. Is a girl whom you see every time and you seem to love her or is she who loves you. She will like you to be her baby but not really one and she is your play mother. Example: When I say to Brenda that I love her to be my mother. You know that I'm not her really child. . . . It's just a game isn't true. In Zulu we say *umama wokudlala. Dladla* means play. *Mama* means mother.

- And they used this writing *to express opinions*. For example,

  I like this teacher. Oh! She's a good teacher. I think the principal's must promote her.

- And they used their free writing *to make conversation comments*.

  Just look how many pages did we write now.

  And

  Bye-bye. Have a nice weekend reading *True Love*.

- They used written English *to express thanks*. One wrote,

Thanks you said to be patient, be patient b_____ Thanks I will be patient

- One student used the writing *to comfort.*

Some of my classmates told me that you have asked him that are you safe here in South Africa. I say Don't be worry, you are safe from *amabutho*, because now we are protected . . . So don't be worry.

- And several used their writing to *reflect.*

I tried many ways to have a friend who is a European who lives in South Africa. But they concerd [consider?] us as nothing. They say that we don't know nothing. But type of people doesn't matter. The matter is that how do you trust each other.

Did you believe that God is a King of the world? Many people said that God is not a king and Bible is same like a story. He [I] beleive that God is a king and Bible is a true.

- Besides writing for their own purposes, these students wrote on their own topics:

If you want to be good in karate you must respect your treiner and do all what he/she tell you. When I was new in karate, the treiner asked me to fight with a girl. The girl kick me on the face and hit me on the chest. When i saw that things are bad, I ran away and everybody laughed at me they said "you are not a brave boy instaed you are the coward boy." When they have laughed at me I was shy.

Sorry, Judith today I want to tell you about a poor people live in Topiya [Ethiopia] That people are very poor and I see in TV and Pacebook thay have no place to sleep and they have no food to eat they become small children and parents of those children I think you are very sorry for this people and I very sorry for this country.

In our school we [have] a child his name is F_____. When is cold she is wearing a jersey which collar is hair of sheep which light brown. She is naught and noise when she laugh she make a noise . . . When she is sit she open the mouth everyday, teachers tell her. "Close the mouth, F_____" and close the mouth. She is 13 years old. She a dirty she clean only day she like to be clean.

I want to tell you about my party. my party was at night on July 30 Its start on a.m. 9.30 up to 1:00 a.m. My mother gave me new dress and she bought a cake, drinks, delicious food my mother cook those food I tell my friends about my party and I take many photograph for my party You like my party? "Judith."

In their dialogue journals these students were creatively constructing their second language. They were forging ways to express their own meanings so that I could understand and respond to them. *Respond*, not correct; respond with meanings and expression of my own. B____ writes to me still. In a letter he sent about six months after I had left South Africa he wrote:

> "Here a secret" One day I was coming from school and I was a lot of work to do and I sit down and rest and I had a call that call was coming from M_____ [a friend of B_____'s from the dialogue-journal writing class, no longer attending the same school as B_____] did you wrote Mr Lindfors, "B_____ [said] Oh yes my friend I write to her every month. And after we finished our talking I went to my bedroom, What I am looking for? "I ask myself" I am looking for the small journal which I was used last year at school. And I found at last but I was very happy to find it. And I read day and day.

Dialogue-journal writing was a "get to" for B_____. It was, and remains, authentic.

The message is clear enough: children's development of language (first or second) is fostered in classroom communication situations that are, purposeful to the child and that engage her in creatively constructing language for herself. We can, of course, ignore this. But if we choose to take it seriously, show and tell, stories, and dialogue journals are good places to begin.

NOTES

1. These examples also occur in Lindfors 1987. I thank Judy Muery, Janet Rothschild, John Henderson, Pat Seawell, Sarah Hudelson, and Judith King for them.
2. The term *authentic* is Edelsky and Draper's. For an insightful and provocative discussion of authenticity and inauthenticity in classrooms, see their article, "Reading/'Reading,' Writing/'Writing,' Text/'Text'."
3. Sarah Michaels's work on sharing-time suggests that, in fact, the teacher (myself in this case) controls this event more than she thinks she does. See, for example, Michaels and Collins 1984.
4. See *Dialogue*, a newsletter from the Center for Applied Linguistics, for descriptions of ways that classroom teachers have been using dialogue journals with first- and second-language learners.

REFERENCES

Calkins, L. M. 1986. *The Art of Teaching Writing*. Portsmouth, N.H.: Heinemann.

Edelsky, C., and K. Draper. In Press. "Reading/'Reading,' Writing/'Writing,' Text/'Text'." In *Reading and Writing: Theory and Research,* edited by A. Petrosky. Norwood, N.J.: Ablex.

Lindfors, J. W. 1983. Exploring in and through Language. In *On TESOL '82: Pacific Perspectives on Language Learning and Teaching*, edited by M. Clarke and J. Handscombe. Washington, D.C.: TESOL.

—. 1987. *Children's Language and Learning*. 2d ed. Englewood Cliffs, N.J.: Prentice-Hall.

Michaels, S., and J. Collins. 1984. Oral Discourse Styles: Classroom Interaction and the Acquisition of Literacy. In *Coherence in Spoken and Written Discourse*, edited by D. Tannen. Norwood, N.J.: Ablex.

Seawell, R. P. M. 1985. A Micro-Ethnographic Study of a Spanish/English Bilingual Kindergarten in which Literature and Puppet Play Were Used as a Method of Enhancing Language Growth. Doctoral dissertation. University of Texas at Austin.

Tassell, F. V. 1983. A Writing Assignment with a Different Flair. *Language Arts* 60 (3): 354–56.

Chapter 15

"Teaching" English Through Content-Area Activities

Sarah Hudelson

If we were to visit any number of elementary and secondary school classrooms, probably the dominant way students would be asked to learn would be through using textbooks. Students would be asked to open their books, to read out loud or silently, to answer oral or written questions, and perhaps later, to be tested on the content. While significant numbers of educators would question this practice for any student, this way of approaching content and texts is particularly inappropriate for students whose native language is not English.

However, ESL students are in the classrooms, and the expectation is that they should receive the school's curricula in the content areas. So what are teachers to do? One way of addressing this problem is to use content-area material as a vehicle for language development (Cantoni-Harvey 1987; Chamot and O'Malley 1987; Terdy 1987). The specific approach proposed here involves examining the content-area objectives that school districts and/or state departments of education create, and then beginning the teaching of content there, rather than with the textbook. But looking at content-area objectives themselves is not enough. What is necessary is the combining of content-area goals with some specific principles of learning in general, and language learning in particular, in order to move from the objectives to sets of activities that will provide meaningful learning experiences for students still developing as English users. The following principles, based on personal interpretations of some recent literature on first- and second-language development, may be used as a starting point for developing learning activities from content-area objectives:

PRINCIPLES

1. Students learn both content and language by being active, by doing things, by participating in activities directly related to specific content, and by using both oral and written language to carry out these activities. Language develops holistically, not in parts. Language develops through use, not through isolated practice (Lindfors 1987). This is true in both a native and a second language.

2. Students learn both content and language by interacting with others as they carry out activities. These "others" may be both other students (peers) and adults who provide input and authentic reasons to communicate (Enright and McCloskey 1985; Krashen 1982; Lindfors 1987; Urzúa 1980). This is true in both a native and a second language.

3. All of the language processes are interrelated, and students become more able language users when they make use of all the processes in classroom activities, when they are asked to use both oral and written language in varied ways and for varied purposes, and when they see the connections between experiences and oral and written language (Allen 1986; Goodman 1987; Hudelson 1984; Rigg and Enright 1986). This is true in both a native and a second language.

4. Students learn to read by interacting with whole, authentic texts (by reading), and they learn to write by creating whole, authentic texts (by writing), by having others react to what they have created, by revising their pieces, and by using their reading knowledge to help them write like readers. The acquisition of written language is a holistic process, as is the acquisition of oral language. Literacy is acquired through use, not through practice, of isolated skills (Goodman 1987; Harste, Woodward, and Burke 1984; Smith 1982). This is true in both a native and a second language.

5. Reading comprehension is facilitated by having prior knowledge of the topic of the text (Barnitz 1985; Rigg 1986). Background knowledge may be activated or developed through classroom activities that involve all of the language processes, including reading from a variety of sources other than the textbook. This is true in both a native and a second language.

APPLICATIONS: INSTEAD OF THE TEXT

Beginning with those principles, the rest of this chapter will illustrate ways that they may be applied to specific content objectives in the development of classroom activities. The objectives used have been developed by Dade County Public Schools, Florida, in the areas of math, science, health, and social studies.

Objective: Children will understand family roles and division of labor within the family. This is a primary-level social studies objective. In the Florida state-adopted social studies texts, children would be expected to read an informational selection, accompanied by pictures, that would talk about the jobs various members of the family are responsible for. They would also read a short piece about a mother going back to work outside the home, and the children feeling that the mother doesn't have time for them anymore. Our concern is the provision of activities for ESL children that will enable them to meet the content-area objective while using English to do so, but in ways that are more sensible than simply being exposed to the text material. What kinds of activities might be organized?

An initial activity might be a chart to fill out that would involve the children answering such questions as: In your family, who cooks the food? In your family, who washes the clothes? In your family, who cleans the furniture? In your family, who buys the groceries? The students would be divided into small groups. Each child would first fill out the chart individually, after which the groups would meet to compare their answers and come up with a group summary of responses to each question. Putting the students into groups means that they can help each other with reading and answering the questions. The group chart assignment will also mean that the children will have to talk to each other about what they have done individually. After the groups have had a chance to share and organize their data, the class would come back together and complete a whole-class chart.

The whole-class charting activity might be followed by a learning log activity. In a learning log, children use writing as a way of reflecting on content they have studied. In this case, children would respond in their learning logs to the following questions: What did you learn about your own family from doing this activity? What did you learn about the families of others in this class?

In addition to these activities, several books or stories that reflect the theme of family interdependence would be shared with the children during storytime and made available for the children to read on their own. Some examples of such titles are: *The Little Red Hen,* Aesop's *The Grasshopper and the Ants*, *Cinderella*, and Lois Lenski's *Family Small*. The stories would also provide an opportunity for groups of children to create a skit or play to share with others. Another activity based on the content and concepts would involve dividing the children into groups, giving them two or three different family situations, and asking the groups to take the roles of family members and act out what the family would do in each situation. All of these activities, spread out over several days or weeks, would give the children the opportunity to use English in both oral and written forms, in varied ways, is they came to understand the concept of family roles.

APPLICATIONS: MAKING THE TEXT READABLE

The activities used demonstrate clearly that it is not necessary or even advisable to be limited to the textbook in terms of content teaching and ESL learners. Content objectives may be achieved by using a variety of materials and activities. But if teachers either choose or feel compelled to use the textbook, a variety of activities could be undertaken to provide the children with necessary background experiences and language that should make their reading of the text successful. When the children do see the text, it is critical to begin their reading with a prereading activity that asks students to list what they already know about the topic, in this case, what they already know about family roles. An alternative would be to construct a semantic map or web of what the children already know about family roles. After what they already know has been listed or mapped, children would read the selection and then compare what they listed to what was actually in the selection. After reading, it is logical to ask, "What else did you learn about family roles from what you just read?" This means that the variety of activities just detailed here may be used as alternatives to the text, or they may be used as background builders to the text. In either case, it is important for the students to spend time working together with a content focus, including reading and writing for various purposes.

APPLICATIONS: MATHEMATICS EXAMPLE

Let's look at another objective, this time from mathematics. An intermediate and junior high math objective in Dade County is the following: *Students will determine probability, meaning equally likely or not equally likely events.* For many learners, the concept of probability might be most understandable if it were considered initially in a nonmathematical way by dealing with the idea of chance in people's daily lives. *Chance* refers to the idea that something might or might not occur. It could happen, but maybe it won't. Here, for example, are some questions that students might be put into groups to answer: "Who will win the city championship in football (or any sport) this year? Will all the members of our class be in school tomorrow? How many members of our class will have perfect math papers this week? Will you see a Toyota car on your way home from school this afternoon?" Students would consider these questions and come up with answers (their best guesses). After students have reported what their groups decided, the teacher could conclude that all of these were chance events, giving students the specific vocabulary for the concept that they have been investigating.

Having demonstrated the concept of chance, students could then begin to consider the concept of probability. In groups once again, students could deal with statements such as: "Which is more likely or more probable, that one of the students or that the teacher will be absent from school tomorrow? Which is more likely, that you will have pizza for breakfast or that you will have pizza for lunch? Which is more likely, that you will go swimming in the summer or in the winter?"

Students might also work in groups to come up with answers to such statements as: "Is it more likely than not that you can find the sum of 324 and 465? In Phoenix, Arizona, in July, is it more likely than not that the sun will be shining at noon?" Then groups could respond to similar statements by categorizing them as certain/uncertain/impossible. Sample statements: "I will use my brain sometime this week. My dog can write his name in Spanish. All new cars will use water instead of gasoline for fuel. We will see the sun tomorrow. I will sleep eight hours on Tuesday night. I will not sleep at all this week." Activities such as these will give students the opportunity to experiment with chance and probability in their own lives, to use their collective experiences and language abilities to consider the statements, and to develop an experiential understanding of probability to which the term *probability* may then be affixed by the teacher. First the concept, then the label.

Following these nonmathematical activities, the mathematical side of probability should be developed. In groups once more, students would solve a variety of probability problems by carrying out sets of written directions that would ask them to do such things as: Toss a coin into the air a certain number of times (twenty, for example) and record whether it lands heads or tails; toss a die a certain number of times and note whether the number of dots on the top face is even or odd; toss a die a certain number of times and note what numbers come up. Small-group charts would be shared with the rest of the class and used to construct entire-class charts.

As the learners solve these kinds of problems and struggle with answers to some of the questions, the learning logs would be a logical vehicle to use for enabling learners to consider what they were learning about probability.

For teachers interested in extending the ideas of chance and probability into other contexts and written material, an amusing book like Remy Charlip's *Fortunately, Unfortunately* could be used, both for a light change of pace and as a possible model for student creation of chance and probability stories. In this book a series of chance occurrences, one after the other, keeps the main character going from something good happening to something bad happening. Students could create their own fortunately/unfortunately, good luck/bad luck sequences which would utilize various chance happenings. All of these activities would serve as background and language builders that should ensure greater success with the probability problems in the mathematics textbooks.

APPLICATIONS: SCIENCE/HEALTH EXAMPLE

Another way to approach the task of combining language and content is to group together a set of related objectives, such as the following set of intermediate science/health objectives: *Children will define the basic food groups, will recognize and understand cultural differences in foods eaten, will define what is needed to stay healthy, will evaluate specific foods and diets in terms of how healthy they are*. What kinds of activities could be organized to help students achieve these objectives?

As an initial activity, children could be asked to keep a record or log of all the food that they eat over a certain period of time (for one or two days). These logs would be kept individually and then brought to school. In school students in groups would share their logs with the goal of determining which foods they all have eaten and which foods they have eaten are unique to them or to their ethnic or cultural group. After small groups have listed the foods eaten, a class list would be developed. Then small groups would work again to put the foods eaten into categories. How would the students categorize the foods they eat? Which foods would they put together, and why? After the groups have reached consensus about food groups (an activity that requires children to use language informatively and persuasively with each other), they might consult their textbooks or other written sources, including informational books, food group posters, etc., to compare their categories to those of nutritionists.

Another activity would involve children in using information about food groups to create their own menus. Using newspaper ads, students would be asked to come up with menus for certain meals. They could put together both menus reflecting what they would eat if they had a choice and menus reflecting well-balanced meals. In many areas ethnic grocery stores advertise their food specials in city and neighborhood newspapers and flyers, so advertising could be chosen that reflects cultural differences in what people eat. Mathematics could be added to the activity if students received a certain amount of money with which they would need to buy groceries for a certain number of meals for a certain number of people. A requirement could be that the meals are well-balanced in terms of representing the basic food groups. Again the text or other written material on the food groups, as well as newspaper advertisements, could be consulted to determine what foods could be used to represent certain groups and how many servings of which were recommended each day.

Still another way to examine foods would be a study of the nutritional elements in certain kinds of packaged foods, such as breakfast cereals. Students could be asked to bring in cereal boxes and then to compare the nutritional elements of their favorite cereals. As an extension, groups of students could create their own breakfast cereals, including name, package design, ingredients, and nutritional elements of the cereal that they created. In addition to the box and nutritional elements, students could create an advertisement for the cereal they had created, and they could try to sell their cereals to the others in the class. The advertising activity also demonstrates that an intermediate social studies/economics objective—understanding advertising as a way of persuading—could be incorporated into the teacher's plans. The students could pitch their cereal and others could vote on which cereal they would most like to eat.

It should be obvious by now that students have used talking, reading, and writing for a variety of purposes. From the point of view of reading, a wide variety of informational reading materials has been utilized. Additionally, reading material such as cookbooks created for children could be used by the students as they consider menus they would like to create. Fun books, such as *Strega Nona* by Tomie de Paola could be shared. *Strega Nona* is the tale of a witch and her magical pasta pot, a pot that runs out of control when Strega Nona leaves Big Anthony alone in her house. De Paola's wonderful wordless picture book *Pancakes for Breakfast* could be used by children to create their own written stories to share with others. Informational books such as those on vitamins and junk foods could be used by the children as sources of information about nutritional elements.

From the point of view of writing, children could create their own recipe books or bring in favorite recipes from home. Cooking could be carried out in the classroom, and taste tests performed to see which ethnic foods students preferred. Learning logs could be utilized as students considered what they had learned about nutrition. And all of these literacy activities necessarily involve students in talking with one another to accomplish various tasks. All of these are examples of the kinds of integrative language activities advocated as crucial to the language and cognitive growth of ESL students.

APPLICATIONS: SOCIAL STUDIES EXAMPLE

Let's look now at content-area objectives from one more perspective, that of objectives which sometimes are divided into content objectives and process or skills objectives. Many of these objectives appear, albeit with some variation, at several educational levels. As an example, at both elementary and secondary school levels, social studies objectives in Dade County deal both with the content of immigration as a factor in United States history and with such "skills" or process objectives as timeline and map construction and interpretation. Both kinds of objectives could be joined together and activities developed that would be of interest and relevance and that would provide for necessary skill development. In terms of ESL, some of the same objectives could be used successfully with different age groups of second-language learners. From the point of view of language development, this kind of recycling of objectives would give students more opportunities to use content-focused language. What might change would be not so much the activities or interactive processes, as the sophistication of the students' products and some of the written materials utilized.

Looking at content objectives in the area of immigration, intermediate group objectives state that students will be able to explain that the people of the United States are immigrants linked to the rest of the world through their immigrant heritages, and that students will be able to tell how their own immigrant heritages link them to the rest of the world. (Obviously, this curriculum is not drawn from states like New Mexico or Arizona, both of which have large populations of ESL speakers whose ancestors preceded English speakers by many, many years.) At senior high level, the expectation is that students will be able to describe the role of immigration in the growth of this country, list chronologically and describe the waves of immigration to this country, and describe the contributions of various immigrant groups to the United States. An examination of the "skills" objectives reveals that students at both levels are expected to be able to use maps of various kinds, identify items on maps, and construct and interpret timelines.

In terms of activities that might enable students to meet these objectives, the most logical place to begin the study of immigration is with something that may be in the students' experiences: their own immigration to this country. One of the things that many students know or can find out about is information about their own families. So an initial assignment could be to ask students to find out where their ancestors came from, when they came to this country, why they came here, and any other important facts in their family's history that they would like to share. Students who didn't have the information on a firsthand basis might interview one or more family members in order to come up with what they needed to share. This might mean that the interview would be conducted in a language other than English, but the sharing in class would be in English. After the students had collected information about their families, they would divide into groups to share what they had learned and to create group charts about group members' ancestry and reasons for coming to this country. Group sharing with the class would result in a whole-class chart that would reflect the heritages of all the class. This should mean that everyone in class would be able to participate, whether their families have been in this country for five years or a hundred years or more.

A *caveat* should be issued here. The purpose of this activity is not to determine who may be here on an undocumented basis. Care must be taken in the use of this activity, so that families do not get the impression that the school is about to turn them in to INS. Also, some refugee students may have suffered such trauma in escaping their native land, perhaps watching members of their families be killed, that they do not feel comfortable with this assignment. The sensitive teacher may decide to explore the possibility of this activity before assigning it.

After a class chart has been developed, maps would be used to locate the countries of the students' ancestors. Countries of origin would be highlighted, as well as routes drawn to the countries. In addition, maps that focus on political changes, economic conditions, and geographic realities as factors in immigration could be used and interpreted.

From the initial activity based at least partially on the students' own experiences, several other projects could be undertaken. The teacher might share the history of his or her family's arrival in this country with the class and demonstrate the use of a timeline as one way of visualizing the chronology of one family coming to this country. The teacher's model could prove useful to students as they created their own individual timelines.

Instead of individual projects, students could be asked to investigate a variety of immigrant groups to this country, different sets of students taking different groups. As a part of a report that each set would prepare for the rest of the class, students would construct timelines illustrating their immigrant group's history and contributions made by the group to this country over the years. As they prepare their reports, students will make use of a variety of written sources, books, encyclopediae, news articles, magazines, maps, atlases, films and filmstrips, television programs, interview data, etc., which the teacher will help them choose and utilize based on what they can handle. Involved in this report-writing will be sharing of information, creating initial drafts, sharing what has been written, and revising and editing.

For a slightly less ambitious project, the teacher might take the text information on immigration and carry out a jigsaw activity by asking students in groups to read different parts of the material and to report to each other. Because each group will report on information that the others have not read, there will be an authentic reason for listening. At the conclusion of the jigsaw activities, students would create a class bulletin board about immigration. For some students, it would be interesting and important to raise issues such as: "Did everyone who came to this country come of their own accord? If not, how were the experiences different?" This would give students the opportunity to compare the concept of immigration, which many would see as voluntary, to the history of slavery in this country.

Report-writing for the purpose of different groups sharing information that they have learned already has been mentioned as one kind of writing students could do. What other kinds of writing could be carried out in terms of the objectives stated? Certainly learning logs could be used, as students were asked on a regular basis to consider what they had learned. Another meaningful writing project would be the construction of student autobiographies, with special emphasis given to each student's immigrant experience, whether this experience took place recently or several generations ago. As with the report projects, the creation of autobiographies could take several days or weeks to complete and the processes of drafting, sharing, receiving reactions, and revising should be utilized, from the point of view of expanding students' language abilities. In all of these activities, the processes students are engaged in should be viewed as at least as important as the final products.

In the examples given so far, little or no mention has been made of utilization of the arts, such as music, dance, and drama. Obviously these could be included here (and in other content areas). Songs such as Neil Diamond's "Coming to America" could be considered in terms of the message the song provides. Music from various countries and its influence in this country could be seen as part of the immigrant heritage and contribution. So could dance. The possibilities are many. From a set of objectives many weeks' interesting and meaningful work, for both teachers and students, may be developed.

SUMMARY

These, then, are some examples of one way of approaching the issue of combining language and content learning in classes, including ESL learners. This chapter has tried to illustrate both that important school content may be viewed as a vehicle for language development, and that language is crucial to students as the major way they have of demonstrating their knowledge of content. The perspective taken is that language and content learning do not mean isolated skills and drill work. The aim of the activities presented has not been to assure that students get the correct answers to questions at the end of the chapter. The perspective presented is not that of the transmission classroom, in which the teacher doles out knowledge or facts (content of some kind), and the students give it back. The aim of considering the objectives is not even that of "covering" all of the objectives in any content area, just so the claim can be made that the students "did" the material. All of the biases or perspectives just stated apply to native English speakers as well as to those developing a second language.

Rather, the major concern is that learners, whether they be ESL students or native speakers of the language, grapple with content-area concepts and information, and that they use language: to share what they know, to work through what they're learning; to ask questions about what they want to know; and to seek answers to their questions both from other people and from varying sources of material. This concern is realized in the activity-based approach delineated in the previous pages. From my perspective, this kind of approach does the following: (1) It provides students with the opportunity to use English in both oral and written forms, for varied purposes. That is, the approach demonstrates to students what English is for. (2) It adds to students' background of experiences, experiences that should help them as they cope with regular classrooms. (3) It adds to students' knowledge of and abilities to deal with English, because of the variety of things learners do and because of the ways they use language to do these things. (4) It demonstrates to students that learning can be fun, exciting, and challenging, and that we believe that our content learning does not mean isolated skills and drills work. I believe that we owe our students, and ourselves, no less.

REFERENCES

Allen, V. G. 1986. Developing Contexts to Support Second Language Acquisition. *Language Arts* 63:61–66.

Barnitz, J. 1985. *Reading Development of Nonnative Speakers of English*. Orlando, Fla.: Harcourt, Brace, Jovanovich, and the Center for Applied Linguistics.

Cantoni-Harvey, G. 1987. *Teaching ESL in the Content Areas*. Reading, Mass.: Addison-Wesley.

Chamot, A. U., and J. M. O'Malley. 1987. The Cognitive Academic Language Learning Approach: A Bridge to the Mainstream. *TESOL Quarterly* 21:227–50.

Enright, D. S., and M. L. McCloskey. 1985. Yes, Talking!: Organizing the Classroom to Promote Second Language Acquisition. *TESOL Quarterly* 19:431–53.

Goodman, K. 1987. *What's Whole in Whole Language?* Portsmouth, N.H.: Heinemann.

Harste, J., V. Woodward, and C. Burke. 1984. *Language Stories and Literacy Lessons*. Portsmouth, N.H.: Heinemann.

Hudelson, S. 1984. Kan Yu Ret an Rayt en Ingles: Children Become Literate in English as a Second Language. *TESOL Quarterly* 18:221–38.

Krashen, S. 1982. *Principles and Practices in Second Language Acquisition*. New York: Pergamon.

Lindfors, J. 1987. *Children's Language and Learning*. 2d ed. Englewood Cliffs, N.J.: Prentice-Hall.

Rigg, P. 1986. Reading and ESL: Learning from Kids. In *Children and ESL: Integrating Perspectives*, edited by P. Rigg and D. S. Enright, 55–91. Washington, D.C.: TESOL.

Rigg, P., and D. S. Enright. 1986. *Children and ESL: Integrating Perspectives*. Washington, D.C.: TESOL.

Smith, F. 1982. *Writing and the Writer*. New York: Holt, Rinehart and Winston.

Terdy, D. 1987. *Content Area ESL: Social Studies*. Palatine, Ill.: Linmore.

Urzúa, C. 1980. A Language Learning Environment for All Children. *Language Arts* 57:38–44.

Chapter **16**

From the Margins to the Center

Vivian Zamel

For years I had created composition courses that explored a particular area of content, based on the conviction that language was best acquired in the context of using it to make sense of rich and complex subject matter. As I planned these courses, I had repeatedly returned to considering content that would deal more explicitly with the situations of my particular students, students who had shared with me the difficulties they had experienced as a result of their minority status, their inability to use English as well as their native speaker counterparts, their sense that they were invisible both at UMass/Boston and within the larger society. My thinking about this was informed by the same conviction that shaped my decisions about other thematically based courses I had created: if students' language and writing are promoted as a result of their engagement with issues they view as intriguing, illuminating, and authentic, then a course that places their realities at the center rather than on the margins would be all the more dramatic in its impact. Yet I continued to shy away from the idea of such a curriculum, afraid of what might happen if we overtly addressed these issues, afraid that this material was far too disturbing, too risky. In retrospect, I realize that this fear stemmed not just from how I thought my students would react to this material but from a concern with how I might be drawn into the center of a course that focused on issues inextricably connected to my life.

The more, however, my students' experiences as outsiders seemed to affect their lives, the more I was drawn to reconsider taking the risk. At the same time, incidents of racism and discrimination at UMass/Boston were on the rise, and the UMass/Boston community was beginning to explore how it could address this problem through its policies and through curricular changes. With these efforts came the institutionalization of a diversity requirement and attempts to create courses that would explicitly acknowledge the "differences" our students brought with them. The combination of these factors gave me the courage to deal directly with the realities that were too often left unrecognized and unrepresented, the voices that had too often been silenced, and the stories that had too often been left untold.

The freshman composition course that evolved was one in which students explored the myth and reality of the American Dream, a dream that almost all of them had embraced uncritically, despite the everyday tensions that seemed to chafe against it. They examined the extent to which the promises of America applied to their realities and raised questions about incidents and events that revealed "broken promises." They tried to come to terms with the factors that had marginalized them, thus allowing them to see that their situations were not just the result of some personal difficulty or problem but were interwoven with larger and far more complex conditions. And given these realizations, they began to understand the ways in which they could transcend their voicelessness, their invisibility, so that rather than being appropriated by the institutions they came in contact with, they could transform them in the same way that all participants in a culture contribute to and shape that culture.

In the context of this course, students read, examined closely, and wrote about key documents and court decisions. They read newspaper accounts and analyzed reports in the media related to immigration experiences and issues. They read pieces by authors (Maxine Hong Kingston and Richard Rodriguez, for example) that uncover issues of identity, loss of a first language, assimilation, and the relationship between language, culture, and authority. One student, Fukiko, created a dialogue with herself in the context of writing her first paper on language, culture, and identity.

A: Why do you suffer with English?

A1: I have freedom of choice. I mean I could go back to Japan anytime, also I can stay in this country.

A: OK, you should go back to Japan. Your English is no good.

A1: I know, but I want to try how much to improve my English. Now I go to school and study English every day.

A: No, No I don't think so. You married with American over ten years. You had lots of chance to practice English until then.

A1: But we never speak English with each other. I was not planning to live in this country, so I didn't need to learn English. I thought. but my husband died so I have to think my own life and I have to bring up our son by myself. Maybe I will go back to Japan after I finish school.

A: Listen! You are not young. You should decide quickly. Don't waste time for learning English.

A1: But I have my child. I'm single mother. Its seems more comfortable to live in this country than Japan. I don't know.

A: Are you OK? you will struggle with English whole your life in this country.

While the paper in which this dialogue appeared was problematic from the standpoint of the assignment, it told movingly of the tensions and struggles Fukiko was experiencing and became the basis for her subsequent revision.

Students read revealing interviews in Studs Terkel's *American Dreams: Lost and Found* and conducted interviews of their own. They read poetry by Langston Hughes, selected work by Martin Luther King, Jr., and autobiographical pieces by Ann Moody and Audre Lourde, and considered the civil rights movement in light of the promises of the American Dream. As the notion of the American Dream was (re)considered, questioned, and (re)constructed, they looked at the way racism had manifested itself with respect to the ethnic groups represented by the students in the classroom, reading and writing about the work of authors from these groups. Students kept observational notebooks in which they recorded events that reflected the ways in which people are marginalized in different settings—the home, the educational institution, and the workplace. In these notebooks students described their observations and recorded their responses to these observations, making connections between the course work and the variety of cultures they inhabit. Students also participated in a semester-long correspondence with a class of graduate students, most of whom were teachers in urban schools who had enrolled in a course on the importance of multiculturalism in education. At some point during this correspondence, the two groups of students met in order to interview one another, and the data collected during these interviews were included in their subsequent papers. Through all of this work, which immersed students in a rich and deep study of these issues, I invited students' reactions, analyses and interpretations, and the connections they made between their work and their own experiences and assumptions.

Organic to this work was a sequence of reading, writing, and firsthand research that built on itself, so that as the semester progressed, students referred back to previous work, both the texts they were assigned to read and those they themselves had written, in order to demonstrate the knowledge they brought with them as well as their growing expertise. This did not produce neat and predictable essays that could be plotted against some standardized continuum. Instead, this kind of work generated compelling and memorable pieces that reflected the questions and issues students were grappling with, their active engagement with the material, and their use of the material to think about the world around them. They became authors alongside the authors they read, thus reclaiming authority for themselves. In short, their work represented their own dialectical interplay with the course content, which clearly spoke to complex issues and questions of central concern to them and allowed them to speak back. As the material exerted an impact on them, they contributed to and transformed it in some fundamental way.

A powerful illustration of the ways in which this dialectical transformation took place was the class poem that we generated after reading Nellie Wong's "When I Was Growing Up," a poem that movingly tells of Wong's desire as a girl "to be white," to be American. Both the students and I could immediately identify with Wong's recollections, and all of us wrote at least one verse reflecting individual responses the poem had triggered. Mine, which revealed some of the conflicts in my own history, including the moment when my name changed from Aviva to Vivian, is the next to the last verse.

When I was growing up,
I dreamed to become a millionaire.
I wanted to come to a place
Where is called Gold Mountain and
Melting Pot.
People could mingle together, hand
By hand, swarm by swarm.
Let us go to pick gold on the street. . . .

When I was growing up
My own language,
I don't know how to write.
My aunt told me, my skin color
Will color all my English.
Perhaps, she has seen who I am
In insulting eyes of my friends parents. . . .

When I was growing up,
I saw western movies.
I saw the white gentlemen behave
Dignified, humorous, and brave.
The white women are pretty and well-treated.
The scenes were so beautiful that
I wanted to be a part of them. . . .

When I was growing up,
I was so proud of having dark hair.
Small eyes. Yellow and short.
When I came to America,
I couldn't be proud of
My dark hair, yellow skin, and small eyes
Anymore.
It seems white skin was best in this country.
How sad!
I wonder why we can't be proud
Of our own country and figure.

When I was growing up.
I had to play with dolls and not with cars.
With dolls that were white with blue eyes
And beautiful dresses. I never had a black one.
I did not know why!
Dancing and singing around girls.

When I was growing up,
During my kindergarten,
I painted a picture
That was a boy; but the color I put in
His face was yellow, and the nun erased it. . . .

When I was growing up,
I found myself in this strange land,
With a small portion of yellow people
Living in a little town.

When I was growing up,
All I saw was white in the walls, lights,
Schools, Presidents, media,
And even the clouds . . . .

When I was growing up,
My parents' language, their accents,
Their quaint ways
Shamed me.
I craved sameness,
I longed to belong.
I changed names.
Was that so wrong?
Now I embrace
My life on the margin.
Now I trace
My roots, my beginnings.
Now I can face
Aviva.

I don't want to be white.
Did I disappoint you?
I feel comfortable being a palette's painting
Where everybody has their stains,
A crop with different grains.
A bearable rainbow through the rain
An accidental landscape
Where the shades have a freeway.
I crave the dawn,
The marriage between the night and the day,
And the childbirth of the dawn.
The sunrise red
The Indian's race.
Did I disappoint you?
Did I give you enough reason?
I'm sorry, but I want to be what I am.
The union of all human beings.

As is obvious even in this excerpt, the poem is full of powerful images that reflect the ways in which we were coming to terms with both our childhood expectations and our realizations about these expectations. Some of these images commented on Nellie Wong's experiences, others referred to pieces we read earlier in the semester, still others allowed students to transcend Wong's worldview.

Other texts students composed were essays that revealed their ability to write about the readings and use them to make meaning for themselves. These texts were as variable as the students' individual voices and perspectives, each representing their original ways of (re)composing these issues. In one text, Thao, influenced no doubt by the number of readings that used the images of color and paintings to refer to the experience of acculturation, began by creating a metaphor that reflected the role that color played in her framework of understanding:

> Coming to campus everyday, have you ever paid attention to the blocks of colored stone on the driveway near the bus stop? And shopping over weekend, have you ever concerned about color of clothes? In my country, no one ever think of coloring a rock and you could rarely find any multicolored, gaudy clothes in the stores. But in this country, colors are extraordinary, so important and so troublesome as well. Colors themselves have their own meaning. And no matter on a piece of cloth, on a painting, or in the society, while colors blend in themselves, they fight to each other so strongly. That is what Sasaki once ironically said: "America was creating a masterpiece and did not want their color." Yes, "America is great because it is composed of almost every race in the world," as Nakasian said. So a masterpiece that Americans made was wonderful because it combines any colors. But since there were people "dirty," "humble and mean," a masterpiece got stained and its color was disliked.

After beginning in this way, she introduced verses from the class poem we had written:

> Colors of this masterpiece! Obviously, we all know that
> "It seems white skin was best in this country,"
> and
> "When I was growing up
> All I saw was white in the walls, lights,
> Schools, Presidents, media,
> And even the clouds . . ."
> (When I was growing up—My class's poem)

She went on to discuss research findings that students had read and written about, shifted again to another verse from the class poem, referred to some of the autobiographical pieces that had been assigned, quoted a verse from Nellie Wong's poem, and then discussed the other readings before returning to the metaphor of color in her final section. This open-ended and recursive movement reflected her impressive ability to shuttle back and forth not only between different texts but between different types of texts. And the connections she was able to make between such disparate pieces, the ways in which she was able to integrate research findings with poetry, for example, resulted in a piece not just *about* multiculturalism, but one that in its very voice, tone, and content *was* multicultural.

Yet another illustration of the kinds of texts students created as they were addressing these critical issues is this one, written later in the semester by Fukiko, which begins powerfully by confronting the reader with a set of troubling questions:

> Who is marginalized in the United States? It is ethnic group and women. Who has pushed them away to the margin? It is people who have power. Who has power in the United States? Usually these people are white, rich males and they never know how it feels to be marginalized so that they don't care about marginalized people. It seems that ethnic groups have been marginalized since their childhood schooling. According to Sonia Nieto in *Affirming Diversity*, she reported, "Teachers tend to pay more attention to their white students than to their students of color." Several of the authors we have read this semester deal with the issue of marginalization in education. I want to discuss how ethnic children are marginalized by teachers at their schools in the U.S.

Fukiko went on to a full discussion of the extent to which Nieto's report is corroborated by some of the accounts of schooling experiences that the class had been assigned to read, after which she turned to the ways in which this issue is related to her own experiences:

> From what I have observed in my class at U.Mass, When I am in E.S.L class, I am so comfortable because E.S.L teachers know the students' diversity or they try to understand about students' diversity. On the other hand, I feel that I am isolated from the majority of students, When I am in the non-E.S.L class. However, I realize often minority students are alienated by themselves in their class and don't communicate in the class with teachers. Usually they don't speak out, and sit in the corner of the classroom. Nieto points out, "Relationships between teachers and students also bear out these findings." Many teachers do not discriminate against ethnic students on purpose. Most teachers want to be a good teacher for every student. But many teachers are unthinking about students' diversity. This reminds me of Takaki's excerpt. He said, "My teachers and text books didn't explain our diversity."

Note the relationships Fukiko saw between the research findings reported in the readings and her own world of experiences. Note, too, that she was not just drawing on her experiences to support what other "experts" had found, but was also foregrounding her own findings and using one of these "experts" to reinforce her own claims. She went on to conclude her paper this way:

> I think teachers should teach more on our diversity than any subject. We must think and educate for generations "what America is." Do we have specific ideas to eradicate marginalization for people of color? Yes, we have one. It is to educate teachers in muticulturalism. Multiculturalism in education is the key that will open the magical doors to equal society.

In the course of writing this paper Fukiko offers a solution to the disturbing and complex problems the class has been grappling with, the very solution that faculty across the curriculum at UMass/Boston and other institutions are trying to enact in their own teaching.

Toward the end of the semester, Fukiko returned to the issue of language and identity as she reacted to the texts of two authors who describe growing up with mothers who were perceived as limited and incapable because of the ways they spoke English. After tracing her own troubling experiences with the English language, explaining how easily she could identify with these women, Fukiko concluded:

> Both Amy Tan's and Manjarrez's mothers are so strong as compared with me. Because I always escaped all troble in my life. May be I should confront all troble by myself in this country. As long as I live in this country I have to deal with identity, language and culture every day. If so, I should enjoy two identities, two languages, and two cultures. May be I might be one lucky persons because I could live with two worlds.

Fukiko has moved dramatically from her initial position, revealed by the dialogue in her earlier paper. She has stopped questioning whether she ought to return to Japan because of her "struggle with English" and has begun to see her "two identities, two languages, and two cultures" as "lucky." She has transcended what she had viewed earlier as her limitations and now values what both a first and a second language, both her own and another perspective, make possible, choosing to embrace multiculturalism as a way of life. Although Fukiko's initial texts were so problematic that I questioned whether she should have been admitted to the course, the strength of her later writing demonstrates what can happen when students are invited into the center of work, when they are recognized as knowers, when their perspectives are not only acknowledged but viewed as essential to our own. It speaks not only to the ways in which educational institutions can foster the language and critical thinking of students but also to the ways in which these students, with their multicultures and their multivoices, can contribute to and transform the very institutions they inhabit and thereby enrich the lives of all of us who work there.

Chapter **17**

Participatory Literacy Education Behind Bars: AIDS Opens the Door

Kathy Boudin

In this article, Kathy Boudin recounts her story as an inmate and literacy educator at Bedford Hills Correctional Facility for women. While the standard literacy education curriculum for the facility emphasized instrumental, workbook-based reading skills, Boudin sought to make the literacy program more relevant to the women's lives and experiences. By working with the women in the literacy program, Boudin incorporated critical literacy teaching practices into the skills-based curriculum, using the subject of AIDS in prison as a means of linking the women's experiences with their acquisition of literacy skills. Although the article focuses on prison education, the women in Bedford Hills are like other women in urban communities for whom literacy is only one of many problems. Thus, the pedagogical and social issues raised here have many implications that extend beyond the prison bars.

> I started hanging out and not taking school seriously when I was a teenager. At seventeen I met my first baby's father, and he had a lot of control over me. After he went to jail, I started using drugs. I had a job for one or two years on and off in a grocery store, running a cash register. But I left that job to sell drugs, because I could earn more money that way. I always wanted to be a bookkeeper, but you have to know how to read, filing, math. Now I think about a porter job in a hospital. Nothing I have to use reading for. I would like to think of nice things: nice clothes, an investigator, a secretary, nice jobs. I see ladies all dressed up, legs crossed. I like things like that, bub-

ble baths, but I can't be thinking too many dreams cause I got five kids. I hope I can make it when I go home.

—Anna, Adult Basic Education student
Bedford Hills Correctional Facility[1]

Prison lies at the end of a road taken. Although women arrive for many reasons, we have one thing in common: we share a deep desire to leave prison and not return. Many of us are looking for alternatives to the actions that brought us here. We are working to imagine new choices, to widen options, and to figure out how to make these real.

When Anna spoke, she was in an Adult Basic Education (ABE) literacy class, hoping it would open doors for her. She was not alone with her literacy problem. In Bedford Hills Correctional Facility, New York State's maximum security prison for 750 women, 63 percent of the incoming women do not have a high school diploma and almost 20 percent do not read at a fifth-grade level (Nuttall, 1988).

Although having limited literacy proficiency is a serious problem, it is only one of many that women in Bedford Hills face.[2] Prior to their imprisonment, most were confronting more pressing problems: poverty, drugs, domestic abuse, neighborhood violence, single-mother parenting, and immigration issues. Many, feeling permanently locked out of the eco-

---

[1]This quote is a verbatim statement taken from an interview with an ABE student with whom I worked. Some of the quotes in the article come from similar interviews, while others come from my own journal entries. Although this article was written when almost all of the women quoted had already left prison on parole, or had transferred to a different prison, I was able to get in touch with the majority of them to tell them that I was doing public writing and to get their permission to use material about or by them. Because some of the women consented to have their real names used and others preferred to remain anonymous, I used fictitious names throughout. The one exception is Juana Lopez, who previously had material written for the ABE class that was published using her real name.

[2] The prisoners in Bedford Hills Correctional Facility are overwhelmingly Black and Hispanic women, mothers, undereducated in a formal sense, frequently poor, and usually single heads of households. The ethnicity of the general prison population in New York State prisons is 50 percent Black, 31 percent Hispanic, and 19 percent White. (The United States population as a whole is 12 percent Black and 7 percent Hispanic.)

The ethnicity of those prisoners with serious reading problems, that is, those under the 5.0 reading level, is 54 percent Black, 37 percent Hispanic, 9 percent White, and 5 percent other. In terms of the education levels of the women who enter the New York State prison system, 18 percent read below a fifth-grade level; 16 percent have math skills below a fifth-grade level; 77 percent dropped out while in high school; and 63 percent do not possess a high school diploma (Nuttall, 1988).

Seventy-three percent of the women in Bedford Hills are mothers (Division of Program Services, 1992), and the majority were single heads of households (Humphrey, 1988). One study showed that over half the women in prisons have received welfare payments during their adult lives (Craig, 1981); in a National Institute of Corrections study of men and women, 80 percent of those who were employed before arrest made less than a poverty-level salary (Bellorado, 1986).

nomic mainstream, were trying to make fast money illegally, usually through involvement with drugs. Basic literacy education meant a time commitment, a slow, long-term investment in a life moving fast, so fast that it got out of control, and ended up with imprisonment. In prison, life slows down enough for these women to take time for such things as a literacy class, yet the women know that when they leave here, most will return to the same broad problems, problems that loom as permanent and intractable. Improved literacy will not be the miracle that will change their lives, especially since the average stay in prison is less than three years (Division of Program Services, 1992) and literacy growth is a slow process. It is rare for a woman to leave Bedford with a goal of changing social conditions, even if she believes those very conditions contributed to her ending up in prison. "You can't change the world" is a commonly held attitude. Trying to deal with immediate issues such as housing, jobs, and child raising are foremost in most women's minds when they leave. The urgent need many of us from a diversity of backgrounds feel is to change the things inside ourselves that landed us here, to be more able to negotiate the system and to cope with the problems we will face when we leave. Improved literacy is part of something bigger, part of their whole struggle to grow. As one woman said, "The only way out . . . is in."

What kind of literacy education would best meet the needs of the women in prison who face these issues? This is the question I grappled with some years ago, when I came to prison, as I became involved in studying and teaching adult literacy. I am an insider, a prisoner myself, a woman and a mother, serving a twenty-to-life sentence. I am also something of an outsider—White, from a middle-class background, college educated, and a participant in the social movements of the 1960s. I had not shared some of the most common realities of the women in the ABE class, realities including racism, drugs, family violence, immigration, or poverty. Nevertheless, twelve years of prison life has broken down barriers: living through the daily experiences such as lock-ins or cell searches, cooking or gossiping; deep friendships; working on AIDS, foster care, and literacy; and sharing the life events such as mothering, deaths, and graduations. All of this has created for me windows into the lives, past and present, of women from different backgrounds and has also led to a new commonality among us.

Early in my master's degree work in adult education (which I undertook when I first entered prison), I learned about Paulo Freire's problem-

---

Forty-four percent of the women in Bedford Hills Correctional Facility were convicted of a drug offense; however, the warden at Riker's Island, which is the largest feeder jail to Bedford Hills, estimates that drugs underlie the incarceration of 95 percent of the female inmates there (Church, 1990). Lastly, in a study done at Bedford Hills in 1985, 60 percent of respondents said they had been victims of abuse (sexual, physical, or emotional) (Grossman, 1985).

solving approach to literacy education, an approach that places literacy acquisition in the context of learners' daily concerns and social reality (Freire, 1970, 1974). I hypothesized that it would be effective at Bedford because it could offer an education in which women could think and act around urgently felt needs while developing their literacy ability.

I, like many other prisoners, wanted to be productive and to do something meaningful with my time in prison, and I looked to teaching literacy as one way to do this. Yet prison administrators usually limit the amount of responsibility and independence a prisoner can have, and teachers who have inmate teacher aides usually use them only in very limited roles. Would I, a prisoner, as a teacher's aide to a civilian teacher, be able to create the space to do meaningful work?

Would it be possible in a prison classroom to create conditions for self-awareness, a space where people felt safe to identify and address their own problems and then struggle toward solutions, to imagine the world as it could be otherwise? Prisons are founded on assumptions of control, obedience, and security. Thus, independent thinking and individual and collective initiative create sharp tensions around these assumptions.

Prison is a metaphor for failure, the failure of those who end up there, while a sense of self-worth is a foundation for active learning, for being willing to take risks. Would it be possible, in the prison atmosphere, to break through the prevailing ideology about prisoners as failures, an ideology that had been internalized to varying degrees by the women themselves, and to release their psychological energy for creative learning? These were among the questions I faced as I began to think about becoming a literacy educator in prison.

In this article, I tell the story of what happened between 1986 and 1990 at Bedford Hills Correctional Facility as I struggled to develop a literacy program that was meaning-based, problem-posing, and relevant to learners' lives. Written from my perspective and observations as both a teacher and a prisoner, with quotes drawn from my detailed journal entries over a five-year period, I start by examining the prison environment, and then relate my experience of teaching while evaluating which educational approach best met the needs of incarcerated women at Bedford. Finally, I discuss the possibilities and constraints that the prison context creates for establishing participatory education.

THE PRISON CONTEXT

The primary missions of prison—control, punishment, and deterrence through social isolation (Sullivan, 1990)—serve to intensify the powerlessness and dependency that many women prisoners have already experienced outside of prison. The loss of the ability to make decisions permeates every aspect of prison life cumulatively in the way it increases powerlessness. The authorities move women freely among the nine female prisons in New York State; thus, within a moment, a woman's entire world may shift. Lack of control over where one lives means lack of control over all the pieces of a life—friends, work, education, routine, possessions, environment, and, of central importance to women, contact with children and family. If a woman is in prison near her children, she can maintain an active relationship with them; when she is moved, the ties are ruptured.

Prison policies dictate what clothing to wear and what colors are permitted. When the telephone rings, a prisoner cannot pick it up. Only guards can open doors. Intimate relationships are illegal and must be hidden. This lack of control extends to life outside prison as well. For example, a woman may learn that her child is in the hospital, but cannot be present to comfort her or him. When a child runs away from home, the mother is helpless to work on the problem. We as prisoners must rely on people outside to help with the details of daily living—from buying clothes, food, and presents for children, to phoning lawyers who don't accept collect calls.

While women's prisons can be brutalizing, they are often infantilizing.[3] The social conditioning in a women's prison encourages a childlike dependency (Burkhart, 1976). For example, at Bedford Hills we constantly have to ask permission to do some of the most basic things: when at work or at school we must ask an officer for toilet paper, and she or he will then tear off a few pieces and hand them to us; we must wait for an officer to turn the lights off or on in our cells, since cell lights are controlled by a key that the officer has; we may stand by a gate or a door for five minutes or more until an officer feels we are quiet enough, and only then will she or he open it. Women operate within the confines of power and control, reward and punishment; women typically express their overall sense of having no control when they refer to authorities and say, "This is *Their* jail."

Although prison intensifies powerlessness, for many women it paradoxically also offers a space for growth. There is a release from the pressures of everyday survival, abusive relationships, family responsibilities, and drug addiction; some women have their first drug-free pregnancy while in prison. Incarceration can be a time for women to reevaluate and reflect on their lives, to get an education and acquire skills they never had a chance or didn't want to get, and to think about issues they may never have thought about.

---

[3]Recent examples of women's prisons in which repressive measures such as extreme isolation or sexual abuse have been documented include the underground prison in Lexington, Kentucky, and the Shawnee Unit in Maryanna, Florida.

There are numerous educational and social programs that women can make use of in prison.[4] These programs are shaped by the conflicting goals of security, control, and punishment on the one hand, and rehabilitation or self-development on the other (Bellorado, 1986; Sullivan, 1990). The various basic education programs at Bedford Hills—ABE, pre-GED, GED, ESL, Bilingual Literacy—can serve either as a means of control (primarily used to keep prisoners occupied and having limited educational goals) or as a fruitful context for deep growth. It was in this environment of constraints and possibilities that I set out to teach.

Entering the Classroom: Education for Control

I started to work as a teacher's aide in the ABE class in February 1986. I requested to work in this class because the teacher had expressed support for my teaching ideas and, from my observation, seemed to have a strong rapport with the students. By this time, I had spent a year-and-a-half in both graduate study and individual tutoring of ABE, GED, ESL, and college students. This range of experience led me to define three goals for my work in the ABE classroom: first, to teach reading and writing; second, to foster participants' intellectual and emotional strengths (e.g., analytical ability, imagination, and self-esteem); and third, to create a context for exploring and possibly acting on personal and social issues faced by women in the prison. When I entered the classroom, I was in for a rude awakening.

On an average day, the women in the ABE class ranged in age from seventeen to seventy, with the vast majority in their mid-twenties. They were primarily African-American or Hispanic, coming from a variety of cultures and places: New York City, the South, Puerto Rico, Jamaica, Colombia, and the Dominican Republic. A few were working-class White women from upstate New York, and some came from other countries (Hong Kong, Yugoslavia, and Israel).

Typically, women arrived in class and took their individual folders and workbooks from a shelf. Their work consisted of reading paragraphs or short passages on various unrelated themes (e.g., popcorn, insects, and newspapers), and then answering multiple-choice questions that focused on skills (e.g., finding the main idea, understanding a particular word, or locating a detail). When a student finished a designated amount of work,

[4]In addition to the basic education programs, some of these programs include: The Parenting and Foster Care Programs of the Children's Center, where women learn about issues related to being mothers; the Family Violence program, where women examine violence in their personal lives and some of the social values and roles that permit or even encourage such violence; the AIDS Counseling and Education (ACE) program, where women have struggled to build a community of support around AIDS-related issues and have trained themselves to become peer educators and counselors; and the four-year college program run by Mercy College, where women can earn bachelor degrees.

the teacher or aide checked the answers against the answer key. The student then tried to correct her wrong responses.

The class was silent, except when the teacher spoke to individual students or when friends exchanged a few words. There was no instruction to the whole class by the teacher. What mattered most was whether the students answered workbook questions correctly. The answer key and the teacher were the only sources of knowledge. The learning process was entirely defined by the teacher, and it was narrowly confined to a limited body of information.

Occasionally, group discussion followed a movie; the teacher might encourage writing a few times a year, for example, during Black History month. Once in a while there was a lesson on a life skill relating to the state-mandated functional competency program or computer work, but these activities were not the norm. Day after day, year after year, women came to class and silently read workbooks in which they repeated discrete skills in preparation for periodic tests.

My first reaction to the classroom was physical. My eyes strained from trying to match up answer sheets with hundreds of tiny boxes, and my mind went dull. I found myself de-skilled and transformed into a clerk. I was neither expected nor able to use any intellectual or emotional aspects of myself. I found no room for choice, judgment, or authentic interaction. The experience of almost two years in this role contributed to passivity, conformity, and a feeling of uselessness, which, as a prisoner, I was constantly struggling against anyway.

For the women in the literacy class, reading paragraphs day after day and taking tests with similar paragraphs resulted in incremental improvement on test scores over time, and, therefore, in some sense of progress and satisfaction. Yet communication and meaning, the essential core of reading, were not the point of the classroom experience. There was no writing, no explicit development of strategies to enhance construction of meaning from texts, no exposure to various literary genres such as poetry, stories, or drama, and no building on interaction between the different language processes of reading, writing, listening, and speaking.

I asked myself what we were telling women about the importance of literacy, when there was no link between literacy and self, no development of literacy as a powerful means to construct a world. What message were we giving the women about themselves and their lives in this classroom, where their thinking and all their experience were irrelevant? The women I taught brought into the classroom a rich tapestry of knowledge, experience, and cultures. They knew firsthand about the social problems of crack, homelessness, the crisis of being mothers behind bars, the immigrant experience; they shared basic human conditions of love and friendship, betrayal, death, community, work. If learning materials did not portray a life that was familiar, did not reflect their reality, did not contain their voices or their languages, what did that tell them about their cultures? If the teacher and the workbooks were the only sources of knowledge and authority, what did that say about their capacity to know and to create?

I believe that this approach, with its excessive emphasis on obedience and limited possibility for initiative or constructive learning, with its lack of attention to self and its undervaluing of affect in learning, was detrimental to basic mental health. This kind of instruction could not foster self-esteem or self-confidence. And, in denying the possibility of making choices, solving problems, looking at different options, or figuring out one's own opinion, it thwarted the possibility of helping women to change their lives.

Educational policy and curriculum for all New York State prisons is set by the Department of Education of the New York State Department of Correctional Services (Nuttall, 1988). The approach used in the prison literacy classes, like that used in many adult literacy programs throughout the country (Fingeret, 1984; Hunter & Harman, 1979), is a decontextualized, subskill model of reading in which content, real life issues, creativity, and imagination are all irrelevant. It is individualized and programmed, precluding interaction or social action (Nuttall, 1983). The reading process is conceptualized as a bottom-up process in which comprehension of the message of the text is slowly built up by accumulating small pieces, sound by sound, word by word, moving from lower to higher levels of complexity (LaBerge & Samuels, 1985). An adult who has failed to learn to read adequately is presumed to be lacking in particular subskills. Initial testing identifies those particular weaknesses, remediates for them and then retests in this diagnostic prescriptive model (Nuttall, 1983). The concept of literacy that guides the curriculum in the ABE class is based on grade level: a literate inmate is defined as one who scores at or above the 5.0 reading level on the standardized achievement tests used throughout the system (Nuttall, 1983).[5]

As in any other teaching context, the rationale for the choice of approach to prison literacy education is informed, in part, by assumptions about learners. A report from the Education Department of the New York State Department of Correctional Services states:

> The most serious obstacle to a successful program and "habilitation" or "rehabilitation" is the make-up of the population itself. For the most part, com-

[5] The Department of Education of the New York State Department of Correctional Services defines literacy by using a combination of grade level and functional competency definitions. The functional competency definition was crystallized into a Life Skills curriculum (Nuttall, 1983). However, in the three-and-a-half years during which I was involved in the ABE class, the Life Skills curriculum was not put into practice except in an occasional lesson.

> mitments to the Department represent individuals who have little education, who have no viable occupational skill, who have a history of substance abuse, and who often have a long history of criminal activity. (Nuttall, 1988, p. 2)

This policy statement characterizes prisoners themselves as the main obstacle to their own rehabilitation. Although it identifies objective problems, it fails to recognize strengths that prisoners bring to the learning process. From my observation, viewing prisoners primarily as a problem meant that correctional services' education personnel were unlikely to involve prisoners in their own education, let alone to think they might make a contribution to society. I knew from my years in prison that this perception of women exclusively as "problems" was inaccurate, and that this prevailing view would never lead to a process of meaningful educational growth.

Women who have committed serious crimes may well have survived serious pressures. Many women have not just survived, but have actively refused to accept a passive or victimized role. While women may have acted in a destructive and/or self-destructive way, assertiveness can be a lever that opens options for new action. The ability to survive and fight back may be a strength on which to build. It is crucial to discover and work with this and other strengths because, however deeply hidden, they are, in the end, women's greatest allies. And so a question began to form and to follow me: Could I create a process whereby the potential and strengths of the women could be expressed and developed, becoming part of the literacy process and fueling it with energy?

An Alternative Vision

I developed an alternative vision through a combination of my past history as a community organizer, my experience in the individual tutoring and ABE class, and the theory and methods that I learned through my graduate studies. In the 1960s, I had been involved in teaching about welfare rights, housing, and health issues. I had worked with women who had little formal education and who were regarded by society as inadequate, or as "victims" to be helped by those who were more educated by formal academic standards. Yet these women and people like them throughout the United States were learning together, acting on their own problems, and, at the same time, providing social insights that affected the entire society. I brought to my classes a certain optimism from my experience as an educator outside the classroom. I believed that, even in the controlled prison environment and in a different historical period, it might be possible to create a participatory learning process in which people felt a relative sense of empowerment.

My studies confirmed that, when literacy was taught as a collection of skills outside of any meaningful context and divorced from any importance in the learners' lives, the work would not fully tap their intellectual capacity. Neither would it draw on their prior knowledge, which, as schema theory had taught me, is so critical in the development of reading proficiency (Anderson, 1985; Bransford, 1985). Taken together, my community organizing experiences, my graduate studies, and my observations of prison classrooms led me to hypothesize that a meaning-driven, whole-language orientation might be more effective in the prison context (Altwerger, Edelsky, & Flores, 1987; Goodman, 1973, 1985; Smith, 1973).

I believed that such an approach would be stronger not only cognitively, but affectively as well. The women whom I taught were once the children who had failed in school or, more accurately for many of them, whose schools had failed them. From my interaction with the women in and out of class, I learned that they brought with them negative feelings about education and about themselves as learners. Attitudes about race, class, and gender undermined their confidence to learn academically, compounding the insecurities about school. I knew from conversations that many were only in the ABE class because it would look good for the parole board or because they had been assigned to be there. It was critical to use an approach that built on the women's intelligence, experience, and culture in order to counter these forces.

The existing classroom process, depending as it did on passivity and the rote learning of isolated skills, did not link literacy learning with the daily needs of the women, nor did it equip them to take an active role in their own education. As such, it ran counter to what we know about adult learning in general: a) the complexity of adult social roles and related responsibilities (spouse, worker, parent, community member) means that adults want learning to be applicable to their needs; b) the broad knowledge and life experience that adults have acquired mean that they have a great deal of prior knowledge that can be used as a strength in developing literacy ability; and c) the independence and self-direction that characterize adults mean that learning—both in content and in process—should be participatory (Ellowitch, 1983; Knowles, 1984).

For the women with whom I worked, the general needs of all adult learners were magnified by the multitude of urgent issues they faced; thus, the need to overcome powerlessness and to create new choices was essential. Freire's approach to literacy education was particularly relevant, as it is rooted in work with marginalized and oppressed groups. His ideas influenced my work in several ways. First, his approach begins with students developing the ability to analyze their experiences and their social reality, as they explore the meanings of this reality in the words and the sentences they are learning to read and write. The literacy class can, at times, become a place where students may even act on issues, using and further developing their literacy ability. Second, his work raises issues about teachers, their methods, and their relationships with their students. I had been frustrated with the one-way street of teaching that left the ABE students in a passive situation. Freire argues that this passivity comes, in part, from the tendency of many middle-class teachers to feel superior to their students from poorer backgrounds. He proposes a "dialogic" method, in which students and teachers together explore a shared set of issues. This dialogue, while not removing the teacher's responsibility to teach a body of knowledge, can unleash an active role for the learners, enhancing not only their present learning, but also their lives beyond the classroom (Freire, 1970, 1974).

These views resonated with my community work with African-American and poor White women, largely from Appalachia, prior to my incarceration. As I had come to know these women and their life stories, I became acutely aware that my formal education represented only one kind of knowledge; in fact, my own background, while having given me certain advantages, also had left me with certain blinders. My work with these women had been a two-way street—we learned from and taught one another. I wanted now to build on both the reality we shared as women prisoners and the differences in our backgrounds and experiences.

The Struggle for Change

For almost two years as a teacher's aide, I struggled to implement this alternative vision. Sometimes I worked with small groups of women, reading a particular text of interest, striving always to keep meaning in front of us. We read plays, did interviews, and read stories. Although each project engaged women and taught them a wider range of literacy skills, nothing altered the overall routine. The women frequently did not want to work with other women, feeling either embarrassed and ashamed of themselves or contemptuous of the others.

In many cases, they did not want to attempt any writing, which was rarely required by the teacher. The classroom context was still set by the teacher and the sub-skill approach; the approach I was using was simply not considered "real work." Moreover, I found myself experiencing the same frustration as other teachers with the "call-out" system (in which students could be pulled from class at any time for appointments). This system, along with transfers to other prisons, pushed the curriculum toward individualized work and away from a content focus, since it was difficult to develop a cohesive unit of study with a constantly changing group of people.

Slowly, the sub-skill model began to seduce me. Although I never lost my aversion to this limited sense of education, I began to become preoccupied with how women were doing in their workbooks and on the tests, measuring my worth as a teacher in these terms. I lost a strong sense of initiative. The structure and machinery of school were undermining my vision of education. I was turning into the teacher I did not want to be. I understood what had happened to other teachers, many of whom encouraged me and seemed to identify with my vision, but didn't have the energy to implement it.

The existing curriculum materials, testing apparatus, and overall conception of literacy set terms for success and failure that brought all of us—teachers and students alike—into its orbit. From my observations in class, and from conversations with the students, it appeared that the students had internalized years of failure in school, and without the confidence in themselves as thinkers they were very open to the safe routine of workbooks. In addition, prison, with its system of rewards and punishments (the ultimate of which was meted out by the parole board), contributed to students' willingness to accept a rote method of learning. By the fall of 1987, after almost two years of trying, I wanted to quit.

While I was wrestling with whether or not to leave teaching, the ABE teacher had resigned; the Educational Supervisor then asked me to teach the class for four months until a new teacher could be hired. This offer was unexpected and unprecedented, since prisoners are permitted only to be aides to civilian teachers. I saw the opportunity to try to implement my vision of education, and I took it, as I felt it would allow me to define the approach to literacy education for the class as a whole, rather than as a side project.

The Education Supervisor, as an educator, was supportive of a problem-posing approach. He knew of my graduate work and was willing to take a risk with me. In allowing me to teach the class, the prison authorities had to balance their personal interest in my ideas about education with the system's policy of limiting an inmate's level of responsibility and influence over other inmates, along with concern not to threaten the civilian teachers' job security and status.[6] According to prison authorities, the decision was possible because it was limited in time, and I would officially remain in the position of teacher's aide to the other ABE teacher who worked with students at a tested reading level of K-3.[7]

---

[6]A recent policy statement of the New York State Department of Correctional Services states, "Although the Department has been reluctant to place inmates in positions where they might possibly acquire influence or authority over other inmates, we have used inmates as teacher's aides and vocational aides and in recent years have begun to employ them as pre-release peer counselors and ASAT aides" (Division of Program Services, 1991, p. 3). This statement is comparable with the long-standing practice of not permitting inmates to teach academic classes, but of encouraging them to do one-on-one tutoring, either as a teacher's aide or volunteer tutor.

[7]In the summer of 1987, the ABE class was divided into two classes defined by level K-3 and level 3-6. I was working with the 3-6 level, and it was this class that I was offered to teach. Beginning with the winter of 1991–1992, the K-3 teacher was laid off, and once again there is one ABE class, level K-6.

The Issue of AIDS Enters the Classroom

The most important challenge facing me was to create a reading class in which concerns that had meaning to the women would "drive" the learning process. The issue of AIDS opened this possibility. In September 1987, the ABE reading class watched a television show on the National AIDS Awareness Test. At that time, AIDS was still largely an issue prisoners did not discuss, although it was deeply affecting their lives. Close to 20 percent of incoming women inmates tested positive for the HIV virus (New York State Commission on Correction, 1988). Women lived in a state of anxiety over whether they might be HIV positive and whether to take the test. Many women had used intravenous (IV) drugs, and many had lovers or spouses who still did. Women were sisters, mothers, daughters, and homemakers for people with AIDS. Here, women shared cooking areas, showers and toilets, and a life together. People were scared—scared of each other, scared for their lives. The stigma that AIDS carried reenforced a sense of guilt and shame that the women already felt as prisoners pronounced "guilty" by the courts and society. There was a fear of just being associated with AIDS. This fear created both a collective silence and a desperate need to talk.

During the television show, I noticed that the women were riveted to the screen, trying to write down information, their voices sounding out rapidly staccato, one after another: "How do you spell 'pneumonia'?" "How about 'disease'?" "And 'infection'?" "What's an antibody?" "What do they mean, 'immune system'?" "Spell 'protection,' 'hemophiliac'." While they tried to hold on to the meaning of new terms, I went to the blackboard to write down all the words they were calling out. AIDS was a powerfully emotional issue; a new sense of urgency entered the classroom.

That night I focused on everything I had learned but, until then, been unable to implement. I prepared a vocabulary worksheet, an activity that was familiar to the women. While the words were typically drawn from a textbook list for children at different grade levels, the words on this list came from the AIDS show. The women studied avidly, learning words far above their difficulty level in their workbook lists. Some words were conceptually familiar but difficult to spell, such as *transmit*, *doctor*, *disease*, *patient*, and *pneumonia*; some led to learning new concepts, such as *immune system*, *antibody*, and *hemophiliac*.

In addition to the vocabulary, I asked three questions that were on all of our minds: *What are the pros and cons of taking the AIDS test and how do you feel about it? If you tested positive would/should you tell somebody and who would you tell? What do you think would be a good program for AIDS here at Bedford Hills?* These questions created an environment in which the students related to real life emotional and social issues; they began addressing problems that they faced both individually and communally. I asked the women what they thought.

"I don't want to take the test. I'm scared to find out. I used needles."

"You have to tell your lover, otherwise you might hurt her."

"I don't even know what the test tells you, do you?"

"I'm not worried now, but what about when I go home? My man, he's been with women while I'm here. Even though he says he hasn't, he's like any other man. I know the real deal."

"I shot up with some people and now they're dead. I don't want to know and then again I do."

Everyone participated. The women speaking to one another turned their orderly rows into an informal circle. I also talked, feeling my commonality with the women because I too had feelings about testing, safe sex, and fears of rejection. I also felt our differences as women spoke about IV drugs in their lives and decided to speak to these differences, making explicit the fact that I didn't know about IV drugs and wanted to know more. This was the first of many times that I would try to make the differences in our backgrounds a point for exchange. In that first discussion, I began to change my role as teacher: I was a prisoner, exploring shared problems; a facilitator, guiding learning and discussion; and a person with specific information I wanted to learn and impart.

Soon, women began to write about personal experiences with AIDS, and even brought unsolicited writings to class. For example, Lucia wrote:

> My friend died from AIDS last year. . . . Since then I've been scared. This is a disease that they haven't found the medicine for. I would like to be one of those persons from the big laboratory to help find the medicine for those people who have AIDS. I'm trying not to think about the disease, but I have a brother and a sister and they are into drugs. They say they don't use anybody's syringe, but still I'm afraid.

Lucia had never written anything in class and had difficulty writing in her native Spanish, as well as in English. When she presented her piece, she was sharing a hidden secret about her family, her fears and her dreams, as well as asking for help in English and writing. The drive to express her intense feelings had led her to take real risks in her writing and use of English.

With reading centered on AIDS-related materials, the women contributed to the curriculum, something that had not happened previously. They brought in newspaper articles and pamphlets to share with the class, which I developed into reading lessons. One day Juana, who was about to transfer to the GED class, came to me holding pages of paper tightly in her hand. She said, "I've written something; it's a story, maybe the class would like it." She had a look of triumph on her face, and a triumph it was! Juana's story, called "Chocolate and Me," was about a relationship between two women in jail, one of whom had AIDS.[8] When she read it, the women listened intently as they felt their own lives being described by one of their class members, and clapped enthusiastically when it was over. Juana worked on it, learning the concept of paragraphs, struggling with sentence structure and spelling. Then I typed it, made copies, and developed a reading lesson from it. The class felt proud that one of their members had written something that they were studying. This was the first of many times that the women's own writings became the reading materials for our class.

Writing a Play: Building on the Strengths of an Oral Tradition

During this time, I proposed to the class that we write our own play.[9] I had several goals: to develop literacy through the process of creating a play in which women would be communicating important thoughts and feelings; to broaden literacy ability through studying the genre of a play and integrating the language forms of reading, writing, talking, and listening; and to develop the strengths of working in cooperation with others.

We began by talking about what a play is, learning about the elements of plot, character, conflict, dialogue, and setting. I gave out vocabulary worksheets with words related to theater. We read plays from a literacy program facing issues similar to those in our own community.[10] This encouraged us: if another basic literacy class could write a play about issues of housing, health, and drugs, then we, too, could write such a play. When one woman asked, "What should the play be about?", another responded, "It should be something about us, our lives." This was one more step by participants in gaining confidence that their own life experiences were significant. When it came time to decide on a focus, the women chose AIDS, because we were increasingly involved with it in class.

During the next weeks, the conflicts around which to base the plot emerged from our real questions and anxieties about AIDS: Should a person take the HIV test or not? If she tests positive, should she tell her par-

[8]Juana's story, "Chocolate and Me," was published by the PWA Coalition in *Surviving and Thriving with AIDS: Collective Wisdom,* vol. I (1988).

[9]The sources of the suggestion and the guidance in using theater with literacy instruction were Dr. Ruth Meyers, my graduate study mentor, who worked with the Creative Arts Team (CAT), a professional educational theater company in residence at New York University, and Klaudia Rivera, who at the time was Director of the Community Language Services Project of the Adult Learning Center at LaGuardia Community College, where literacy and theater work was developed.

[10]The plays were written by different classes of the Community Language Services project (CLS) of the Adult Learning Center at LaGuardia Community College in 1986, under the coordination of Klaudia Rivera, coordinator of the program.

ents? Her lover? The work on the play allowed women to reflect on their day-to-day experiences, and the play changed along with their reflections. One day Elena said, "A friend of mine told me last night that she just tested positive. She's supposed to go home in four months. She had so many dreams—traveling, having kids—now those dreams have all gone down the drain. Maybe I shouldn't push so hard for testing."

Jackie added, "Yeah, I agree, here I am in the play, pushing Anna to take the test, but I'm scared. I'm not ready to deal with it; I know I'm not, and I bet I'm not the only one." From this discussion, the group decided to make the dialogue in the play less pressured toward taking the test.

As we improvised dialogue around each conflict, plot and characters slowly developed. When it was time to create a script, two or three people followed each person's spoken words and wrote down whatever they could. We then pieced the entire dialogue into a whole. Finally we put all the scenarios on the blackboard and made choices as to the sequence of action.

The theater framework allowed participants to try out different resolutions to conflict, to experience the emotions they most feared, and to learn from the process. During one rehearsal, we focused on the woman who was the counselor in the play. "Try to get into it more, try to really put yourself into it," the women coached and pushed. Suddenly Teresa burst into tears. "I think I'm afraid," she said, "afraid to put myself in it completely because then it makes it real, and I guess no matter how calm I seem to all of you, really I'm afraid to think about AIDS." Women went to her and hugged her. After that moment, she did put herself more into the acting and was more open about her experiences and fears.

Work on the play further molded my changing role as teacher. The women urged me to take a part in the play. For a moment I hesitated, wondering if it was appropriate for a teacher to do that. Then I laughed at myself, realizing I was feeling afraid I might lose my authority. Taking the part strengthened my teaching, as I identified with the women in working on a shared problem.

Theater gave the Hispanic and African-American women an opportunity to build on a strong oral tradition. They were able to use their own language, dialects, informal speech, and body language. Some of the women who had the greatest problems developing their reading and writing were outstanding in the development of dialogues and acting. The theater process accentuated the strengths of some women, while valuing the strengths of each as language, communication, reading, and writing all developed.

A Community Develops in the Classroom

The students' growing consciousness of themselves as part of a community, first in the classroom and then in the prison, became a positive factor in literacy development. The classroom had been a place in which each person individually felt locked into her own sense of failure. "I hate being in this class, people think it's for dummies. Maybe it is," Anna had said. No one wanted to be identified with being in the ABE class, "the lowest spot on the totem pole,"just as no one wanted to feel like they were part of the prison.

But as people began to talk about their fears and questions concerning AIDS, something changed in the classroom. A sense of community, an awareness of common experiences, and a feeling of support began to grow. The most emotional moment reflecting this came when Lucia shared with the class that she had just found out that her brother was hospitalized with AIDS. I wrote in my journal:

> When Lucia came back into the classroom, people said they were sorry and wanted to be there for her. Elena suggested that Lucia write about her feelings. So Lucia spent the rest of the class writing about what is happening with her brother.

When people arrived at class in the morning, they now spoke with each other differently, with an openness, a sense of identification, and growing trust. As one woman wrote, "In our class we talk about a lot of things and learn a lot of reading. Sometimes we talk about real things that make our tears come out. . . ."

The support for one another expressed itself in the classroom in many ways. For example, when a woman got sick, everyone made a card for her; when a woman made parole, people had a celebration for her. The class organized a Christmas party, something that had never before happened in an ABE class. The most significant articulation of community occurred when we were picking a title for the play. When someone said, "Let's call it *Our Play* because it is about us," there was enthusiastic agreement. That sense of there being an "us" had never existed before, and the title expressed a pride in the "us" that had emerged.

ABE class members carried this ethos of support beyond the class and into the prison population. Word began to get out that the ABE class was talking about AIDS in a supportive way; other prisoners now sought out women in the ABE class as confidantes on their living units. One day Ching came to class and said to me, "A woman on my floor found out she has AIDS and tried to kill herself. I'm the one person she told. I know why she tried. She came to me, I'm the person she talks to." Ching's eyes filled with tears. I saw then that the knowledge that the ABE class was accumulating was also bringing with it awesome responsibilities.

The feeling of community influenced literacy ability, as well as intellectual and emotional growth. People took risks in reading and writing because they were no longer afraid. They felt less ashamed of themselves and were willing to express their thoughts more freely. As they brought increasingly complex reading materials to class and began to teach one another, recognizing that each one could teach as well as learn, a tentative grouping of learners and teachers emerged. One of many examples of this occurred when the women were preparing for a spelling test. "I'll help Jamie," said Ms. Edna, who was seventy years old. They worked for a while, and then Ms. Edna brought the test over to me. They had gotten 100 percent on it. They were beaming at their mutual success.

A growing social awareness laid the basis for the next critical leap: the desire to change the conditions that were causing problems. "What can we do with everything we're learning?" Jackie asked. "People are coming to me, asking me things," Alicia added. Instead of seeing AIDS as an individual problem, people began to see it as a common one, and one they could work on together. First the women worked on an article for the school journal, hoping to share what they had learned. I took the class through the process of writing a composition, focusing on what they wanted to say about AIDS. After five hard-working sessions, the article, *Alert to Aids*, was done, and was published not long after with all the class members' names on it. Although the feeling of community had first grown inside the class, it now extended beyond the class into the prison as a whole. The women continued to use their developing literacy skills to make a difference. *Our Play* became the means of accomplishing this.

Are We Really Learning to Read and Write?

The transformation that was taking place in the classroom challenged participants' notions about what counts as education. In place of filling out multiple choice questions from workbooks, the women were learning from their own experiences and reading materials that did not have "yes" or "no" answers. The range of literacy activities was far beyond those normally carried out in the ABE class. Yet, it was not an easy transformation, and not everyone was comfortable with the process. The students had questions, and so did I. Randy said, "I feel I've learned a lot about AIDS, I'm learning to write a composition, I'm reading lots of articles, and I'm actually writing a play, but I'm just not sure I'm really learning." Many women wanted a clear sense of right and wrong answers. The workbooks had provided this, as well as a sense of progress because of the movement through the book and from one level to the next. Some women did not like working in groups. Others wanted to know whether their progress would show up on the test scores.

During the work on the play, one woman playing a major role did not do as well on the quarterly TABE test as she had hoped. She announced that she was quitting the play to go back to the workbooks. Everyone wanted her to come back to the play and eventually she did, with renewed commitment. However, I knew that I had to take her concerns seriously, and that they were shared by others. I, too, was worried about whether this work would give them the needed test preparation.

During this period, when I encountered both a variety of student resistance and my own insecurities as a relatively new teacher of literacy, I asked myself whether I was imposing on the women an educational approach that I thought was best for them, but that they didn't want. Perhaps my views were linked to the differences in my background. Would it give them adequate test preparation? With time, the range of reading materials, the explosion of writing, and the students' engagement and personal growth all made me more confident about my approach. And now, having established a meaning-driven context within the classroom, I was able to begin focusing on problem areas. I took readings and developed lessons similar to those in the workbooks. This, I felt, would allow the women to feel a relationship between the past and the new learning experiences. I tried to develop a better balance between group and individual work, spending time with each person on specific areas of need. Many of the women needed work on both the sound symbol relations and the basic structure of English language. Finally, I developed lessons on test-taking skills.

Performing the Play: Empowerment within a Prison

By mid-December of 1987, we were ready to put on the play. We were all nervous. AIDS was still a subject associated with fear and stigma. Those who were taking the risk to open up a hidden subject were not seen by either themselves or other inmates as potential educators, because they were in the lowest level academic class.

The play was performed six times, and each time the audience reacted beyond all dreams. It brought into the open fears, questions, and issues in a safe social setting, breaking the silence so that people could together begin to deal with the epidemic. Women cried as a father rejected his daughter, moving his chair away from her after she told him she had tested positive. Yet the tears were mixed with embarrassed laughter, because they knew that they, too, might move away from someone whom they thought to have AIDS. When a woman told her lover she had tested positive, there was a dead silence as people waited for the lover's reaction. Everyone was able to identify with one of the women or the other; they were living through what they themselves might face. When the support group in the play came together for the last scene and told each other of the good and of the difficult reactions they had gotten from family and friends, the audience stood up and cheered, feeling the strength that came from people supporting each other.

After several performances, we held discussions with the audiences about what could be done to deal with the crisis of AIDS here at Bedford Hills. The audience asked for support groups and a program to be built like the one depicted in the play. Members of the prison administration came to watch one of the performances. The superintendent requested that the class put on the play for the civilian counselors in the prison, and the class made a video of it.

Several months later, a group of women separate from the ABE class, including myself, formed an organization for peer education and counseling called AIDS Counseling and Education (ACE). The ACE Program has created a major difference in attitudes, medical care, mental health, knowledge, and support in the prison around AIDS-related issues.[11] It uses the video of *Our Play* to help women deal with the emotional issues that AIDS raises.

After the play, the ABE class did its first evaluation of their learning experience, another step in the women's self-consciously helping to mold their own education. The Education Supervisor, who facilitated the evaluation, asked, "What did the work in the AIDS unit accomplish for you?" The answers included, "Writing skills, vocabulary, recognizing words, spelling, how to write a play, learning about conflicts and resolutions."

"Learning about AIDS."

"How to put on a play and how to act."

"How to respect people's feelings, how to speak louder, and how to express our feelings."

"I liked the counseling group because it involved counseling each other."

"We gave people a message, we helped people."

"The play brought a level of emotions, awareness to help learn."

"I feel wise, learning how other people feel."

"The play gave me a mirror to look at my own life."

I believe that these quotes reflect how the women in the ABE class felt empowered in different ways, both as individuals and as a group. The classroom experience allowed individuals to understand their own lives more clearly. Their self-concept changed from being poor learners to people who could teach others. Although the process had begun with one peer educator, myself, the participatory problem-posing approach generated many others, as women taught one another in the classroom, and as the ABE class educated the population through informal discussions and

[11]For more information about the ACE Program see J. Clark and K. Boudin (1990), "A Community of Women Organize Themselves to Cope With the AIDS Crisis: A Case Study From Bedford Hills Correctional Facility," and K. Boudin and J. Clark (1991), "A Community of Women Organize Themselves to Cope with the AIDS Crisis: A Case Study from Bedford Hills Correctional Facility."

writing the play. A sense of efficacy and agency developed for all of us—myself as teacher, the women in the class as students, and all of us as prisoners. As a group, the class knew that they had made a major contribution to the entire prison population by breaking the silence about AIDS, using their growing literacy ability to do so. The play had helped to create conditions whereby an ongoing program developed. Three years later, I asked one of the ABE class participants in *Our Play*, who is presently a member of ACE teaching others about AIDS, how she felt about her experience in the ABE class and the play. She said to me:

> The play made people more aware. Some people didn't want to face it, some people went around judging people that have AIDS. The play helped change that. I felt good about myself. I didn't know what AIDS was before I came to Bedford. It made me feel good that I'm educated and how I can help educate others. I grew in the process, that was a step, and a step makes for progress.

The Model Repeats: A Multicultural Community Expresses Itself

Was the intense student involvement during the unit on AIDS tied only to the issue of AIDS, or was it linked to the new way of teaching? Clearly AIDS was an issue of great emotional urgency, and it did provide the initial energy to transform the educational approach. Once the ABE class openly embraced the issue of AIDS and owned it as a shared human problem instead of as a badge of guilt, then, paradoxically, the very issue that led to oppressing and denying people their humanity became a vehicle of transformation and hope. As women freed themselves from the dehumanization of stigma and prejudice, proclaiming their own self-worth and humanity, an energy was created that drove the learning process, the desire for knowledge, the confidence to create.

Once the women had experienced a literacy education that focused on issues of importance, they wanted it to continue. Fundamentally, it was the educational approach that had provided the glue to overcome the fragmented reality that is debilitating to prisoners and teachers alike. Fragmentation was overcome when the learning process tapped into the whole person, and when a sense of community was created so that people felt committed to each other, as well as to broader goals.

An indication of the power of such an educational approach occurred when the new teacher was hired and reestablished the individualized, basic skills model, sending all of us—students and myself—back to the workbooks and multiple-choice questions. I felt a sadness, almost as if there had been a death of a fragile new life. The students evidently felt the same way and, as the weeks went by, many of them complained to the teacher and to administrators, asking for a return to teaching in which their ideas and issues mattered. This active role of ABE students requesting a certain type of education was unprecedented at Bedford Hills.

The AIDS unit had generated enough support for a participatory approach that not only the education supervisor, but also higher prison authorities were interested in seeing it continue in some form. The new teacher, who was troubled by declining attendance, and was also open to the problem-posing approach, agreed to let me teach the class two out of five days, during which time he would be present in the classroom. This arrangement left him in authority, yet gave credence to my work.

The model repeated itself as the ABE class explored other thematic units over the next year. In one called "Mothers and Daughters," we explored our mothers' lives, our relationship to them as daughters, and our own role as mothers. In another, we explored issues of personal experiences and values with money. Finally, for a six-month period, we took on a major project—writing a handbook for incoming inmates, entitled *Experiences of Life: Surviving at Bedford Hills.*

For two days a week, the class became a writers' workshop. It began with the women, myself included, sharing what was on our minds the first night we arrived in prison. Then we brainstormed about what we had known, feared, and wondered about prison life in Bedford Hills before arriving here. I found writings by other prisoners about these concerns and used them as the basis for structured reading lessons. They triggered intense writing, from several sentences to several pages, until enough material was created for the book. The chapters included, "Advice for How to Survive in Prison," "Coming from Another Country," "Being Pregnant in Bedford Hills," and "Mothers and Children."

The exploration of each new issue deepened participants' sense of themselves and of shared realities. Out of the cumulative experience of feeling our commonality as prisoners and women, a trust developed that made it possible for us to explore our cultural, racial, ethnic, and linguistic differences. Literacy acquisition interacted with the exploration of cultural identity. One among many examples of this occurred when it came time to edit the handbook. We looked at the different forms of language that were found in the writings of the women in the handbook: Standard American English, informal speech, Black English, and slang. For the first time, many women heard that the Black English, which always had been corrected as "wrong," was a dialect reflecting a culture.

The class had a long discussion about what style of language to use for the handbook. Some wanted it to be in Standard American English because they felt that new women coming in should see that the ABE students knew the standards of accepted grammar. Other women wanted to leave some of the informal language or slang and Black English dialect in order to facilitate communication with the new women. A Chinese woman proposed a solution: to leave it in the style that the particular woman had written if she wanted, but to explain in the beginning of the book that the decisions about language had been a conscious, educated choice. Thus, the readers would know that the ABE students knew enough to distinguish between and to choose different types of language. This was how it was done.

Prisoners as Educators

As a prisoner teaching, I experienced a shifting of roles and identities. I was an inmate, reminded of that reality by a twenty-to-life sentence and the day-to-day experiences of being strip-searched after a visit, separated from my son, and locked down; yet, at times I felt myself to be a teacher in training, headed for an identity as an educator, occasionally asked by another inmate, "Are you a teacher or a prisoner?", until they noticed my green pants and gave me a knowing nod. In my role as educator, teachers would sometimes speak to me with respect, almost as a peer; some were genuinely excited about the work and supported my educational growth. Yet there was an ambivalence about me as an educator. One example can be seen in the words of a teacher who was familiar with the quality of the AIDS work, yet who introduced me as her "inmate clerk." At times I would be a translator, negotiating between two worlds. Then the reality of control and limits would bring everything back into focus. Although there was a shifting of roles, I found that the primary tendency of the system was to define me as prisoner. It was always a struggle to transcend the limitations of that role.

To what extent was the participatory approach tied to a prisoner being the one teaching? In the class evaluation, the women addressed this issue, responding to the Education Supervisor's question, "How was Kathy's teaching like past teachers or different from them?" The women responded, "In the past a teacher was always just a teacher, but she (Kathy) was both part of it and also a teacher."

"She was learning also. She was also like a counselor."

"Teachers never participated in learning, past teachers taught 'what to do,' not 'how to'." The Education Supervisor asked, "Could a civilian do it, not just a prisoner?" One woman said, "Yes, but they would have to be sympathetic to the group and have to pick up on the vibes. It wouldn't happen as fast, have to build rapport, that takes time." To the question, "How do you build rapport?", someone responded, "Show care, speak what you're about, you open up to us, we'll open up to you, forget that you're a civilian."

There was a strength in the peer education process, of a prisoner teaching prisoners. It allowed for a shared exploration of issues that became the basis of literacy curriculum development. Additionally, as a prisoner I shared the powerlessness felt by the students and had a deep stake in creating a participatory learning process, in which we as prisoners were ourselves making decisions, taking on problem-posing and problem-solving.

Yet the very strength of the peer education process was also its weakness in the prison context. Although most of the prison administrators with whom I dealt expressed personal enthusiasm toward the educational approach I was using, they also expressed a dilemma when the question of whether I could actually teach arose: how could they permit me real responsibility as an educator without giving me too much responsibility as a prisoner? How could such an empowering group process be initiated by prisoners without it becoming a threat to security?

Future Prospects

> The paradox of education is precisely this—that as one begins to become conscious, one begins to examine the society in which one is being educated. The purpose of education, finally, is to create in a person the ability to look at the world for oneself, to make one's own decisions, to say to oneself this is black or is white, to decide for oneself whether there is a God in heaven, or not. To ask questions of the universe, and then to learn to live with those questions, is the way one achieves one's own identity. But no society is really anxious to have that kind of person around. What societies really ideally want is a citizenry which will simply obey the rules of society. (Baldwin, 1988, p. 4)

If creating a liberating education is difficult and paradoxical within the society at large, as James Baldwin writes, then it is all the more so within a prison, an institution of authoritarian control. Yet, after a year-and-a-half of utilizing a problem-posing approach in the classroom, there was change. The experience was so positive that it moved not just inmates, but also some teachers, educational administrators, and some prison officials towards supporting more of this kind of teaching.[12] This support led me to ask: could a problem-posing approach to literacy become an ongoing part of the educational programs in the prison? Was the experience simply a

---

[12]In December 1987, Educational Supervisor Rob Hinz wrote about my teaching after the completion of the AIDS unit: "Her use of Dr. Freire's theoretical work on praxis combining thought and action in a dialectical approach to the teaching of reading to adults has had remarkable results. The women with whom she was working are technically classified as technically illiterate, yet she was able in three months time to provide classroom instruction on AIDS . . . and to, using the vehicle of a play, have these women writing and reading while at the same time boosting their self-image and confidence."

chance occurrence, or was it consonant enough with the prison goal of rehabilitation to imagine extending it to involve more classes and more inmates as peer educators?

Three education supervisors agreed to work with me on a proposal to implement a problem-posing curriculum more widely. We addressed the question: Who were the most appropriate people to do the teaching? We agreed that inmates would bring particular strengths to the process, namely that of identification with the learners. Moreover, a program using peer educators meant extending the rehabilitative process beyond the students in the literacy classes to those women with higher educational backgrounds. In this prison alone, more than one hundred women are either in college or have bachelor degrees; therefore the potential number of literacy peer educators was large, and developing teaching skills, carrying out work that required self-reliance, and contributing to the broader community was clearly within the concept of penal rehabilitation.

The final proposal involved training peer educators from among prisoners to work four hours per week in every basic education class, using a problem-posing curriculum developed in cooperation with the students. The Superintendent approved the program and productive meetings began with education administrators, teachers, and interested peer educators. Then, midway through the planning period, the prison Administration disapproved it.

Both the support and the withdrawal of support for the peer education program can only be understood as aspects of the broad contradictions among the primary prison goals of control, punishment, and deterrence, and that of rehabilitation. These conflicting goals manifest themselves in many ways, including what type of behaviors are rewarded or sanctioned, the perspective towards inmates, and different education models. How this contradiction is resolved at any moment in time depends on specific conditions. In this case, a number of conditions as diverse as personnel and social climate changed between the time of approval and disapproval: 1) The key education supervisor, who was the critical link between the teachers and our group of inmate peer educators and who supported the program, left the prison for another job; 2) The New York State financial crisis led to education cutbacks, and teachers were laid off. I knew from conversations with teachers and administrators that this increased anxiety among remaining teachers about their jobs made them more resistant to,

---

In the spring of 1988, the prison authorities gave permission for the ABE class video to be shown at an ABE conference of educators in New York City, with a presentation of the teaching methods done by Klaudia Rivera.

In the winter of 1988–1989, the Bedford Hills Correctional Facility Education Department sent a copy of the ABE class handbook to Albany as an example of an education product.

and threatened by, inmates teaching or even inmates playing an active role in their own learning; 3) There was an increasing tendency towards law and order policies and attitudes within the society with concomitant social-service cutbacks. The general political climate was more antagonistic towards prisoners, inmate initiative, and program innovation. The prison administration reacted to all these factors by canceling a program involving inmates' critical thinking and initiative.

The current education crisis facing most prisons illustrates the impact of these conflicting goals. Prison populations are swelling due to drug-related crimes—in New York State, they have grown from 35,000 to 55,000 since 1985, when crack became a driving force in crime, and prison officials estimate that 75 percent of the inmates are incarcerated for drug-related offenses (Browne, 1991). The need for basic education programs has grown with the population increase.

Conversely, the budget cutbacks in education mean elimination of classes taught by civilian teachers. The first layoffs at Bedford Hills, in January 1991, led to the elimination of the ABE class for those inmates reading at the K-3 level and also of the ESL class; the GED class has also suffered significant cutbacks. Between 1989 and 1993 the number of academic and vocational teachers was cut from 25 to 9. The crying need for educational services could be alleviated by allowing inmates to be peer educators and by using participatory methods in which learners actively work on problems they face. Yet prison authorities are reluctant to allow such a problem-posing curriculum to develop or to allow inmates to teach classes. In short, while prison administrators may talk about providing an education for rehabilitation, they rarely do what is necessary to make it happen.

These contradictory needs and goals are integral to the structure of the prison system and, as such, cannot be transcended. At the same time, however, they frame the conditions under which struggle can occur; the very existence of these contradictions offers possibilities for change.[13]

Prisons, like other societal institutions, contain cracks and openings for change—conflicting goals and policies, a diversity of people, changing historical directions. At Bedford Hills, due to a particular combination of

---

[13]An example of how the contradictory needs and goals present opportunities for change is reflected in a recent development in the New York State Department of Correctional Services. The enormous increase in the prison population has created the need for a greatly increased work force inside the prison. Looking toward inmates to partially meet this need has led to a reformulation of a philosophy about inmates: "In keeping with our new emphasis on training inmates to meet the needs of the Department and encouraging and recognizing individual inmate responsibility, it is now our intention to make even greater use of properly trained and qualified inmates. We plan to establish new job titles of 'Inmate Program Associates.' The Program Associates will work in such areas as classrooms, orientation, pre-release, libraries, and counseling" (Division of Program Services, 1991, p. 3). It is too soon to know how this new philosophy will actually manifest itself.

these variables, it became possible to create a liberating form of education that lasted for several years. This experience is now an immutable part of the educational history at Bedford Hills, a basis upon which to build.

The enormous expansion of prison populations suggests that prisons mirror and are part of a larger social crisis. This connection is reflected in the words of one New York State Department of Corrections spokesperson who said that prisons "probably give out more high school equivalency diplomas than ninety percent of the high schools in the state. Why do people have to come to prison to learn to read and write and get drug treatment?" (Browne, 1991). Human potential, which will be wasted or encouraged, is crowding into prisons. The challenge that problem-posing education raises in prison is part of a larger challenge facing the entire society: will social problems be dealt with by measures of control from above or through mobilization and education from below?

CONCLUSION

One never knows what improved literacy ability in itself will do for women in prison. One person may gain in self-esteem, while another will make practical improvements in letter writing, filling out forms, or reading to her child. For some, the ability to compete in the job market may increase, but indications are that for most it will not. For the adults with whom I work, the kinds of improvements necessary to increase job opportunities involve great effort over an extended period of time.

What if one embeds literacy acquisition in a broader education that has at its heart problem-posing, critical thinking and acting on shared problems? How might that affect people's personal growth, family relationships, jobs, and their ability to create the lives they want? Although the answer to this clearly depends on many unknowns, these are questions I have asked myself as I have thought about the struggle to build a problem-posing approach and about the women with whom I work and live.

One story in particular illustrates the complexity of this issue. When Anna was here, she participated fully in the AIDS unit, in the play, and in every successive unit during the year-and-a-half that the educational program existed. She, as much as anyone, felt empowered by the entire experience. When Anna went home, she started by getting a job in a flower shop. When the father of her children came out of prison, she made a decision to go back to him in spite of their problems with drugs, because he offered economic and emotional security. Soon afterward she became pregnant and, during her pregnancy, her husband began seeing another woman. Anna went back to drugs. She was rearrested on a parole violation and came back to Bedford Hills for eight months before going home again.

When Anna was in the play and learning to read and write, while also learning about AIDS, this approach to education seemed like the answer. There were moments when I felt that the human potential and creativity that were emerging in the classroom would allow the women to take on the world, or at least in their own lives, and remake them to fit their dreams. Then, when Anna came back and told me her story, I felt the crushing limitations of even the most positive educational experience in light of what Anna and other women face, including personal scars and the need for social and economic changes.

As educators, we are often forced to accept more limited results than we envision in our hopes and dreams. The success of a short-term literacy program, one that meets our best vision, cannot be measured by one set of tangible standards; the social forces are too complex. Thus, despite Anna's return to prison, I believe that her learning experience and that of the others in the ABE class affirms an approach to teaching literacy based on the lives and experiences of the women themselves. Anna and the others so often have spoken with great pride of what they read and wrote, of the things they learned and taught to others. The participatory approach encouraged a feeling of their own worth and capacity. Although it contains no guarantees, it does offer a powerful hope, because it involves the full potential of participants. Lucia, who is among the many who have not returned to prison, said before she left, "I never thought I would be doing this. I never even did it on the street. I never thought I would act in a play and here I am reading everything. I can go home to my kids and say, 'I've done something!' "

REFERENCES

Altwerger, B., Edelsky, C., & Flores, B. M. (1987). Whole language: What's new? *The Reading Teacher, 41,* 144–145.

Anderson, R. C. (1985). Role of the readers' schema in comprehension, learning and memory. In H. Singer & R. B. Ruddell (Eds.), *Theoretical models and processes of reading* (3rd ed., pp. 372–384). Newark, DE: I.R.A.

Baldwin, J. (1988). A talk to teachers. In R. Simonson & S. Walker (Eds.), *The Graywolf Annual Five: Multi-cultural literacy*. St. Paul, MN: Graywolf Press.

Bellorado, D. (1986). *Making literacy programs work: Vol. I. A practical guide for correctional educators* (Grant No. FZ-7). Washington, DC: U.S. Government Printing Office (Stock No. 027-000–1293-1).

Boudin, K., & Clark, J. (1991). A community of women organize themselves to cope with the AIDS crisis: A case study from Bedford Hills Correctional Facility. *Columbia Journal of Gender and Law, 1,* 47–56.

Bransford, J. D. (1985). Schema activation and schema acquisition: Comments on Richard Anderson's remarks. In H. Singer & R. B. Ruddell (Eds.), *Theoretical models and processes of reading* (3rd ed., pp. 385–397). Newark, DE: I.R.A.

Browne, A. (1991, February 10). Cuomo: Release nonviolent cons. *The Daily News,* pp. 3, 24.

Burkhart, K. W. (1976). *Women in prison*. New York: Popular Library.

Church, G. J. (1990). The view from behind bars [Special Issue: Women: The road ahead]. *Time*, pp. 20–22.

Clark, J., & Boudin, K. (1990). A community of women organize themselves to cope with the AIDS crisis: A case study from Bedford Hills Correctional Facility. *Social Justice, 17* (2).

Craig, G. M. (1981, July). The development of literacy/conscientization program for low-literate women in prison. *Dissertation Abstracts International, 42*, p. 68. *(University Microfilms No. 81-12, 793)*

Division of Program Services. (1991). *Division of Program Services action plan*. New York: New York State Department of Correctional Services.

Division of Program Services. (1992). *Female cluster program services action plan*. New York: New York State Department of Correctional Services.

Ellowitch, A. (1983). *Women and the world of work*. Philadelphia: Lutheran Settlement House Women's Program.

Fingeret, A. (1984). *Adult literacy education: Current and future directions*. Columbus: Ohio State University, National Center for Research in Vocational Education.

Freire, P. (1970). *Pedagogy of the oppressed*. New York: Seabury Press.

Freire, P. (1974). *Cultural action for freedom*. Cambridge, MA: Harvard Educational Review (Monograph Series No. 1).

Goodman, K. (1973). Psycholinguistic universals in the reading process. In F. Smith (Ed.), *Psycholinguistics and reading*. New York: Holt, Rinehart & Winston.

Goodman, K. (1985). Unity in reading. In H. Singer & R. B. Ruddell (Eds.), *Theoretical models and processes of reading* (3rd ed, pp. 813–840). Newark, DE: I.R.A.

Grossman, J. (1985). *Domestic violence and incarcerated women: Survey results* (Prepared by New York State Department of Correctional Services; administered in July 1985 to female inmate population at Bedford Hills Correctional Facility). New York: Department of Correctional Services.

Humphrey, C. (1988). *Female, new court commitments (1976–1987)*. New York: Department of Correctional Services.

Hunter, C., & Harman, D. (1979). *Adult illiteracy in the United States: A report to the Ford Foundation*. New York: McGraw Hill.

Juana. (1988). Chocolate and me. In *Surviving and thriving with AIDS: Collective wisdom* (vol. 1). New York: PWA Coalition.

Knowles, M. (1984). *Andragogy in action*. San Francisco: Jossey-Bass.

LaBerge, D., & Samuels, S. J. (1985). Towards a theory of automatic information processing in reading. In H. Singer & R. B. Ruddell (Eds.), *Theoretical models and processing of reading* (3rd ed., pp. 689–718). Newark, DE: I.R.A.

New York State Commission on Correction. (1988). *Acquired immune deficiency syndrome: A demographic profile of New York State inmate mortalities 1981–1987*. New York: Author.

Nuttall, J. H. (1983). *Reducing inmate illiteracy in New York State*. New York: Department of Correctional Services.

Nuttall, J. H. (1988). *An update of illiteracy in New York's correctional system*. New York: Department of Correctional Services.

Smith, F. (1973). *Psycholinguistics and reading*. New York: Holt, Rinehart & Winston.

Sullivan, L. E. (1990). *The prison reform movement: Forlorn hope*. Boston: Twayne.

Reflection and Inquiry

REFLECTING ON THE READINGS

1. The chapters in this unit address different populations of learners and a variety of content areas. Yet these readings share a common philosophical perspective. Identify some of the principles that link two or more of these readings.

2. Examine the extent to which any of the issues, theories, or principles presented in Unit Four (chapters 14–17) contributes to your understanding of the issues, theories, or principles presented in Unit Three (chapters 10–13). For example, you might select a description of a particular classroom and discuss the ways in which it illustrates one or more of the theories discussed in chapters 10–13.

3. Consider how the practices described in a given reading in this unit can be applied to a different population. For example, how can Lindfors' suggestions for the teaching of children (chapter 14) be adapted for the teaching of adolescents or adults? What might be inappropriate for adolescents or adults?

4. Lindfors claims that "what is good for the first-language learner is good for the second" (chapter 14). Do you agree with this perspective? If so, how does it resonate with your own experiences as a student and/or teacher? If not, how does you own experience refute or challenge this view?

5. Boudin recounts her history as a graduate student, community organizer, and teacher and describes the kinds of changes she tried to imple-

ment in prison (chapter 17). What did you find compelling, surprising, or intriguing about her attempts to implement "an alternate vision"? Could you identify with the challenges and tensions she faced? To what extent do you agree with Boudin that the pedagogical and social issues she raises "have many implications that extend beyond the prison bars"? Can you provide any specific examples of how these implications might be played out in a classroom in which you are a student, teacher or observer?

6. Have you ever been a student, teacher, or observer in a language classroom in which language was not an end in itself but rather a means to learn about a particular content area? Drawing on the readings in Units Three and Four, discuss the extent to which the study of this subject matter promoted language acquisition. How could you determine that this was the case?

7. Imagine that you are attending an in-service professional day on engaging learners in purposeful and relevant language activities. After the presentation, a colleague turns to you and shares her conviction that students need classes that focus on grammar instruction if students are to succeed academically. Drawing on the readings in Units Three and Four, you respond. Write the dialogue that ensues between you and your colleague.

8. Imagine that you have been hired to teach writing in a program where everyone is obligated to use a textbook that focuses on grammar-based language work. Drawing on the readings in Units Three and Four, how might you add to and adapt this work so that it engages learners in meaningful language activities?

9. Select a text that you might want to teach some day. This could be a written text, a photo, a movie, a poem, in short, any text that can be "read." Drawing on the readings in this unit, what kinds of activities could you plan in order to help students engage with this text? How could the reading of this text be connected to or extended by activities that involve speaking and/or writing? What other text(s) could you use to relate to and build on the first text?

10. Select a passage (one sentence or several sentences) from one of the readings in Unit Four that struck you in some way. For example, it may be a passage that resonates with your own experience, that reminds of you something else you've read or seen, or that makes an important point. Highlight or copy the passage and then reflect on why you chose it.

READING FOR FURTHER REFLECTION

1. Read the following poem, "English as a Second Language," by Lisel Mueller and write a response. What strikes or moves you? What relationship do you see between the poem and your ongoing understanding of teaching and learning?

- If you have written an earlier response to this poem (in Unit One), compare your two responses. What does this process teach you about the nature of reading? What implications do you see for the teaching of reading?
- If possible, share your (two) response(s) with other students. What does this process teach you about the nature of reading? What implications do you see for the teaching of reading?

ENGLISH AS A SECOND LANGUAGE
Lisel Mueller

The underpaid young teacher
prints the letters *t, r, e, e*
on the blackboard and imagines
forests and gardens spring up
in the tired heads of her students.

But they see only four letters:
a vertical beam weighed down
by a crushing crossbar
followed by a hook,
and after the hook, two squiggles,
arcane identical twins
which could be spying eyes
or ready fists, could be handles,
could be curled seedlings, could take root,
could develop leaves.

2. Read the following excerpt from "The Importance of the Act of Reading" by Paolo Freire. How do Freire's recollected experiences as a student and teacher extend your understanding of teaching language and literacy?

I would like to go back to a time when I was a secondary school student. There I gained experience in the critical interpretation of text I read in class with the Portuguese teacher's help, which I remember to this day. Those moments do not consist of mere exercises, aimed at our simply becoming aware of the existence of the page in front of us, to be scanned, mechanically and monotonously spelled out, instead of truly read. Those moments were not *reading lessons* in the traditional sense, but rather moments in which texts, including that of the young teacher Jose Pessoa, were offered to us in our restless searching.

Sometime afterward. . . . I experienced intensely the importance of the act of reading and writing—basically inseparable—with first-year high school students. I never reduced syntactical rules to diagrams for students to swallow, even rules governing prepositions after specific verbs, agreement of gender and number, contractions. On the contrary, all this was proposed to the students' curiosity in a dynamic and living way, as objects to be discovered within the body of text, whether the students' own or those of established writers, and not as something stagnant whose outline I described. The students did not have to memorize the description mechanically, but rather learned its underlying significance. Only by learning the significance could they know how to memorize it, fix it. Mechanically memorizing the description of an object does not constitute knowing the subject.

3. Read the following excerpt from Esmeralda Santiago's *When I Was Puerto Rican* in which she describes a classroom in Puerto Rico. What strikes you? Does it remind you of any of your own school experiences? You might want to contrast this piece with the piece by Julia Alvarez in Unit Three, Reading for Further Reflection.

"Today," Sra. Leona said, "we will write a composition using the words you were assigned."

She wrote the words on the blackboard. Someone asked if we were supposed to use all ten words, and she laughed and said that would be impossible.

"Use as many as you can, but not less than five."

It was a stupid assignment. I hated her.

I wrote the words at the top of the page. Sra. Leona walked up and down the aisles between our seats, and stopped and hovered over me.

"Esmeralda, try to form those letters better. I always have trouble reading your handwriting."

The point on my pencil broke. She looked at me though her thick glasses, and I wished I were bigger and could punch her.

"Go sharpen your pencil."

She treated me like I had a disease. If I died and never came back to school, she'd probably be happy. But not for long. I'd come back to haunt her. I'd fill her inkwell with glue. I'd put hot peppers in her face cream. I'd curl a snake under her pillow.

I sat down to write the stupid composition using her ten stupid words. I would use all of them, just because she thought I couldn't. *Incandescent* and *Carmelize* must go together somehow. *Bannister* and *Delimitation. Boundary.* "A Cartographer draws the Delimitation of Boundaries in maps." There, I'd even given her a word bigger than the assigned ones. What else could I say about cartographers? I had to think.

The door of the classroom was open. Across the hall, someone recited a poem I knew by heart.

"Esmeralda, is there something in the hall you'd like to share with us?"

Kids laughed. Sra. Leona hated it when my mind went elsewhere than her classroom.

"I was just thinking, Sra. Leona."

She curled her lip.

"Well. This is not time for daydreaming. You're supposed to be writing, not thinking."

4. Read the following excerpt from Mike Roses' *Lives on the Boundary*. What strikes you? What does the text reveal about the nature of language acquisition, about writing, and about promoting learning?

> Over Chin's bent head arches a trellis packed tight with dried honeysuckle and chrysanthemum, sea moss, mushrooms, and ginseng. His elbow rests on the cash register—quiet now that the customers have left. He shifts on the stool, concentrating on the writing before him: "A young children," he scribbles, and pauses. "Young children," that doesn't sound good, he thinks. He crosses out "children" and sits back. A few seconds pass. He can't think of the right way to say it, so he writes "children" again and continues: "a young children with his grandma smail . . ." "Smail." He pulls a Chinese-English dictionary from under the counter.
>
> In front of the counter and extending down the aisle are boxes of dried fish: shark fins, mackerel, pollock. They give off a musky smell. . . . Chin has found his word: It's not *smail*, it's *smile*. "A young children with his grandma smile . . ." He reaches in the pocket of his jeans jacket, pulls out a piece of paper, and unfolds it. There's a word copied on it he has been wanting to use. A little bell over the door jingles. An old man comes in, and Chin moves his yellow pad aside.
>
> Chin remembers his teacher in elementary school telling him that his writing was poor, that he didn't know many words. He went to middle school for a few years but quit before completing it. Very basic English—the ABCs and simple vocabulary—was, at one point, part of his curriculum, but he lived in a little farming community, so he figured he would never use it. He did, though, pick up some letters and a few words. He immigrated to America when he was seventeen, and for the two years since has been living with his uncle in Chinatown. His uncle signed him up for English classes at the community center. He didn't like them. He did, however, start hanging out in the recreation room, playing pool and watching TV. The English on TV intrigued him. And it was then that he turned to writing. He would "try to learn to speak something" by writing it down. That was about six months ago. Now he's enrolled in a community college literacy program and has been making strong progress. He is especially taken with one tutor. . . . who encourages him to write. So he writes for her. He writes stories about his childhood in China. He sneaks time when no one is in the store or when customers are poking around, writing because he likes to bring her things, writing, too, because "sometime I think writing make my English better."
>
> The old man puts on the counter a box of tea guaranteed to help you stop smoking. Chin rings it up and thanks him. The door jingles and Chin returns to his writing, copying the word from his folded piece of paper, a word he found in *People* magazine: "A young children with his grandma smile *gleefully*."

SUGGESTED PROJECTS FOR INQUIRY

Select a project that you would like to pursue.

1. Examine several textbooks designed for teaching English to speakers of other languages.

- What kinds of activities and assignments are included? What are the purposes of these activities and assignments?
- Are there ideas that you might like to incorporate or adapt for your own teaching? Which ones? Why?
- How might you adapt a particular chapter to make it more meaningful? What activities or assignments would you plan in order to enrich the work?
- What theories or assumptions seem to inform these textbooks? Characterize each textbook in light of the theories and principles presented in Units Three and Four.

2. Search the internet for websites on ESOL pedagogy. You may want to limit your search to a particular level (e.g., beginning ESL) or population (e.g., adult ESL) or competency (e.g., reading).

- What kinds of activities and assignments are included? What are the purposes of these activities and assignments?
- Are there ideas that you might like to incorporate or adapt for your own teaching? Which ones? Why?
- How might you adapt a particular activity to make it more meaningful? What activities or assignments would you plan in order to enrich the work?
- What theories or assumptions seem to inform these sites? Characterize the site(s) in light of the theories and principles presented in Units Three and Four.

3. Develop a thematically-based sequence of work for engaging a particular population of students in meaningful language and literacy activities.

- Consider what kind of theme would be of interest and/or relevance to these students. Plan to integrate speaking, listening, reading, and writing so that they contribute to and build on one another. Draw on a range of source material (e.g., essays, poems, "real objects," movies, photos, musical lyrics) to enact this process.
- If possible, implement this project in a classroom and observe its impact on students and their learning. To what extent did your plan "work"? How do you account for this? If you were to do this project again, what would you keep, add, or change?

4. Observe a classroom or continue in your ongoing observations of a classroom. Determine the extent to which the teacher enacts a curriculum that attempts to keep language meaningful. What do the activities and assignments reveal about the purpose of the work in this classroom? To what extent do the activities and assignments contribute to and build on one another? What do you note about the students' reactions to the work they are asked to undertake? What does the teacher use as a basis for evaluating the students' learning?

5. Observe a classroom or continue your ongoing observations of a classroom, focusing on classroom verbal interactions. To what extent do the teacher's questions engage students? What kinds of contributions are students expected to make? In what ways does the teacher extend or build on the students' contributions? How do the conditions for learning in this classroom promote interactions among students?

6. Through interviews or in writing, ask a number of individuals to share their experiences with learning a language in a classroom context. What kinds of work do they recollect being asked to do? What seems to have promoted their learning? What did these individuals find problematic? Are there any patterns across these individuals' experiences? To what extent do these recollected experiences illustrate the importance of keeping language meaningful?

Unit V

QUESTIONING ASSUMPTIONS ABOUT LANGUAGE AND IDENTITY

BEFORE READING

Respond to one or more of the following:

- What does the term *standard English* mean to you? How did you come to this understanding?
- What does the term *native speaker* mean to you? How did you come to this understanding?
- If you use more than one language, think about your relationship with each language. Reflect on one or more of the following questions: Are there specific attitudes, behaviors, abilities, or circumstances associated with each language? Do you think that each of your languages is linked to a particular identity? To what extent does one language contribute to or interfere with the other language?

Chapter 18

The Ownership of English

H. G. Widdowson

The following is the text of a plenary address delivered in April, 1993, in Atlanta at the 27th Annual TESOL Convention. The oral character of the presentation has been preserved.

Given the theme of this convention, Designing Our World, and at a time when territorial disputes and matters of ownership and identity are so prominent in the affairs of the world in general, this is perhaps an appropriate occasion to raise the question of how we stake out our own territory as English teachers in delimiting and designing our world. And to ask who does the designing and on what authority.

To start with, who determines the demarcation of the subject itself? We are teaching English and the general assumption is that our purpose is to develop in students a proficiency which approximates as closely as possible to that of native speakers. But who are these native speakers?

One answer might be: the English. And why not? A modest proposal surely. England is where the language originated and this is where the English (for the most part) live. The language and the people are bound together by both morphology and history. So they can legitimately lay claim to this linguistic territory. It belongs to them. And they are the custodians. If you want real or proper English, this is where it is to be found, preserved, and listed like a property of the National Trust.

Of course English, of a kind, is found elsewhere as well, still spreading, a luxuriant growth from imperial seed. Seeded among other people but not ceded to them. At least not completely. For the English still cling tenaciously to their property and try to protect it from abuse. Let us acknowledge (let us concede) that there are other kinds of English, offshoots and outgrowths, but they are not real or proper English, not the genuine article.

As an analogy, consider a certain kind of beverage. There are all kinds of cola, but only one which is the real thing. Or, further afield, an analogy, from the French. They have, until just recently, successfully denied others the right to use the appellation *Champagne* for any wine that does not come from the region of that name where Dom Perignon first invented it. There may be all kinds of derivative versions elsewhere, excellent no doubt in their way, but they are not real or proper Champagne, even though loose talk may refer to them as such. Similarly, there is real English, Anglais real, Royal English, Queen's English, or (for those unsympathetic to the monarchy) Oxford English. The vintage language.

I do not imagine that such a view would gain much support in present company. The response is more likely to be outrage. You cannot be serious. Well, not entirely, it is true. As I have expressed it, in somewhat extravagant terms, this position is one which very few people would associate themselves with. It is reactionary, arrogant, totally unacceptable. And the argument is patently absurd. Perhaps as I have expressed it. But then why is it absurd? The particular associations of England, Queen and country, and Colonel Blimp which I have invoked to demonstrate the argument also in some respects disguise it. If we now remove the position from these associations and strip the argument down to its essential tenets, is it so readily dismissed? Is it indeed so uncommon after all? I want to suggest that the ideas and attitudes which I have just presented in burlesque are still very much with us in a different and less obvious guise.

To return briefly to Champagne. One argument frequently advanced for being protective of its good name has to do with quality assurance. The label is a guarantee of quality. If any Tom, Jane, or Harry producing fizzy wine is free to use it, there can be no quality control. Recently an English firm won a court case enabling it to put the name Champagne on bottles containing a nonalcoholic beverage made from elderflowers. Elderflowers! The Champagne lobby was outraged. Here, they said, was the thin end of the wedge. Before long the label would be appearing on bottles all over the place containing concoctions of all kinds calling themselves Champagne, and so laying claim to its quality. The appellation would not be *controllée*. Standards were at stake. The same point can be made, is made, about the local Georgian beverage. There can only be one. This is it. Be wary of variant products of lower quality.

And the same point is frequently made about English. In this case, you cannot, of course, preserve exclusive use of the name and indeed it would work against your interests to do so, but you can seek to preserve standards by implying that there is an exclusive quality in your own brand of English, aptly called standard English. What is this quality, then? What are these standards?

The usual answer is: quality of clear communication and standards of intelligibility. With standard English, it is argued, these are assured. If the language disperses into different forms, a myriad of Englishes, then it ceases to serve as a means of international communication; in which case the point of learning it largely disappears. As the language spreads, there are bound to be changes out on the periphery; so much can be conceded. But these changes must be seen not only as peripheral but as radial also and traceable back to the stable centre of the standard. If this centre does not hold, things fall apart, mere anarchy is loosed upon the world. Back to Babel.

In itself, this argument sounds plausible and it is difficult to refute. But for all that, there is something about it which is suspect. Let us replay it again. Standard English promotes the cause of international communication, so we must maintain the central stability of the standard as the common linguistic frame of reference.

To begin with, who are we? Obviously the promoters of standard English must themselves have standard English at their disposal. But to maintain it is another matter. This presupposes authority. And this authority is claimed by those who possess the language by primogeniture and due of birth, as Shakespeare puts it. In other words, the native speakers. They do not have to be English, of course, that would be too restrictive a condition, and one it would (to say the least) be tactless to propose especially in present company, but they have to be to the language born. Not all native speakers, you understand. In fact, come to think of it, not most native speakers, for the majority of those who are to the language born speak nonstandard English and have themselves to be instructed in the standard at school. We cannot have any Tom, Jane, and Harry claiming authority, for Tom, Jane, and Harry are likely to be speakers of some dialect or other. So the authority to maintain the standard language is not consequent on a natural native-speaker endowment. It is claimed by a minority of people who have the power to impose it. The custodians of standard English are self-elected members of a rather exclusive club.

Now it is important to be clear that in saying this I am not arguing against standard English. You can accept the argument for language maintenance, as indeed I do, without accepting the authority that claims the right to maintain it. It is, I think, very generally assumed that a particular subset of educated native speakers in England, or New England, or wherever, have the natural entitlement to custody of the language, that the preservation of its integrity is in their hands: their right and their responsibility. It is this which I wish to question. Not in any spirit of radical rebellion against authority as such but because I think such questioning raises a number of crucial issues about the learning and teaching of the language.

Consideration of who the custodians are leads logically on to a consideration of what it is exactly that is in their custody. What is standard English? The usual way of defining it is in reference to its grammar and lexis: It is a variety, a kind of superposed dialect which is socially sanctioned for institutional use and therefore particularly well suited to written communication. In its spoken form it can be manifested by any accent. So it is generally conceded that standard English has no distinctive phonology. The same concession is not, however, extended to its graphology. On the contrary, it is deviant spelling which, in Britain at least, is most frequently singled out for condemnation. There is something of a contradiction here. If standard English is defined as a distinctive grammatical and lexical system which can be substantially realized in different ways, then what does spelling have to do with it? It is true that some spelling has a grammatical function (like the *'s* which distinguishes the possessive from the plural) but most of it does not. If you are going to ignore phonological variation, then, to be consistent, you should surely ignore graphological variation as well and overlook variations in spelling as a kind of written accent.

The reason it is not overlooked, I think, is that standard English, unlike other dialects, is essentially a written variety and mainly designed for institutional purposes (education, administration, business, etc.). Its spoken version is secondary, and typically used by those who control these institutions. This means that although it may not matter how it is spoken, it emphatically does matter how it is written. Furthermore, because writing, as a more durable medium, is used to express and establish institutional values, deviations from orthographic conventions undermine in some degree the institutions which they serve. They can be seen as evidence of social instability: a sign of things beginning to fall apart. So it is not surprising that those who have a vested interest in maintaining these institutions should be so vexed by bad spelling. It is not that it greatly interferes with communication: It is usually not difficult to identify words through their unorthodox appearance. What seems to be more crucial is that good spelling represents conformity to convention and so serves to maintain institutional stability.

Similar points can be made about grammatical features. Because language has built-in redundancy, grammatical conformity is actually not particularly crucial for many kinds of communicative transaction. What we generally do in the interpretative process is actually to edit grammar out of the text, referring lexis directly to context, using lexical items as indexical clues to meaning. We edit grammar back in when we need it for fine tuning. If the reason for insisting on standard English is because it guarantees effective communication, then the emphasis should logically be on vocabulary rather than grammar. But the champions of standard English do not see it in this way: On the contrary, they focus attention on grammatical abuse. Why should this be so? There are, I think, two reasons.

Firstly, it is precisely because grammar is so often redundant in communicative transactions that it takes on another significance, namely that of expressing social identity. The mastery of a particular grammatical system, especially perhaps those features which are redundant, marks you as a member of the community which has developed that system for its own social purposes. Conversely, of course, those who are unable to master the system are excluded from the community. They do not belong. In short, grammar is a sort of shibboleth.

So when the custodians of standard English complain about the ungrammatical language of the populace, they are in effect indicating that the perpetrators are outsiders, nonmembers of the community. The only way they can become members, and so benefit from the privileges of membership, is to learn standard English, and these privileges include, of course, access to the institutions which the community controls. Standard English is an entry condition and the custodians of it the gatekeepers. You can, of course, persist in your nonstandard ways if you choose, but then do not be surprised to find yourself marginalized, perpetually kept out on the periphery. What you say will be less readily attended to, assigned less importance, if it is not expressed in the grammatically approved manner. And if you express yourself in writing which is both ungrammatical and badly spelled, you are not likely to be taken very seriously.

Standard English, then, is not simply a means of communication but the symbolic possession of a particular community, expressive of its identity, its conventions, and values. As such it needs to be carefully preserved, for to undermine standard English is to undermine what it stands for: the security of this community and its institutions. Thus, it tends to be the communal rather than the communicative features of standard English that are most jealously protected: its grammar and spelling.

I do not wish to imply that this communal function is to be deplored. Languages of every variety have this dual character: They provide the means for communication and at the same time express a sense of community, represent the stability of its conventions and values, in short its culture. All communities possess and protect their languages. The question is which community, and which culture, have a rightful claim to ownership of standard English? For standard English is no longer the preserve of a group of people living in an offshore European island, or even of larger groups living in continents elsewhere. It is an international language. As such it serves a whole range of different communities and their institutional purposes and these transcend traditional communal and cultural boundaries. I am referring to the business community, for example, and the community of researchers and scholars in science and technology and other disciplines. Standard English, especially in its written form, is their language. It provides for effective communication, but at the same time it establishes the status and stability of the institutional conventions which define these international activities. These activities develop their own conventions of thought and procedure, customs and codes of practice; in short, they in effect create their own cultures, their own standards. And obviously for the maintenance of standards it is helpful, to say the least, to have a standard language at your disposal. But you do not need native speakers to tell you what it is.

And indeed in one crucial respect, the native speaker is irrelevant. What I have in mind here is vocabulary. I said earlier that the custodians of standard English tend to emphasize its grammatical rather than its lexical features. I have suggested that one reason for this is that grammar is symbolic of communal solidarity. "Ungrammatical" expressions mark people as nonmembers. What you then do is to coax or coerce them somehow into conformity if you want to make them members (generally through education) or make them powerless on the periphery if you don't. So much for grammar. What then of lexis.

It is said that standard English is a variety, a kind of dialect, in that it is defined by its lexis and grammar. In fact, when you come to look for it, standard lexis is very elusive. It is my belief that it does not actually exist. And on reflection it is hard to see how it could exist. To begin with, the notion of standard implies stability, a relatively fixed point of reference. So if I invent a word, for example, it is not, by definition, standard. But people are inventing words all the time to express new ideas and attitudes, to adjust to their changing world. It is this indeed which demonstrates the essential dynamism of the language without which it would wither away. So it is that different groups of users will develop specialist vocabularies, suited to their needs but incomprehensible to others. When I look at my daily newspaper, I find innumerable words from the terminology of technology, law, financial affairs, and so on which I simply do not understand. They may claim to be English, but they are Greek to me. Are they standard English? One way of deciding might be to consult a standard reference work, namely a learners' dictionary. But most of these words of restricted technical use do not appear. This is because, reasonably enough, the dictionary only contains words of wide range and common occurrence. If this is the way standard is to be defined, then these words of restricted use do not count by definition. Yet they are real enough, and indeed can be said to represent the reality of English as an international language. For the reason why English is international is because its vocabulary has diversified to serve a range of institutional uses.

As I indicated earlier, the custodians of standard English express the fear that if there is diversity, things will fall apart and the language will divide up into mutually unintelligible varieties. But things in a sense have already fallen apart. The varieties of English used for international communication in science, finance, commerce, and so on are mutually unintelligible. As far as lexis is concerned, their communicative viability depends on the development of separate standards, and this means that their communication is largely closed off from the world outside.

The point then is that if English is to retain its vitality and its capability for continual adjustment, it cannot be confined within a standard lexis. And this seems to be implicitly accepted as far as particular domains of use are concerned. Nobody, I think, says that the abstruse terms used by physicists or stockbrokers are nonstandard English. It is generally accepted that communities or secondary cultures which are defined by shared professional concerns should be granted rights of ownership and allowed to fashion the language to meet their needs, their specific purposes indeed. And these purposes, we should note again, are twofold: They are communicative in that they meet the needs of in-group transactions, and they are communal in that they define the identity of the group itself.

The same tolerance is not extended so readily to primary cultures and communities, where the language is used in the conduct of everyday social life. Lexical innovation here, equally motivated by communicative and communal requirement, is generally dismissed as deviant or dialectal. Take, for example, the two words *depone* and *prepone*. The first is a technical legal term and therefore highly respectable. The second *prepone* is not. It is an Indian English word of very general currency, coined to contrast with *postpone*. To postpone an event means to put it back, to prepone an event is to bring it forward. The coinage exploits the morphology of English in an entirely regular way. It is apt. But it is also quaint. An odd Indian excrescence: obviously nonstandard. And yet there is clearly nothing deviant in the derivational process itself, and indeed we can see it at work in the formation of the related words *predate* and *postdate*. But these are sanctioned as entirely ordinary, proper, standard English words. What, then, is the difference? The difference lies in the origin of the word. *Prepone* is coined by a nonnative-speaking community, so it is not really a proper English word. It is not pukka. And of course the word *pukka* is itself only pukka because the British adopted it.

Where are we then? When we consider the question of standard English what we find, in effect, is double standards. The very idea of a standard implies stability, and this can only be fixed in reference to the past. But language is of its nature unstable. It is essentially protean in nature, adapting its shape to suit changing circumstances. It would otherwise lose its vitality and its communicative and communal value. This is generally acknowledged in the case of specialist domains of use but is not acknowledged in the case of everyday social uses of the language. So it is that a word like *depone* is approved and a word like *prepone* is not.

But the basic principle of dynamic adaptation is the same in both cases. And in both cases the users of the language exploit its protean potential and fashion it to their need, thereby demonstrating a high degree of linguistic capability. In both cases the innovation indicates that the language has been learned, not just as a set of fixed conventions to conform to, but as an adaptable resource for making meaning. And making meaning which you can call your own. This, surely, is a crucial condition. You are proficient in a language to the extent that you possess it, make it your own, bend it to your will, assert yourself through it rather than simply submit to the dictates of its form. It is a familiar experience to find oneself saying things in a foreign language because you can say them rather than because they express what you want to say. You feel you are going through the motions, and somebody else's motions at that. You are speaking the language but not speaking your mind. Real proficiency is when you are able to take possession of the language, turn it to your advantage, and make it real for you. This is what mastery means. So in a way, proficiency only comes with nonconformity, when you can take the initiative and strike out on your own. Consider these remarks of the Nigerian writer, Chinua Achebe (1975):

> I feel that the English language will be able to carry the weight of my African experience. . . . But it will have to be a new English, still in communion with its ancestral home but altered to suit its new African surroundings. (p. 62)

Achebe is a novelist, and he is talking here about creative writing. But what he says clearly has wider relevance and applies to varieties of English in this country and elsewhere. The point is that all uses of language are creative in the sense that they draw on linguistic resources to express different perceptions of reality. English is called upon to carry the weight of all kinds of experience, much of it very remote indeed from its ancestral home. The new English which Achebe refers to is locally developed, and although it must necessarily be related to, and so in communion with, its ancestral origins in the past, it owes no allegiance to any descendants of this ancestry in the present.

And this point applies to all other new Englishes which have been created to carry the weight of different experience in different surroundings, whether they are related to specialist domains of use or to the contexts of everyday life. They are all examples of the entirely normal and necessary process of adaptation, a process which obviously depends on nonconformity to existing conventions or standards. For these have been established elsewhere by other people as appropriate to quite different circumstances.

The fact that these people can claim direct descent from the founding fathers has nothing to do with it. How English develops in the world is no business whatever of native speakers in England, the United States, or anywhere else. They have no say in the matter, no right to intervene or pass judgement. They are irrelevant. The very fact that English is an international language means that no nation can have custody over it. To grant such custody of the language, is necessarily to arrest its development and so undermine its international status. It is a matter of considerable pride and satisfaction for native speakers of English that their language is an international means of communication. But the point is that it is only international to the extent that it is not their language. It is not a possession which they lease out to others, while still retaining the freehold. Other people actually own it.

As soon as you accept that English serves the communicative and communal needs of different communities, it follows logically that it must be diverse. An international language has to be an independent language. It does not follow logically, however, that the language will disperse into mutually unintelligible varieties. For it will naturally stabilize into standard form to the extent required to meet the needs of the communities concerned. Thus it is clearly vital to the interests of the international community of, for example, scientists or business people, whatever their primary language, that they should preserve a common standard of English in order to keep up standards of communicative effectiveness. English could not otherwise serve their purposes. It needs no native speaker to tell them that. Furthermore, this natural tendency towards standardization will be reinforced by the extending of networks of interaction through developments in telecommunications and information technology. For there is little point in opening up such amazing new transmission systems if what you transmit makes no sense at the other end. The availability of these new channels calls for the maintenance of a common code. And these are therefore likely to have greater influence on stabilizing the language than the pronouncements of native speakers.

The essential point is that a standard English, like other varieties of language, develops endo-normatively, by a continuing process of self-regulation, as appropriate to different conditions of use. It is not fixed by exo-normative fiat from outside: not fixed, therefore, by native speakers. They have no special say in the matter, in spite of their claims to ownership of real English as associated with their own particular cultural contexts of use.

And yet there is no doubt that native speakers of English are deferred to in our profession. What they say is invested with both authenticity and authority. The two are closely related, and a consideration of their relationship brings us to certain central issues in language pedagogy. An example follows.

Over recent years, we have heard persuasive voices insisting that the English presented in the classroom should be authentic, naturally occurring language, not produced for instructional purposes. Generally, what this means, of course, is language naturally occurring as communication in native-speaker contexts of use, or rather those selected contexts where standard English is the norm: real newspaper reports, for example, real magazine articles, real advertisements, cooking recipes, horoscopes, and what have you. Now the obvious point about this naturally occurring language is that, inevitably, it is recipient designed and so culturally loaded. It follows that access to its meaning is limited to those insiders who share its cultural presuppositions and a sense of its idiomatic nuance. Those who do not, the outsiders, cannot ratify its authenticity. In other words, the language is only authentic in the original conditions of its use, it cannot be in the classroom. The authenticity is nontransferable. And to the extent that students cannot therefore engage with the language, they cannot make it their own. It may be real language, but it is not real to them. It does not relate to their world but to a remote one they have to find out about by consulting a dictionary of culture. It may be that eventually students will wish to acquire the cultural knowledge and the idiomatic fluency which enable them to engage authentically with the language use of a particular native-speaking community by adopting their identity in some degree, but there seems no sensible reason for insisting on them trying to do this in the process of language learning. On the contrary, it would seem that language for learning does need to be specially designed for pedagogic purposes so that it can be made real in the context of the students' own world.

The importance of getting students engaged with the language, cognitively, affectively, personally, is widely accepted as established wisdom. Let the learners be autonomous (at least up to a point), allow them to make the language their own, let them identify with it, let not the teacher impose authority upon them in the form of an alien pattern of behaviour. Very well. But this injunction is totally at variance with the insistence on authentic language, which is an imposition of another authority, namely that of native-speaker patterns of cultural behaviour. If natural language learning depends on asserting some ownership over the language, this cannot be promoted by means of language which is authentic only because it belongs to somebody else and expresses somebody else's identity. A pedagogy which combines authenticity of use with autonomy of learning is a contradiction. You cannot have it both ways.

The notion of authenticity, then, privileges native-speaker use (inappropriately, I have argued) as the proper language for learning. But it also, of course, privileges the native-speaker teachers of the language. For they, of course, have acquired the language and culture as an integrated experience and have a feel for its nuances and idiomatic identity which the nonnative speaker cannot claim to have. Indeed, native speakers alone can be the arbiters of what is authentic since authenticity can only be determined by insiders. So if you give authenticity primacy as a pedagogic principle, you inevitably grant privileged status to native-speaker teachers, and you defer to them not only in respect to competence in the language but also in respect to competence in language teaching. They become the custodians and arbiters not only of proper English but of proper pedagogy as well.

But what if you shift the emphasis away from contexts of use to contexts of learning, and consider how the language is to be specially designed to engage the student's reality and activate the learning process? The special advantage of native-speaker teachers disappears. Now, on the contrary, it is nonnative-speaker teachers who come into their own. For the context of learning, contrived within the classroom setting, has to be informed in some degree by the attitudes, beliefs, values and so on of the students' cultural world. And in respect to this world, of course, it is the native-speaker teacher who is the outsider. To the extent that the design of instruction depends on a familiarity with the student reality which English is to engage with, or on the particular sociocultural situations in which teaching and learning take place, then nonnative teachers have a clear and, indeed, decisive advantage.

In short, the native-speaker teacher is in a better position to know what is appropriate in contexts of language use, and so to define possible target objectives. Granted. But it is the nonnative-speaker teacher who is in a better position to know what is appropriate in the contexts of language learning which need to be set up to achieve such objectives. And that, generally speaking, is not granted. Instead what we find is that native-speaker expertise is assumed to extend to the teaching of the language. They not only have a patent on proper English, but on proper ways of teaching it as well.

So it is that the approaches to pedagogy which are generally promoted as proper are those which are appropriate to contexts of instruction in which native-speaker teachers operate. And their prestige, of course, exerts a powerful influence so that teachers in other contexts are persuaded to conform and to believe that if the approaches do not fit, it is their fault.

So it is that native speakers write textbooks and teachers' books, make pronouncements and recommendations, and bring to remote and hitherto benighted places the good news about real English and good teaching to lighten their darkness. Real English: their English. Good teaching: their teaching. But both are contextually limited by cultural factors. Their English is that which is associated with the communicative and communal needs of their community, and these may have little relevance for those learning English as an international language.

And their teaching is suited to particular contexts of instruction which in many respects are quite different from those which obtain in the world at large. Consider, for example, a language school in England, with English as the ambient language outside the classroom, the students well off and well motivated, but quite different in linguistic and cultural background both from each other, and from the teacher. In such a context it is, of course, necessary to focus on what can be established as a common denominator. Everybody is here in England, for example, and everybody is human. And so you devise an approach to teaching which combines authenticity with an appeal to universal natural learning and humanistic response. This is an example of appropriate pedagogy: Such an approach is necessary and of course it works in these local conditions. Highly commendable. But it is exclusive in that it excludes possibilities which might be particularly appropriate elsewhere—translation, for example. The problem is when an absolute virtue is made of local necessity by claims of global validity, when it is assumed that if the approach works here it ought to work, or be made to work, everywhere else. This is a denial of diversity.

For of course there is no reason why it should work elsewhere where quite different conditions obtain. It is difficult to resist the conclusion that such an approach, which makes a virtue of necessity, is only privileged because of the authority vested in the teachers by virtue of their native-speaker status. This is not to say that it may not offer ideas worth pondering, but then these ideas have to be analysed out of the approach and their relevance evaluated in reference to other contexts. You should not assume, with bland arrogance, that your way of teaching English, or your way of using English, carries a general guarantee of quality. To put the point briefly: English and English teaching are proper to the extent that they are appropriate, not to the extent that they are appropriated.

TESOL has recently made public its opposition to discrimination against the nonnative teacher, as a matter of sociopolitical principle. This is obviously to be welcomed. But if it is to be more than a token gesture, such a move needs to be supported by an enquiry into the nature of the subject we are teaching, what constitutes an appropriate approach, what kinds of competence is required of teachers—in other words an enquiry into matters of pedagogic principle which bring sociopolitical concerns and professional standards into alignment. In this convention we are concerned with designing our world. Our world. Possessive. Who are we then? What is this world we own? TESOL has designs upon us. Us. I think we need to be cautious about the designs we have on other people's worlds when we are busy designing our own.

REFERENCES

Achebe, C. (1975). The African writer and the English language. In *Morning yet on creation day*. London: Heinemann.

Chapter 19

Language Identity and Language Ownership: Linguistic Conflicts of First-Year University Writing Students

Yuet-Sim D. Chiang
Mary Schmida

> *How can I give myself an American identity if I cannot even feel connected to the American language itself? By saying connected, I mean the feeling of owning the language and, therefore having full authority over it. It does not matter how frequently I use English, somehow I can never feel that I own it.*
>
> —Hai Nguyen

> *I am a native speaker of English because English is the language I know best.*
>
> —Peter Mack

> *I communicated with my sisters at home only through English in the midst of mom yelling, "Speak Korean! Aren't you Korean?"*
>
> —Jane Kim

> *Now, the only time I speak Vietnamese is to my parents. Unfortunately, I don't talk to them much, only when necessary; it's not very often that I speak their native tongue. I speak English fluently now and this is the reason why I don't talk to my parents very often.*
>
> —Christine Nguyen

Recently, a body of research has emerged that views language and literacy acquisition from a broad-based sociocultural perspective; a perspective that seeks to explain success or failure of learning from within a social and political context in which the language learning occurs (Lantolf, 1996;

Peirce, 1995; Rampton, 1995; Siegal, 1996). It is within this theoretical framework that we align ourselves.

Our study is somewhat different than those conducted by researchers before us, however, in that this study deals *not* with immigrant populations learning the language of the dominant society, but with U.S. born children of immigrant parents who must define and negotiate the boundaries of language and identity.

Despite this new trend in considering the construction of identity in language and literacy acquisition, however, there is still a shortage of research-based studies that specifically examine the conflicting constructions of English literacy, language identity, and native language loss among speakers of non-English language background (NELB). The lack of study is not coincidental; rather, we argue that it is a culmination of several factors that include: (a) the traditional and unchallenged division of native and nonnative speakers, (b) an oversimplification of English learning at the college level into arbitrary categories such as (mainstream) English and English as a second language (ESL), and (c) a lack of theoretical discussion of the literacy practices of language users caught on the language borderlands of these three subcategories.

Although the linguistic gaps between first language (L1) learning and native language loss have been documented by linguists at a macro level, and acknowledged by leading Asian American writers (e.g., Fong-Torres, 1994; Tan, 1989) at a personal level, the social, cultural, and emotional tensions of the disharmony have yet to be framed carefully within the theoretical and pedagogical frameworks of applied linguistics studies.

THE STUDY

The Institution: College Writing Programs

This year-long study was conducted during the fall semester 1995 and the spring semester 1996 within the College Writing Programs (CWP) at the University of California (UC), Berkeley, where both researchers were instructors. The aim and scope of the CWP, as stated in the college writing handbook, is to help students ground their own literacy within the demands of the larger language community, while simultaneously helping them to develop fluency and control over their own language skills. In both the reading and writing activities, students' language experiences are an integral part of the classroom discourse. This six unit, one-semester course, College Writing 1A, fulfills the Subject A requirement as well as

English 1A. Students who pass this course with a C or better may enroll directly in an English 1B course.

All freshmen entering the UC, Berkeley must fulfill an English proficiency requirement which is called the Subject A requirement. Students can meet the Subject A requirement before coming to Berkeley by passing the university's writing proficiency Subject A essay exam, which involves reading a short selection and writing an essay within 3 hours. Students who receive a combined score of 6 or below (out of a possible 12 points) must take College Writing 1A.

The Participants

In the state of California, the Asian population of NELBs is predicted to increase from 5.2 million in 1976 to 8.3 million in 2000, a jump of 36% (Oxford-Carpenter, Pol, Lopez, Stupp, Gendell, & Peng, 1984). Within the CWP, where this study was conceived and conducted, Asian American students make up approximately 56% of the student population (Simons, Perrow, Stritikus, Schmida, & Ponte, 1997). Because of these figures, this study was limited to Asian American students.

Although statistically it appears that the Asian population has maintained its home language (50% of the Asian American students in our study reported that they speak their ethnic language at home, vs. only 15% of the Chicano students), these categories do not tell the true story. It was through student interviews that the reality of language loss and the tension between linguistic identity and language ability emerged.

Research Questions

This study focused on the following questions:

1. How are the boundaries among English literacy, language identity, cultural identity, and native (heritage) language loss manifested, defined, and maintained?
2. What are the social, cultural, and emotional consequences/implications of the phenomena of language use and language identity for this particular linguistic group?
3. How do NELB students negotiate between the borders of English language use and L1 (e.g., Chinese) identity?
4. What is the impact of the disharmony among language use, language identity, and language ownership on their development as English language users?

Stages of Study

This study was conducted in two main stages. Stage 1 consisted of pretesting the survey questions that came out of an analysis of students' literacy experiences from Chiang's class. This student information was gathered over a period of two academic years (1995 and 1996) by compiling students' "Literacy Life History" essays, writing in which students examine their own literacy journeys. *Literacy journey* in this context refers to the students' relationships with literacy and language, both written and spoken. Twenty-five questions were posed to the students as writing prompts in this assignment, and included both open-ended questions (Writing is:____; English is:____;) as well as more directed questions (When were you first aware of using language? Who were the people involved? What is good writing?). The survey questions were later refined and then administered to the larger group of 471 students enrolled in any of the 14 sections of College Writing 1A.

The answers given by the students in the large survey were examined and from those, 20 randomly selected students who reported that they were Asian American were chosen to participate in individual open-ended interviews with the researchers. These taped interviews lasted anywhere from 1 to 2½ hours.

DATA ANALYSIS

Data analyzed consisted of responses from surveys from this section (termed *general response 1*), students' written responses in the survey, detailed transcriptions from the 20 interviews, and students' writing portfolios.

Method of Analysis

The constant comparative method outlined in Bogdan and Biklen (1982) was used in the analysis of the collected data. The constant comparative method allowed for the delimiting of the ongoing hypotheses in which tentative theories were generated and which, in turn, were either rejected or supported by the collected data, for example, surveys versus literacy biographies versus personal essays versus interviews.

Data collected from the program-wide written survey were coded quantitatively when appropriate; the open-ended survey and interview questions were coded according to themes that emerged from the students' responses. Themes included such categories as: emotional attachment to English, dominance of English in society, notions of what it means to be a nonnative or a native speaker of a language, code-switching, English as a tool, bilingualism, definitions of self, and cultural and linguistic bonds to a language.

Of the students surveyed, 60% of the Asian American students reported that they were nonnative English speakers (NNES), and 91% reported they were bilingual according to their responses on the survey. Interestingly, although 91% of the students designated themselves as bilingual, only 37% reported they spoke both their ethnic (heritage) language and English at home. And among the 40% of the Asian American students who labeled themselves as native speakers of English, only 28% of those same students reported learning English as a first language. What this points to is that 12% of the 40% of students who labeled themselves as native speakers of English actually began speaking English as a *second* language (L2), not as a first language. Perhaps these students label themselves as native English speakers because they think that their primary language—the language of school and economic success in the United States—is and has been English.

RESEARCH FINDINGS

"The act of learning language[,] is also learning the culture through language. The semantic system which he is constructing becomes the primary mode of transmission of the culture" (Halliday, 1975, p. 66).

The scope of this chapter does not allow us to address the multilayered issues of language, identity, and literacy that have emerged from the study. Instead, we devote our discussion to a dominant theme captured in the study; namely, the conflicts between linguistic identity and linguistic ability, and how these conflicts are manifested in students' self-definitions of the following categories: bilingual identity versus bilingual literacy, native versus nonnative speaker, and cultural identity versus linguistic identity.

Bilingual Identity Versus Bilingual Literacy

By the students' own definition, a *bilingual individual* is one who *identifies* with a language other than English. In other words, their self-definition does not necessitate an ability to speak, read, and write in their heritage language, but rather a traditional cultural *affiliation* with the heritage language. Throughout the study, we note that the students' self-definition is not grounded in a clear or competent ability to speak the ethnic language; instead, it is informed by a sense of cultural identification as the following attests:

Wong:	I find it hard to speak to my grandparents, because I don't speak it [Chinese] anymore, and so I can't communicate with them what I want to.
Researcher:	Why is that important to you?
Wong:	I just think it is. I guess the most important reason is I want to be able to talk with my grandparents . . . and I remember a time when it was really easy for me to talk to [my grandmother]. Now, if I try to say the words, I have a very strong English accent and it's kind of a shock that I didn't realize I was losing my Chinese so quickly, but I was. I want to get it back, trying to get at least the sound right.

In fact, in many instances, language for these students is being used as a synonym for culture. This double-edged consciousness—culture as language—operates at a very complex level, often forcing students to position themselves as in between worlds in spite of the publicly self-proclaimed bilingual identity. The following excerpts capture the dilemma many students feel in terms of language use and the positionality of their two worlds:

Excerpt 1:

Student:	You either speak really good English or you're kind of in between.
Researcher:	What do you mean by "you're kind of in between?"
Student:	It's like me. I can't really speak really well in English. Like right, you know? But I can't do really good in Chinese either. So I'm kind of in between.

Excerpt 2:

Researcher:	You wrote in the written response that you're "bilingual." What do you mean by this?
Wong:	I don't know if I am really bilingual because I don't really bond with—I don't really connect with the English culture. American culture. I'm kind of in between, I guess. I don't really speak [Chinese] that well, therefore I'm non-native Chinese. But language and the culture are kind of connected, I think.
Researcher:	Do you consider yourself bilingual?
Wong:	To a point.

Researcher: To an extent?

Wong: Yeah. But I think more English 'cause I don't use Chinese on a regular basis. . . . I don't feel emotionally attached to it, but sometimes I feel guilty when I don't . . . But I feel I should be Chinese. I, like I said, when I, I think in English. It's so, it's easy. When I think in Chinese, I have to think for a while. It's hard . . . I never really thought in Chinese for really anything. . . I feel like a, like a, you know if I were to use a term, a bamboo. Like um, yellow on the outside and white on the inside.

It seems that for this group of linguistic minorities, the collapsing of language and culture into one category allows them to name their allegiance to their ethnic heritage without impeding their linguistic ability in English. However, this seemingly benign conceptualization is problematic for it raises crucial questions of the core and essence of being literate. What these students are experiencing seems to be serious disjunctures between the way they conceptualize their linguistic identities. That is, on the one hand, they are not fully comfortable with speaking, reading, or writing their heritage language, whereas on the other hand, they are not fully integrated into the culture of mainstream, academic English by the virtue of the label, linguistic minority. Although at ease with their ethnic culture, these students do not possess the full linguistic facility to participate fully as members of a cultural group, particularly so if we view language learning as a transmitter of culture. Their inability to have full participation at the cultural level is captured in the following excerpt:

Soo Kim: The only time I can talk to my parents is when I speak Konglish or in broken English.

Researcher: When you talk about family problems, is English used then? Or Korean? In conflicts, what language is used?

Soo Kim: Um. I think English is used when dealing with family problems and with other people. But if I have a problem, I'll talk with them in both Korean and English. Because sometimes I feel like when I talk to them in Korean, I can really get their attention. You know, really grasp hold of them when I talk in Korean because it's their whole language. Maybe it'll penetrate their psyche or something, you know.

Researcher: What happens when you try to do so but you do not have adequate vocabulary and terms and all that?

Soo Kim: I have to speak English. I find myself doing that. I would just start talking in English.

Researcher: So then you have a combination of both?

Soo Kim: Yeah. But that doesn't happen too often. I can usually talk to my parents in basic Korean most of the time.

Researcher: What do you mean by basic Korean?

Soo Kim: Just non-complicated vocabulary. There's nothing complicated. Just regular phrases, conversational dialogue, that kind of thing. Nothing complicated.

Researcher: So for complicated or complex concepts, you use English?

Soo Kim: Yes. I use English, yeah. I just ask them how to say it in Korean.

If, as Halliday (1975, p. 66) posited, "the act of learning language [is] also learning the culture through language[,] the semantic system which [the student] is constructing becomes the primary mode of transmission of the culture," and if indeed the semantic system is the primary mode of transmission of the culture, it raises questions of whose culture, and whose semantic systems are being privileged in English learning.

Another dominant thread is that these students identify with their heritage language, even if they do not speak it (indeed, they *all* reported that they were bilingual). It is as if by claiming the language, they claim a linguistic identity that perhaps exists in their minds, but not in their tongues. Even as they assert that they are native speakers of English, they are also asserting that they are bilingual (even if their heritage language use is devoid of any language transactions involving complex negotiations). One student said, "I am a Chinese American. So, I guess I'm bilingual," as if one begets the other, or vice versa. Language exists in the mind; for these students, it remains there, and they identify with it by considering themselves "bilingual" even when their bilingualism is not supported by a clear literacy competence (indeed, most of the students reported that they cannot read or write in their heritage language).

What is most troubling is that although school literate in English, these very students are not able to fully "bond" with the language because of the ways in which they perceive speakers of English in relation to themselves (as "they," "them," and the "other.") And although they feel connected to their home culture, they are not able to connect with it linguistically, often needing to resort to "konglish," "vietnamish," "chinglish," "broken English" or "English substitutions." More often than not, their linguistic lack in the heritage language compelled them to simplify the naming of their complexed realities to simple or broken English. They are faced with the double whammy of having a cultural home language in which they have the culture but not the full linguistic ability, and with English (for many a home and school language) in which they have the linguistic ability (however varying it is) but not the culture that, according to the students, means mainstream culture.

NATIVE VERSUS THE NONNATIVE ENGLISH SPEAKER

The constant waverings in the bilingual identification also seem to complicate the way students define themselves in terms of the native speaker identification. Although a majority of the students interviewed were either born here or came to the United States at a preschool age, and in spite of the clear documentation (indeed, UC Berkeley undergraduates are from the top 12% of California schools) that they could only read and write English, many of them did not claim the native-speaker identity. The following three excerpts are typical of the spectrum of student responses when asked to elaborate on their native or nonnative affiliation:

Excerpt 1:

Chan: A native speaker—to me, I think it's somebody who can speak English very well. I mean, it doesn't matter where you were born. A couple of my friends came here when they were small and they speak English perfectly. So shouldn't that be native? . . . I don't really know how to define myself. Am I a native speaker of English, too?

Researcher: How would you define a nonnative speaker?

Chan: Nonnative speakers. Hmm. Are they supposed to be less of an English speaker? Do they speak not as well as the people that are born here? I think that language is basically your culture, by your family. So when you're not born here, I think you don't speak well, maybe. Maybe that's how they define it. Nonnative: You're not born here and you don't speak as well because you don't culturally, like, bond.

Excerpt 2:

Researcher: How do you define the "native" speaker?

Nguyen: It [English] is just the way they speak in America.

Researcher: And what about Vietnamese?

Nguyen: My native language.

Researcher: What does the term nonnative speaker mean to you?

Nguyen: A person that English wasn't their first language.

Researcher: And how about when you hear the word "native English speaker?"

Nguyen: Like, they constantly use English, and I think, like, their first language.

Researcher: Are you a native or a nonnative speaker of Vietnamese?

Nguyen: I'm not sure. I don't know. [pause] I think I'm a nonnative 'cause my Vietnamese isn't that great.

Researcher: And what about English?
Nguyen: I think I'm native.

For many of these students, despite their sometimes contradictory ambivalence in the native and nonnative categories, we discovered that when questioned about their "thinking" language, English predominates:

Shun: I think the native speaker is probably either English was your first language or English is a language you're fluent at. But native sounds like to me, it's your first language. But that's complicated because I actually learned Korean first. . . . Then I took on English and then my fluency in English took off, whereas with Korean, it just gradually . . . I don't know. It's complicated.
Researcher: So you consider yourself a nonnative speaker of English.
Shun: I don't think so. Probably because I'm so fluent at it. So if I said I was a nonnative speaker, it would sound funny because I would say, "Wait. But I speak it fluently." So I can't be. It just contradicts itself.

With other students, the ambivalence is less defined even as they "other" the native-speaker:

Researcher: So what is a native speaker?
Cheng: I . . . I'm not sure. It's like other people in class, when they have to speak English, they have to think first right? So, their original language is like their natural instinct; that's how it is for me. English is, it's natural. I think in English.

These identification labels that the students create illustrate their dissatisfaction with the inherent binary categories with respect to their bilingual identity, which force them to categorize their identity into an either–or sort of framework, when in fact they may not perceive it in such clear-cut distinctions. At the beginning of the interview, Cheng talks about her bond to the Chinese culture, and how she understands it better than she understands U.S. culture. Dominating her literacy narrative is the self-imposed nonnative speaker. However, when asked to define a native speaker, she answers, "I'm not sure." In fact, her linguistic identity dramatically turns around when she talks about the "natural instinct" and how to her, "English is natural." Cheng even goes further to say that she "thinks in English" even as she holds on to a nonnative identity. It is as if to say that she could not be a native speaker of English because of her more primal bond to Chinese. Many of the students said that they hear the heritage language spoken at home, between parents and grandparents, or at family gatherings, and that because of this they feel a connection to the language. It seems that regardless of their linguistic inability to fully communicate with the language, the students' emotional connection to the heritage language remains deep and complex.

Another point of interest is that with some students, the native speaker label comes not by conscious choice, but by default as the following responses attest:

Shennie: I describe myself as a native English-speaking student because I was born and educated under the U.S. system. The English I've learned in public schools was the same for both White and non-White students, regardless of the home language.

Lee: I think I'm a native speaker of English because I'm proficient in it even though I learned a language before hand [meaning Taiwanese] but there's a cultural language which is Chinese; it's like my language that I can always be at, I can always like, I can always revert back to, because it is, it is innate in me in some ways, you know. . . . But to me a native language is a language that you continually speak, that you write an essay on it. You know like I just wrote an essay for College Writing and, and there's no way I could have put those ideas into Chinese. So, and that's why I like, just creating ideas and creating new thoughts is like what I think is a native language just because that's how you advance.

So despite the fact that these students use English to create "ideas and new thoughts" and that English is primary in their lived realities, they still distance themselves from English, often times reducing it to "a tool." "English is a great tool, a tool you know, tool for me that I use as a language, and you know, to write my papers and stuff like that, useful things" (Wong, Interview 1). And despite the fact they could not read, write, and can barely speak in their heritage language, these students still see it as their bond to their cultural roots: "Chinese to me is uh, in the essence, it is me."

Perhaps because of their difficulty in labeling their own linguistic abilities, many of these students refer to English-speaking people, and the English-speaking world, in terms of "other." Although most of the students were born in this country, and English is primary in their lived realities, they are unable to fully assert themselves as native speakers. In fact, to many of these students, native speakers are the Americans, the "they" and the "them." Although English-dominant, these students are not as ready to identify with the language, in terms of the native label, as they perhaps do with their heritage language, although many are not speakers of that language.

BLURRED BOUNDARIES: REVISIONING THESE STUDENTS

The varying contradictions in students' definitions of bilingual identity, bilingual literacy, and their ambivalence toward defining themselves as a native versus a nonnative speaker raise some important questions of the way literacy experiences of linguistic minorities are defined. Our students do not neatly fit into clear-cut categories such as mainstream English speaker, ESL speaker, or bilingual students. Neither does it seem that their literacy journeys are duly served by the arbitrary and ill-challenged categories of language minority students, ESL, and international students.

Category 1: Mainstream English Speakers

The students we interviewed shared many of the literacy needs and orientations of mainstream students—literacy as an act of making meaning, literacy as an act of self-definition, and literacy as a way to engage with the world even as they are tagged with the nonnative English-speaking label. That many resisted enrolling in a nonnative English-speaking section (an option available to ESL students), and that all our students interviewed were from the native English-speaking section further attest to their mainstream affiliation. For many of the students, the reality is that English is more than a functional tool, or an L2; in many aspects, it is their primary language.

Although the needs of these students cannot be adequately addressed under the mainstream English speakers category, ironically, they are as mainstream as can be. The students we have are considered the model students. They are enrolled in three or four other classes in addition to their college writing class, and are successful in meeting the academic demands of the university. These are the students who are seen as having made it; whose education is smooth sailing, whose relationship with the English language has gotten them all As.

Paradoxically, another indication of their primary affiliation to English (part of the mainstream linguistic identity) is in their struggle with their linguistic and cultural loyalties. Perhaps, had these students not had such a primary and emotional bond with English, they would not have been so split in their struggles with, contradictions, and uncertainties about their cultural and linguistic identities.

Category 2: Language Minorities

The label *language minority* is used to group and homogenize language learners of non-English language background. The underlying sociopolitical assumption is that these "linguistic minorities" do not speak English as a primary language. Instead, what is often assumed in this reductionist term is that English is an add-on, that is, students are assumed to have primary affiliation with their heritage language—be it Spanish, Vietnamese, Cantonese—and a lesser/secondary affiliation with English. The complex juxtaposition of home language and the primacy of English in their lived realities is eclipsed by the term *language minority*.

The student responses suggest that English and the students' heritage tongue are not viewed in competition with one another. Home language and school language (i.e., English) are felt to coexist comfortably at various levels; English is understood to work in parallel with their mother tongue.

Indeed, although many of our students may be termed as *language minorities*, their literacy journey indicates that English is really their primary language even when they seem to flip flop between the two languages. The primacy of English reverberates throughout their literacy narratives. Significant, too, is the use of English when students articulate their need to combine two languages to express their complex thoughts:

> For everyday, routine speech, I would think in Chinese when I want to speak Chinese, and in English when I want to think in English. For abstract thinking, I would think in English or most of the time, and in Chinese for concepts that are not readily expressed by English. Therefore, when I "flip-flop" between Chinese and English, I am relying on *both* at the same time in order to help express my ideas.

Yet, in as much as these students are aware of that need to combine the heritage and the learned/school language, their sense of their own language deficiency plagues their journey, as the following excerpts revealed:

> **Excerpt 1:**
>
> Therefore, I do not have a well-founded mastery of either language but a superficial knowledge of both languages, with each language being only capable in expressing my basic thoughts. (It is only when I combine the two language that I can express my complex thoughts.)
>
> **Excerpt 2:**
>
> Because I do not have a solid language foundation in one language, I will have trouble communicating my complex ideas with using one language. [i.e., Chinese and English]. . . . As a result, my weak language foundation affects my learning and writing English or Chinese.

Category 3: ESL Speaker

The biggest assumption (and perhaps the most homogenized category) is that of ESL. The embedded hierarchy indicates the secondary importance of English in relation to the native tongue. In other words, because English is their second language, students are assumed to have difficulties with the language. As noted by Reyes, "in classrooms and schools, as in larger societal structures, educators and policymakers are conditioned to ignore differences and to treat them as deficiencies" (Reyes, 1992, p. 437). The educational society expects them to make ESL mistakes; they are expected to stumble over the English language for it is not their native tongue. Students in our study often internalize this ill-defined assumption even when their affiliation to English is primary rather secondary. And this internalization often leads them to see themselves as incapable of owning the language as captured in the following:

> I am unsure about writing. I am confused. I am frustrated. I think I will never become a good writer because I am Asian. It is excusable for me not to be good at writing. I am not supposed to be good anyway. People expect me to be geared toward science and math. This expectation gives me an excuse to avoid writing. "People don't expect me to do well anyway," or "Why bother?" I will never learn how to speak and write like natives," I always say to myself.

It is further assumed that they have their first or native tongue to fall back to. Whereas they are not expected to have English mastery because it is their second tongue, they are presumed to have mastery in their native tongue. In many instances, this may be the case, but this is not true for all our students. Almost without exception, each expressed great difficulties in using their native or mother tongue:

> Because I learned both languages at a relatively early age, I spoke both English and Cantonese without any accent. However, my Cantonese vocabulary was limited to that of a five-year-old.

To compensate for their linguistic limitations in the heritage language, many students either resorted to keeping their thoughts simple so they have enough words to express them, or to the use of broken English to keep up communication when speaking to family members, or to combining English with the heritage language such as in "konglish," "Vietnamish," or "Chinglish." As Jane Kim describes in one of her portfolio pieces:

> I communicated with my sisters at home only through English in the midst of my mom yelling "Speak Korean! Aren't you Korean?" Then I would start to break out in "Konglish" whenever my mom was nearby. I felt my English had to compensate for what I lacked in my knowledge of Korean. Although I don't speak Korean with a heavy accent, it's still difficult to communicate in the language. My vocabulary is very limited and my reading and writing power is very weak.
>
> Many people are surprised that I can speak as well as I can for someone who has practically lived in America all her life. I'm still saddened at the fact that I can't communicate to my parents the same way my sisters are able. If I talk to my mom, it's usually just simple questions I need to ask her; otherwise I'd ask my sisters to ask for me.

Characterizing Jane Kim's English as her second language does not capture the full complexity of her linguistic experience. Kim's experiences with language and literacy, particularly in the home context, seem to depict someone who turns to English for stability and a sense of self.

Therefore, a further limitation in the ESL characterization is that English is really the primary medium students use to articulate their complex realities. They depend on it to help them weave in and out of their everyday communication interactions. Their race and/or ethnicity does not preclude them from relying on English to express their multifaceted realities and to make the necessary transitions between home and school.

CONCLUSIONS

What we strive to do in this chapter is to highlight the cultural and linguistic web of home language and English for students from NELB. Essentially, we hope that the insights of their multifaceted experiences provoke language educators to question and think beyond the narrow confines of a monolithic English ideology, and reorientate themselves to the sociocultural politics of English literacy in a multicultural and multilingual world.

In addition, we wish to suggest the following educational implications:

- The need for language teachers to be adequately trained and professionally prepared to recognize and attend to the increasingly blurred cultural and linguistic boundaries of linguistically diverse students. Whereas categories like ESL, bilingual, and linguistic minority do indeed serve to delineate some students, these categories are inadequate when it comes to capturing the literacy journey of students whose lived realities often waver between cultural and linguistic borderlands.

- The urgency to reexamine the categorization of native versus nonnative students and reconceptualize the labels. As our study has indicated, the nonnative labels are neither adequate in capturing the complexities of their literacy experiences, nor resonant in representing their paralleling cultural and linguistic ties to English and their heritage language. Perhaps the overarching question should be less whether these linguistically diverse students are native or nonnative, but rather how primary English fits their literacy and linguistic identity. The reorientation will not only serve in recentering the primacy of English literacy as an act of constructing one's social, cultural, and political place in the world, but it will also heighten the role of English as a world language.
- The need for greater interaction and exchanges among leaders of National Council of Teachers of English, Teachers of English to Speakers of Other Languages, National Association of Bilingual Education, and World Englishes and their obligation to provide more informed and cross disciplinary insights into the multiplicity of English learning in a pluralistic world. With the increasing dominance of English across the world, it is no longer sufficient to work within the narrow paradigms and specificities contained within each linguistic field. Instead, researchers need to view commonalties and contradictions and come up with new insights and models formed from multiple perspectives. This kind of interdisciplinary model will add to a fuller understanding of the literacy journey of a diverse student population.
- The need to not only acknowledge but accommodate the intersections of race, culture, and ethnicity in the sociopolitical constructions of English literacy. As pointed out by Peirce (1995), which our study supports, "the individual language learner is not ahistorical and unidimensional but has a complex and sometimes social identity, changing across time and space" (pp. 25–26).

REFERENCES

Bogdan, R., & Biklen, S. (1982). *Qualitative research for education: An introduction to theory and methods*. Boston: Allyn and Bacon, Inc.

Fong-Torres, B. (1994). *The rice room: Growing up Chinese-American: From number two son to rock 'n roll*. New York: Hyperion.

Halliday, M. A. K. (1975). *Learning how to mean: Explorations in the development of language*. London: Edward Arnold.

Lantolf, J. (1996). SLA theory building: Letting all the flowers bloom! *Language Learning, 46*, 713–749.

Oxford-Carpenter, R., Pol, L., Lopez, D., Stupp, P., Gendell, M., & Peng, S. (1984). *Demographic projections of non-English language background and limited English proficient persons in the United States to the year 2000 by state, age, and language group*. Rosslyn, VA: National Clearing House for Bilingual Education.

Peirce, B. N. (1995). Social identity, investment, and language learning. *TESOL Quarterly, 29(1), 9–31.*

Rampton, B. (1995). *Crossing: Language and ethnicity among adolescents.* New York: Longman.

Reyes, M. (1992). Challenging venerable assumptions: Literacy instruction for linguistically different students. *Harvard Educational Review, 62*(4), 427–446.

Siegal, M. (1996). The role of learner subjectivity in second language sociolinguistic competency: Western women learning Japanese. *Applied Linguistics, 17*(3), 356–382.

Simons, H., Perrow, M., Stritikus, T., Schmida, M., & Ponte, E. (1997). *Participating in academic conversation: An evaluation of college writing.* Unpublished report, University of California at Berkeley.

Tan, A. (1989). *The joy luck club.* New York: Putnam.

Chapter 20

ESL and the Colonial Legacy: A Teacher Faces Her 'Missionary Kid' Past

Stephanie Vandrick

A hidden aspect of teaching English as a Second Language (ESL) students—in writing classes or elsewhere—is the colonial legacy of the profession, a legacy that in some senses taints those of us who teach these students. This legacy can involve, on some unspoken and mainly unacknowledged level, a feeling of superiority of West to East, of English to other (especially non-European) languages, so that teaching English becomes a kind of preaching "a better way" to the "natives." We who teach ESL classes, as well as composition classes that include nonnative English speakers, must confront the possible consequences of this colonial shadow.

This "colonial" attitude is not (generally) intentional. And of course what we ESL teachers do is "good," isn't it? Isn't learning new languages intrinsically a good thing? And isn't English an important and even essential (perhaps the most important and most essential) worldwide language? These have been basic assumptions in the field of ESL. And, after all, don't students *demand* English classes?

All of the above assumptions may be legitimate. But we ESL teachers must at least think about the possibility of a "colonial shadow" over our profession, along with the effects of such a shadow. Do we on some level believe English is superior? And therefore that English speakers are superior? And that native speakers—and especially speakers of Western Englishes—are particularly superior? And do we believe that those who learn it gain some of our superiority (only some—they can never quite catch up)? If we do in fact believe these things on some level, all of these beliefs enhance our self-image as ESL teachers; look how "good" we are, sharing the valuable treasure of our language, and by extension, our culture and our power.

I believe that all of us who teach English language and writing classes to nonnative speakers of English are affected by this colonial legacy, but some of us have been even more immersed in it than others because of our life circumstances. We don't often look at our own backgrounds and how they lead us to teach ESL, and how they affect the way we teach. We are more likely to discuss *students'* backgrounds—nationality, ethnicity, race, class, gender, educational background, and so on—and how these factors affect their motivation, achievement, and classroom interactions. But it makes sense that instructors' backgrounds would have an enormous effect on their motivation, teaching philosophies and styles, and attitudes toward and interactions with students. Elsewhere I have explored the effects of both students' and teachers' identities, particularly hidden identities, on classroom interactions. Similarly, Spack points out that

> As teachers and researchers, we have been reading our classrooms—including actual texts and students as texts—but, for the most part, we have not turned our gaze on ourselves. Yet given the cultural work that many of us are doing, we need to understand who we are as historical, political, social, and cultural beings in order to gain a fuller sense of the complexity of the relationship between teacher, student, and text. (10)

It is becoming increasingly recognized that one of the best ways to build knowledge is to share stories (see, for example, Coles; Casanave and Schecter). Some of those who have reminded us of this are black storytellers, oral historians, and feminists in consciousness-raising groups. In particular, autobiography can be powerful. Hesford writes that because "teachers reward students for writing texts that preserve myths of objectivity and the impartiality of scholarship," for students to write autobiographical texts in academic settings can be powerful because of its allowing of room to write "against the grain by challenging and displacing the academy's authority through constructing disruptive subject positions and discourse" (134). Although faculty/scholars are expected to write in such a way that will "preserve the myths of objectivity and the impartiality of scholarship," writing autobiographically may provide another way for them as well to make knowledge.

We are beginning to see more "teachers' stories." Particular aspects of a teacher's family or individual history may affect her or his teaching. Clearly each teacher has her or his own story and we cannot generalize about ESL (or any) teachers based on any one story, but perhaps if we share enough stories, we will begin to see patterns.

IN INDIA

Thus I share here my own story of having been an "MK," a "missionary kid," the child of missionary parents. I have only recently looked at this story in a new light, a light made possible by more than thirty years of distance. I grew up as an "MK" in India, graciously dispensing gifts, hand-me-downs, prizes, trinkets, wisdom, religion, and Western culture to the "natives." My parents—and by extension my brothers and I—were caught up, unwittingly, in a historical phenomenon: the colonial spread of Western culture to the East, whether through government, trade, or religion. And on the part of some, at least, this phenomenon was well-intentioned. Doris Lessing, whose British father worked in both Persia and Rhodesia (now Zimbabwe), writes of her parents' belief that "they represented God's will, working by agency of the British Empire, for the good of the world" (qtd. in Schinto 31). In retrospect, I can see how immersed we were in a very colonial mode.

Now I teach ESL to students of the world, graciously dispensing the gifts, prizes, and wisdom made available through the English language, "American culture," and academic skills for the American university. What is the connection? I used to believe that I became an ESL teacher partly because of my growing up overseas, which gave me a simple interest in other cultures and other languages. Now, thirty-three years after leaving India, and twenty-seven years after beginning to teach ESL, I am finally beginning to see and acknowledge another, more complicated, aspect of the connection. Was it being steeped in the colonial project—albeit indirectly, through a Canadian church mission—that made ESL teaching seem oh-so-familiar and oh-so-comfortable that very first day I, as an eager and naive graduate assistant, stood up in front of my first ESL class full of "natives" from Asia, Africa, and the Middle East? Was I once again in the position of the generous but condescending Lady Bountiful dispensing my valued linguistic and cultural favors to the uncivilized (non-Western) natives?

When, years after growing up in India as an "MK," I "fell into" ESL teaching without consciously planning to, I immediately felt "at home." The obvious explanation for my immediate sense of comfort with ESL teaching might be that I was used to being in a different culture and to hearing and speaking several languages, that I enjoyed interaction with people from different cultures, and that those factors in combination with my love of language and literature made ESL teaching a logical and happy "fit" for me. For years I assumed that this innocuous explanation was true. And in a way, it was and is in fact true. But looked at from a different angle, and from the vantage point of nearly three decades of teaching and thinking, there is another truth, a perhaps less straightforward and comfortable truth. I was a child in a missionary family; my parents went to India to provide assistance to Indian people. Let me say here that my parents are the kindest, most well-intentioned people one could meet, and that they dedicated a good part of their life, at considerable sacrifice, to give their talents and skills to help people. My father is a doctor who did surgery in village hospitals, set up clinics in the jungle, and worked with lepers. My mother helped in hospitals and schools, while raising four children. They made an enormous and tangible contribution, changing and even saving many people's lives. They did so because of their religious faith, but they did not impose their religion on anyone. (I realize that the latter is not true of all missionaries, but it was true of my parents.) I myself could never and will never make the kind of sacrifices most missionaries had to make, and it is unlikely that anything I do will change people's lives and help people in such concrete ways as my parents' work did.

But—despite these caveats—there was a "missionary mentality" that I unconsciously absorbed. My brothers and I grew up in the India of the 1950s and 1960s, just after Indian Independence. We were very attached to India, as most children are attached to the places where they grow up. My life there is a huge and essential part of me, and of who I am. But in many senses we were never really part of India. Since we moved there so soon after the British had left India, the colonial tradition was still very strong, still very much present. And my parents and their North American colleagues had clearly come from the West to share their (by implication superior) Western religion, expertise, and resources. Although India had so recently become independent, Indians still deferred (at least outwardly) to whites, still the "sahibs," in many ways. It takes a long time for cultural change to catch up with political change.

Although my family was far from wealthy by North American standards, our house was much larger than the other houses in the village we lived in, and we had several servants to manage the cooking, housework, and garden, all of which demanded much time and energy, as there were very few labor-saving appliances available in India at that time. We took the servants for granted, and were genuinely fond of some of them, but there was not a sense of equality with them . . .

* * *

The closest relationships we children had with Indians were with our *ayahs* (Indian nannies) when we were little, especially one named Perongani, whom we missed terribly when she left to get married. Although my mother didn't work full-time when we were small, we spent a lot of time with this young Indian woman and were very fond of her. We thought she was beautiful. We were sometimes naughty and disobedient, and we somehow knew she didn't have any ultimate authority over us. But we loved her and felt a great sense of loss when she left. When another, less pretty, less "fun" *ayah* took her place, we were unhappy and uncooperative. Our story echoes those of all the British and other colonial families in India, Africa, the Philippines, and elsewhere with *ayahs* and servants. Our story also resonates with those of white families in the South with black "mammies," and with those of American families with Mexican nannies/housekeepers even now. In all of these stories, there was between the families and *ayahs*/mammies/nannies a strange closeness, intimate yet decidedly unequal, unbalanced.

* * *

We children played with Indian children, but not much, and again, not on a truly equal basis. I remember with embarrassment that we used to show off our North American toys, enjoying the attention from the Indian children who crowded around to see them. . . . Arriving back in India after three years home in the United States and Canada on furlough, we four children greeted our newly delivered big boxes of belongings with fervor and raced to unpack them and try them out. We took everything out on the wide veranda that circled our spacious bungalow, on a compound set back from the village road and surrounded by gardens and trees. We ostentatiously set out our pile of bicycles, sports equipment, toys . . . all the accouterments of Western childhood, commonplace "back home" but envied treasures here in an Indian village. We then proceeded to play with them all, systematically yet somewhat frantically. I particularly remember jumping on a pogo stick over and over . . . bounce, bounce, bounce . . . We were still unsettled, a little hyperactive, and were acting out a bit, showing off. My brothers played an impromptu game of badminton. We threw Frisbees wildly, and laughed loudly. We knew quite well that we had an audience, that we were objects of curiosity, and we assumed that we were objects of admiration and envy. We were very aware that crowds of village children were watching us from the road, through the fence around the compound, and though we didn't speak of it to each other, we each knew that the others knew that we were performing. We were reaching out to connect with the Indian children, but in a way that was in effect establishing our "superior" place in the hierarchy. Bounce, bounce . . . sneak a look at the crowds of children watching . . . affect nonchalance . . . bounce, bounce, bounce some more . . .

* * *

Our mission ran a boarding school for Indian village girls that was right next door to our compound. I rarely played with "the boarding girls." Sometimes I would swing on the rope swing hanging from a tree right next to the wall around the boarding school, and as I sailed into the sky I would sing, partly for the benefit of the Indian girls. I imagined them envying me my swing, big house, my freedom, and my obviously superior position in the world. One of the few times I visited the boarding school and spent time with the girls, it was viewed on both sides as a kind of royal visit. I was about ten years old. I was treated with great deference (though I have no idea what they were actually thinking about me or about their being required to appear deferential to me). It seemed quite justified to me that they should be happy I was visiting them. I brought some candy and small gifts. In any case, the girls gathered around me, politely praising me and asking me questions. They were particularly interested in my hair since it was light brown, almost blond. They asked if they could comb it, and they did. A couple of days after this visit, I found I had head lice. I felt, mostly unconsciously, that it was shameful to have lice, and that this shameful condition was a natural consequence of mixing too much with the boarding school girls. The proper order of things had been upset, the proper separation between "them" and "us" had been violated. I never played with the boarding girls again.

* * *

When we went to the local church and sat through long services in a language we did not know, or when we went to the Christmas party at the hospital or at one of the schools, it was because it was our duty to do so, to "make an appearance" there; in fact, there was a sense of *noblesse oblige*. The missionary family feeling of *noblesse oblige* became, perhaps, most explicit in the Christmas parties we gave, first for our servants and then for the workers in the small mission hospital my father ran. A large meal was served. Everyone sat on the floor on the veranda, and steaming food was piled onto the stitched-together banana leaves that served as plates. Curiously, I cannot remember who cooked and served the meals for the servants. Did they double as cooks/servants and guests? Did my parents hire other servants to serve our servants? After the meal, gifts were handed out to each person. One of the adults would call the name of each servant or worker, and indicate the gift intended for that person (most often a piece of clothing, or a length of material to be used for clothing). We children were invited to hand the gifts out as each person stepped forward. We looked forward to this ritual, which allowed us to feel both generous and superior. How did the adult Indians feel, having to act subservient and grateful to a white child handing them a gift?

* * *

For a large part of the year, we four children were away at a boarding school in a hill resort town with other children of Western missionaries, diplomats, and businessmen. Although we were thousands of miles from "home," we easily preserved the rituals of American adolescence, only a year or two behind the latest trends "back home." We saw Hollywood movies, listened to and danced to American and British rock music, and envied those who had recently been in the United States and had brought back the latest music and clothes and slang. It was assumed that our time in India was temporary, and that we would all go home eventually; as much as we loved India, our futures would not be there. I have a very clear memory of thinking, one day when I was about six or seven years old, that of course the United States and Canada were the "main" places, in other words the center of the universe, and that everywhere else was peripheral. Later on, after graduation from high school, when one of my fellow students, another "missionary kid," chose to stay in India for the rest of his life, most of us felt he had "gone native," and couldn't imagine doing the same.

I do not mean to say that we—the "we" of my family, and the "we" of many of the Western people who lived in India—didn't respect or value Indians; we did. But in day-to-day life, we had our own way of doing things, our own lives, and it seemed quite natural to us that these did not intersect very much with the lives of the people who lived there, the Indians. We didn't question the situation; it was just the way things were. There was an implicit assumption of the superiority of Western people and ways, although we would have been surprised and embarrassed to hear that assumption spoken aloud. If questioned, we would probably have denied that we had such an assumption, but we would have done so with a vague sense of uneasiness.

BECOMING AN ESL TEACHER

When I began graduate school, my assistantship involved teaching ESL to international university students, and from the first day of class I loved the teaching and felt "at home" in the ESL classroom. I assumed that I felt so comfortable and happy in this teaching situation at least partly because it reminded me of my childhood years overseas, and that I was a world citizen type after all, despite my six years away from that identification. But now I wonder if that immediate connection was, at least partly, with the colonial aspects of my missionary kid background, rather than with my living in India per se. Perhaps the teaching situation "clicked" for me because (unconsciously) it was a kind of "ministering to the natives" all over again. They—in this case the international students in my classes—lacked something that I had (the English language, knowledge of Western academe and culture), something that I could magnanimously provide for them. I could be the generous colonial lady, or perhaps the missionary coming to "help" the natives. Also, perhaps, this situation provided a gratifying ego boost; when one teaches, one is in a position of knowledge and power, and teaching one's native language, one is clearly "in the right" and can't be easily challenged. Again, all of this was unconscious . . .

* * *

"Thank you, teacher," my students often said, smiling at and sometimes even bowing to me. They seemed so grateful, so appreciative. How kind I felt, how wise, how generous.

* * *

I also strongly believed that I was free of prejudice because I had grown up in India, experiencing living with people of various ethnic backgrounds and economic levels. But I have recently become much more conscious of some of the sense of privilege I carry, along with some of the unconscious racism that infects almost everyone with privilege, including "colonial" privilege. Reading McIntosh and then Wildman on "white privilege" has helped me understand how this unconscious, absolutely taken for granted, privilege pervades every aspect of a white person's life.

I have also realized that when students are not "properly appreciative," I feel, unconsciously or consciously, somewhat annoyed, even resentful. I find myself feeling, to my surprise, that they *should* appreciate this wonderful opportunity they have to study English in the United States. And they shouldn't criticize too much: not me, nor English, nor the United States. . . . Sometimes students come uncannily close to home with their comments, little realizing how I may react . . .

* * *

Recently my advanced ESL reading class read Chinua Achebe's short story "Dead Man's Path," which describes an African headmaster who has received his education in missionary schools. He prides himself on his education and his modern attitude, and condescendingly scoffs at the beliefs of the villagers regarding the spirits of their ancestors. During the class discussion, I spoke about colonialism, including the missionaries' role in it, and expounded upon the difficulties caused when colonial cultures clashed with traditional cultures. One of my students interrupted, "So, missionary means arrogant?" "No, no," I replied. "Well, SOMETIMES some missionaries are arrogant, but not all." ("Not my parents," I think.) How can I explain the problems of colonialism, yet not criticize all colonizers, all missionaries? I feel myself becoming defensive. Should I tell my class that my parents were missionaries, that I grew up as a missionary kid? No, it would be too complicated to explain. I don't want to deal with explaining. . . . So, perhaps wisely, or perhaps out of cowardice, I don't reveal my personal connection to the question, and we move on to analyze other aspects of the story.

ENGLISH, THE COLONIAL LEGACY, AND PRIVILEGE

This sense of privilege, along with its part in the colonial legacy influencing those teaching the English language, has been discussed by some theorists and researchers in ESL and linguistics, particularly those concerned with language planning (see, for example, Canagarajah; Phillipson; Tollefson). Areas in which the quasi-colonial attitude is questioned include arguments that immigrants in the United States are taught a kind of utilitarian "survival" English, an English that will be "good enough" for their needs and that will help them fit into their (fairly lowly) place in the system. Auerbach and Burgess, for example, are concerned that "Survival ESL" curricula "prepare students for subservient social roles and reinforce hierarchical relations within the classroom" (475). Tollefson "challenges the survival English taught to refugees . . . for its ideological content (e.g., refugees are taught that if they work hard and apply themselves, they too will be equipped to join our consumer society)" (paraphrased in Leki 241). We especially note the possible signs of the colonial legacy as we see the English language being taught and proliferating in non-Western countries. In many countries, English is being promoted as the language of technology and commerce, the language that is necessary to compete in the world today. In non-Western countries that already have a history of using the English language, those colonized by England or the United States, we can see a different aspect of the colonial attitude: British or American English is held up as the standard, and the various other Englishes that have developed, such as Indian English, are considered inferior and even laughable by many. In recent years we have been sensitized to this type of condescension by such authorities on World Englishes as Kachru.

Here, however, although my thinking draws on all of the above sources, I particularly want to explore the way we as individual teachers—"we" signifying, broadly, ESL instructors who are native speakers of Western Englishes—may be unconsciously influenced by the colonial mode of thinking and how it may manifest itself in our teaching. The word *unconsciously* is critical here because most ESL teachers are well-intentioned and caring people. The colonial aspect I discuss here is something that operates below the surface, something that we have absorbed with our culture in many subtle ways.

Even in classrooms that are not specifically ESL but are, for example, freshman writing classes with students from various national, ethnic, and cultural backgrounds (the kind of classroom that is increasingly common in today's institutions of higher education), there is an imposition of Western values and of standard English. De and Gregory state that in such classrooms, "Students whose thinking differs substantially from or lies on the margins of the epistemic practices dominant in a Western metropolitan academy are liable to be 'colonized' by the theoretical methods they encounter on entering" (118). They go on to say that "Writing teachers widely recognize that culturally diverse students who succeed in the United States university do so because they have been successfully socialized into Western argumentative discourse. This socialization often occurs at the expense of students' culture-specific ways of interacting with reality" (119). For students in such writing classes as well as those in ESL classes, there is a need to learn Western academic discourse, yet a need to preserve their own styles of writing, which are determined by their own cultural assumptions and practices. The conflict between these two needs can be very painful (see Fox; Shen).

COLONIAL IMAGES, COLONIAL ATTITUDES

I have gone on to teach for many years, and have continued to enjoy it and feel it is a way to make a contribution. But the realizations outlined here have made me question much about that teaching. If in fact I (and perhaps other ESL teachers) am influenced by the colonial legacy, in what ways is that manifested in the classroom? Shafiei quotes an adult ESL student describing his teacher's behavior as follows: "My teachers were kind, but I was ashamed to talk because I felt like a little baby, and my teacher acted like my mother" (10). Shafiei notes that many ESL instructors speak loudly and make large gestures, and goes on to point out that ESL students often feel condescended to, including being excessively and exaggeratedly praised for any achievements, as if teachers are surprised by the ESL students' success. Also, do ESL teachers, along with much of American academe, always use the West, and particularly the United States, as the central reference point, so that everything else is marginalized, and dealt with only in terms of its relationship to the West, or in terms of how it measures up to Western standards? Is the English language, and particularly the "standard" English of the United States or Great Britain, central, with all other languages, especially non-European languages, marginal? Do we feel that we are giving our students a gift by sharing our language and culture with them, and that they should be properly grateful for this gracious gift, and should show their gratitude appropriately? Do we, consciously or unconsciously, penalize students who don't appear to be properly cognizant of the favor we are doing them, and therefore don't show proper signs of gratitude?

It is not fair to generalize about other ESL faculty from my story or my speculations here. However, I believe that my story may to some extent reflect the experiences and attitudes of other ESL teachers who are children of missionaries, and perhaps of other American or British ESL teachers who grew up in countries where (Western) Englishes were not the first language. It is possible that my story also overlaps in some ways the experiences of those who have themselves worked in countries outside the United States and Great Britain (and Canada and Australia), such as Peace Corps volunteers, teachers in international schools, diplomats, and employees of multinational corporations. And I believe that some of the colonial attitudes that I absorbed living in India are also absorbed by many, if not most, people in Great Britain and the United States, including ESL teachers. Such attitudes are part of the culture, the media, the literature, the air itself, and it is a rare person who can totally avoid or counteract them.

It is also not fair to be too judgmental, of ourselves or of others; we are all creatures of our time and place in history, and it is not necessarily fair to impose today's knowledge and standards on yesterday's attitudes. But it is important to be aware of ways in which colonial history influences us, and to grapple with these issues, both as individuals and as a profession.

WORKS CITED

Achebe, Chinua. "Dead Man's Path." *The International Short Story: An Anthology with Guidelines for Reading and Writing about Fiction*. Ed. Ruth Spack. New York: St Martin's Press, 1994. 113–115.

Auerbach, Elsa Roberts, and Denise Burgess. "The Hidden Curriculum of Survival ESL." *TESOL Quarterly* 19 (1985): 475–495.

Canagarajah, A. Suresh. "Critical Ethnography of a Sri Lankan Classroom: Ambiguities in Student Opposition to Reproduction Through ESOL." *TESOL Quarterly* 27 (1993): 601–626.

Casanave, Christine Pearson, and Sandra R. Schecter, eds. *On Becoming a Language Educator: Personal Essays on Professional Development*. Mahwah, NJ: Erlbaum, 1997.

Coles, Robert. *The Call of Stories: Teaching and the Moral Imagination*. Boston, MA: Houghton, 1989.

De, Esha Niyogi, and Donna Uthus Gregory. "Decolonizing the Classroom: Freshman Composition in a Multicultural Setting." Severino 118–132.

Fox, Helen. *Listening to the World: Cultural Issues in Academic Writing*. Urbana, IL: NCTE, 1994.

Hesford, Wendy S. "Writing Identities: The Essence of Difference in Multicultural Classrooms." Severino 133–149.

Kachru, Braj B. *The Other Tongue: English Across Cultures*. 2d ed. Urbana: University of Illinois Press, 1993.

Leki, Ilona. "Cross-talk: ESL Issues and Contrastive Rhetoric." Severino 234–244.

Mcintosh, Peggy. "While Privilege and Male Privilege: A Personal Account of Coming to See Correspondences Through Work in Women's Studies." Working paper No. 189. Wellesley, MA: Wellesley College, Center for Research on Women, 1988.

Phillipson, R. *Linguistic Imperialism*. Oxford: Oxford University Press, 1992.

Schinto, Jeanne. "Lessing in London." Rev. *Walking in the Shade: Volume Two of My Autobiography, 1949–1962*, by Doris Lessing. *The Nation* 13 Oct. 1997: 31–33.

Severino, Carol, Juan C. Guerra, and Johnella E. Butler, eds. *Writing in Multicultural Settings*. New York: MLA, 1997.

Shafiei, Masoud. "Treating IEP Students as Knowledgeable Adults (Part I)." *TESOL Matters* (Aug.–Sept. 1997): 10.

Shen, Fan. "The Classroom and the Wider Culture: Identity as a Key to Learning English Composition." *College Composition and Communication* 40 (1989): 456–459.

Spack, Ruth. "The (In)visibility of the Person(al) in Academe." *College English* 59 (1997): 9–31.

Tollefson, James W. *Planning Language, Planning Inequality: Language Policy in the Community*. London: Longman, 1991.

Tollefson, James W., ed. *Power and Inequality in Language Education*. Cambridge: Cambridge University Press, 1995.

Vandrick, Stephanie. "The Role of Hidden Identities in the Postsecondary ESL Classroom." *TESOL Quarterly* 31 (1997): 153–157.

Wildman, Stephanie M. *Privilege Revealed: How Invisible Preference Undermines America*. New York: New York University Press, 1996.

Chapter 21

The Language We Know

Simon J. Ortiz

I don't remember a world without language. From the time of my earliest childhood, there was language. Always language, and imagination, speculation, utters of sound. Words, beginnings of words. What would I be without language? My existence has been determined by language, not only the spoken but the unspoken, the language of speech and the language of motion. I can't remember a world without memory. Memory, immediate and far away in the past, something in the sinew, blood, ageless cell. Although I don't recall the exact moment I spoke or tried to speak, I know the feeling of something tugging at the core of the mind, something unutterable uttered into existence. It is language that brings us into being in order to know life.

My childhood was the oral tradition of the Acoma Pueblo people—Aaquumeh hano—which included my immediate family of three older sisters, two younger sisters, two younger brothers, and my mother and father. My world was our world of the Aaquumeh in McCartys, one of the two villages descended from the ageless mother pueblo of Acoma. My world was our Eagle clan-people among other clans. I grew up in Deetziyamah, which is the Aaquumeh name for McCartys, which is posted at the exit off the present interstate highway in western New Mexico. I grew up within a people who farmed small garden plots and fields, who were mostly poor and not well schooled in the American system's education. The language I spoke was that of a struggling people who held ferociously to a heritage, culture, language, and land despite the odds posed them by the forces surrounding them since 1540 A.D., the advent of Euro-American colonization. When I began school in 1948 at the BIA (Bureau of Indian Affairs) day school in our village, I was armed with the basic ABC's and the phrases "Good morning, Miss Oleman" and "May I please be excused to go to the bathroom," but it was an older language that was my fundamental strength.

In my childhood, the language we all spoke was Acoma, and it was a struggle to maintain it against the outright threats of corporal punishment, ostracism, arid the invocation that it would impede our progress towards Americanization. Children in school were punished and looked upon with disdain if they did not speak and learn English quickly and smoothly, and so I learned it. It has occurred to me that I learned English simply because I was forced to, as so many other Indian children were. But I know, also, there was another reason, and this was that I loved language, the sound, meaning, and magic of language. Language opened up vistas of the world around me, and it allowed me to discover knowledge that would not be possible for me to know without the use of language. Later, when I began to experiment with and explore language in poetry and fiction, I allowed that a portion of that impetus was because I had come to know English through forceful acculturation. Nevertheless, the underlying force was the beauty and poetic power of language in its many forms that instilled in me the desire to become a user of language as a writer, singer, and storyteller. Significantly, it was the Acoma language, which I don't use enough of today, that inspired me to become a writer. The concepts, values, and philosophy contained in my original language and the struggle it has faced have determined my life and vision as a writer.

In Deetziyamah, I discovered the world of the Acoma land and people firsthand through my parents, sisters and brothers, and my own perceptions, voiced through all that encompasses the oral tradition, which is ageless for any culture. It is a small village, even smaller years ago, and like other Indian communities it is wealthy with its knowledge of daily event, history, and social system, all that make up a people who have a many-dimensioned heritage. Our family lived in a two-room home (built by my grandfather some years after he and my grandmother moved with their daughters from Old Acoma), which my father added rooms to later. I remember my father's work at enlarging our home for our growing family. He was a skilled stoneworker, like many other men of an older Pueblo generation who worked with sandstone and mud mortar to build their homes and pueblos. It takes time, persistence, patience, and the belief that the walls that come to stand will do so for a long, long time, perhaps even forever. I like to think that by helping to mix mud and carry stone for my father and other elders I managed to bring that influence into my consciousness as a writer.

Both my mother and my father were good storytellers and singers (as my mother is to this day—my father died in 1978), and for their generation, which was born soon after the turn of the century, they were relatively educated in the American system. Catholic missionaries had taken both of them as children to a parochial boarding school far from Acoma, and they imparted their discipline for study and quest for education to us children when we started school. But it was their indigenous sense of gaining knowledge that was most meaningful to me. Acquiring knowledge about life was above all the most important item; it was a value that one had to have in order to be fulfilled personally and on behalf of his community. And this they insisted upon imparting through the oral tradition as they told their children about our native history and our community and culture and our "stories." These stories were common knowledge of act, event, and behavior in a close-knit pueblo. It was knowledge about how one was to make a living through work that benefited his family and everyone else.

Because we were a subsistence farming people, or at least tried to be, I learned to plant, hoe weeds, irrigate, and cultivate corn, chili, pumpkins, beans. Through counsel and advice I came to know that the rain which provided water was a blessing, gift, and symbol and that it was the land which provided for our lives. It was the stories and songs which provided the knowledge that I was woven into the intricate web that was my Acoma life. In our garden and our cornfields I learned about the seasons, growth cycles of cultivated plants, what one had to think and feel about the land; and at home I became aware of how we must care for each other: all of this was encompassed in an intricate relationship which had to be maintained in order that life continue. After supper on many occasions my father would bring out his drum and sing as we, the children, danced to themes about the rain, hunting, land, and people. It was all that is contained within the language of oral tradition that made me explicitly aware of a yet unarticulated urge to write, to tell what I had learned and was learning and what it all meant to me.

My grandfather was old already when I came to know him. I was only one of his many grandchildren, but I would go with him to get wood for our households, to the garden to chop weeds, and to his sheep camp to help care for his sheep. I don't remember his exact words, but I know they were about how we must sacredly concern ourselves with the people and the holy earth. I know his words were about how we must regard ourselves and others with compassion and love; I know that his knowledge was vast, as a medicine man and an elder of his kiva, and I listened as a boy should. Mv grandfather represented for me a link to the past that is important for me to hold in my memory because it is not only memory but knowledge that substantiates my present existence. He and the grandmothers and grandfathers before him thought about us as they lived, confirmed in their belief of a continuing life, and they brought our present beings into existence by the beliefs they held. The consciousness of that belief is what informs my present concerns with language, poetry, and fiction.

My first poem was for Mother's Day when I was in the fifth grade, and it was the first poem that was ever published, too, in the Skull Valley School newsletter. Of course I don't remember how the juvenile poem went, but it must have been certain in its expression of love and reverence for the woman who was the most important person in my young life. The poem didn't signal any prophecy of my future as a poet, but it must have come from the forming idea that there were things one could do with language and writing. My mother, years later, remembers how I was a child who always told stories—that is, tall tales—who always had explanations for things probably better left unspoken, and she says that I also liked to perform in school plays. In remembering, I do know that I was coming to that age when the emotions and thoughts in me began to moil to the surface. There was much to experience and express in that age when youth has a precociousness that is broken easily or made to flourish. We were a poor family, always on the verge of financial disaster, though our parents always managed to feed us and keep us in clothing. We had the problems, unfortunately ordinary, of many Indian families who face poverty on a daily basis, never enough of anything, the feeling of a denigrating self-consciousness, alcoholism in the family and community, the feeling that something was falling apart though we tried desperately to hold it all together.

My father worked for the railroad for many years as a laborer and later as a welder. We moved to Skull Valley, Arizona, for one year in the early 1950s, and it was then that I first came in touch with a non-Indian, non-Acoma world. Skull Valley was a farming and ranching community, and my younger brothers and sisters and I went to a one-room school. I had never really had much contact with white people except from a careful and suspicious distance, but now here I was, totally surrounded by them, and there was nothing to do but bear the experience and learn from it. Although I perceived there was not much difference between *them* and *us* in certain respects, there was a distinct feeling that we were not the same either. This thought had been inculcated in me, especially by an Acoma expression—*Gaimuu Mericano*—that spoke of the "fortune" of being an American. In later years as a social activist and committed writer, I would try to offer a strong positive view of our collective Indianness through my writing. Nevertheless, my father was an inadequately paid laborer, and we were far from our home land for economic-social reasons, and my feelings and thoughts about that experience during that time would become a part of how I became a writer.

Soon after, I went away from my home and family to go to boarding school, first in Santa Fe and then in Albuquerque. This was in the 1950s, and this had been the case for the past half-century for Indians: we had to leave home in order to become truly American by joining the mainstream, which was deemed to be the proper course of our lives. On top of this was termination, a U.S. government policy which dictated that Indians sever their relationship to the federal government and remove themselves from their lands and go to American cities for jobs and education. It was an era which bespoke the intent of U.S. public policy that Indians were no longer to be Indians. Naturally, I did not perceive this in any analytical or purposeful sense; rather, I felt an unspoken anxiety and resentment against unseen forces that determined our destiny to be un-Indian, embarrassed and uncomfortable with our grandparents' customs and strictly held values. We were to set our goals as American working men and women, singlemindedly industrious, patriotic, and unquestioning, building for a future which ensured that the U.S. was the greatest nation in the world. I felt fearfully uneasy with this, for by then I felt the loneliness, alienation, and isolation imposed upon me by the separation from my family, home, and community.

Something was happening; I could see that in my years at Catholic school and the U.S. Indian school. I remembered my grandparents' and parents' words: educate yourself in order to help your people. In that era and the generation who had the same experience I had, there was an unspoken vow: we were caught in a system inexorably, and we had to learn that system well in order to fight back. Without the motive of a fight-back we would not be able to survive as the people our heritage had lovingly bequeathed us. My diaries and notebooks began then, and though none have survived to the present, I know they contained the varied moods of a youth filled with loneliness, anger, and discomfort that seemed to have unknown causes. Yet at the same time, I realize now, I was coming to know myself clearly in a way that I would later articulate in writing. My love of language, which allowed me to deal with the world, to delve into it, to experiment and discover, held for me a vision of awe and wonder, and by then grammar teachers had noticed I was a good speller, used verbs and tenses correctly, and wrote complete sentences. Although I imagine that they might have surmised this as unusual for an Indian student whose original language was not English, I am grateful for their perception and attention.

During the latter part of that era in the 1950s of Indian termination and the Cold War, a portion of which still exists today, there were the beginnings of a bolder and more vocalized resistance against the current

U.S. public policies of repression, racism, and cultural ethnocide. It seemed to be inspired by the civil rights movement led by black people in the U.S. and by decolonization and liberation struggles worldwide. Indian people were being relocated from their rural homelands at an astonishingly devastating rate, yet at the same time they resisted the U.S. effort by maintaining determined ties with their heritage, returning often to their native communities and establishing Indian centers in the cities they were removed to. Indian rural communities, such as Acoma Pueblo, insisted on their land claims and began to initiate legal battles in the areas of natural and social, political and economic human rights. By the retention and the inspiration of our native heritage, values, philosophies, and language, we would know ourselves as a strong and enduring people. Having a modest and latent consciousness of this as a teenager, I began to write about the experience of being Indian in America. Although I had only a romanticized image of what a writer was, which came from the pulp rendered by American popular literature, and I really didn't know anything about writing, I sincerely felt a need to say things, to speak, to release the energy of the impulse to help my people.

My writing in my late teens and early adulthood was fashioned after the American short stories and poetry taught in the high schools of the 1940s and 1950s, but by the 1960s, after I had gone to college and dropped out and served in the military, I began to develop topics and themes from my Indian background. The experience in my village of Deetziyamah and Acoma Pueblo was readily accessible. I had grown up within the oral tradition of speech, social and religious ritual, elders' counsel and advice, countless and endless stories, everyday event, and the visual art that was symbolically representative of life all around. My mother was a potter of the well-known Acoma clayware, a traditional art form that had been passed to her from her mother and the generations of mothers before. My father carved figures from wood and did beadwork. This was not unusual, as Indian people know; there was always some kind of artistic endeavor that people set themselves to, although they did not necessarily articulate it as "Art" in the sense of Western civilization. One lived and expressed an artful life, whether it was in ceremonial singing and dancing, architecture, painting, speaking, or in the way one's social-cultural life was structured. When I turned my attention to my own heritage, I did so because this was my identity, the substance of who I was, and I wanted to write about what that meant. My desire was to write about the integrity and dignity of an Indian identity, and at the same time I wanted to look at what this was within the context of an America that had too often denied its Indian heritage.

To a great extent my writing has a natural political-cultural bent simply because I was nurtured intellectually and emotionally within an atmosphere of Indian resistance. Aacquu did not die in 1598 when it was burned and razed by European conquerors, nor did the people become hopeless when their children were taken away to U.S. schools far from home and new ways were imposed upon them. The *Aaquumeh hano*, despite losing much of their land and surrounded by a foreign civilization, have not lost sight of their native heritage. This is the factual case with most other Indian peoples, and the clear explanation for this has been the fight-back we have found it necessary to wage. At times, in the past, it was outright armed struggle, like that of present-day Indians in Central and South America with whom we must identify; currently, it is often in the legal arena, and it is in the field of literature. In 1981, when I was invited to the White House for an event celebrating American poets and poetry, I did not immediately accept the invitation. I questioned myself about the possibility that I was merely being exploited as an Indian, and I hedged against accepting. But then I recalled the elders going among our people in the poor days of the 1950s, asking for donations—a dollar here and there, a sheep, perhaps a piece of pottery—in order to finance a trip to the nation's capital. They were to make another countless appeal on behalf of our people, to demand justice, to reclaim lost land even though there was only spare hope they would be successful. I went to the White House realizing that I was to do no less than they and those who had fought in the Pueblo Revolt of 1680, and I read my poems and sang songs that were later described as "guttural" by a Washington, D.C., newspaper. I suppose it is more or less understandable why such a view of Indian literature is held by many, and it is also clear why there should be a political stand taken in my writing and those of my sister and brother Indian writers.

The 1960s and afterward have been an invigorating and liberating period for Indian people. It has been only a little more than twenty years since Indian writers began to write and publish extensively, but we are writing and publishing more and more; we can only go forward. We come from an ageless, continuing oral tradition that informs us of our values, concepts, and notions as native people, and it is amazing how much of this tradition is ingrained so deeply in our contemporary writing, considering the brutal efforts of cultural repression that was not long ago outright U.S. policy. We were not to speak our languages, practice our spiritual beliefs, or accept the values of our past generations; and we were discouraged from pressing for our natural rights as Indian human beings. In spite of the fact that there is to some extent the same repression today, we persist and insist in living, believing, hoping, loving, speaking, and writing as Indians. This is embodied in the language we know and share in our writing. We have always had this language, and it is the language, spoken and unspoken, that determines our existence, that brought our grandmothers and grandfathers and ourselves into being in order that there be a continuing life.

Chapter 22

Mother Tongue

Amy Tan

I am not a scholar of English or literature. I cannot give you much more than personal opinions on the English language and its variations in this country or others.

I am a writer. And by that definition, I am someone who has always loved language. I am fascinated by language in daily life. I spend a great deal of my time thinking about the power of language—the way it can evoke an emotion, a visual image, a complex idea, or a simple truth. Language is the tool of my trade. And I use them all—all the Englishes I grew up with.

Recently, I was made keenly aware of the different Englishes I do use. I was giving a talk to a large group of people, the same talk I had already given to half a dozen other groups. The nature of the talk was about my writing, my life, and my book, *The Joy Luck Club.* The talk was going along well enough, until I remembered one major difference that made the whole talk sound wrong. My mother was in the room. And it was perhaps the first time she had heard me give a lengthy speech, using the kind of English I have never used with her. I was saying things like, "The intersection of memory upon imagination" and "There is an aspect of my fiction that relates to thus-and-thus"—a speech filled with carefully wrought grammatical phrases, burdened, it suddenly seemed to me, with nominalized forms, past perfect tenses, conditional phrases, all the forms of standard English that I had learned in school and through books, the forms of English I did not use at home with my mother.

Just last week, I was walking down the street with my mother, and I again found myself conscious of the English I was using, and the English I do use with her. We were talking about the price of new and used furniture and I heard myself saying this: "Not waste money that way." My husband was with us as well, and he didn't notice any switch in my English. And then I realized why. It's because over the twenty years we've been together I've often used that same kind of English with him, and sometimes he even uses it with me. It has become our language of intimacy, a different sort of English that relates to family talk, the language I grew up with.

So you'll have some idea of what this family talk I heard sounds like, I'll quote what my mother said during a recent conversation which I videotaped and then transcribed. During this conversation, my mother was talking about a political gangster in Shanghai who had the same last name as her family's, Du, and how the gangster in his early years wanted to be adopted by her family, which was rich by comparison. Later, the gangster became more powerful, far richer than my mother's family, and one day showed up at my mother's wedding to pay his respects. Here's what she said in part:

"Du Yusong having business like fruit stand. Like off the street kind. He is Du like Du Zong—but not Tsung-ming Island people. The local people call putong, the river east side, he belong to that side local people. That man want to ask Du Zong father take him in like become own family. Du Zong father wasn't look down on him, but didn't take seriously, until that man big like become a mafia. Now important person, very hard to inviting him. Chinese way, came only to show respect, don't stay for dinner. Respect for making big celebration, he shows up. Mean gives lots of respect. Chinese custom. Chinese social life that way. If too important won't have to stay too long. He come to my wedding. I didn't see, I heard it. I gone to boy's side, they have YMCA dinner. Chinese age I was nineteen."

You should know that my mother's expressive command of English belies how much she actually understands. She reads the *Forbes* report, listens to *Wall Street Week*, converses daily with her stockbroker, reads all of Shirley MacLaine's books with ease—all kinds of things I can't begin to understand. Yet some of my friends tell me they understand 50 percent of what my mother says. Some say they understand 80 to 90 percent. Some say they understand none of it, as if she were speaking pure Chinese. But to me, my mother's English is perfectly clear, perfectly natural. It's my mother tongue. Her language, as I hear it, is vivid, direct, full of observation and imagery. That was the language that helped shape the way I saw things, expressed things, made sense of the world.

Lately, I've been giving more thought to the kind of English my mother speaks. Like others, I have described it to people as "broken" or "fractured" English. But I wince when I say that. It has always bothered me that I can think of no way to describe it other than "broken," as if it were damaged and needed to be fixed, as if it lacked a certain wholeness and soundness. I've heard other terms used, "limited English," for example. But they seem just as bad, as if everything is limited, including people's perceptions of the limited English speaker.

I know this for a fact, because when I was growing up, my mother's "limited" English limited *my* perception of her. I was ashamed of her English. I believed that her English reflected the quality of what she had to say. That is, because she expressed them imperfectly her thoughts were imperfect. And I had plenty of empirical evidence to support me: the fact that people in department stores, at banks, and at restaurants did not take her seriously, did not give her good service, pretended not to understand her, or even acted as if they did not hear her.

My mother has long realized the limitations of her English as well. When I was fifteen, she used to have me call people on the phone to pretend I was she. In this guise, I was forced to ask for information or even to complain and yell at people who had been rude to her. One time it was a call to her stockbroker in New York. She had cashed out her small portfolio and it just so happened we were going to go to New York the next week, our very first trip outside California. I had to get on the phone and say in an adolescent voice that was not very convincing, "This is Mrs. Tan."

And my mother was standing in the back whispering loudly, "Why he don't send me check, already two weeks late. So mad he lie to me, losing me money."

And then I said in perfect English, "Yes, I'm getting rather concerned. You had agreed to send the check two weeks ago, but it hasn't arrived."

Then she began to talk more loudly. "What he want, I come to New York tell him front of his boss, you cheating me?" And I was trying to calm her down, make her be quiet, while telling the stockbroker, "I can't tolerate any more excuses. If I don't receive the check immediately, I am going to have to speak to your manager when I'm in New York next week." And sure enough, the following week there we were in front of this astonished stockbroker, and I was sitting there red-faced and quiet, and my mother, the real Mrs. Tan, was shouting at his boss in her impeccable broken English.

We used a similar routine just five days ago, for a situation that was far less humorous. My mother had gone to the hospital for an appointment, to find out about a benign brain tumor a CAT scan had revealed a month ago. She said she had spoken very good English, her best English, no mistakes. Still, she said, the hospital did not apologize when they said they had lost the CAT scan and she had come for nothing. She said they did not seem to have any sympathy when she told them she was anxious to know the exact diagnosis, since her husband and son had both died of brain tumors. She said they would not give her any more information until the next time and she would have to make another appointment for that. So she said she would not leave until the doctor called her daughter. She wouldn't budge. And when the doctor finally called her daughter, me, who spoke in perfect English—lo and behold—we had assurances the CAT scan would be found, promises that a conference call on Monday would be held, and apologies for any suffering my mother had gone through for a most regrettable mistake.

I think my mother's English almost had an effect on limiting my possibilities in life as well. Sociologists and linguists probably will tell you that a person's developing language skills are more influenced by peers. But I do think that the language spoken in the family, especially in immigrant families which are more insular, plays a large role in shaping the language of the child. And I believe that it affected my results on achievement tests, IQ tests, and the SAT. While my English skills were never judged as poor, compared to math, English could not be considered my strong suit. In grade school I did moderately well, getting perhaps B's, sometimes B-pluses, in English and scoring perhaps in the sixtieth or seventieth percentile on achievement tests. But those scores were not good enough to override the opinion that my true abilities lay in math and science, because in those areas I achieved A's and scored in the ninetieth percentile or higher.

This was understandable. Math is precise; there is only one correct answer. Whereas, for me at least, the answers on English tests were always a judgment call, a matter of opinion and personal experience. Those tests were constructed around items like fill-in-the-blank sentence completion, such as, "Even though Tom was ______, Mary thought he was ______." And the correct answer always seemed to be the most bland combinations of thoughts, for example, "Even though Tom was shy, Mary thought he was charming," with the grammatical structure "even though" limiting the correct answer to some sort of semantic opposites, so you wouldn't get answers like, "Even though Tom was foolish, Mary thought he was ridiculous." Well, according to my mother, there were very few limitations as to what Tom could have been and what Mary might have thought of him. So I never did well on tests like that.

The same was true with word analogies, pairs of words in which you were supposed to find some sort of logical, semantic relationship—for example, "*Sunset* is to *nightfall* as ______ is to ______." And here you would be presented with a list of four possible pairs, one of which showed the same kind of relationship: *red* is to *stoplight*, *bus* is to *arrival*, *chills* is to *fever*, *yawn* is to *boring*. Well, I could never think that way. I knew what the tests were asking, but I could not block out of my mind the images already created by the first pair, "*sunset* is to *nightfall*"—and I would see a burst of colors against a darkening sky, the moon rising, the lowering of a curtain of stars. And all the other pairs of words—red, bus, stoplight, boring—just threw up a mass of confusing images, making it impossible for me to sort out something as logical as saying: "A sunset precedes nightfall" is the same as "a chill precedes a fever." The only way I would have gotten that answer right would have been to imagine an associative situation, for example, my being disobedient and staying out past sunset, catching a chill at night, which turns into feverish pneumonia as punishment, which indeed did happen to me.

I have been thinking about all this lately, about my mother's English, about achievement tests. Because lately I've been asked, as a writer, why there are not more Asian Americans represented in American literature. Why are there few Asian Americans enrolled in creative writing programs? Why do so many Chinese students go into engineering? Well, these are broad sociological questions I can't begin to answer. But I have noticed in surveys—in fact, just last week—that Asian students, as a whole, always do significantly better on math achievement tests than in English. And this makes me think that there are other Asian-American students whose English spoken in the home might also be described as "broken" or "limited." And perhaps they also have teachers who are steering them away from writing and into math and science, which is what happened to me.

Fortunately, I happen to be rebellious in nature and enjoy the challenge of disproving assumptions made about me. I became an English major my first year in college, after being enrolled as pre-med. I started writing nonfiction as a freelancer the week after I was told by my former boss that writing was my worst skill and I should hone my talents toward account management.

But it wasn't until 1985 that I finally began to write fiction. And at first I wrote using what I thought to be wittily crafted sentences, sentences that would finally prove I had mastery over the English language. Here's an example from the first draft of a story that later made its way into *The Joy Luck Club*, but without this line: "That was my mental quandary in its nascent state." A terrible line, which I can barely pronounce.

Fortunately, for reasons I won't get into today, I later decided I should envision a reader for the stories I would write. And the reader I decided upon was my mother, because these were stories about mothers. So with this reader in mind—and in fact she did read my early drafts—I began to write stories using all the Englishes I grew up with: the English I spoke to my mother, which for lack of a better term might be described as "simple"; the English she used with me, which for lack of a better term might be described as "broken"; my translation of her Chinese, which could certainly be described as "watered down"; and what I imagined to be her translation of her Chinese if she could speak in perfect English, her internal language, and for that I sought to preserve the essence, but neither an English nor a Chinese structure. I wanted to capture what language ability tests can never reveal: her intent, her passion, her imagery, the rhythms of her speech and the nature of her thoughts.

Apart from what any critic had to say about my writing, I knew I had succeeded where it counted when my mother finished reading my book and gave me her verdict: "So easy to read."

Reflection and Inquiry

REFLECTING ON THE READINGS

Respond to one or more of the following:

1. On the basis of the readings in this unit, how would you explain the terms "standard English" or "native speaker"? To what extent have the readings challenged or confirmed your prior understandings of these terms?
2. How do the sociocultural issues raised by the authors in this unit contribute to your own understanding of (a) what it means to be an English language learner and (b) what it means to teach English language learners?
3. How can Widdowson's concept of the ownership of English (chapter 18) be brought to bear on the autobiographical experiences of Vandrick (chapter 20), Ortiz (chapter 21), or Tan (chapter 22)?
4. Vandrick explores the implications of her past experiences for her present teaching (chapter 20). Reflect on your own past and consider the impact it may have on your present or future teaching.
5. Vandrick discusses how a legacy of colonialism may play out in the English language classroom (chapter 20). Can you think of other ways in which such a legacy is enacted? How might you address/redress these situations?
6. Ortiz refers to the songs and stories in his own language that contributed to his becoming a learner and writer in English (chapter 21). Re-

flect back on your own family stories and songs. In what ways did these influence your own history as a learner? What implications for teaching do you draw from Ortiz's and your own experiences?

7. Tan comes to recognize that she uses "different Englishes" (chapter 22). Consider the different Englishes that you may use (or the different variations of another language that you may use) and the circumstances that give rise to these variations. How would you apply your understanding of Tan's and your own experiences to the teaching of English in a classroom setting?

8. Imagine that Tan's mother is a student in your adult education classroom, and said:

> "Why he don't send me check, already two weeks late. So mad he lie to me, losing me money."

Drawing on the perspectives and practices of the authors in this and other units, what issues would you bring to bear on the way you respond to her English?

9. Imagine that you are attending an in-service professional day on teaching linguistically diverse learners. During the session one of the participants says, "The reason these students are not succeeding is that they don't speak English at home." Having read Chiang and Schmida's study about students' relationships with the languages they use (chapter 19), you feel compelled to respond. Write the dialogue that might ensue between you and the other participant.

10. To what extent does one of the personal experience essays by Vandrick (chapter 20), Ortiz (chapter 21), or Tan (chapter 22) provide a framework for your understanding of an abstract theory delineated in another reading in this book? To what extent does the theoretical perspective of an academic article in this book provide a framework for your understanding of an individual writer's personal experience?

11. Imagine that you are approached by a colleague who teaches another subject area in your institution. He is concerned about a student who completed the ESOL program the year before. According to this colleague, the student "works hard and fulfills all the assignments," but his writing is not "standard English." Your colleague wants to know why this student is no longer taking ESOL courses. Drawing on the readings in this unit, consider how you might respond to this colleague.

12. Select a passage (one sentence or several sentences) from one of the readings in Unit Five that struck you in some way. For example, it may be a passage that resonates with your own experience, that reminds of you something else you've read or seen, or that makes an important point. Highlight or copy the passage and then reflect on why you chose it.

READING FOR FURTHER REFLECTION

Respond to one or more of the following:

1. The following journal entries were written in an ESOL writing course in which students were asked to reflect on their attitudes toward writing in English. What surprises or intrigues you about these journal entries? What do these entries reveal about the relationship between language and identity? What do they reveal about the nature of literacy acquisition?

- Personally, I love writing in English . . . I much prefer writing in English than in my native language. I feel very rhythmical when writing in English. What I mean is I can get along with developing words easily. Although it may sound strange, now that I learned to write something in English, I feel awkward a little bit when I am writing in Japanese. The words do not come up in my head so smoothly. This may be because I do not spend time for writing in Japanese as much as in English.
- I like writing, it's my hobby. However, I don't feel comfortable writing in English because English is not my native language. I don't have enough vocabulary to express my ideas. Furthermore, different languages have different textures to compose a writing, some words which are used in this context have different meaning in another context. . . . I truly feel different in writing in my native language. It's much easier. I feel confident when I write in my native language.

2. Read the following excerpt from *French Lessons* by Alice Kaplan who learned French as a second language and now teaches it. What strikes you? What do Kaplan's experiences reveal about her relationship with her second language? To what extent do her reflections represent your own experiences with two (or more) languages? What do her experiences suggest about the benefits of acquiring another language? How does her perspective influence what she seems to value in her language teaching?

> I go back and forth in my thinking about my second language. . . . I think, why have I confined myself to teach in this second language, this language which will never be as easy as the first one?
>
> Then something will happen, in the classroom, and I'll see this French language as essential *in its imperfection*: the fact that we don't have as many words is forcing us to say more. The simplicity of our communication moves us, we're outside of cliché, free of easy eloquence, some deeper ideas and feelings make it through the mistakes and shine all the more through them.

In French class I feel close, open, willing to risk a language that isn't the language of everyday life. A sacred language.

3. Read the following excerpt from Marjorie Agosin's essay, "Always Living in Spanish." What strikes you? What do Agosin's experiences suggest about the relationship between language and identity? To what extent do her reflections represent your own experiences with your languages? Contrast her reflections with those of Kaplan (in #2, above).

> I had left a dangerous place that was my home, only to arrive in a dangerous place that was not: a high school in the small town of Athens, Georgia, where my poor English and my accent were the cause of ridicule and insult. The only way I could recover my usurped country and my Chilean childhood was by continuing to write in Spanish, the same way my grandparents had sung in their own tongues in diasporic sites.
>
> The new and learned English language did not fit with the visceral emotions and themes that my poetry contained, but by writing in Spanish I could recover fragrances, spoken rhythms, and the passion of my own identity. . . .
>
> I miss that undulating and sensuous language of mine, those baroque descriptions, the sense of being and feeling that Spanish gives me. . . . To write in Spanish is for me a gesture of survival.

4. Read the following excerpt from the essay, "California Palms," by lê thi diem thûy. What strikes you? What does this text suggest about the complex relationship between the languages that an individual uses?

> I think I became a writer in part because I wanted to convey in English the quality of my father's voice as he sang a song in Vietnamese or the peculiar truth of my mother's accented English speaking for General Electric when she declared, "G.E. We bring good things to lie." . . . I have arrived at English through Vietnamese and can't hear one language without feeling the presence of the other.

5. Read the following poem, "Crossing Over" by Lisel Mueller and write a response. What strikes or moves you? What does the poem reveal about the complicated relationship between language and identity?

Crossing Over
by Lisel Mueller

There comes a day when the trees
Refuse to let you pass
Until you name them. Stones
Speak up and reveal themselves
As the poor of your new country.
Then you see that the moon

Has chosen to follow you here
And find yourself humming the music
You stuffed your ears against.
You dream in rhyme, in a language
You never wanted to understand.
When you pick up the telephone,
The voices from home arrive
Sighing, bent by the ocean.
Their letters bear postage stamps
That surprise you with their strange, bright birds.

6. Read the following excerpt from *A Hunger of Memory* by Richard Rodriguez. What strikes you? Reflect on the implications or consequences of bringing the language of school into the home.

Because I wrongly imagined that English was intrinsically a public language and Spanish an intrinsically private one, I easily noted the difference between classroom language and the language of home. At school, words were directed to a general audience of listeners. ('Boys and girls.') Words were meaningfully ordered. And the point was not self-expression alone but to make oneself understood by many others. The teacher quizzed: 'Boys and girls, why do we use that word in this sentence? Could we think of a better word to use there? Would the sentence change its meaning if the words were differently arranged? And wasn't there a better way of saying much the same thing?' (I couldn't say. I wouldn't try to say.)

Three months. Five. Half a year passed. Unsmiling, ever watchful, my teachers noted my silence. They began to connect my behavior with the difficult progress my older sister and brother were making. Until one Saturday morning three nuns arrived at the house to talk to our parents. Stiffly, they sat on the blue living room sofa. From the doorway of another room, spying the visitors, I noted the incongruity—the clash of two worlds, the faces and voices of school intruding upon the familiar setting of home. I overheard one voice gently wondering, 'Do your children speak only Spanish at home, Mrs. Rodriguez?' While another voice added, 'That Richard especially seems so timid and shy.'

That Rich-heard!

With great tact the visitors continued, 'Is it possible for you and your husband to encourage your children to practice their English when they are home?' Of course, my parents complied. What would they not do for their children's well-being? And how could they have questioned the Church's authority which those women represented? In an instant, they agreed to give up the language (the sounds) that had revealed and accentuated our family's closeness. The moment after the visitors left, the change was observed. '*Ahora*, speak to us *en inglés*,' my father and mother united to tell us.

At first, it seemed a kind of game. After dinner each night, the family gathered to practice 'our' English. . . . We played with strange English sounds, often over-anglicizing our pronunciations. And we filled the smiling gaps of our sentences with familiar Spanish sounds. But that was cheating, somebody shouted. Everyone laughed. . . . The scene was inevitable: One Saturday morning I entered the kitchen where my parents were talking in Spanish. I did not realize that they were talking in Spanish however until, at the moment they saw me, I heard their voices change to speak English. Those *gringo* sounds they uttered startled me. Pushed me away. In that moment of trivial misunderstanding and profound insight, I felt my throat twisted by unsounded grief. I turned quickly and left the room. But I had no place to escape to with Spanish. (The spell was broken.) My brother and sisters were speaking English in another part of the house.

SUGGESTED PROJECTS FOR INQUIRY

1. Ask a group of people for whom English is an additional language (e.g., students in a class that you are teaching, observing, or attending) to write a linguistic autobiography in which they describe in detail their experiences with their first and second languages. Identify any patterns that emerge in these writings. What do these students see as the relationship between their first and second languages? What do they see as the relationship between their identities and their languages?

2. Generate a series of questions in order to gain a better understanding of the language backgrounds and linguistic identities of students in a particular classroom. Have students respond to these questions in writing and/or through interviews. What do the students' responses reveal about students' linguistics experiences, identities, and attitudes? Compare your findings with the findings of Chiang and Schmida (chapter 19).

3. Select a site where a person or people whose first language is not English might interact with a person or people whose first language is English. Observe the interactions between these different language users for 15 or more minutes. Take notes to record what you see and hear. How do the readings in this unit illuminate your observations?

4. Observe a classroom, or continue your ongoing classroom observations, by recording the following fieldnotes in order to discover who "owns" the language in a classroom:

- Note how the teacher responds to students' use of spoken English. (For example, if a student's language is unintelligible, does the teacher try to paraphrase? request repetition? request help from another student? ignore the speaker? move on to another student? etc.)?
- Note how students respond to each other's use of spoken English.

- If students switch to another language, note (1) the circumstances under which that happens, (2) the way the teacher responds, and (3) the way other students respond.
- Note who determines who gets to speak and under what circumstances.
- Note who tends to speak the most.
- Note who is silent and how others respond to the silence.
- Note how students get turns to speak.
- Note anything else related to the use of oral language in this classroom.

What do these notes reveal about language ownership and attitudes in this classroom?

5. Examine a test (e.g., a teacher's classroom-designed test or a standardized test) that is being used to assess students' understanding of language and literacy. What kinds of items and activities does this test consist of? What do these items and activities reveal about underlying assumptions about English language use? Do these items and activities reflect the theories and principles discussed in the readings in this book? If not, what would you change or add to this test in order to make it more congruent with these theories and principles?

Credits

- Mueller, Lisel. English as a Second Language and Crossing Over. Reprinted by permission of Louisiana State University Press. From *Alive Together: New and Selected Poems*, by Lisel Mueller. Copyright © 1996 by Lisel Mueller.

Chapter 1

- Clarke, Mark, & Silberstein, Sandra. Problems, Prescriptions, and Paradoxes in Second Language Teaching. *TESOL Quarterly, 22.4* (1988): 685–700. Copyright © 1988 by Teachers of English to Speakers of Other Languages, Inc. Reprinted with permission.

Chapter 2

- Holliday, Adrian. Teachers' and Students' Lessons. From *Appropriate Methodology in Social Context*, by Adrian Holliday. Cambridge: Cambridge University Press, Copyright © 1994, pp. 142–159. Reprinted with the permission of Cambridge University Press.

Chapter 3

- Roller, Cathy. Classroom Interaction Patterns: Reflections of a Stratified Society. *Language Arts, 66.5* (September, 1989): 492–500. Copyright © 1989 by the National Council of Teachers of English. Reprinted by permission.

Chapter 4

- Pennycook, Alastair. Method, Interested Knowledge, and the Politics of Language Teaching. *TESOL Quarterly, 23.4* (1989): 589–618. Copyright

© 1989 by Teachers of English to Speakers of Other Languages, Inc. Reprinted with permission.

Chapter 5

- Fanselow, John. 'Let's See': Contrasting Conversations about Teaching. *TESOL Quarterly, 22.1* (1988): 113–130. Copyright © 1988 by Teachers of English to Speakers of Other Languages, Inc. Reprinted with permission.

Chapter 6

- Losey, Kay. Gender and Ethnicity in the Development of Verbal Skills in Bilingual Mexican Women. *TESOL Quarterly, 29.4* (1995): 635–661. Copyright © 1995 by Teachers of English to Speakers of Other Languages, Inc. Reprinted with permission.

Chapter 7

- Harklau, Linda. ESL Versus Mainstream Classes: Contrasting L2 Learning Environments. *TESOL Quarterly, 28.2* (1994): 241–272. Copyright © 1994 by Teachers of English to Speakers of Other Languages, Inc. Reprinted with permission.

Chapter 8

- Hull, Glynda, Rose, Mike, Losey Fraser, Kay, & Castellano, Marisa. Remediation as Social Construct: Perspectives from an Analysis of Classroom Discourse. *College Composition and Communication, 42.3* (1991): 299–329. Copyright © 1991 by the National Council of Teachers of English. Reprinted with permission.

Chapter 9

- Genishi, Celia. *Language Arts, 66.5* (1989): 509–515. Copyright 1989 by the National Council of Teachers of English. Reprinted with permission.

Chapter 10

- Krashen, Stephen. Theory Versus Practice in Language Training. From *Innovative Approaches to Language Teaching*. Edited by Robert Blair. Cambridge: Newbury, 1982, pp. 15–30. Reprinted with the permission of Robert Blair.

Chapter 11

- Krahnke, Karl, & Christison, Mary Ann. Recent Language Research and Some Language Teaching Principles. *TESOL Quarterly, 17.4* (1983): 625–649. Copyright © 1983 by Teachers of English to Speakers of Other Languages, Inc. Reprinted with permission.

Chapter 12

- Clarke, Mark. On the Nature of Technique: What do We Owe the Gurus? *TESOL Quarterly, 18.4* (1984): 577–594. Copyright © 1984 by Teachers of English to Speakers of Other Languages, Inc. Reprinted with permission.

Chapter 13

- Auerbach, Elsa Roberts. What is a Participatory Approach to Curriculum Development? Reprinted from *Making Meaning, Making Change: Participatory Curriculum Development for Adult ESL Literacy*. Center for Applied Linguistics and Delta Systems, Inc. (1992), pp. 5–22. Copyright © 1992. Reprinted with the permission of Center for Applied Linguistics, Washington, DC, and Delta Systems, Inc., McHenry, IL.

Chapter 14

- Lindfors, Judith Wells. The Classroom: A Good Environment for Language Learning. Reprinted from *When They Don't All Speak English*, edited by Pat Rigg & Virginia G. Allen. Urbana, IL: NCTE, 1989, pp. 139–151. Copyright © 1989 by the National Council of Teachers of English. Reprinted with permission.

Chapter 15

- Hudelson, Sarah. Teaching Language Through Content-Area Activities. *When They Don't All Speak English*, edited by Pat Rigg & Virginia G. Allen. Urbana, IL: NCTE, 1989, pp. 39–54. Copyright © 1989 by the National Council of Teachers of English. Reprinted with permission.

Chapter 16

- Zamel, Vivian. From the Margins to the Center. From *Discovery of Competence: Teaching and Learning with Diverse Student Writers*. By Eleanor Kutz, Suzy Q. Groden, & Vivian Zamel. Portsmouth, NH: Boynton/Cook Heinemann, 1993, pp. 183–191. Copyright © 1993. Reprinted with the permission of Boynton/Cook Heinemann.

Chapter 17

- Boudin, Kathy. Participatory Literacy Education Behind Bars: AIDS Opens the Door. *Harvard Educational Review, 63.2* (Summer, 1993): 207–232. Copyright © 1993 by the President and Fellows of Harvard College. All rights Reserved.

Chapter 18

- Widdowson, Henry. The Ownership of English. *TESOL Quarterly*, 28 (1994): 377–389. Copyright © 1994 by Teachers of English to Speakers of Other Languages, Inc. Reprinted with permission.

Chapter 20

- Vandrick, Stephanie. ESL and the Colonial Legacy: A Teacher Faces Her 'Missionary Kid' Past. Reprinted from *The Personal Narrative: Writing Ourselves as Teachers and Scholars*, edited by Gil Haraoian-Guerin. Copyright © 1999 by Calendar Islands Publishers. Reprinted with the permission of Calendar Island Publishers.

Chapter 21

- Ortiz, Simon. The Language We Know. Reprinted from *I Tell You Know: Autobiographical Essays of Native American Writers*, edited by Brian Swann & Arnold Krupat by permission of the University of Nebraska Press. Copyright © 1987 by University of Nebraska Press.

Chapter 22

- Tan, Amy. Mother Tongue. Copyright © 1990 by Amy Tan. First appeared in *The Threepenny Review*. Reprinted by the permission of the author and the Sandra Djikstra Literary Agency.